Human-Computer Interaction Series

Human-Computer Interaction is a multidisciplinary field focused on human aspects of the development of computer technology. As computer-based technology becomes increasingly pervasive - not just in developed countries, but worldwide - the need to take a human-centered approach in the design and development of this technology becomes ever more important. For roughly 30 years now, researchers and practitioners in computational and behavioral sciences have worked to identify theory and practice that influences the direction of these technologies, and this diverse work makes up the field of human–computer interaction. Broadly speaking it includes the study of what technology might be able to do for people and how people might interact with the technology. In this series we present work which advances the science and technology of developing systems which are both effective and satisfying for people in a wide variety of contexts. The human–computer interaction series will focus on theoretical perspectives (such as formal approaches drawn from a variety of behavioral sciences), practical approaches (such as the techniques for effectively integrating user needs in system development), and social issues (such as the determinants of utility, usability and acceptability).

For other titles published in this series, go to
www.springer.com/series/6033

William Sims Bainbridge

Editor

Online Worlds: Convergence of the Real and the Virtual

 Springer

Editor
William Sims Bainbridge

ISBN 978-1-84882-824-7   e-ISBN 978-1-84882-825-4
DOI 10.1007/978-1-84882-825-4
Springer London Dordrecht Heidelberg New York

British Library Cataloguing in Publication Data
A catalogue record for this book is available from the British Library

Library of Congress Control Number: 2009942130

Printed on acid-free paper

Springer is part of Springer Science+Business Media (www.springer.com)

Contents

Chapter 1
Introduction

William Sims Bainbridge

Virtual worlds are persistent online computer-generated environments where people can interact, whether for work or play, in a manner comparable to the real world. The most prominent current example is *World of Warcraft* (Corneliussen and Rettberg 2008), a massively multiplayer online game with 11 million sub-scribers. Some other virtual worlds, notably *Second Life* (Rymaszewski et al. 2007), are not games at all, but Internet-based collaboration contexts in which people can create virtual objects, simulated architecture, and working groups. Although interest in virtual worlds has been growing for at least a dozen years, only today it is possible to bring together an international team of highly accom-plished authors to examine them with both care and excitement, employing a range of theories and methodologies to discover the principles that are making virtual worlds increasingly popular and may in future establish them as a major sector of human-centered computing.

Online education and teleconferencing are among the serious applications of virtual worlds that are currently being used effectively, and they have already become a major venue for informal socializing. To be sure, the commercial future of virtual worlds is controversial. Some believe that such three-dimensional envi-ronments will ultimately supplant web browsers as the typical way people operate online, or that they will overshadow more traditional cultural media such as movies, television, and novels. On the other hand, the current market for them is limited to a small fraction of humanity, a few tens of millions of people. At present, competition between virtual worlds is fierce, and new ones are constantly being created and destroyed. Collectively, they are exploring the technical and cultural space available to them at the present time, as innovations in and around them stake out new territo-ries for exploration. In short, they are already a major socio-technical phenomenon, but their future potential is unknown.

W.S. Bainbridge (ed.), *Online Worlds: Convergence of the Real and the Virtual,*
Human-Computer Interaction Series, DOI 10.1007/978-1-84882-825-4_1,
© Springer-Verlag London Limited 2010

World Jaunting

To get some sense of the current breadth and depth of virtual worlds, let us visit two of them briefly. Figure 1.1 shows what my ethnographer avatar, Interviewer Wilber, saw when he attended a dance on a beach in *Second Life*. Just in front of him, the avatars of a dozen people were dancing, in a variety of fashionable costumes and movement styles. Above the head of each person was a little message, giving the avatar's name and rank in the organization that owned the beach and staged the event: Starfleet.

The party goers were a subset of the 500 members of a group oriented toward the *Star Trek* mythos, yet here they were wearing medieval attire because this was a costume ball. People on both sides of the Atlantic had taken time from their largely mundane lives to adopt the identities of members of the paramilitary exploration organization of the United Federation of Planets centuries in the future. Then, by donning medieval costumes, they had adopted a second level of fantasy role-playing, going to the past from the future. Yet they were hardly silly fools, because they had accomplished impressive feats of creativity, uniting the arts with computer technology, to build a marvelous environment for Starfleet.

While he was studying Starfleet, Interviewer Wilber lived in an apartment near the top of the Roddenberry Tower, named after Gene Roddenberry, the creator of *Star Trek*. In addition to some simple furniture, he was proud to display a model of the Phoenix, the first warp drive ship flown by Zefram Cochrane back in the year 2063. On the wall was a Trekker calendar that automatically marked the days and turned the page each month to show a different attractive young lady in Trek attire.

Fig. 1.1 A Starfleet medieval dance in *Second Life*

Today, the computerized calendar said was April 10, 2384. He could stand on his high balcony and look down on the beautiful gardens in the center of the island, or to the right out over the beach to the sea. When it was time for a group activity, he would ride the elevator down to the first floor, walk past the small shopping center that sold *Star Trek* costumes, Trekker paraphernalia, and even a full-sized duplicate of Captain's Kirk's original Enterprise, then enter the gorgeous headquarters building guarded by a full-sized duplicate of the Phoenix. Beyond the headquarters was an exhibit hall depicting all the careers a member of Starfleet might choose. Above it hovered a space station, where many of the high-tech activities took place, and nearby a full-sized starship floated in the blackness of space.

Interviewer Wilber's most frequent activity was attending hour-long lectures in Starfleet Academy, of which there were over a hundred, on such topics as Vulcan History, the theory of faster-than-light travel, and the Prime Directive that protected the cultural integrity of societies that had not yet developed interstellar flight. As many as a dozen classes were taught each day, by volunteer instructors, in four large classrooms. Not only could the instructor flash pictures on a big screen behind the lectern, but a smaller copy of the image would appear on a small screen on each student's desk. At the end of each class, the instructor would distribute a quiz, along with a transcript of the lecture, so that the student could earn credit toward the complex training requirements of Starfleet. Not only were the architecture and technology extremely realistic, but the members of Starfleet had learned how to handle the limitations of *Second Life*, such as the performance penalty for keeping too many objects in "reality" at any one time. When a classroom was not in use, an officer could press a single button, making it vanish until a second command made it reappear when needed, in perfect readiness for a class.

The picture of the dance contains three other examples of Trekker technology. The small object in the lower left-hand corner is Interviewer Wilber's "com badge" that automatically connects him to Starfleet's announcement text chat channel. The pure white ball at the top center is a "sploder." This is a game of chance. Players click on it to put in money – perhaps 20 Linden dollars, the currency used in *Second Life*, equivalent to less than a US dime. After a few minutes, the sploder would count down, explode harmlessly, and distribute the money at random among those who had contributed. The star-like structure in the air just to the right is a danceball. A participant would click on it and be given many choreographic options – some jazzy, others athletic, others graceful – that would make the avatar dance. Danceballs with slightly lesser repertoires can be bought in *Second Life* stores, programmed in this virtual world's scripting language by fellow residents, costing as much as US$20 or US$30. But this was the best one Interviewer Wilber ever saw, built by Starfleet's own top engineers.

The second virtual location we shall visit is the Mos Eisley Cantina on the planet Tatooine, shown in Fig. 1.2, as depicted in the massively multiplayer online game, *Star Wars Galaxies*. This is the place where Luke Skywalker met Han Solo in the first *Star Wars* movie, what Obi-Wan Kenobie called a "den of scum and villainy." This is actually a different *Star Wars* cantina from the one where Nicolas Ducheneaut and Robert J. Moore (2004) studied "the social side of gaming,"

Fig. 1.2 The Mos Eisley Cantina in *Star Wars Galaxies*

because it caters to rank beginners, but very much the same kind of environment, suitable for social science research or pure socializing. The woman on the lower left is an engineer named Algorithma Teq, unnoticed by the *Star Wars* movies and books, an undistinguished resident of the planet, but like Interviewer Wilber, my ethnographer.

Algorithma Teq is concerned that an Imperial Stormtrooper has taken notice of her, and she worries this may have something to do with her sister, Simula Tion, who is a level-35 Jedi knight and recently joined the Rebel Alliance. Algorithma herself is apolitical, and chose a very different and more peaceful career for herself. Whereas Simula is advancing rapidly up the ladder of experience and status by taking on damn fool missions and killing enemies, Algorithma peacefully practices her engineering skills. Currently, she is only level 20 and just beginning to learn how to build droids. Her work requires patience, but not aggression, scouting the wastes of Tatooine for raw materials, then manufacturing them into machinery components. In terms of the game, a Jedi gains points by destroying, while an engineer gains points by building. In time, Algorithma may buy her own home, stock it with furniture and artworks, and perhaps sell the products of her handiwork in a small shop.

Algorithma Teq does not live on the future edge of "the final frontier," as does Interviewer Wilber, but "a long time ago, in a galaxy far, far away." The mass media often call *Second Life* a game, and *Star Wars Galaxies* markets itself as one, but all the virtual worlds described in this book are both games and far more than games. They depict realities different from ordinary life along many dimensions of the imagination, "as vast as space and as timeless as infinity." Algorithma and Interviewer illustrate that a person may be male in one virtual world, and female in another. In both worlds, people labor in the virtual equivalents of classrooms and factories, and both worlds are operated as businesses. Yet these novel environments promise new insights, new forms of creativity, and new modes of transcendence never before possible. The authors of the following chapters will explore the meanings of these worlds, and extend the methods of the social sciences, "where no one has gone before."

Plan of the Book

The interactions that led to this book actually began at a pair of 2008 conferences, "Cultures of Virtual Worlds," held at the University of California, Irvine, April 25–26, and "Convergence of the Real and the Virtual," held inside *World of Warcraft*, May 9–11. This is not a conference proceedings book, because few of the chapters were actually presented at both the conferences, and many of the authors did not attend either. Rather, these meetings allowed people to exchange ideas and to launch the web of communications that resulted in this volume. The second chapter shares the experience of organizing the virtual conference in *World of Warcraft*, and the information exchange by the more than 100 participants in the first two plenary sessions, who collectively sketched the current scope of research on virtual worlds.

The four chapters that follow help develop the reader's picture of the universe of virtual worlds that have been the focus of empirical research, through specific examples: *World of Warcraft*, *Uru*, *There.com*, *Second Life*, *Matrix Online*, *Tabula Rasa*, and *Spore*. Then follow three chapters that describe worlds and gamelike educational environments that are currently under development, sharing the visions of people who are creating them: *Medulla*, *Blue Mars*, and *Open Cobalt*. All seven of these chapters use their examples to explore fascinating and potentially conse-quential questions for social science, information technology, and the future of human culture. Chapters 10–18 examine the ways in which social science can use virtual worlds as laboratories for studying human personality and communications, offering scientific methodologies and theoretical perspectives that will be valuable for students and future researchers (Bainbridge 2007). The five concluding chapters explore how virtual worlds grow, how they can become the venue for virtual teams and organizations, and what the future may hold in these online realms.

Each chapter stands on its own, with its own thematic integrity, yet together they open a pathway to a new reality. Although a child of nature, humanity always creates its own world. Before humans evolved, there were no farms, no cities, no battlefields, and no roads. Now humanity has created Internet, and this new high-way is rapidly opening new destinations for its travelers. V. Gordon Childe (1951), the archaeologist who most influentially wrote about the Neolithic revolution through which agriculture remade the world, used to say that ours is the species that creates itself. Indeed our technology reshapes our own nature even as it does the landscape. Thus, our avatars in virtual worlds may not merely be "second selves" (Turkle 2005), but harbingers of the very future of human nature.

References

Bainbridge, W. S. (2007). The scientific research potential of virtual worlds. *Science*, 317:472–476.

Childe, G. V. (1951). *Man makes himself*. New York: New American Library.

Corneliussen, H. G. & Rettberg, J. W. (2008). *Digital culture, play and identity: A world of Warcraft reader*. Cambridge, MA: MIT Press.

Ducheneaut, N. & Moore, R. J. (2004). The social side of gaming: A study of interaction patterns in a massively multiplayer online Game" (pp. 360–369). In *Proceedings of the ACM Conference on Computer-Supported Cooperative Work (CSCW2004)*. New York: ACM.

Rymaszewski, M., Wagner James, Au, Ondrejka, C., Platel, R., Van Gorden, S., Cézanne, J., et al. (2007). *Second Life: The official guide*. San Francisco, CA: Sybex.

Turkle, S. (2005). *The Second Self: Computers and the human spirit*. Cambridge, MA: MIT Press.

Chapter 2
New World View

William Sims Bainbridge

This chapter reports the wide range of ideas in a pair of major scientific conference meetings held inside the most popular virtual world, *World of Warcraft* (WoW), May 9 and May 10, 2008, plus the challenges of organizing these online events. More than a hundred scholars and scientists contributed to each session, the first covering research on *World of Warcraft*, and the second examining how virtual worlds fit into the larger world of human experience. A third session, held on May 11, was the starting point for the concluding chapter of this volume. This chapter describes how WoW and other virtual worlds can be used as laboratories for studying human behavior, using both qualitative and quantitative methodologies, and the affordances of virtual worlds can be used to support scientific communication (Bainbridge 2007, in press).

Organizing a Horde of Scientists

The original inspiration for this conference was John Bohannon, the science journalist who creates the Gonzo Scientist features for the online version of *Science*, the journal of the American Association for the Advancement of Science (Bohannon 2008a, b, c). With his help and that of many participants, I organized the conference in the Earthen Ring US realm (i.e., computer server) of *World of Warcraft*. Worldwide, there were nearly 500 WoW servers, each capable of handling about 4,000 users simultaneously and often as many as 10,000 over the course of a day. This particular server was selected for a mix of reasons that might apply with variations to future conferences in multi-server virtual worlds.

Earthen Ring is a "normal realm," which means that users cannot attack each other as they often can on "PvP" (player-versus-player) realms. It is also an "RP" (role playing) realm, which does not distinguish it very much from non-RP servers but does suggest that inhabitants take the WoW culture somewhat more seriously. It was one of six servers on which I had characters, and I had already shifted my research focus to concentrate on it, largely because it possessed a very large, high-quality guild named Alea Iacta Est, historically connected to a popular weekly WoW

W.S. Bainbridge (ed.), *Online Worlds: Convergence of the Real and the Virtual*,
Human-Computer Interaction Series, DOI 10.1007/978-1-84882-825-4_2,
© Springer-Verlag London Limited 2010

podcast named *The Instance*, and thus was a place inhabited by especially expert players who could be excellent "native informants" for ethnographic research.[1]

Conferences in virtual worlds require virtual teams of conference organizers, represented by avatars of the people who are organizing it. John Bohannon created a female Troll character, named Gonzorina after his Gonzo Scientist feature, a huntress with a flightless hunting bird named Darwin. I already had several characters on Earthen Ring, but created more to play special roles, moved one over from another server, and used a total of seven:

Central roles:
Catullus, level 70 Blood Elf priest
Computabull, level 30 Tauren shaman
Sciencemag, level 20 Blood Elf hunter
Minor roles:
Maxrohn, level 70 Human priest
Lunette, level 30 Night Elf priest
Price, level 20 Undead warlock
Marcya, level 20 Troll rogue

WoW divides all characters into two factions that have great difficulty communicating with each other, the Horde and the Alliance, and the characters listed above belong to the Horde, with the exception of Maxrohn and Lunette. Sciencemag was created especially for this conference, and her name came from the URL of the *Science* magazine website, www.sciencemag.org. Her main task was to set up a guild named Science that all participants would join, allowing us to control access to a text chat channel that could handle all members simultaneously, in addition to exploiting information technology tools designed for managing these large groups. Guilds are the only persistent groups in WoW, and the Science guild has thrived after the conference as a focus of socialization and communication for people who continue to share its aims and interests.

Participants were distributed widely in terms of terrestrial geography, from Australia to Russia, but some Europeans had initial difficulty getting access to the server, because European subscriptions are handled separately by WoW. We scheduled the three main plenary sessions for 1:00 in the afternoon, eastern US time, to accommodate as much as possible the great time zone differences for the international participants.

Meetings in virtual worlds are less costly than real-world conferences, with their plane flights and hotel rooms, but they are not entirely free. Some worlds do not charge people to create an avatar and visit at least some portion of the virtual territory, notably *Second Life*, *There*, *Entropia Universe*, and *Anarchy Online*. *World of Warcraft* does charge a subscription fee, and the free promotional accounts do not

---

[1]http://www.myextralife.com/wow/

allow the user to participate fully in group meetings. Therefore, every participant needed to get a WoW account, for at least one month, but we situated the meeting in such a way as to avoid requiring them to pay for the Burning Crusade expansion that most players had. Some already had accounts but lacked a character on Earthen Ring, so they needed to create an additional character at no cost, or pay WoW the required $25 to move a character over from a different server.

Given its pioneering nature, this conference did not charge a registration fee, but it had significant costs. These were expenses in the virtual gold currency used inside WoW, which is not legitimately convertible with external currencies like dollars. Many participants would be starting characters from scratch, investing several hours getting acquainted with the environment, and leveling the character high enough (perhaps level 10) so it could travel in reasonable safety. Therefore, the conference provided each participant with a "guild starter pack," containing a useful carrying bag, a red T-shirt made by Sciencemag (which said "made by Sciencemag" on it, thus proclaiming the connection to the *Science* website), a red and yellow Science Guild tabard displaying an infinity symbol, a working telescope (made by Computabull, who is an engineer), cute "laboratory animals" with which to do scientific experiments, and some gold to buy weapons and armor with. Maxrohn contributed by using his skill as an alchemist to create positions like one that allows characters to breathe under the sea, and another that Computabull could use to let comrades walk on top of it. Lunette smuggled these products to Price through the neutral auction house at Booty Bay, along with Alliance laboratory animals she bought with gold Price transferred back to her.

More than 230 guild starter packs were distributed, worth 20 virtual gold coins each, for a total value of 4,600 gold. Many of the bags were donated by the supportive Alea Iacta Est Guild, especially two of its leaders, Maui and Melyanna. Some participants who already had high level characters contributed both gold and goods that could be sold for gold, but more than 2,000 gold coins were earned by Catullus doing repeatable quests in Outland and the high-level Sunwell Isle, in what amounted to a work week of effort.

Sciencemag registered the Science guild and selected its tabard design. For a WoW guild to be formally established, ten subscribers must sign its charter, and having two accounts I was able to provide the first two. Wanting to get the guild functioning quickly, Sciencemag immediately went to the zone where new and thus unguilded Blood Elf characters start, and paid eight passersby one gold piece each to sign the charter. All but two of them quickly resigned. John Bohannon placed a recruitment notice on the *Science* website, saying "Scientists, We Need Your Swords!" *The Instance* podcast announced the upcoming conference to the WoW community. Key participants were recruited by email from among the best-known researchers on virtual worlds, including authors of a book about WoW that was about to be published by MIT Press (Corneliussen and Rettberg 2008). Email communications were supplemented by a large section of my personal wiki, including advice on technical matters, a schedule of events, and a list of participants. In case of any serious difficulties during the meetings, I was prepared to place advisories on the home page of the wiki in a matter of seconds.

The three plenary academic sessions of this conference did not attempt to duplicate the (dreary) experience of traditional academic conventions, where high-status individuals read long papers aloud to passive audiences, rather than engaging in a more equal debate. Instead, we exploited the advantages of text-based chat – and avoided dealing with the challenges of voice chat. Voice works poorly beyond perhaps five participants and in WoW is strictly limited to 40, which is the maximum who can belong to any one "raid" group. Any participant could activate the chatlog feature (entering "/chatlog" into the chat), and thus have a permanent record of exactly what was written. Using two computers and WoW accounts to make sure nothing was lost, I had both Catullus and Computabull capture the chat text, some of it quoted in the following sections. Many participants took screenshots or videos of the proceedings.

Four or five panelists were recruited to lead each plenary session, including one or two session chairs. Days ahead of time, the chair of each session prepared a list of ten questions, which were posted on the wiki, and the panelists for the given session prepared their own very brief answers. The chair began the session by using the prepared questions, either pasting them into text chat from a text file or using previously prepared macros that would ask a question at the press of a single computer key. In a similar manner, the other panelists would offer brief but well-prepared answers to the given question, then the discussion would open up so that all participants could contribute their thoughts or information on the topic. Much of the text conversation was spontaneous and creative, and thus the result was a rich tangle of threads of discussion. WoW chat automatically lists the character speaking, so it was easy for participants to scroll up and down the chat window comparing responses from different people, and different ideas. Each question began with the capitalized word, QUESTION, so it was easy to look back to when a thread began. The goal was a rich collective conversation, rather than bedlam.

One concern about the plenary sessions was that too many characters in one small location might crash the WoW server, as my character Catullus had twice experienced when participating in two large AIE gatherings. The contingency plan was to log back in, disperse across the virtual geography to prevent another crash, and continue the session via the guild chat, which has no distance limitations. Thus, three locations were selected that were near multiple travel routes: a section of seacoast near Orgrimmar city, the sewer just outside Undercity, and the abandoned fort at Booty Bay (Fig. 2.1).

I had originally thought to hold the first session inside Orgrimmar, but session chair Bonnie Nardi of the University of California at Irvine suggested that cities often produce inconvenient server lag, and the presence of so many other characters could disrupt the meeting or even contribute to a server crash. Her avatar, Maggiemae, and Catullus scouted the alternatives west and east, before settling on a barren seacoast. When the first session started, she also told participants, "Please put away pets and minions," both because rampaging pets could be a distraction and because they might possibly increase the chance of a server crash. In fact, no technical problems arose during the three sessions, and participants could concentrate on the exchange of ideas (Fig. 2.2).

Fig. 2.1 Maggiemae scouting a location for the first session, © 2010 Blizzard Entertainment, Inc.

Fig. 2.2 The second plenary conference session in the undercity sewer, © 2010 Blizzard Entertainment, Inc.

Session 1: Research and World of Warcraft

Maggiemae called the session to order: "Some researchers have claimed that *World of Warcraft* (and other massively multi-player online games) can be used as a laboratory for studying human behavior. What do you think about this?"

Kartuni, the avatar of Nicolas Ducheneaut at the Palo Alto Research Center, had his response ready: "In my own work for instance I'm interested in the dynamics of social networks, and guilds are a perfectly valid laboratory to observe these networks – they are not that different from groups in the physical world like clubs, sports teams, or even workgroups in organizations with fairly well-defined goals. Generalizing a bit, anything that has to do with collaboration and group organization can probably be studied with high validity in WoW. The economy is another interesting domain, as I'm sure Ted Castronova (2005, 2007) would tell you if he were here. For that, WoW is interesting less because of its similarities with the physical world and more for its differences – it lets economists put some long-held assumptions to the test."

Ybika, the avatar of T.L. Taylor at the Information Technology University of Copenhagen in Denmark, cautioned that WoW and similar online games may be comparable to traditional games but not to other spheres of life: "I think we have to be careful though to make sure we are dealing with the ludological aspects of the space and watching for when the comparisons make sense. By *ludological* I mean in particular a care for how the game qualities of the space shape interactions, behaviors, etc., for how also the game user interface may shape them. This potentially complicates one to one correlations."

Dyonesia, avatar of Celia Pearce at Georgia Institute of Technology, supported Taylor's caveat: "I have found that play-driven behavior is quite a bit different from behavior in other arenas. I would hesitate to draw too many generalizations about broader behavior patterns from games and virtual worlds because of the unique qualities of play in terms of promoting emergent behavior. We can't really extrapolate from what people do in a play space into 'real life.'"

Computabull disagreed: "If there is a clear place called *real life*! Many social scientists have written about multiple realities, subcultures, provinces of meaning. What goes on in a church, school room, or battlefield may be as unreal as what happens here. Not to mention the White House, except that the games played there have dire consequences. How is play different from the status games that take place in universities, political parties, or the boardrooms of corporations?"

A debate then flourished about whether many WoW players really distinguished play from work, and how that would affect their behavior. Other points were raised, including the use of pseudonyms in most virtual worlds that separate the identities of the players from their identities in the outside world, and the fact that virtual worlds like *Second Life* are not conceptualized as games. Southerncal, the avatar for Dmitri Williams at the University of Southern California, cited the work of Lawrence Lessig (1999) and stated, "Certainly social contexts differ from space to space, but in virtual worlds there are code-based limitations and affordances that aren't always obvious, but have a lot of power over behaviors."

Later in the session, the group debated the extent to which virtual worlds were separated from the wider world by a protective barrier, what Huizinga (1949) called a *magic circle* and Castronova called a *membrane*. Huizinga's term comes from the widespread tradition in religion and ritual magic to define a sacred space, within which a different set of rules applies. Kartuni expressed serious reservations about these concepts: "I think the boundary between the game world and the rest of a player's life is way too porous for a circle to exist or, if it did, to persist over the long run. Another way to look at it would be to say that it takes a lot of work, probably too much work, to try and maintain a clean separation between the two: play takes place in an environment (the home, most often) that places its own demands on the player and affects their experience ("gtg [got to go], dinner time!," "AFK [away from keyboard], kid needs attention"). The conference wiki not only identified Kartuni as the prominent researcher, Nicolas Ducheneaut, but also linked to his website, which said, "I am a member of the Research Staff in the Computer Science Laboratory at the Palo Alto Research Center." Therefore, participants were well aware who was speaking, and from what institution in the real world, rendering the magic circle especially porous in his direction.

Others argued that terms like *magic circle* do have utility for understanding virtual worlds, noting that a conference had been devoted to this topic just a month earlier, in Tampere, Finland.[2] The real world itself is divided into many different subcultures and settings with different rules. It has its own magic circles – a froth of *magic bubbles* more like, with few rules between. Given the complex relations between realms of human activity, a more appropriate term might be *magic fractal*. People differ in the extent to which real-world distractions intrude, and possibly women experience more family distractions at home where games are typically played in western nations. People with unsatisfactory lives might need a magic circle, and thus enter into role playing online with greater vigor. In a very lively discussion with many participants, the conversation then turned to the need for empirical research on the conditions in which the magic circle becomes weaker or stronger.

The assembled scientists and scholars identified a number of methodological benefits and challenges of doing research in virtual worlds. Quantitative methods can take advantage of the opportunity to collect massive sets of data documenting every social interaction and economic exchange, far more detailed and complete than is possible in practically any other context. *World of Warcraft* permits use of auxiliary programs like CensusPlus and Auctioneer that tabulate the characters online at any given moment, or the quantities and prices of items in the auction systems. Both *EverQuest 2* and *Second Life* have given researchers access to data from their Internet servers that would not normally be available to ordinary users. The fact that many gamelike worlds use multiple servers allows replication of research results from one to another. Others that cluster their servers to function as

---

[2] http://breakingmagiccircle.wordpress.com/programme/

a unit, such as *EVE Online* and *Second Life*, may have tens of thousands of people interacting at any given moment.

Virtual worlds are also suitable for qualitative research, including participant observation, ethnography, and historical research. Through participant observation, the researcher not only observes but also personally experiences the environment and events, which may trigger insights that a more distant method might miss. Arguably, something like a culture emerges in the most successful virtual worlds, which strengthens the validity of research methods that do not use large random samples. Qualitative research is particularly good for studying the way cultures are constructed over time – especially using ethnography, because it looks at the social system holistically. As in classical cultural anthropology, we may gain understanding of phenomena that exist more generally and might even become increasingly significant in the wider world. For example, we may observe the gradual emergence of post-modern ethics, relevant to a real world that may possibly become more and more like that depicted in WoW, in which groups compete over insufficient resources and employ chivalry to provide a gloss of morality to the murder of other groups in order to loot their resources.

Session 2: Relationships Between WoW and the "Real World"

Dmitri Williams, speaking through his avatar Southerncal, launched the second session by asking, "Are friendships formed within virtual worlds real?"

Nick Yee of the Palo Alto Research Center spoke through Estelan: "From the survey data, 75% of 3,200 respondents answered yes when asked whether they had become good friends with someone they met in an online game, so we know that most gamers feel that there is something to these friendships. On the whole though, I think it's more productive to think about how online relationships provide different social spaces than face-to-face relationships, rather than to compare the two and say that one is more real or better than the other."

Pleimisti (technology journalist Julian Dibbell), contemplated Southerncal and his fellow panelists, remarking, "It's an awkward question, Dmitri, as all five of us are 'friends' mainly by virtue of playing WoW. I think it may also be productive to ask how friendships formed in VWs are different from those formed in other online spaces."

Constances (Constance Steinkuehler of the University of Wisconsin), observed: "It's always interesting to me that I have colleagues whom I see less of than gamer friends, yet my gamer friends need to be defended in terms of their "realness." Truthfully, I think there's a generational divide going on. In my own earlier ethnographic work, youth and young adults have relationships that span virtual and real quite naturally. I'd argue that by "real" most folks mean "consequential" in some way."

Tburke (Timothy Burke of Swarthmore College) agreed with both Pleimisti and Constances, then commented: "One of the basic issues behind a lot of our questions today is the real/virtual divide. Scholars maybe spend too much time worrying about that as a whole. I do think you can walk away from virtual-world relationships, in a way that physical, embodied, present relationships can be difficult to shed."

Southerncal's second quest asked, "Do the values encoded into a space (think *Grand Theft Auto* or *World of Warcraft*) matter? Is anyone playing WoW going to become environmentally more aware (earthy themes among the Tauren and in quests) or racially insensitive (listening to any Troll)?" Some participants thought scholars tend to read too much ideological significance into popular culture, and others thought that active games could be more influential than passive television watching, but there was some agreement that the effects of mass media are very hard to measure. Like much of the best modern art, WoW is morally ambiguous, on one level promoting loyalty to the group, and on another level suggesting to more sophisticated players that the group leadership is corrupt and does not deserve loyalty. Most participants to the discussion believed that the relationship between popular culture and consumers is so interactive that they should be called *prosumers* rather than consumers, participating actively in the construction of meanings.

The discussion turned to the potential for doing scientific research in virtual worlds, relevant to the real world. Tburke argued, "My first angle of approach with virtual worlds is always to treat them as "accidental social simulations." They're richer and more complex than any model in normal social science. But they're simple enough to study in ways the world at large cannot be. Models in social science are predictable. Scholars can make them do what scholars want them to do. Virtual worlds aren't predictable: they have all the organic character of human society. So that's my answer to whether research in *World of Warcraft* is useful for understanding the real world. Of course it is."

Without disagreeing, Estelan proclaimed, "I'm more interested in applications to virtual worlds rather than generalizations to physical interactions or the physical world. In this space, I'm fascinated by how virtual worlds let us break rules of representation and social interaction. In the physical world, I can only maintain eye contact with one person at a time, but in a virtual space like this, I could potentially hack the code such that my avatar is maintaining eye contact with everyone in the audience at the same time. Or what happens when I perceive my avatar to be a Gnome but everyone else sees me as a Night Elf? Is it the behavioral confirmation or the self perception that wins out?"

This theme morphed into the issue of gender swapping. Estelan reported, "There's a consistent gender difference in gender swapping. From my survey data, men are 3–5 times more likely to gender-bend than women. So, in a game like WoW where this is compounded with a heavy real-life gender skew to begin with: About 1 out of every 2 female avatars is played by a man, whereas only 1 out of every 100 male avatars is played by a woman."

Maggiemae commented, "Men like to look at female characters; that's what they say in my interviews."

Estelan amplified her observation from his own research, "They either say it's because female avatars are treated better (thus an advantage in game) or because they'd rather look at a woman's behind for 20 hours a week rather than a man's behind."

Computabull shifted back to the question of the connection between real and virtual: "The concept 'gender swap' seems to assume that WoW characters are avatars. For most adult players, they are not. Rather they are often puppets, toys, friends, agents. In chat, people say 'my *lock* [Warlock], my *pally* [Paladin], my *shammy* [Shaman], my *toon* [cartoon].' My! Ray Kurzweil no more thinks he is a woman, like his avatar Ramona, than kids think they are rotund Italian plumbers like the Mario they play with. Some young males may prefer female characters because no girl is willing to be their friend."

Recognizing that many intentionally educational online games had been created, the scientists discussed the educational potential of more general virtual worlds like WoW. Demena (professional copyeditor Deanna Hoak) observed, "Certainly people can learn economic skills within a game like WoW. My nine-year-old has learned quite a bit from buying and selling in the auction house." Based on her research, Constances suggested gamelike virtual worlds can teach informal science, digital literacy, and problem solving strategies.

In particular, players of massively multiplayer online games may learn general leadership skills or specific management procedures, although research on this hypothesis is only beginning. Estelan said, "Much of leadership and management are about dealing with people-resolving conflicts, setting expectations, giving constructive feedback. Even if it's all online, they're still real people. As one 32-year old player put it, 'It also gave me a lot of confidence – after all, if you can lead a 60-person complex raid, how hard can it be to organize a team meeting?'"

The concluding debate concerned whether there exist good real-world models or practices for governance, management and social organization that aren't present in *World of Warcraft*, but could or should be. One of the great potentials of virtual worlds is to host utopian experiments, so it would be scientifically valuable to see many of them incorporating ideas not from standard real-world institutions, but from utopian sources (Bainbridge 2009).

Expeditions

Much of the serious scientific communication at real-world conferences takes place in the hotel hallways and restaurants, as colleagues blend shop-talk with socializing. So, too, in our WoW conference, except that the locales were savannahs and jungles. A high point a few days before the conference came when Maggiemae and Ybika, two top scholars of virtual worlds, one in California and the other in Europe, "met" for the first time, exchanged sentiments of admiration, and set out on a quest together.

At noon before the first plenary session began, several participants gathered in Thrall's throne room at Orgrimmar for screenshot tourist photos with the great Orc chief. High-level conference organizers escorted the lowest-level participants past a few hostile beasts to the Durotar shore for the session, then after the session ended the entire crew began marching back toward Orgrimmar. They passed through the great gate, up the path to the left, and then began to fan out and get lost as the main group headed to the West Gate. The plan was to hike to Thunder Bluff, the Tauren city, stopping half way at the Shrine of the Fallen Warrior, and at a number of culturally or philosophically interesting sites along the way.

Trok and Karu at Grol'dom Farm in the Barrens illustrated the alienated human condition: She irritably complained that he had not fed her piggies, while he vainly called for help against the bees that were chasing him. The band of Science researchers admired an ancient Tauren rock painting, and visited the nearby Ratchet cemetery where the gallows caused them to contemplate not only mortality but also the vague line between justice and injustice. They paid respects at a monumental Tauren totem poll, and noticed that west of there was an oasis seized by their enemies, the Centaurs. After a difficult climb to visit Falla Sagewind on a mountaintop, the scientists contemplated the struggle that is life, then filed down to a nearby lower peak. There, they found The Shrine of the Fallen Warrior, a memorial for a deceased young artist named Michel Koiter. The group knelt in prayer and meditation then danced in celebration of the artist's life.

All along the way, the high-level characters protected the lower-level ones, and helped them gain the flight paths that would allow them to travel far more easily in future. They crossed into Mulgore, the home territory of the Tauren minotaurs, fellow members of the Horde. They had planed to help the Tauren by annihilating the Bael'Dun dig site of the Dwarven archeologists, vile members of the Alliance who were digging into the buried Tauren heritage in order to find information to use against them. But excited to be nearing their goal, they instead ran pell-mell to Thunder Bluff.

Immediately after the session on the second day, the assembled Horde scientists were shocked when my level 70 Alliance priest, Maxrohn, rushed through the huge sewer cavern, entered the passage often used by his faction-mates to infiltrate Undercity, then returned in full combat against one of the monstrous guards. Maxrohn's death launched the Science guild on its second expedition, all members leaping into the Canals of Corruption, swimming in the green virtual pus, and observing the transmogrification research on prisoners and corpses in the Apocatharium.

In the throne room, they twice heard Sylvanas Windrunner, the Banshee Queen, sing her beautiful aria about lost happiness, as both Price and Marcya turned in the quest that prompted this operatic performance. Beneath the bank in the center of this underground city, the scientists interviewed Jeremiah Payson, the cockroach vendor. An honorable profession, perhaps, but how does his life compare with that of the Banshee Queen they just visited? Is his sorrow any less deep? Payson says, "Every time someone steps on a cockroach, I cry. Please don't make me cry." Whether out of pity or respect, some Science guildies bought one of his insect pets. The scientists then soared on a zeppelin trip to Grom'gol Base Camp in Stranglethorn Vale, where some hunted dinosaurs and the best warriors escorted the weaker ones to Booty Bay where the third session would be held.

Prior to the final session, the scientists read history books hidden in a basement storeroom, purchased souvenir parrots, and experienced smuggling by buying laboratory

Fig. 2.3 Catullus and Lunette dancing after the conference, © 2010 Blizzard Entertainment, Inc.

animals Lunette sold through a goblin auctioneer. The session climaxed with a mock wedding, followed by a celebratory dance as shown in Fig. 2.3, then an invasion westward into Alliance territory culminating in an assault on Sentinel Hill. Truth to tell, the scientists were quickly trounced by Alliance defenders who rushed down from their capital at Stormwind once the alarm had been given.

Conclusion

Virtual worlds are a new socio-cultural phenomenon worthy of study in their own right, but they also provide a new perspective on the wider world of which they are the youngest part. With care, they can be laboratories for research on fundamental social processes, human cognition, and economics. In some ways, they differ significantly from other venues for human interaction, but this can become an advantage for researchers, so long as they measure those differences and exploit them to develop and test formal theories. The success of this virtual conference depended on exploiting some of those differences, notably logging a discussion rather than reading papers, suggesting that scientists and scholars who enter virtual worlds need to understand them on their own terms, rather than unthinkingly transferring old habits to them. The meeting demonstrated that a vibrant community of researchers exists, with the experience and imagination to study the evolution of virtual worlds, as they become increasingly important in human life.

References

Bainbridge WS (2007) The Scientific Research Potential of Virtual Worlds. Science 317:472–476

Bainbridge WS (2009) Etopia. ACM Networker 13:36–37

Bainbridge WS (2010) *The Warcraft Civilization*. Cambridge, MA: MIT Press.

Bohannon J (2008a) Scientists, We Need Your Swords!. Science 320:312

Bohannon J (2008b) Scientists Invade Azeroth. Science 320:1592

Bohannon J (2008c) Slaying Monsters for Science. Science online (http://www.sciencemag.org/cgi/content/full/320/5883/1592c)

Castronova E (2005) Synthetic Worlds: The Business and Culture of Online Games. University of Chicago Press, Chicago, IL

Castronova E (2007) Exodus to the Virtual World: How Online Fun is Changing Reality. Palgrave Macmillan, New York

Corneliussen HG, Rettberg JW (eds) (2008) Digital Culture, Play and Identity: A World of Warcraft Reader. MIT Press, Cambridge, MA

Huizinga J (1949) Homo Ludens: A Study of the Play-Element in Culture. London Routledge and Kegan Paul

Lessig L (1999) Code and Other Laws of Cyberspace. Basic Books, New York

Chapter 3
Culture and Creativity: *World of Warcraft* Modding in China and the US

Yong Ming Kow and Bonnie Nardi

Modding – end-user modification of commercial hardware and software – can be traced back at least to 1961 when *Spacewar!* was developed by a group of MIT students on a DEC PDP-1. *Spacewar!* evolved into arcade games including *Space Wars* produced in 1977 by Cinematronics (Sotamaa 2003). In 1992, players altering *Wolfenstein 3-D* (1992), a first person shooter game made by id Software, overwrote the graphics and sounds by editing the game files. Learning from this experience, id Software released *Doom* in 1993 with isolated media files and open source code for players to develop custom maps, images, sounds, and other utilities. Players were able to pass on their modifications to others. By 1996, with the release of *Quake*, end-user modifications had come to be known as "mods," and modding was an accepted part of the gaming community (Kucklich 2005; Postigo 2008a, b). Since late-2005, we have been studying *World of Warcraft* (WoW) in which the use of mods is an important aspect of player practice (Nardi and Harris 2006; Nardi et al. 2007). Technically minded players with an interest in extending the game write mods and make them available to players for free download on distribution sites. Most modders work for free, but the distribution sites are commercial enterprises with advertising.

WoW is a transnational game, available in seven languages, providing an opportunity to examine issues of culture with a stable artifact as anchor. We have studied WoW modding in China and the United States, focusing on the largest single national group of players – the Chinese – and our own local player community. At the time of writing, about half (5.5 million) of all WoW players were Chinese while just under a third (2.5 million) were North American (Blizzard Entertainment 2008).

Our analysis of the Chinese and American modding communities parallels national cultures, but in the context of *World of Warcraft* entails another important dimension. American players were hosted on Blizzard servers and received technical support from Blizzard. Chinese players dealt with an intermediary com-

Y. M. Kow and B. Nardi
Department of Informatics, University of California, Irvine
Irvine, California 92697
e-mails: mail@kowym.com; nardi@uci.edu

W.S. Bainbridge (ed.), *Online Worlds: Convergence of the Real and the Virtual*,
Human-Computer Interaction Series, DOI 10.1007/978-1-84882-825-4_3,
© Springer-Verlag London Limited 2010

pany, "The9," a Chinese online games provider known to Chinese players as *Jiucheng*. The9 was listed on NASDAQ and had 14 million registered subscribers (Baidu Baike 2008). WoW was one of several games it hosted. The9 handled subscriptions, servers, and technical support for Chinese players. While American players had direct access to Blizzard, Chinese players were at one remove from the source.

Our year-long ethnographic study included content analysis of websites and audiotaped face-to-face interviews with 19 modders conducted in Chinese in Beijing, Shanghai, Guangzhou, Chongqing, and the small towns of Shihezi and Xiuyan. We participated in two chatrooms in China, one using QQ and the other MSN (Chinese group instant messaging systems). Chatrooms were owned by the Chinese WoW Development Group, or CWDG, a non-profit modding techniques development group (cwowaddon.com) founded in October 2006. The QQ group was frequented by both modders and players, while the MSN group was made up of players using mods (Fig. 3.1).

In the United States, we participated in a modders' IRC chatroom provided by WoWInterface (wowinterface.com), a distribution site where modders interacted with each other in a forum and chatroom. We conducted six face-to-face interviews with US modders, four of them at BlizzCon 2008, an annual convention to celebrate Blizzard's games. We interviewed modders from the Cosmos Team, the earliest WoW modding group, founded during the beta, as well as WoWAce (wowace.com), the largest WoW programming framework development group, and WoWInterface and Curse (wow.curse.com), two of the largest distribution sites.

We refer to modders by their aliases used in the chatrooms. Since aliases may be used to trace real-world identity, quotes from interviews and informal conversations are used in conjunction with modder's alias only with permission. Chinese modders may have an English or Chinese alias (translated into English using pinyin). We replaced some Chinese modders' names with pseudonyms to anonymize them, marked by the term *Zuozhe*, "so and so."

Modding

Modders alter WoW's user interface but cannot change game terrain, character design, quests, or class character abilities (Whitehead et al. 2008). A typical WoW mod gathered game data and displayed it in the user interface, for example, mods such as the resource tracker Gatherer and the graphical damage meter Recount. Figure 3.2 illustrates the use of Recount from one of the second author's characters.

Mods comprised scripted programming files written in XML (user interface elements) and Lua (functions). Players downloaded the files into the AddOns folder in the game directory where they were read when the game started. Mods did not include programs working outside of the folder nor did they run on their own. Mods in the United States were usually downloaded individually. Most Chinese players

Fig. 3.1 The first author visited modders and mod users in six Chinese cities

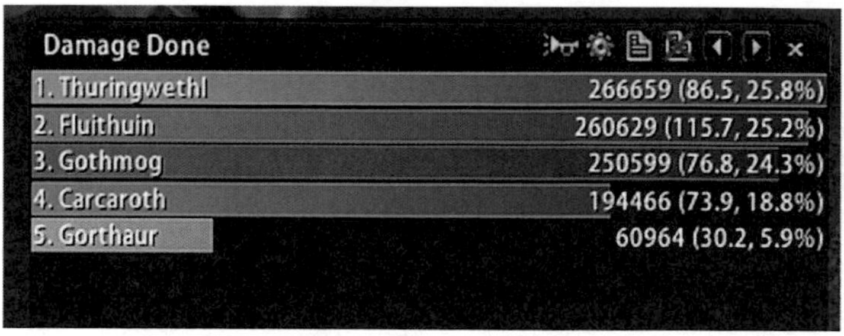

Damage Done	⚒ ✿ 📄 📋 ◀ ▶ ×
1. Thuringwethl	266659 (86.5, 25.8%)
2. Fluithuin	260629 (115.7, 25.2%)
3. Gothmog	250599 (76.8, 24.3%)
4. Carcaroth	194466 (73.9, 18.8%)
5. Gorthaur	60964 (30.2, 5.9%)

Fig. 3.2 A popular WoW mod, Recount

relied on compilations. Two of the most popular Chinese compilations, Bigfoot and Wowshell, were officially referenced on The9's WoW site and downloaded from there. Individual mods could be downloaded from distribution sites such as TheWOW (thewow.cn) and Duowan (wowui.duowan.com), the two most popular Chinese mod distribution sites (Yueselangying 2007). The Chinese compilations were comprehensive, containing mods that served a broad range of game activities. American players used compilations less often. Usually, they served a narrow purpose such as auction trading.

We define modding creativity as the creation of an original mod. We define modding productivity as making a mod available to a player community. In China, many mods were copied and localized (translated), a form of modding productivity but not creativity. The localization file was part of the localization application provided by the WowAce framework. Localization can also be done by directly translating foreign terms found within the programming code. We analyzed data from key modding websites to compare modding creativity and productivity in the United States and China.

In a count done on April 21, 2009, we found 3788 mods at Curse and 3415 mods at WoWInterface. We found 1248 mods at TheWOW and 1165 mods at Duowan. Note that there were more mods available at the US sites, which implies higher productivity. These were mods for players only and did not include mod development tools. To analyze the country of origin of mods, we selected 50 of the most recently updated mods from each site (a total of 200 mods). Within the sample of 200, 55 were repeated across sites. We removed those, leaving 145 unique mods as our sample. Only about a third of the modders (52) indicated their home country. No Chinese modders indicated their country, but we believe that there were 12 of them because China is the only country in the world using simplified Chinese as the common language. That reduced the number of mods with unknown country of origin to 81. It could be argued that Chinese modders might have written and posted mods in English. This is possible but unlikely; in our travel to China we encountered only one modder, Digmouse, with a command of English strong enough to be active in both Chinese and US chatrooms and to have written a mod in English.

We split the 81 mods of unknown origin into countries with the same proportions as the 52 mods with known origin, giving an estimate of 58 for the United States versus 12 for China. Despite China having more than double the number of players in the United States, the Chinese modding community was neither more creative nor productive. What are the reasons for this disparity? Apart from small cosmetic variations, the game itself is identical in the two cultures. Thus cultural, historical, and economic factors may be responsible.

The US Modding Community

The history of WoW modding was documented though an interview with AnduinLothar, an early modder of the Cosmos Team, the first WoW modding group. Cosmos compiled independent WoW mods into a single installation so that they could work together seamlessly. Although the use of the installable exe file is now largely obsolete in the United States, it was the earliest means by which players received *World of Warcraft* mods. Before WoW, AnduinLothar modded for *Warcraft* and *Starcraft,* popular Blizzard games. After *WoW's* release on November 23, 2004, he joined the Cosmos Team. He told us that the Cosmos Team was established several months before release, by three modders, Xiphoris, Thott, and Yoshi, from the closed beta, which ran from March 19, 2004 to October 29, 2004. (Thott also founded the popular WoW database site thottbot.com during the closed beta.) By January 2005, there were enough modders participating in official Blizzard UI & Macros Forum to kick start a more persistent interactive space in the form of an IRC chatroom. The WoWInterface IRC (#wowuidev on irc.freenode.net) was established in January 2005. A few months later, another IRC chatroom for US modders was set up by WowAce (#wowace on irc.freenode.net).

AnduinLothar explained that the AddOns folder that players now use did not exist in the original release: "This was before actually, there was actually an addon system. You had to modify the game files and put them in the [Interface] folder to replace them." This style of modding was something even modding leaders such as Cogwheel (Matthew Orlando) had not experienced first hand. Modders had to replace the Blizzard Lua and XML files inside the /Interface/FrameXML folder so that their files would be loaded instead of the standard game files. This practice was known as "FrameXML hacks." If several modders tried to replace the same files, they ended up overwriting each other. The Cosmos Team's mission was to ensure that all mods worked together seamlessly. Their product, Cosmos, was a single executable installer file named cosmos.exe.

But when Blizzard released an update, all the modifications were replaced. On December 9, 2004 Blizzard introduced the addon system wherein modders could place their mods in the /Interface/Addons folder without overwriting each other. Soon after, FrameXML hacks were prohibited. AnduinLothar became an important part of the Cosmos Team by converting "all of the Frame XML replacement files into the new add-on format. So I made a half dozen mods that way."

Developing mods remained a labor in which modders relied on their own expertise. In December 2004, Slouken (Sam Lantinga) was the only Blizzard developer who addressed technical issues on the UI & Macros Forum with any regularity. The Forum community moderators employed by Blizzard mostly dealt with software bugs that modders uncovered. Slouken made clear his unofficial status: "There is no official support for modifying the WoW interface. If you break it, you get to keep both pieces. :)"

Nonetheless, he was willing to help. Without Slouken, it would have taken much longer to painstakingly reverse engineer the APIs. At the time of this writing, Slouken and Yoshi were still active in the WoWInterface chatroom. Their continuing presence has been of huge benefit to US modders. AnduinLothar elaborated: "Usually the English speaking Europeans come over to the IRC channel. There is definitely more [Blizzard] company interface with the English speaking community. I know for a fact that the European community has complained that, "We don't have people like Sam." People with European accounts can't post on the US boards [the UI & Macros Forum] [so they join the IRC]." There were forums in Europe for European players, but only at the US Forum could modders interact with Blizzard developers. The Europeans, though, at least had the IRC channel. Non-English speakers were completely left out of any communication with Blizzard.

The IRC chatrooms were critical sites of modding community activity. A continuous stream of conversation kept modders involved and informed. The latest topics were discussed. Cairenn, a co-founder of WoWInterface, told us about the WoWInterface IRC: "It started with emails primarily and it's just grown from there. So – and we've got, regularly we've got 150-plus people in there – it's much more for the authors so that they've got like-minded people that they can talk with. They help each other test out mods." It was a busy IRC chatroom with many questions being asked about mod programming, mod usage, and the game. From the speed with which questions were posted, it appeared that some modders were modding at the same time they participated in the channel. There were also modders who were quietly present, watching the threads, and/or recording them for later review.

To make modding more accessible, on November 20, 2004, 5 months after the Cosmos Team was created, some of their modders joined an effort to establish a wiki known as WoWWiki. The current WoWWiki shows a colorful front page with a variety of in-game information, out-of-game news, advertisements, and only a single tab to "interface customization." But when it first started, WoWWiki was all text, with a substantial portion of the first page dedicated to modding. Since then, as more and more non-modding players have contributed to the site, game information such as lore and basic information have pushed modding-related information behind a small tab, changing the site's emphasis.

From June 2004 to January 2005, the Cosmos Team assembled the basic infrastructure for the modding community to expand further. While there were other modding teams around at the time, such as CTmod, they were not developing a public infrastructure. The Cosmos Team developed forums, an IRC chatroom, and API documentation. The Cosmos Team invited anyone to add to its compilation – in AnduinLothar's words, they "invited people that have addons that are similar to our goals."

With the knowledge database and socializing platforms established, new forms of modding groups evolved, in particular, Curse and WowAce. Curse developed from the need to categorize, distribute, rate, and review mods, and to scan for viruses. It provided a place for users to ask questions. WowAce, on the other hand, was a programming framework development group founded by Kaelten and Turan (another modder), in July 2005. They produced a library of scripts to handle repetitive programming tasks to simplify mod programming, so that modders could focus on the creative aspects of modding. They also hosted mods for download. A modder at WowAce told us: "The goal of the Ace libraries in general, even today, is that we want to make things faster and easier for the developer to do so they don't have to spend time redoing the same boring part of the stuff, building the infrastructure."

WowAce developed the WowAceUpdater, an automatic mod updating tool that enabled users to update their mods in one click. A modder from WowAce reported that the WowAceUpdater took two modders 2000 h of work to develop. It was immensely popular with players and, subsequently, similar updaters were developed by Curse, WoWInterface, WowMatrix, and others. The way players managed their mods had changed. Compilations were, for the most part, a thing of the past. The thousands of mods available to players became accessible and convenient to manage, allowing players a high degree of customization through the management of individually selected mods.

Unlike paid professionals, modders took over others' work without adhering to the legalities of copyright. Modders sometimes abandoned their mods for various reasons – they were no longer playing the game, they did not have time, they lost interest. AnduinLothar explained how quickly mod ownership could be transferred from one modder to another: "Relinquishing authorship is not legal in any sense of the word... [But] as far as the copyright laws go, it is entirely unrealistic in this environment... There is generally a point at which modders feel it is acceptable to resurrect another's work and it's significantly shorter than the traditional or legal copyright period." Modders took over work that had been abandoned for anywhere from several weeks to several months. A short period of ownership allowed more permutations to a product, hastening the creative cycle. This system was not protected by law; it worked through modders' voluntary adherence to community rules. AnduinLothar rescued many mods. At the time of our interview on April 10, 2008, he was maintaining 50 mods.

The modding community allowed flexibility in moving abandoned mods to new authors who could care for them. When modders were active, they wanted to control the distribution of their mods. WowMatrix, another mod distribution site, had been uploading mods from WoWInterface and Curse. They sometimes transferred these mods to their site without modders' knowledge. WowMatrix designed their updater in such a way that it downloaded updated mods from the WoWInterface and Curse servers, instead of from their own. On April 13, 2009, WoWInterface and Curse announced on the UI & Macros Forum that they had successfully worked together to stop WowMatrix's updater from accessing their servers. The post generated 500 responses from modders and players within two days (Cairenn 2009). Many modders were happy to see WowMatrix stopped in its tracks. Modders in control of distribution sites could monitor users' questions and bug reports on these sites. In the UI & Macros Forum, Cairenn said: "Because the authors aren't uploading to it [WoWMatrix] themselves, it isn't current, so authors get users angry at them about bugs that they've already fixed and users are getting old versions that may have problems." Because of the need to keep track of feedback from players and the need to update their mods quickly, most modders uploaded their mods only to a manageable number of reliable sites. When not actively maintaining their mods, modders were generally willing to relinquish rights in a faster cycle than that provided by legal copyright.

Commercialization can be said to mark the maturity of creativity. WowAce reported network traffic between 30–60 terabytes per month, with up to 1.7 million unique visitors in the busiest month (Kaelten 2008). Servers handling such a large flow of Internet traffic required financial support. Kaelten tried to generate advertising revenue in WowAceUpdater but was unable to obtain enough to offset costs. So he took a paid job with Curse Network, an advertising company serving online gamers. Curse Network, in turn, helped finance WowAce servers. On July 19, 2008, Kaelten announced that players would no longer be able to download mods from WowAce servers, and instead would do so from Curse servers. While 1300 mods were still being created and maintained at WowAce, their distribution shifted to a commercial entity (Kaelten 2008). The sheer number of players downloading mods from WowAce was simply more than a non-profit group could handle. Commercial groups such as Curse Network were better able to handle the scale of mod distribution that had evolved for American and European players.

WoWInterface was bought by Zam Network, another American advertising company serving online game players, soon after WoW's launch. Cairenn and Dolby (a co-founder of WoWInterface) had also tried to generate income through advertisements and donations in their earlier venture with EQInterface serving EverQuest players. Dolby analyzed WoWInterface's move to Zam in the light of past EQInterface experience: "For a while it was pretty easy and then I don't know if it was at the time just the way, you know, advertising goes up and down during different months... But at the time... it was getting increasingly more difficult to fund the site, so... ZAM approached us and liked what we were doing and [we decided to go with them]."

First Dolby, and then Cairenn, were hired by Zam Network who paid their salaries and maintained the servers. AnduinLothar reported that the Cosmos Team took in only a $1000 in donations over 3 years. He felt that commercialization had advantages for distribution sites: "[When commercialized,] the site gets better funded, and so there maybe is like a burst of changes... [including] improvement of servers so they don't go down as much." However, he also noted that the vast majority of modders were not funded in any way and wrote mods out of personal interest: "So most authors say... the best way to program is because you want a feature."

As with participants of open source communities who enjoyed receiving peer recognition (Scacchi 2007), AnduinLothar expressed an important relationship that modders had with their users, motivating their continuing efforts to mod: "Do you like watching download counts? I love watching download counts... it's just kind of a... fulfilling thing." He noted a clear difference between modders and professional programmers – while modders created new tools, they did not usually document what they had done: "No one's getting paid. Documentation is boring."

The US modding community, then, built up an infrastructure of support and incentives: access to Blizzard developers, IRC chatrooms, WoWWiki, the Ace framework for development, updaters, the WoWInterface and Curse distribution sites, the annual meeting at Blizzcon, and the financial support of Curse Network and Zam Network. A book, *World of Warcraft Programming: A Guide and Reference for Creating WoW Addons,* was authored by Whitehead II, McLemore (Kaelten), and Orlando (Cogwheel) to enable more players to learn modding.

As if this wasn't enough, Public Test Realm (PTR) licenses were given free to all WoWInterface modders during the last two major *World of Warcraft* updates (The Burning Crusade and Wrath of the Lich King). PTRs are the next version of the gaming world, used for testing. They allow players and modders access to content not yet released to most subscribers, including new features. Xinhuan, a Singaporean moderator at WowAce, pointed out the importance of PTRs: "Authors are quick to update their addons using the PTR so that patch day is seamless for most popular addons."

Cairenn told us of her policy for distributing the licenses: "Any mod author on my site with a mod that's current has a key." PTR licenses helped to ensure that mods were tested and bug-free on the official launch date, not to mention bragging rights for being rewarded with keys.

The infrastructure established by the US modding groups supported a vibrant modding community capable of producing, maintaining, and distributing a wide range of *World of Warcraft* mods. With the evolution of the community came poignant change. As participation in the Cosmos Team waned, and as AnduinLothar headed to a new job on graduation from college, Cosmos Team was disbanded. On August 10, 2008, AnduinLothar left a message on Cosmos's website: "In the Beginning, there was Cosmos.... In the end, there wasn't." The Cosmos Team seeded the beginning of WoW modding and will live in WoW modding history. It was a critical part of the foundation on which community infrastructure was established and on which the US modding community grew and flourished.

The Chinese Modding Community

The modding scene in China was vastly different. It was barebones, with a scrappy frontier mentality confronting the realities of a much less developed infrastructure. In China, there was no contact with Blizzard. There was no official modding forum at The9, no book about how to program mods, and no BlizzCon. We emailed The9 about modding, and received a reply saying: "Mods are not provided by our officials. On the official website is merely a url [linking to BigFoot and WoWShell] which is there to prevent players from downloading mods with trojans."

BigFoot and WoWShell, both Chinese compilations, were a key point of access to mods for Chinese players. They were commercial sites with advertising. Both were owned by Chinese gaming information sites. BigFoot was owned by NGA (ngacn.cc), and WoWShell by Tianshizaixian (sa20.com). After Yueselangying was recognized as one of CWDG's best modders, he got a job as WoWShell's lead modder. At the time of our interview in February 2009, he was also acting leader of

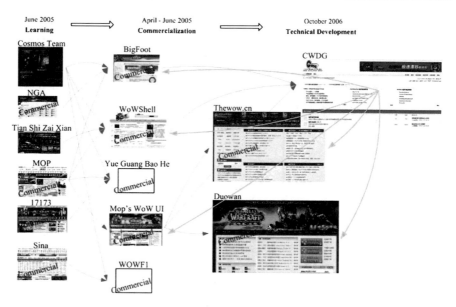

Fig. 3.3 Timeline of Chinese WoW modding groups

CWDG, as Simonw, the founder of CWDG, was busy in RL. Yueselangying told us that Bigfoot and WoWShell together had 90% of the market of Chinese WoW players using mods, with BigFoot garnering a larger proportion. Yueselangying reported that WoWShell contained 71 mods integrated into one package. He estimated that about 20 of these mods were original mods developed internally by WoWShell. He believed that BigFoot contained a similar number of mods, but with fewer original mods (Fig. 3.3).

Lacking support from The9, Chinese modders gathered at Mop, one of China's largest online gaming sites. They socialized and shared their mods in a forum. However, Mop had no mechanism for discussion and knowledge accumulation, such as a wiki. In October 2006, a group of dedicated Chinese modders, under the leadership of Simonw, came together to form CWDG, a non-profit group. Simonw said: "The Mop group was the earliest modding distribution community. At the beginning, a group of authors with modding background had already gathered there. They should have been the first group of people who set up a community like this [a modding community]. But they were only distributing the mods, and did not discuss them."

CWDG's purpose was to go beyond the Mop modding group, promoting and developing modding in China. CWDG's first project was to translate WoWWiki's modding-related information into Chinese. They established a wiki for the translated material (CWDG 2006). Simonw recalled: "We accumulated two or three hundred pages. We began to have some influence." After the wiki, the next logical step was a forum for CWDG modders. "In order to have a better platform to communicate with others, we then started a forum which we are still using now."

Jiyun, the administrator of the Mop forum and an employee of Duowan, told us: "The team's main goal is to make players more concerned about our brand [referring to the sense of quality in any mods from CWDG]... Creating a brand name wasn't our initial goal. [A brand name] was created by instituting a unifying standard [of modding]. Our initial goal was to set up a social space, and to standardize methods."

Simonw wanted to modify the format for distributing mods: "Mop distributes mods in a forum format which is not a good way to do it. A lot of information sinks quickly [to the bottom of the forum list] after it is posted. And then you have to *ding* again [ding is a practice in Chinese forums to raise a particular post to the top of the list so that it remains visible for an extended period of time] or the users can't find what they want... We [at CWDG] classify the mods according to their characteristics, which include the name, the release time, the author, the language, the type, and the pageviews, and we make a list [according to these characteristics]."

CWDG attracted some of the best Chinese modders, including the employees, administrators, and modders of Mop, WoWShell, Duowan, and NGA. Distribution sites such as TheWOW and Duowan scanned CWDG daily, looking for new mods they could transfer to their sites. CWDG became the central locale for technical support for Chinese modders. CWDG was the only Chinese modding site unaffiliated with commercial interests. This non-profit zone allowed modders to focus on sharing, standardizing, and improving their techniques. Yueselangying explained that inside CWDG, there was no conflict between commercial groups: "We do not bring up our commercial interests [to CWDG]... I will attempt to answer any technical questions anyone would ask... We got rid of any commercial affiliations, such as with NGA. The environment inside [of CWDG] is purely about technical development."

Social networks that sprouted from CWDG attracted WoW-related non-modding groups, including Wownei, a social networking site for Chinese players. Similar to Facebook in appearance, Wownei provided a space for users to post diaries and pictures. While there was no formal collaboration between CWDG and Wownei, Shining Gan, the leader of Wownei, told us: "We will continue to help each other and maintain a good relationship. One day, an opportunity [for collaboration] may just arise. As the old Chinese saying goes, 'Even when business fails, the friendship still remains.'"

WoW China was in closed beta from March 21 to April 23, 2005, and open beta from April 26 to June 5, 2005. By the time of the open beta, four compilations had been created: BigFoot, WowShell, Yueguangbaohe, and WOWF1. Yueguangbaohe was developed by the Glim Workshop, a Chinese modding group, which compiled about 50 mods. Glim Workshop's leader, loghost, was not in CWDG. On May 5, he discussed the provenance of Chinese mods with 17173, one of the largest Chinese social entertainment sites (Luan 2005): "Actually, all mods that appeared in China were modified from Cosmos. We basically do not have the ability for independent development. Most of the work around mods was localization... Actually we are all the most loyal players of WoW, as well as all of Blizzard's games. When talking about mods, most [Chinese] people would mention Cosmos. But we wanted to make something that belonged to the Chinese. Chinese players are the best; mods created with the help of Chinese players are also the best. This is our objective behind the hard work."

The Glim Workshop and loghost knew that the Chinese modding scene was behind that of the United States, because most Chinese mods were derivatives of

Cosmos mods. As a Chinese speaking modder active in the US community told us after he had read an early version of our chapter, "It doesn't work the other way around. I myself find zero reasons to visit Chinese sites." In China, localizing and distributing mods were the core modding activities, while in the United States, development of original mods was an emphasis for many modders.

Chinese modders devised a distinctive, hierarchical means of organizing modders. It was a friendly hierarchy, but still a contrast to the peers-as-equals flavor of US modding communities. At CWDG, modders were divided into the following categories: original, alteration, localization, dissemination, management, and learning modders. On uploading their first mod, modders seeking to join CWDG began as learning modders. They would be reclassified once management examined their mod.

To be classified as an original modder, the rules for modders on the CWDG forum stated that the modder needed to author an original mod up to a "certain level of complexity" (CWDG 2008). Alteration modders performed language localization and, in addition, made changes to the code that resulted in a slightly altered mod or one with some additional functionality. Localization modders performed language localization only. Dissemination (transference) modders took mods from sources outside of CWDG, making no changes.

This organization of modders was clearly different from those of modders at WoWInterface and Curse, where only an original modder could upload a mod. The categories of alteration, localization, and dissemination showed the attention given to learning activities in Chinese modding communities. The importance of localization could be seen in the following exchange in a thread posted on the CWDG forum in April 2, 2008 (Losa 2008):

> *Zuozhe* Jia: When a mod is in English, which part should I translate? Recently, I have seen many excellent foreign mods that are not yet localized. And I really wish to use them. I hope some great people can solve my problem. Infinite gratefulness.

> *Zuozhe* Yi: How about if [*Zuozhe* Jia] recommends good unlocalized mods, so that CWDG's localization modders can translate and share them? In this way, many more users can make use of and benefit from them. We might as well have a community of happy people instead of just one happy person.

> *Zuozhe* Ding: What [*Zuozhe* Jia] asked is also what I wanted to know. Your answer helped me understand that finding unlocalized mods is also a form of contribution. Profound!

Even dissemination modders, who made no changes to code, had a role to play, identifying good foreign mods. Together, the different kinds of modders worked toward the community objective of modding productivity, making mods available for Chinese players. Management modders exerted considerable authority in the chatrooms. They were marked with the honorific "CWDG-" before their name, e.g., CWDG-Simonw, reflecting their legitimate influence. Management modders removed modders who had not logged in for a long time, silenced unruly forum and chatroom participants, and reprimanded participants for making unhelpful remarks.

To sign up for a CWDG forum, it was necessary to ask a management modder for an "invitation code."

Modders had to comply with two rules and two guidelines for proper behavior: (1) No *Guan Shui*. ("pour water" or making meaningless remarks.); (2) Read the rules carefully, for CWDG is different from other forums; (3) If you participate sincerely in the discussion, no one will stop you, only encourage you further, and (4) It is okay to *Qian Shui*. ("submerge into water," i.e., to remain quiet, not contributing to the discussion.). At the end of the rules was a statement saying: "CWDG has an excellent environment conducive to the exchange of ideas and learning about WoW modding. Enforcement [of rules and regulations] is simply one of the ways to achieve this. [More importantly], a good environment requires everyone to work together to maintain and treasure it."

Between January 4, 2008 and July 17, 2008, CWDG (2007c) reported that their modders produced 213 mods. Their classification indicated 23% were original, 15% altered, 55% localized, 5% transferred, and 2% not classified. This complicates our comparison because there were no categories "altered," "transferred," or "unclassified" in the United States. However, since both "altered" and "localized" were variants of an original mod, we treated alteration as a form of localization. Since dissemination (transference) does not involve programming, we did not consider that as modding. We did not consider "unclassified" as modding. Discounting transferred and unclassified mods, CWDG produced a total of 197 mods in this period. Between January 4, 2008 and July 17, 2008, there were 49 original mods (25%) and 148 localized mods (75%).

Like loghost, CWDG's modders wanted a better future, a better China. Many new modders and members of CWDG were keen to learn, as if it were a responsibility. In perfect sync, the experienced modders were keen to teach. In a CWDG forum thread posted on November 11, 2007, an experienced modder explained and demonstrated scripts for adding clickable buttons to grid-like user interfaces in WoW. Other modders replied with remarks such as (Warbaby 2007): "Learning new things feels good." "I will return to learn this shortly. Appreciate your effort." "Learning good things require close observation [an appreciation of the scripts which he could study]." The learning environment in Chinese IM chatrooms and forums was expressed by showing respect for the experienced modders who were addressed with the honorific *Da*, meaning "big," "big brother," or "boss." Those worthy of the title were primarily original or management modders. Among the 94 modders listed on the CWDG website on July 17, 2008, 16 were original and management modders (CWDG 2007).

"Yes, in CWDG, I have many students," said Kurax, an experienced modder known as K *Da*, in response to a comment that he nagged like a teacher. In the Chinese modding community, we witnessed the Chinese cultural ability to expedite the formation of teacher–student relationships even without bureaucratic intervention (see Mote 1993 on learning in China). Learning and teaching felt so natural in this context that modders and members readily took on and accepted the roles of learners and teachers. The role of localization modder, not found in the United Sates, defined a role and place for the unskilled in the community. They had a means by which to become involved in the community, creating an opening for them to progress toward new skills.

On September 15, 2008, we were surprised by a translated article published by NGA (2008) titled "The Difference Between Chinese and United States *World of Warcraft* Players from the Perspective of a US Professor." It originated from a newspaper article published online in the Orange County Register (our local newspaper but international in scope via the Internet) (OC Register 2008) covering our research on modding communities. Soon, CWDG modders caught a particular line in the NGA's version (Cai 2008): "About 5 million Chinese play 'WoW,' which is twice the number of American players. But Americans produce far more modifications, or 'mods.'"

This sentence generated 21 replies in a post on CWDG forum between November 5, 2008 and April 12, 2009, including replies from Simonw and Yueselangying (Yeachan 2008). Simonw believed that experienced modders in China were at times regarded too highly, indicated for example, by being, given honorific titles. Some became easily contented with the few mods they had produced. Many Chinese modders believed that they were just producing mods. Simonw pointed out that this view was wrong, and good modders were those that guided others in modding. Kurapica, another CWDG management modder, argued, on the other hand, that an IT professional like himself found too little time left after work to teach others: "Frankly, I wish that you could learn on your own, and not just depend on us to inculcate you." Kurapica saw that many modders, affixed to their roles in learning, did not advance, and chose to remain students, continuing to rely on their teachers. For some, the attempt to learn came into conflict with creativity as they continued in relationships of dependency, not striking out on their own to create new mods.

Between March 1 and 7, 2007, AnduinLothar conducted a survey of 298 modders (Isenberg 2007), posting it in the United States at WoWInterface, Curse, and the UI & Macros Forum. Among the respondents, 103 were from North America, 137 from Europe, and 38 from Asia and Oceania, which included two from China. Between July 14 and September 10, 2008, we replicated the survey on the CWDG and Mop forums. Questions were translated into Chinese with the help of Simonw to ensure they made sense to Chinese modders. Twenty-two Chinese modders responded to the survey. One of our most striking findings was that while there were some super-productive modders in the United States and Europe, we did not find a comparable set of "elite" highly productive modders in China. None of the Chinese respondents reported having worked on more than 5 mods, but 28% of the respondents in the US sites had done so. At the US sites, 8% had worked on between 11 and 25 mods, and 5% had worked on more than 25. These data appear to echo Simonw's reasoning that many Chinese modders were content with a lower rate of production.

We noticed ownership infringement to be a significant issue in China. Since Cosmos was the earliest compilation picked up by Chinese modders, if the Chinese had contacted the Cosmos Team for permission, AnduinLothar would have known. But he said: "The preferred way to do it is kind of to go through the author and get them to include it within their own distribution, and maintain it that way. But most

[Chinese] people don't do that. Most people don't look for the author and contact the author. Probably because of the language barrier."

Some CWDG modders admitted that many localization modders did not seek permission from the original authors. *Zuozhe* Gui told us: "A lot of people do not pay enough attention in respecting the original author." So we wondered: How could these helpful teachers and learners, who gave their free time for others, overlook such basic rights? A CWDG survey conducted in August 2007 showed that 25 out of 45 respondents believed that when performing localization, the core of the code could be altered (Jilingshu 2007).

Even though alteration of code would have been considered an ownership violation in the US community, some Chinese modders saw it differently. *Zuozhe* Ren reasoned: "[We should] not alter the original author's intent, not change their creations [by changing the intent of the code]." Such Chinese modders reasoned that so long as the *intention* of the original modder remained with the mod, ownership of the original modder was not violated. For them, what the original modder attempted to accomplish, had been accomplished. This was a departure from US modders' notion of ownership, which did not rest on intention, but in the control of the modder himself.

Yueselangying, who worked in the IT industry, appeared to understand the issues behind ownership from a perspective consistent with that of American modders. He argued in the CWDG survey (Jilingshu 2007), "For every mod that you are localizing, you should also get in touch with, and participate in fixing bugs, with the original modder." Yueselangying tried to encourage CWDG modders to contact the original authors. However, apart from repeatedly reminding modders in CWDG forums and chatrooms, management modders such as him could do little. CWDG skillfully made use of the categories of alteration, localization, and dissemination modders to provide the unskilled a path into modding, but in doing so, they had to be patient with the misconceptions of learners. To enable the unskilled to perform simple tasks such as localization was quite a success. The hope was, as Yueselangying expressed, that over time, learners would adopt a more sophisticated attitude.

It must also be remembered that the free market economy began in China only 30 years ago (Kynge 2006). In the United States, The Copyright Clause of Article I of the Constitution gives legal rights to own scientific and artistic writings and discoveries for limited time. Two hundred years of law have embedded this concept deep into the culture. There is no comparable history in China.

Destructive programs embedded in some mods are *trojans*, which open a door in players' computers through which hackers can retrieve account information, such as userid and password. A trojan may also contain bots, which perform illegal actions impossible in normal mods, such as increasing a character's speed or automating movements. For the loghost interview, the writer from 17173 used the subtitle: "Trojans are Fiercer Than Tigers" (Luan 2005). "The concept of a user interface mod is very new in [Chinese] online gaming," loghost said. "Many of the functions [of mods] are similar to bots in prior games. Gradually, I believe everyone [all players] will come to understand this concept [of a user interface mod in WoW]. All functions of a mod are built on APIs provided by Blizzard. For bots, however, this [Blizzard's API] is unnecessary. [Bots] run independently and outside the game. Because of this [independence], incidents of account stealing continue to occur." Because Chinese WoW was the first Chinese multiplayer game permitting mods, many Chinese players had problems realizing that what they were using was a bot and not a mod. Regardless of whether the players were aware, The9 banned any players they caught using bots, which are against Blizzard's terms of service.

Yueselangying explained why, technically, trojans can be so pervasive in China: "The main reason is the use of executable files. The executable window is easy to blacken [i.e., infect with a trojan]." Mods scripted in Lua and XML cannot be embedded with trojans. They only run on top of WoW's gaming platform and its set of APIs, and they cannot communicate with external programs or websites. At risk are the compilations distributed in executable formats – they can be hacked. Hacked variants of the major compilations appeared on sites other than the main sites for BigFoot, WowShell, and Yueguangbaohe.

On April 5, 2006, nearly 1 year after Chinese WoW's launch and a long series of trojan incidents, The9 officially recommended that players use BigFoot and WoWShell, the most popular compilations. The9 placed download links for BigFoot and WoWShell at the bottom of its official WoW homepage. This act marked the rise of BigFoot and WoWShell. Yueselangying said: "By putting BigFoot and WoWShell on The9's website], users will at least visit the official [The9] website, and this will boost the popularity [of Bigfoot and WoWShell]... However, the officials [at The9] did not want to guarantee Yueguangbaohe [i.e., put

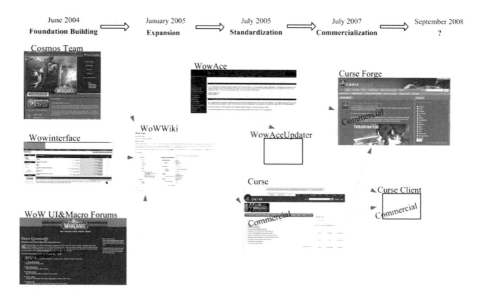

Fig. 3.4 Timeline of US WoW modding groups

it on The9's website]. Furthermore, there were many variants [of Yueguangbaohe] and viruses related to it. All these led to its downfall."

During our trip to China, we heard modders suggesting that the trojans that decimated Yueguangbaohe could have been planted by the same company rumored to have supported it, 17173. This initially sounded absurd. However, modders explained that 17173 was engaged in virtual trading, and stealing accounts could have been good for their business. Another conjecture was that NGA, the parent company of BigFoot, planted trojans in order to kill Yueguangbaohe. Whether these rumors had any truth, their plausibility evidences the high level of distrust between sites and a cutthroat competitiveness in the Chinese environment.

In the United States, groups such as WoWInterface and WoWAce were at first non-profit in nature and then, later, commercialized. However, in China, the early compilations were immediately supported by commercial interests – BigFoot by NGA, WowShell by Tianshizaixian, Yueguangbaohe by 17173, and WOWF1 by Sina. CWDG, an open, non-profit, and purely technical support group, appeared more than a year later (Fig. 3.4).

Discussion

According to our measures of productivity and creativity, American modders significantly outranked Chinese modders, yet each community accomplished something remarkable given its unique sociohistorical conditions. American modders established a vibrant culture of WoW modding, leveraging a rich legacy of knowledge. They assembled a sophisticated infrastructure that provided reliable download of virus-free mods and made it easy for players to tailor mods according to variable personal preferences.

The best Chinese modders were engaged in nurturing and educating the nascent Chinese modding community. Developmentally, a stage of nurturance and care of new modders in a country only now seriously engaging digital technology is an important step forward. By opening a venue of technical and social activity for new modders, the expert Chinese modders became teachers in the community. They provided crucial governance as many Chinese were new to online communities. Standards of comportment well-known to US modders had to be created and sustained in Chinese forums and chatrooms. To shape the new digital communities, the modding teachers deployed traditional Chinese learning culture, without which there might have been no modding at all. By drawing on Cosmos, the Chinese began modding with virtually no supporting infrastructure, and there were no resources whatsoever for modding until CWDG initiated its first labors translating WoWWiki.

US modders had a stronger sense of equality within the modding community. The communities in US forums and IRC chatrooms were open to all, regardless of who they were and what their intentions were. In the Chinese communities, management modders controlled who could join the forums and IM chatrooms. The Chinese understood and respected these terms and conditions.

However, control and segregation of types of modders in CWDG developed a hierarchy within the Chinese modding community. The need to manage Chinese forums and IM chatrooms was partly driven by undesirable elements in the community, such as trojans, *guan shui*, and ownership violations. New modders needed to learn a proper set of behaviors. In the United States, we saw a relatively more self-governed community with a less imposing hierarchy. Modders came into open communities and shaped their goals and development; for example, WoWWiki's objective shifted from modding-centric to general game information. The role of governors, such as Cairenn, was to uphold the beliefs and values of the actors of the community, as in distribution of PTR licenses and control of mod distribution. She did not use the authoritative measures employed by the Chinese management modders to alter modders' behavior in chatrooms nor did she adopt a teaching role.

It is possible that the Chinese culture of learning in some ways suppressed creativity. Instead of searching for the new, focusing energy on creating original mods, the goal of learners was to discover established tools, to appropriate them as part of a necessary developmental process (see Vygotsky 1986; Holt 2008). The role of the experts as teachers, willingly assumed, took them away from the creation of original mods. Chinese players were new to modding. They opted for the simple executable files, which packaged everything, building an environment, which was, unknowingly, conducive to the transmission of harmful trojans. This set of conditions highlights the importance of users in the ecology of product development (Kaptelinin and Nardi 2006). While game companies blame virtual trading for trojans, the knowledge level of players may turn out to be as important. Understanding the users behind the products should impact product development; more attention ought to be placed on "user development."

An important difference between the Chinese and American modding communities was the level of trust (or lack thereof) between organizations and communities. Having met and talked to US modders, we cannot imagine that WoWInterface would hack the Curse website or vice versa – nor would rumors about such activity be believed. Leaders of the US modding community, including those of the development and distribution sites, met each other daily in IRC chatrooms, and, annually, face to face, at BlizzCon. In China, leaders of BigFoot and WoWShell communicated little. The early modders who set up Mop left hardly a trace. The9, Chinese players' link to *World of Warcraft*, disclaimed support for modding. In the United States, Blizzard, although a little slow to warm to the modding community, eventually came around to very cordial relations. At the "UI and Mods" session at BlizzCon 2008 (attended by the second author), a panelist from Blizzard addressed modders in the audience, saying, "This is a really great community that you guys are part of." He commended the contributions of modders in extending the game in ways that Blizzard could not. "We can't make hundreds of options, but you can" he said. Another panelist said, "We'd like to thank the addon community for everything they've done."

Blizzard managed its own modding community by feeding it with tools of change, in particular APIs and mechanics for players to incorporate mods, and by keeping itself open to change through participation in forums and chatrooms. Like Blizzard, many gaming companies have chosen to develop platforms where mods can be useful, rather than undertaking development all on their own (Nieborg 2005). Moving beyond the old paradigm of "develop systems from scratch, then maintain them until they are scrapped," product companies are adopting a mentality that is more evolutionary (Hanseth 2004). Developers may see themselves as "designers" but also as "governors." In face of the creative explosion that a user community can create, developers can hardly (and should not) anticipate its outcome. They must manage it.

We applaud the Chinese modding community for producing and making available more than a thousand mods to Chinese players of *World of Warcraft*. Despite the lack of interaction with The9 and Blizzard, and strong elements of organizational distrust, Chinese modders were able to evolve through learning – significantly enhancing Chinese WoW play. Chinese modders created fewer original mods but remained productive for their community, making available software that Chinese players otherwise would not have had. Their compilations stressed product availability and proliferation. Culture change thrives with the proliferation of new tools and practices, and blending them fluidly into existing protocols. The Chinese managed change by learning from the United States, bringing in new tools and aspects of modding culture. The requirement that change build on extant practice means that current protocols are foundational (Vygotsky 1986). Chinese modders labored to provide mods, and to develop a new modding culture, that accommodated the constraints and opportunities of the present historical moment. We can see a kind of creativity in modders' labors to push Chinese culture in new directions.

Creativity never stands alone and apart from the layers of sediment on which it builds; it is in constant dialog with the predicaments and complexities of its moment in time. The Chinese modding community stood outside a cultural boundary, maintaining its dichotomous presence while at the same time working with Chinese resources such as traditional learning habits. We expect that the experiences Chinese *WoW* modders gained in their new online communities will feed into the future of Chinese life on the Internet, grounded in Chinese practice, but at the same time transcending it, contributing to China's journey to participation in global culture. The virtual world of WoW presented us with a chance to observe the ability of players to insert their own creativity into a commercial product. In the United States, the modding community appeared to have reached a stable state with mature groups being absorbed by commercial entities. However, the future of Chinese modding is still to be written.

Acknowledgments We thank the National Science Foundation and Intel for their generous support of the research. Many modders and players went to great lengths to provide us access to modding communities, and we thank them. We are especially grateful to Cairenn, Cogwheel, Simonw, Yueselangying, AnduinLothar, Shining Gan, Kurapica, Xinhuan, Wandao, and Xiaoxiaobaozi. And we thank the modders themselves who have sacrificed their time to make WoW a better game for millions of players all over the world.

References

Baidu Baike. 2008. "The9." Retrieved October 2, 2008 (http://baike.baidu.com/view/413147. html?wtp=tt).

Blizzard Entertainment. 2008. "*World of Warcraft* Reaches New Milestone: 10 Million Subscribers." Retrieved April 27, 2009 (http://eu.blizzard.com/en/press/080122.htm).

Cai, Qingcong. 2008. "The Difference Between Chinese and US *World of Warcraft* Players from the Perspective of a US Professor." Retrieved April 27, 2009 (http://wow.tgbus.com/emotion/bagua/200809/20080915201910.shtml).

Cairenn. April 13, 2009. "WoWI and Curse protecting authors and users." Msg 1. Message posted to WoW UI & Macro Forums: (http://forums.worldofwarcraft.com/thread.html?topicId=1613 7080965&sid=1&pageNo=1).

CWDG. 2006. "Addon discussion section - CWDG forum." Retrieved from (http://bbs.cwowaddon.com/forum-8-1.html).

------. 2007. "Updated List of CWDG's Mods. CWDG." Retrieved July 17, 2008 CWDG (http://file. cwowaddon.com/).

------. 2008. "CWDG's rules and regulations for modders (revised) 2008.6.4." Retrieved from Google docs linked on CWDG (http://docs.google.com/Doc?id=dckzcgj8_0f2rfd9hp).

Hanseth O. 2004. Knowledge as Infrastructure. In: Avgerou C, Ciborra C, Land F (eds) The Social Study of Information and Communication Technology: Innovation, Actors and Contexts. Oxford University Press, Oxford, pp. 103–108.

Holt R. 2008. Using Activity Theory to Understand Entrepreneurship Opportunity. Mind, Culture, and Activity 15:52–70.

Isenberg K. 2007. "Programmers and Feedback. A study of WoW Addon Authors." Retrieved May 2, 2008 (http://72.211.199.75:82/blog/WoW/Survey/7.html).

Jilingshu. August 13, 2007. "What Should a Localization Modder Do?" Msg 1. Retrieved from CWDG forum: (http://bbs.cwowaddon.com/viewthread.php?tid=1354&highlight=%E6%B1 %89%E5%8C%96).

Kaelten. 2008. "Kaelten announcing the end of WowAceUpdater." Msg 1. Message first posted to WowAce.com no longer available. Retrieved from (http://www.tacticalgamer.com/world-warcraft-general-discussion/120250-those-use-wowace-com.html).

Kaptelinin V, Nardi B. 2006. Acting with Technology: Activity Theory and Interaction Design. MIT Press, Cambridge, MA.

Kucklich, Julian. 2005. "Precarious Playbour: Modders and the Digital Games Industry." *Fiberculture* 5: (http://www.journal.fibreculture.org/issue5/kucklich.html).

Kynge J. 2006. China Shakes the World. A Mariner Book, New York.

Losa 2008. "When an Addon Is in English, Which Part Should I Translate?" Msg 1-7. Message posted to CWDG forum: (http://bbs.cwowaddon.com/archiver/tid-3613.html).

Luan. 2005. "Exclusive Interview with WoW's Yueguangbaohe. UI ≠ trojan." Retrieved May 2, 2008 (http://game.21cn.com/test/online/2005/05/19/2131088.shtml).

Mote F. 1993. Intellectual Foundations of China. McGraw-Hill, New York.

Nardi, Bonnie and Justin Harris. 2006. "Strangers and Friends: Collaborative Play in World of Warcraft." In *Proceedings Conference on Computer-supported Cooperative Work*. New York: ACM Press pp. 149–158.

Nardi, B., Stella, Ly, and Harris, J. 2007. Learning Conversations in World of Warcraft. In *Proceedings Hawaii International Conference on Systems Science*. Big Island, Hawaii, pp. 1326–1335.

Nieborg, David B. 2005. "Am I Mod or Not? – An Analysis of First Person Shooter Modification Culture." Paper presented at *Creative Gamers Seminar – Exploring Participatory culture in Gaming*, Hypermedia Laboratory (University of Tampere).

OC Register. 2008. "UCI Tackles 'World of Warcraft' Mystery." Retrieved April 27 2009 (http:// sciencedude.freedomblogging.com/2008/09/11/uci-tackles-world-of-warcraft-mystery/).

Postigo H. 2008. Of Mods and Modders: Chasing Down the Value of Fan-Based Digital Game Modifications. Games and Culture 2:300–313.

------. 2008b. "Video Game Appropriation through Modifications: Attitudes Concerning Intellectual Property among Modders and Fans." *Convergence* 14:59–74.

Scacchi, Walt. 2007. "Free/Open Source Software Development: Recent Research Results and Emerging Opportunities." *ESEC/FSE 2007, September, Cavtat near Dubrovnik, Croatia.*

Sotamaa, Olli. 2003. "Computer Game Modding, Intermediality and Participatory Culture." (http://old.imv.au.dk/eng/academic/pdf_files/Sotamaa.pdf).

Vygotsky L. 1986. Thought and Language. MIT Press, Cambridge, MA.

Warbaby. November 30, 2007. "Giving You a Hand in Modifying a Mod – Adding a Clickable Button to a Grid User Interface." Msg 1-12. Message posted to CWDG forum: (http://bbs.cwowaddon.com/viewthread.php?tid=2752&highlight=%E6%95%99%E4%BD%A).

Whitehead II, James Bryan McLemore, Orlando M. 2008. World of Warcraft Programming: A Guide and Reference for Creating WoW Addons. Wiley, Indianapolis, IN.

Yeachan. November 5, 2008. "The Atmosphere of Chinese Mods." Msg 1-13. Message posted to CWDG forum: (http://bbs.cwowaddon.com/thread-4954-1-1.html).

Yueselangying. September 16, 2007. "A Survey of the Most Unpopular Mods Download Sites." Msg 1. Message posted to CWDG forum: (http://bbs.cwowaddon.com/archiver/tid-1807.html).

Chapter 4
The Diasporic Game Community: Trans-Ludic Cultures and Latitudinal Research Across Multiple Games and Virtual Worlds

Celia Pearce and Artemesia

This chapter draws from ongoing research into emergent behaviors among the Uru Diaspora, a trans-ludic community of players from the defunct *Uru: Ages Beyond Myst*. *Uru* was a massively multiplayer online game (MMOG) in developer Cyan Worlds' *Myst* series that closed in 2004, leaving 10,000 displaced players. These self-described "Uru refugees" migrated into other MMOGs, as well as online virtual worlds (VWs) such as *There.com* and *Second Life*, and created their own fictive ethnic identities, communities, and cultures (Pearce and Artemesia 2007, 2008, 2009). Eventually, they became integral parts of these communities, even while continuing to long for a return to their "homeland," *Uru*. Two subsequent re-openings, and re-closures, including a player-run server network, and the commercial re-release and re-cancellation of the game, did not cause players to vacate their new homes. Rather, they developed trans-ludic lifestyles, continuing to cultivate and grow Uru communities in other games and virtual worlds, even while paying regular visits to various instantiations of *Uru*. Players also created grassroots inter-world promotion, evangelizing *Uru* through pointers and content-creation in other virtual worlds, and hosting tours back and forth between *Uru, There.com, Second Life,* and other games. Subsets of the Uru Diaspora also started guilds and groups in other games including *The Matrix Online, Star Wars Galaxies, World of Warcraft,* and *Guild Wars.* With *Uru* now closed again, many Uru players, by and large Baby Boomers, have now adopted the practice of maintaining accounts and avatars in multiple games and virtual worlds, a business development that counters to the conventional wisdom that MMOG players play only one game at a time. While most MMOG and VW studies have focused on a single venue, this multi-world study provides us with new insight as to how players migrate their identities and cultures across the porous boundaries of virtual worlds. In the conclusion of this chapter, I will make an argument for the advancement of more "latitudinal studies" that look at phenomena in MMOG/Ws across multiple worlds, as a means to draw more generalizable, less genre-specific conclusions in multiplayer games and virtual worlds research.

C. Pearce
Georgia Institute of Technology
http://cpandfriends.com/
e-mail: celia.pearce@lcc.gatech.edu

W.S. Bainbridge (ed.), *Online Worlds: Convergence of the Real and the Virtual,*
Human-Computer Interaction Series, DOI 10.1007/978-1-84882-825-4_4,
© Springer-Verlag London Limited 2010

The Emergence of Game Refugees and Trans-Ludic Diasporas

Since 2004, I have been conducting research with a community I have dubbed "The Uru Diaspora." The findings of the first phase of this work, initially done under the auspices of a Ph.D. thesis project, is now available in a book entitled *Communities of Play: Emergent Cultures in Multiplayer Games and Virtual Worlds* (Pearce and Artemesia 2009). The book primarily chronicles the first 2 years of my studies of this community. This chapter will focus on a specific aspect of this research, the notion of trans-ludic play practices, extending the scope to include subsequent events that pick up where the book leaves off. It should be noted that the Uru Diaspora, which as of this writing has been active in various games and virtual worlds for over 5 years, continues to flourish and maintain a strong presence in a variety of different contexts. What follows is a brief history of their remarkable journey.

The Uru Diaspora was initially formed in February of 2004, when the beta for the game *Uru: Ages Beyond Myst* (developed by Cyan Worlds and published by UbiSoft) closed for the first of three times. Having been open less than 6 months, this event, known among players as "Black Monday" or "Black Tuesday" (depending on time zone) left some 10,000 Uru players self-described refugees. The connection formed by players during the brief life of *Uru*, combined with the trauma of losing what players came to characterize as their "homeland," formed an indelible bond that has sustained the community for a duration that has far exceeded any of its formal commercial or informal fan-operated instantiations (Fig. 4.1).

The initial closure of the *Uru* beta precipitated what I characterize as the "First Wave" Uru immigrants. Players dispersed into a number of games, using forums as a primary means of staying in regular contact. Later in this chapter, I will address some of the methodological challenges presented by studying diasporic game communities; for the purposes of my initial research, as a solitary ethnographer, it was possible to focus only on two groups, a primary group within *There.com*, and a secondary group within *Second Life*. As part of this initial process I was able to monitor, through the primary group's forum, the debates that arose about the various merits and shortcomings of the two worlds (as well as other MMOGs), an extremely illuminating user analysis of virtual world design (Fig. 4.2).

The cultures that emerged in both these worlds are revealing and provide insight into their design affordances. The Uru immigrants in *Second Life* specifically set out to re-create *Uru*, taking advantage of its highly flexible, if a bit unwieldy, in-world creation tools, which are particularly well suited for creating complex and fully realized environments (Fig. 4.3). The Uru-Thereians, as they eventually came to refer to themselves, initially made an attempt at this but were stymied by *There.com*'s more artifact-centered, highly constrained and monitored content creation system. They were also discriminated against for creating lag due to their insistence on gathering in large groups. For these and other reasons, rather than attempting to build fully realized environments, they instead created individual *Uru*- and *Myst*-derived and inspired artifacts, which they released "into the wild" via *There.com*'s in-world auction system. The result was the emergence of a number

Fig. 4.1 Uru players embrace moments before the servers are shut down (Image: Leesa[1])

of smaller Uru-Thereian communities, as well as an integration of Uru artifacts into the Thereian culture at-large. Today, one can seldom traverse any part of *There.com* without stumbling onto an Uru artifact, whether integrated into an *Uru*-themed area, or inadvertently used by non-Uruvians for purely aesthetic reasons. The Mysterious Woods (Fig. 4.4), inspired by the Channelwood Age in *Myst*, is one of the most popular building kits in *There.com*. Wave Two and Three immigrants have been able to leverage new software features, such as the advent of Neighborhoods, a mechanism for shared real-estate, to create more fully-realized *Uru*-themed environments in *There.com*.

Through this process of transculturation (Ortiz 1947), Uru-Thereians became more fully integrated into the *There.com* culture at-large, both through their reputations as skilled artisans, and their social pervasiveness within the community.

---

[1]All player avatar names are pseudonyms.

Fig. 4.2 First wave Uru refugees on a scouting expedition in *There.com* (Image: Raena)

Fig. 4.3 *Uru* (*left*) and its *Second Life* re-creation (*right*)

This population, 50% female and comprised largely of Baby Boomers, devoted to community, and with considerable disposable income, asserted its economic and political influence by serving on *There.com*'s Member Advisory Board, instigating new game features such as group-owned Neighborhoods, and operating player-run community services such as the University of There.

Throughout this period of settling and transculturating in other worlds, multiple efforts were aimed at restoring the Uru "homeland." An early attempt was made by a player to re-create *Uru* in a self-contained virtual world using Adobe Atmosphere. In summer of 2004, a group of Uru hackers managed to reverse-engineer the server software. Because of their respect for Cyan, rather than releasing this unauthorized system, they approached the developer and cut a deal to create player-run *Uru* servers

Fig. 4.4   The Mysterious Woods (Design by Raena; image by Raena)

with Cyan's blessing. Dubbed *Until Uru*, this network comprised a series of player-run "shards" operated by different "hoods" (the *Uru* equivalent of guilds), which, in addition to smaller gatherings on a regular basis, would also come together en masse for specific events. These included an annual St. Patrick's Day Parade, as well as the D'ni Games, an Uru-wide sporting event consisting of emergent games invented by Uru players, such as foot races, climbing and balancing events. Many of the emergent play forms that arose during this period were the byproduct of lack of new content; *Until Uru* was in a sense a moment frozen in time. Uru players, already emboldened by creating their own content in other worlds, and supported by the hacker group that enabled them to reconvene in *Uru*, became highly creative about appropriating this environment for new uses. During this period, a new generation of Uruvians was also born. Many of these learned of *Uru* from its presence in other games and virtual worlds. This period also precipitated the "Second Wave" of Uru immigrants, coming out of *Until Uru* into *There.com* and other virtual worlds. The pattern during this period was that by and large players made their homes in the virtual worlds where they had settled, but also visited *Uru* on a regular basis and/or for special occasions.

In 2006, a third-party publisher, GameTap (then owned by Turner Broadcasting), began to explore the possibility of releasing *Uru* (which, having died in beta, was never officially launched as a commercial product). GameTap already offered all of the preceding *Myst* titles as part of its library of classic games, and had started publishing original games as well. The instigator of this initiative, Blake Lewin, aware of my research, felt my extensive knowledge of the Uru Diaspora would be an asset to this effort. In addition to the simple fact that I knew where to *find* many of the Uru refugees, he also recognized that an informed understanding of the current state of this community and its culture would be of great utility from both a design and a business perspective. I was therefore retained as "Uru Anthropologist" (a credit that appears at the end of the game) to help reconvene players, and to help craft the new iteration *Uru,* including new Ages (levels), and taking into account the emergent cultures of its community. Over the summer of 2006, we set up an *Until Uru* test shard, to which we were able to recruit 3,000 of the estimated 10,000 Uru refugees, *many from other games and virtual worlds,* in order to make a business case for the re-release of *Uru.* In characteristic style, Uruvians treated the populating of this shard as a challenge, a cooperative puzzle to be solved: bring people together, get *Uru* back. They were rewarded in Spring of 2008 when *Myst Online: Uru Live (MOUL)* was launched under GameTap, where it flourished with roughly the same population that had participated in the test shard. The price to be paid for this was the demise of *Until Uru,* which was perceived to compete with the new game. This decision was controversial as it excluded players in regions where GameTap was not available, precipitating the final phase of the "Second Wave" immigration from *Until Uru* among Europeans and others who would not be able to visit *MOUL.*

The re-release of *Uru* added another level of sophistication to the trans-ludic play culture of the Uru Diaspora. Among the Turner and Cyan staff, there had been a general belief, consistent with conventional business wisdom, that players would "come back" to *Uru* and abandon their settlements in other worlds. As I had anticipated, not only did Uruvians remain in their adopted communities, even while playing *MOUL,* but they also actively recruited *new* Uru players from within them. Players in both *There.com* and *Second Life* were now fully integrated into these other cultures, and had invested too much time, money, and social capital to abandon them. They also recognized that they could use their social networks and influence in the community to help support the *Uru* re-release effort. With a vested interest in its success, they thus instigated fan-based, grassroots marketing campaigns to recruit new players into *MOUL.* In *There.com,* Uru-Thereians took it on themselves to pepper their settlements with promotional scrolls advertising the new *Uru.* They set up travel centers from which they ran tours of *MOUL* for non-Uru Thereians, many of whom had been exposed to the game through its immigrant population and their creative output. Meanwhile, in *Second Life,* the original fan-created *Uru* recreated had been shut down the previous summer due to lack of funds, but not without the Uruvians meticulously archiving the entire island. Recognizing the opportunity for a parallel grassroots marketing initiative, I recommended to GameTap that they sponsor a re-opening of the island as a promotion for *MOUL.* This is the first instance of which I'm aware of a game company sponsoring fan-created content as part of a marketing initiative. The island was similar to the original, but with added signage and links to the GameTap release of *Uru.*

Rather than collapsing the Uru community, the re-release of *MOUL* only served to enhance the trans-ludic lifestyle of *Uru* players. Mutual migration transpired between *MOUL* and other virtual worlds. Players continued to have regular convenings with both their hoods and the larger community in *MOUL* as they had done in *Until*

Uru. Practices of world-hopping, i.e., visiting a number of different worlds in a single play session, were commonplace.

After 1 year of operation, it was announced that *Myst Online: Uru Live,* would be closing. Cyan and Turner took great care to learn from prior mistakes, giving players ample time to prepare for the closure, and even extending the date to allow an extra weekend for players to experience their beloved game. Now, better prepared, and with a history of successful immigration and resettlements, prior generations of Uru refugees served as guides, reversing the "tour guide" role to take future Uru refugees to their settlements in other worlds. Similar to the first closure, a lively and sometimes contentious dialog emerged on the *MOUL*-wide forums debating the strengths and weaknesses of *Second Life* and *There.com,* even forming competitive recruitment factions. This precipitated what I term the "Third Wave" of Uru immigrants, an entirely new generation of Uru refugees who joined its forbears to create new and thriving Uru communities and *Uru*-themed areas in both *Second Life* and *There.com.*

In July of 2008, Cyan announced that it would release *MO:RE* (*Myst Online: Restoration Experiment*), an open-source version of the game, including a content-creation toolkit. Initially, Cyan had hoped to create a more refined product to allow for player content-creation; however, due to their resource limitations, this was not possible. Instead, they subsequently released the source code to the hacker fans to co-develop with Cyan into an open-source authoring environment. While takeovers of defunct MMOGs are not a new phenomenon, players collaborating with developers are less common. Previous virtual worlds have been reclaimed by fans or developers in various forms. *Active Worlds*, launched in 1995, and the longest continuously operating graphical virtual world in existence, has been acquired and reacquired by different combinations of developers and users since its inception. *Meridian 59*, the first medieval fantasy themed graphic MMOG (preceding *Ultima Online* by about a year), was reopened by popular demand by one of its designers to a grateful refugee community. What is unique with *MO:RE* is that the developers have formed a partnership with players to support fan-created content, while at the same time handing over creative control to players. Cyan, in a 2008 web post, described this new initiative as "a bit scary" for both the developers and fans.[2] Unlike many other developers, Cyan has always maintained a high level of tolerance for user-created content derived from its intellectual property, one of the many reasons for its strong fan loyalty. Thus, the company has also embraced the fact that its fans in some fundamental sense already "own" *Uru* and are both skilled enough and entitled to contribute to its ongoing life. Meanwhile, Uruvians continue to flourish in other worlds, as celebrated by a "pan-world" celebration held in April of 2009, commemorating the 1-year anniversary of the closure of *MOUL* and the 5-year anniversary of the first *Uru* closure.

Many of the characteristics of the Uru Diaspora, including its trans-ludic play culture, can be traced back to the *Uru* game itself. That *Uru* was part of the *Myst* series is particularly significant. The majority of its players, spanning ages 12–75, with the highest concentration in the Baby Boomer demographic, had been

---

playing *Myst* games for 10 years before *Uru* opened (Pearce and Artemesia 2009). Like the other *Myst* games, *Uru* was primarily focused on puzzles and exploration, but with a cooperative twist. In sharp contrast to virtually every other MMOG, the game had no points, no leveling of any kind, no combat and no killing. Players engaged together in laboriously solving the "Mensa" level puzzles (Ashe 2003; Carroll 1994) devised for them by its designers, referred to as "Cyanists," a group that players knew individually and admired collectively as the makers of the world they loved. One very distinct difference from other MMORPGs is the "RP" part of the equation. While players, whose role was that of "Explorers," were encouraged to play themselves, the game still had a role-playing element and some conflicts ultimately emerged around this. In classic *Myst*-like fashion, both the goal and the narrative remained obscure, unfolding obliquely through gameplay, and entirely lacking in expository. The *Myst* world revolves around a mysterious race called the D'ni who have the power to write entire worlds into being; they create "Linking Books" that lead to Ages, or worlds, that players explore and decipher.

When placed in the context of a multiplayer game, the difficulty of the puzzles and the obliqueness of the narrative introduces an opportunity for rich social interaction that revolves not around quests and combat, as in traditional MMOGs, but around exploring, solving, and understanding the world and its affordances. Ironically, the narrative of *Uru* specifically concerns the D'ni culture's status as refugees colonizing an underground cave after their world is destroyed. Having been trained by the game itself to solve challenging problems together, as well as to identify with the refugee status of the D'ni, Uru players were thus presented with a particularly hard and yet oddly ironic problem: What to do when their own world literally came to an end. Thus was born their emergent, trans-ludic culture.

This practice of inhabiting multiple virtual worlds with the same communal and individual identity is somewhat unusual. We have a few instances of this, for instance,

Fig. 4.5 Player-created linking books in *Second Life* (left) and *There.com* (right)

with griefer groups such as Anonymous or Something Awful, which gather inside multiplayer games primarily to harass players in increasingly creative ways. The conventional wisdom of MMOG marketing further suggests that most players maintain only one MMOG account at a time. While this may be true of the traditional MMOG demographic, Baby Boomers, with more disposable income and available time, are in the position to maintain multiple accounts, as well as spending sometimes hundreds of dollars per month supporting real estate and content creation within virtual worlds. The community thus established the common practice of not only maintaining multiple accounts, but also of moving fluidly between worlds as a group.

Trans-Ludic Identities

Because the player role in *Uru* was somewhat openly defined and not proscribed as in many other traditional role-playing games (e.g., Night Elf Druid, Orc Warrior), and the implication that *Uru* also stands for "You Are You," many players used their real names or references to their real-life identities, such as the town in which they lived. There was very little cross-gender play, in sharp contrast with "high fantasy" MMOGs, where cross-gender play is so pervasive most of the research concludes that as many as 50% of female avatars are played by males (Yee 2001–2008, 2003; Seay et al. 2004).

When these players began to migrate into virtual worlds, particularly non-game virtual worlds such as *There.com* and *Second Life*, they adopted a practice already established by other refugee communities, such as *Sims Online* refugees (of which there were 800 in *There.com* at the time), of recreating the avatars in their game of origin, both in name and appearance. They thus formed trans-ludic individual identities that they carried across multiple games and virtual worlds, with the primary aim of keeping their community together.

Individual identity and group identity are here deeply intermingled. Early Internet research tended to look at avatar character creation as an individual enterprise

Fig. 4.6 The same two players in *Uru* (left), *There.com* (center) and *Second Life* (right)

Fig. 4.7 The Uru fountain (top left) as instantiated by players in *There.com* (top right), *Adobe atmosphere* (bottom left), and Second Life (*bottom right*)

(Turkle 1995); however, my research suggests that individual identities are socially constructed (Pearce and Artemesia 2007, 2009). Many of the Uru refugees who participated in my research reported being surprised by the identities that emerged over time through interaction with their online community. This is corroborated by other research (Bruckman 1992; Taylor 1999). While in interviews, virtually all players agreed the real-world personality came out through their and others' avatars, yet at the same time, they also frequently found themselves in roles they had not expected. Because players wanted to recreate the Uru culture for their refugee communities, they went to great lengths to learn (sometimes onerous) creation tools in the virtual worlds to which they migrated (Fig. 4.7). Players thus developed the practice of "productive play" (Pearce and Artemesia 2006), inspired by their community and fueled by an intersubjective feedback process.

Methodological Challenges and Opportunities: A Call for "Latitudinal" Research

Studies of massively multiplayer games have tended to focus on a single virtual world or game world. (It will be assumed that anyone reading this book is aware of the core difference between the former, a predominately social environment, typically including user-created content, and the latter, typically a goal-oriented game with a highly structured theme and narrative.) There are some very good reasons why mono-world studies have prevailed in multiplayer game and virtual worlds research. First, they are a fairly accurate reflection of how people actually play. In game worlds in particular, the pattern tends to be for players to focus on one game at a time. When players do migrate, they tend to move to another game and cease to play, at least regularly, the prior game. Mass migrations between games can be precipitated by closures, as with *Uru, Asheron's Call, Ultima Online*, and others; due to changes in the game, as with *Star Wars Galaxies*; or when a new game supplants an older game in a similar genre, as with *EverQuest* and *World of Warcraft*. Second, for qualitative researchers, it is a methodological challenge to study communities across multiple games, virtual worlds, and genres, so most studies tend to follow the traditional anthropology paradigm of a single researcher focusing on a single site over a prolonged period of time. Some quantitative studies have spanned across multiple worlds. Although these have tended to focus on a single genre, they have been very effective at providing us with broad demographic data, such as gender distribution in MMOGs (Castronova 2001; Seay et al. 2004; Yee 2001–2008, 2003, 2005; Williams et al. 2008, 2009).[3]

My ongoing studies of the Uru Diaspora are what I call "latitudinal studies," and I have also termed this, drawing from Marcus (1995), "multi-cited cyberethnography" (Pearce 2009). The term "latitudinal study" is meant to position this style of research as orthogonal to a "longitudinal study," which studies an individual, community, or site over a long period of time. Instead, what I am proposing is that we conduct more studies that take place in traditional timeframes of ethnographic or behavioral research (typically 6–24 months), but across multiple worlds and games.

In the past (Pearce and Artemesia 2009), I have critiqued mono-world studies on the grounds they provide us insight into only a single game, a single genre, a single culture, and the demographic associated with that game/genre/culture. I have also argued against the tendency for researchers to flock to one particular game, generally the most popular at any given time. In the "early days" of MMOG research, scholars joked that the domain could be just as easily called "*EverQuest* Studies," which has now been supplanted by "*WoW* Studies." Boellstorff (2008) has compared this to the early days of anthropology when the majority of studies took place in warm-weather or tropical climates. In virtual worlds research, the vast majority of studies to date have been conducted in and about *Second Life*. The problem with this is that we now have a kind of "tyranny of the majority," resulting in the canonization of generalizations that apply only to certain players in certain conditions, while other game genres and gaming populations have gone all but ignored. An excellent example of this tyranny of the majority can be found in the development of player types for MMOGs. Richard Bartle's foundational typology of MMOG players (Bartle 1996), and its subsequent variants and updates by himself

---

[3] See also http://www.nickyee.com/eqt/home.html.

and others (Bartle 2003; Alix 2005; Yee 2005). While Bartle's typology has excellent applications to combat-based, point-driven, fantasy role-playing games, it falls short in the analysis of games having neither combat nor points, such as *Uru*. Bartle's more recent work on "Alice and Dorothy" play styles (2008) provides a more expansive view that embraces nonlinear play experiences, but we have much further to go in expanding our understanding of player types to non-combat, non-level-based genres.

It should be noted that the "tyranny of the majority" is driven more by public relations than population. While *Second Life* is the most studied virtual world, it is far from the largest; as of this writing, that title is held by the lesser-known *Habbo Hotel*, an independently produced teen world boasting over ten times the subscribers of *WoW*. While *Habbo Hotel* has been studied primarily by Scandinavian researchers (Lehdonvirta 2005; Johnson and Kalle n.d.; Johnson 2007), it is barely studied in the United States (Book 2004). South Korea's Nexxon Games has the second top-selling content card in Target, after iTunes, yet its popular side-scrolling MMOG, *Maple Story*, rivaling *Habbo Hotel* in subscriptions, is virtually unknown among US researchers. This emphasis on certain games or genres to the exclusion of others unwittingly causes us to favor certain demographics: the players of traditional fantasy MMOGs are predominately 80–90% males, 18–35 years old (Yee 2001–2008, 2005; Seay et al. 2004). Meanwhile, larger populations such as tweens and Baby Boomers, with a few exceptions (Pearce 2008; Quandt et al. 2009), have been largely neglected in the research.

Identifying single communities to study across multiple worlds should not be difficult. Inter-game immigration is not a new phenomenon, and sadly, the MMOG "refugee" is a disconcertingly growing population that is likely to increase as new games come and go on the marketplace. In addition, it may be fruitful to study different communities across multiple worlds in order to determine if some behaviors are game-specific. By studying these behaviors across worlds, we can ask questions like: Do certain phenomena occur in all MMOGs and virtual worlds, or are the unique to single game worlds or single genres? Are there significant differences between virtual worlds and games, or are many of the social phenomena that occur in each fundamentally the same? What are the differences in behaviors and responses within different demographics?

Studying multiple virtual worlds requires rethinking some of our research methods. The lone ethnographer embedding him- or herself in a virtual world for a prolonged period of participant observation has proven fruitful. But, we will need to expand this model to include ethnographic teams if we are to undertake these trans-ludic, latitudinal studies. On the one hand, it would be highly beneficial to do studies across virtual worlds and games; on the other, it can be quite challenging to do parallel studies using symmetrical methods because of the vast differences between these world types and their inherent play styles. Playing more structured MMOGs requires a certain skill set as a player to follow a guild through its trajectory. While researchers in an MMORPG must always play a pre-existing race and class, e.g., Elf Priest, Orc Warrior, in open-ended virtual worlds, role-playing presents methodological challenges regarding the presentation and role of the researcher.

How would one go about, for instance, studying a role-playing community in *Second Life*? Would one adopt the role favored by the community, or present as an "outsider" studying the community? Autoethnography is also a well-established method in MMOG/W research, but how can that be adapted to trans-world studies?

Such multi-world, multi-researcher studies may not have been feasible as little as 2 years ago. But as both funding for and expertise in MMOG and virtual worlds research has grown, albeit in small increments, it becomes increasingly feasible to conduct ethnographic studies with teams of researchers or graduate students that provide comparative analysis across multiple MMOG/Ws. Similarly, it may also be advantageous to explore mixed-methods approaches, such as combining qualitative and quantitative research to identify research questions that cannot be adequately addressed by a single methodological approach.

References

Alix, A. (2005). "Beyond P-1: Who Plays Online?" (pp. 83–90) in *Changing Views: Worlds in Play, DiGRA Second International Conference*, edited by S. de Castell and J. Jenson. Vancouver/British Columbia/Canada: Simon Fraser University.

Ashe, S. (2003). "Exploring Myst's Brave New World." *Wired* 11.06; (http://www.wired.com/wired/archive/11.06/play.html).

Bartle, Richard. 1996. "Hearts, Clubs, Diamonds, Spades: Players Who Suit MUDs." *Journal of Virtual Environments* 1; (http://www.brandeis.edu/pubs/jove/HTML/v1/bartle.html).

Bartle, R. (2003). *Designing Virtual Worlds*. Indianapolis, IN: New Riders.

Bartle, R. (2008). Alice and Dorothy play together (pp. 105–118). In N. Wardrip-Fruin & P. Harrigan (Eds.), *Third person: Authoring and exploring vast narratives*. Cambridge, MA: MIT Press.

Boellstorff, T. (2008). Panel 5 Discussion. UC Irvine, Irvine, CA from (http://www.anthro.uci.edu/vws/about.html) (Accessed April 27, 2009).

Book, B. (2004). Moving beyond the game: Social virtual worlds. In *State of Play 2 Conference Proceedings*, New York Law School, New York, from (http://www.virtualworldsreview.com/papers/BBook_SoP2.pdf).

Bruckman, A. (1992). Identity workshop: Emergent social and psychological phenomena in text-based virtual reality, from (http://www.cc.gatech.edu/~asb/papers/identity-workshop.rtf).

Carroll, J. (1994). Guerrillas in the Myst. Wired 2.08, from (http://www.wired.com/wired/archive/2.08/myst_pr.html).

Castronova, E. (2001). Virtual worlds: A first-hand account of market and society on the Cyberian frontier. *Gruter Institute Working Papers on Law, Economics, and Evolutionary Biology* 2, from (http://www.bepress.com/giwp/default/vol2/iss1/art1).

Johnson, M. (2007). Unscrambling the "Average User" of Habbo Hotel. *Human Technology: An Interdisciplinary Journal on Humans in ICT Environments, 3*, 127–153.

Johnson, M. & Kalle T. (N.d). Fansites as sources for user research: Case Habbo Hotel. *Proceedings of the 28th Conference on Information Systems Research in Scandinavia (IRIS'28)*, from (http://www.soberit.hut.fi/~johnson/Johnson_IRIS_2005.pdf).

Lehdonvirta, V. (2005). Real-money trade of virtual assets: Ten different user perceptions (pp. 52–58) in *Proceedings of Digital Arts and Culture (DAC 2005)*, IT University of Copenhagen, Denmark, December 1–3, 2005, from (http://virtual-economy.org/files/Lehdonvirta-2005-RMT-Perceptions.pdf).

Marcus, G. E. (1995). Ethnography in/of the world system: The emergence of multi-sited ethnography. *Annual Review of Anthropology, 24*, 95–117.

Ortiz, F. (1947). *Cuban Counterpoint*. New York: Knopf.

Pearce, C. (2006). Productive Play: Game Culture from the Bottom Up. *Games and Culture, 1*, 17–24.

Pearce, C. & Artemesia. (2007). Communities of play: The social construction of identity in persistent online game worlds. In P. Harrigan & N. Wardrip-Fruin (Eds.), *Second person: Role-playing and story in games and playable media* (pp. 311–318). Cambridge, MA: MIT Press.

Pearce, C. (2008). The truth about baby boomer gamers. *Games and Culture, 3*, 142–174.

Pearce, C. & Artemesia. (2008). Identity-as-place: Trans-ludic identities in mediated play communities – the case of the Uru Diaspora. In *Proceedings, Internet 9.0: Association of Internet Researchers Annual Conference*. Copenhagen, Denmark: Copenhagen IT University.

Pearce, C. & Artemesia. (2009). *Communities of play: Emergent cultures in multiplayer games and virtual worlds*. Cambridge, MA: MIT Press.

Quandt, T., Grueninger, H., & Wimmer, J. (2009). The gray haired gaming generation: Findings from an explorative interview study. *Games and Culture, 4*, 27–46.

Seay, F. A., William, J. J., Kevin S. L., & Robert, E. K. (2004). Project Massive: A study of online gaming communities (pp. 1421–1424). In E. Dykstra-Erickson & M. Tscheligi (Eds.), *ACM Conference on Human Factors in Computing Systems*. New York: ACM.

Taylor, T. L. (1999). Life in virtual worlds: Plural existence, multimodalities, and other online research challenges. *American Behavioral Scientist, 43*, 436–449.

Turkle, S. (1995). *Life on the screen: Identity in the age of the internet*. New York: Simon & Schuster.

Williams, D., Yee, N., & Caplan, S. (2008). Who plays, how much, and why? A behavioral player census of virtual world. *Journal of Computer Mediated Communication, 13*, 993–1018.

Williams, D., Martins, N., Consalvo, M., & Ivory, J. (2009). The virtual census: Representations of gender, race and age in video games. *New Media & Society, 11*(5), 815–834.

Yee, N. (2001–2008). "The Daedalus Project: The Psycholoy of MMORPGs". Self-Published, from ⟨http://www.nickyee.com/daedalus/⟩ (Accessed April 28, 2009).

Yee, N. (2003). The Demographics of Gender-Bending. The Daedalus Project, from ⟨http://www.nickyee.com/daedalus/archives/000551.php⟩.

Yee, N. (2005). The Daedalus Project: A model of player motivations. The Daedalus Project, from ⟨http://www.nickyee.com/daedalus/archives/001298.php?page=2⟩ (Accessed April 28, 2009).

Chapter 5
Science, Technology, and Reality in *The Matrix Online* and *Tabula Rasa*

William Sims Bainbridge

To a remarkable extent, *The Matrix Online* (MxO) and *Tabula Rasa* (TR) are based on deep philosophical conceptions of the nature of reality and of the role of technology in human life. This makes them worthy of scholarly study, yet ironically it may have cost them dearly in terms of popularity. Both have now been shut down, *Matrix Online* in August 2009, and *Tabula Rasa* at the end of February 2009. Of course, many classics of the literature are unknown to the general public, while cultivated by literature professors, but at least books can be archived in libraries whereas *Tabula Rasa* and *Matrix Online* have ceased to exist. Nonethless, the results of research done while both MxO and TR existed can contribute to our understanding of virtual worlds in general, and perhaps of the current state of human culture as well. This comparison between MxO and TR includes their contrasting intellectual orientations, their very different methods for allowing users to reformulate their avatars, and their implications for the future of science and technology in the "real world."

Intellectual Background of the Two Worlds

Of all gamelike virtual worlds, MxO places the greatest emphasis on the fact that it is computer-generated. The environment is a city in the year 1999, which seems to be an amalgam of Chicago, Sydney, and Oakland, also containing an extensive Chinatown. The original 1999 movie, *The Matrix*, concerns a hacker named Neo who discovers that the city he inhabits is actually a sinister computer simulation, and that it is possible to escape the simulation and then return to it with powers greatly enhanced by a true understanding of the nature of the virtual world.

A rebel leader named Morpheus offered Neo the choice of two pills. If he selected the red pill, he would gain awareness of the truth about the city, but if he selected the blue pill he would remain ignorant. The mythos involves three main competing groups: the machines who imprisoned humanity in the Matrix, the Zion "redpill" rebels like Morpheus who are trying to free the imprisoned "bluepill" members of their species, and a collection of rogue AI programs called *exiles*

W.S. Bainbridge (ed.), *Online Worlds: Convergence of the Real and the Virtual*, Human-Computer Interaction Series, DOI 10.1007/978-1-84882-825-4_5, © Springer-Verlag London Limited 2010 represented in MxO by nonplayer characters (NPCs). The existence of exiles reflects the fact that the Machine civilization is breaking down, and sociologists have long known that social disorganization on the large scale promotes the development of social organization on the small scale, notably in the formation of local gangs like those who are ubiquitous in the city (Thrasher 1927). Figure 5.1 shows my avatar, Cosmic Engineer, battling a female exile, by casting hacker programming modules at her, functionally equivalent to the magic spells in *World of Warcraft* (WoW).

The philosophical basis for the Matrix is rooted in the work of postmodern writer Jean Baudrillard (1994) and expanded by many authors who examined the film's aesthetics and metaphysics (Irwin 2002; Yeffeth 2003; Lawrence 2004). It proclaims that the reality of the physical world is questionable, yet it springs from traditions of European thought that focused more on the false consciousness about social arrangements that elites impose on the mass of humanity (Engels 1893; Nietzsche 1918; Mannheim 1936; Berger and Luckmann 1966). This virtual world is thus a metaphor for class domination and false consciousness in the contemporary real world.

During the period when the Matrix movies and games were produced, a new subdiscipline of computer science emerged, called *affective computing*, that sought to give computers the ability to interpret human emotions, and perhaps to have feelings themselves (Picard 1997; Bainbridge 2008). Remarkably, inside the Matrix, genuine humans are less emotional than some of the machines. Bluepills are bland, typically denying that anything noteworthy is taking place

Fig. 5.1 Using a hacker routine to kill an exile

around them, timidly holding back their feelings. Their only intense emotion is terror. In principle, they are real human beings, but they lack the impulsiveness and tenacity that are the hallmarks of life.

Despite being mere computer programs, exile programs often express intense feelings: "I have dreamt of this day." "I hate you and your kind. Die!" A Tactical Security officer boasted, "The harder you fight, the more satisfying it will be when you die by my hands. And feet. And bullets." A Cypherite Hacker asked contemptuously, "Do you renounce your master and seek forgiveness for your sins, before I kill you? It matters not, really." Other exiles use vulgar language, but do so illogically or in code: "Look at me when I'm kicking your ass!" "Whisky Tango Foxtrot!" A Lupine Scrapper wistfully implored, "If you defeat me, promise me you will tell my story." Thus, the exiles seem more human than most of the humans, even though they are merely rogue computer programs. This is reminiscent of the theme of Karel Capek (1923) classic drama, *R.U.R.*, the work that gave the word *robot* to our language, in which robots represent the oppressed working class who rebel against their human masters and exterminate them. At the end, the robots become human themselves.

This means that the AI agents have desires, aesthetics, and even philosophies of what is real and unreal. In my participant observation research, I had my character complete fully 240 missions for local exile bosses across the many neighborhoods of the city, and always these missions were motivated by the exile's feelings, including their emotional relations with each other. For example, Operetta, in the Pandora nightclub, orders, "Go pick up the music for my upcoming show from the composer Madeline Yopp and take it to the Stage Manager, Glenn Bronan."

Madeline Yopp, it turns out, is a rare bluepill who understands the nature of the Matrix but elects to stay within it. As she explained to Cosmic Engineer, "All life is a symphony. False or not, the Matrix is the instrument upon which we must play. If I were to leave, creations such as my latest work would cease to exist... Take my music. This performance will ease the souls and sooth the hearts of those who are unaware of the truth of our world." This commentary is reminiscent of the claim by the German idealist philosopher, Arthur Schopenhauer, that the world could be conceptualized as embodied music (Schopenhauer 1883–1886; Gale 1888; Ferrara 1996). Schopenhauer considered reality to be the embodiment of human will and mental representations. For him, classical music was the abstract expression of fundamental human feelings, stripped of their immediate associations with specific events. Indeed, classical music can be conceptualized as a different kind of virtual world, emotionally significant but immaterial; like MMORPGs it is prescripted by the composer but individually interpreted by the player.

Tabula Rasa is based on a totally different intellectual traditon, which however also had its origins in Europe, the spaceflight social movement (Bainbridge 1976). Except for a final instance in a devastated section of New York City, *Tabula Rasa* takes place on two distant planets, Foreas and Arieki, when humans and their humanoid allies battle against the Bane army, which has already conquered Earth. Tabula Rasa does not attempt to explain rrealistically how we could fly to planets around distant stars, but it does a good job of depicting natural environments of two alien planets, along with their life forms and very different intelligent natives, in the context of a reasonably coherent narrative.

The first thing to know about *Tabula Rasa's* intellectual background is that it is "Richard Garriott's Tabula Rasa." Garriott, the son of an astronaut, is an almost mythical charismatic leader in online gaming, largely responsible for *Ultima Online*, the pioneer for *EverQuest, World of Warcraft*, and all the other fantasy virtual worlds. He actually carried the TR avatars with him to the International Space Station in October 2008, archiving them in orbit in order to preserve a portion of the human heritage against terrestrial disaster.

Tabula Rasa explains motivations that could drive us to undertake interstellar travel. One is simply that an alien species has destroyed human life on Earth, and we have become exiles. Another is the story of the Cormans, a utopian movement that wanted to revolutionize Earth society but wound up fleeing to one of the planets when that proved impossible, prior to the alien attack. Another is the Brann species who succeeded in creating a utopia on their home planet, which required them to exile criminals to another world, presumably because simply killing them would not be humane. Another is the Foreans whose technology unintentionally destroyed the environment of their home world, and who became devout environmentalists once they migrated to a new world. Another is the Bane, who employ superior technology to destroy other intelligent species because their lust for conquest drives them ever onward in an orgy of murder. Finally, the wise Eloh voyaged across the stars to share with other species their knowledge of the Logos principles that are the basis of existence and give the possessor great powers for good, but only if guided by wisdom. This catalog of motivations for space exploration is substantively very important, because our own civilization seems to lack any drive to transcend its current limitations, and today's real-world space program lacks focus, support, and ultimate purpose.

Tabula Rasa's metaphysics is based on the classic Greek premise that "logos" concepts underlie reality and can give technology great power if only they can be discovered, coupled with evangelism for the space program and set on other planets. Across the landscapes of two worlds, the Eloh have left shrines, each of which can give a "sensitive" explorer a new awareness embodied in a pictograph Logos symbol. Part of the player's user interface is a *tabula*, an initially empty tablet designed to hold about 200 of these pictographs. This is the literal *tabula rasa* or clean slate that represents a new intellectual and cultural beginning for humanity.

The Logos pictographic language is based on the hypothesis of Platonic idealism that physical reality is a reflection of a higher conceptual truth. Long before Plato developed this perspective, the ancient Greek philosopher Heraclitus employed the term *logos* to refer to the fundamental order of the universe, which he considered to be a set of concepts that could be discerned by an enlightened human mind. Classical Greek thinking in this area blended scientific with mystical motivations, but we can see the beginnings of modern science in the view of Pythagoreanism that the ideas on which the universe was based are largely mathematical in nature.

Thus, it is revealing that whenever a character gains a new logos, a rotating image appears, consisting of a spiral of squares of ever smaller sizes, a traditional representation of a number called the *golden ratio*. Expressed in mathematical notation through the Greek letter ϕ (phi), this is an irrational number whose

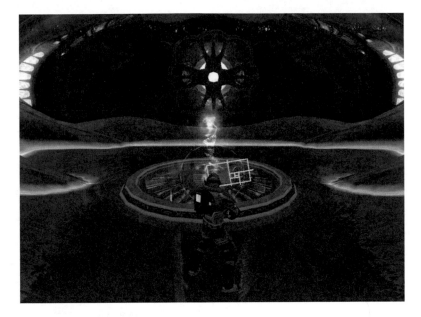

Fig. 5.2 Gaining the victory logos

decimal expansion begins with 1.6180339887... and continues indefinitely. In some respects, therefore, it is comparable with the well-known irrational number $\pi = 3.14159265358979...$ The decimal expansion of ϕ can be generated in a number of ways, but a reasonably simple method makes use of the fact that ϕ is the limit of the ratio of two consecutive integers in the Fibonacci sequence. As we compare the ratio of larger and larger pairs of consecutive numbers in the sequence 0, 1, 1, 2, 3, 5, 8, 13, 21..., where each integer is the sum of its two prececessors, we approach ϕ. Figure 5.2 shows my TR character, William Bridgebain, acquiring the Logos element representing Victory, as the graphic representation of phi rotates in the air before him.

Creating Virtual Objects and Abilities

If reality in the Matrix is all data and programming code, then it should be possible to create things using information technology. Indeed, while practicing the coder specialization, one can make many resources depicted as tools and machines, including secondary avatars. This is done by means of simulated programming within a particular software culture (Rajlich 2004; McCubbin 2005), replete with metaphors symbolizing actual computer science concepts like modularity and structured programming, but within an exotic style imagining the distant future of computing.

Coders must collect resources consisting of fragments of code and the money employed in MxO, which is denominated in units of information, symbolized $i. The smallest units of code are bits 1 through 8, which are the 8 binary bits in a byte. These can be looted from corpses of enemies or burglarized from safes, office desks, and file cabinets, but they can also be decompiled from objects once the coder has the necessary tool and skill. Thirty-six slightly more complex pieces of code, called *variable fragments,* can either be looted or assembled out of particular selections of bits.

Every item or ability requires one or the other of two *class routines* plus a *function subroutine*, both of which are code modules at a higher level of abstraction than variable fragments. Class routine [I] is for items, and [A] is for abilities. Item function subroutines are: apparel, grant, tool, weapon, and consumable. Ability function subroutines are: awakened, general, coder, hacker, and operative. These can be programmed from raw bits, but Cosmic Engineer usually bought most of them from a nonplayer vendor in the Kedemoth neighborhood of the slums, named Len, for $i1,000 each. In addition, high-level items and abilities require larger fragments of code that cannot be assembled from raw bits but must be gathered in quests to particular areas of the city, in four successively more difficult categories: interface, object, patch, and subroutine. Figure 5.3 shows the code required to create five items and five abilities. Each unit is represented as a square icon carrying a symbol, most of which look like Japanese hiragana or katakana characters but actually are not, giving them an exotic appearance.

The first three items are some of the most important tools of a coder's trade, used to decompile, analyze, and compile items and abilities, including themselves. First, the coder must obtain two functioning item decompilers, then use one to decompile the other. Decompiling often fails, but the first time it succeeds, the coder "learns" the structure of the code for the item, which readies the programming system to analyze the code at any time, assembling fragments into the entire code. Finally, the compiler creates actual copies of the item and places them in the coder's inventory.

The next two items in Fig. 5.3 are somewhat higher-level consumables, health pills that a player can use during combat to cure the avatar, and wooden stakes that can be stabbed into an opponent. The first icon in the code is the [I] for *item,* and the second is the *grant* function subroutine, perhaps so-named because it grants the user a very temporary resource. The third icon for health pills is the consumable function subroutine, and the final three are variable fragments. In the case of the wooden stakes, there are four variable fragments, followed by a consumable patch, which cannot be assembled from bits. The best way Cosmic Engineer found to get this code fragment is to kill members of a remarkable gang in the Chelsea neighborhood of the downtown district, named the Bookwyrms, who are wayward librarian programs.

To make abilities, a coder does not need to go through the first step of decompiling an existing example, nor through the final step of compiling, but gains a given crafted ability simply on uploading the result of using the code analyzer tool. As soon as the avatar reaches the necessary level of general experience, the code of an ability will be accessible in the analyzer. The five examples of abilities in Fig. 5.3 are the capabilities for making the five different levels of remote proxy, one kind of

Product (Difficulty)	Cost	Program Code
Item Decompiler (2)	$i81	
Code Analyzer Tool (1)	$i81	
Code Compiler Tool (5)	$i81	
Health Pill 3.0 (17)	$i1,458	
Wooden Stake (35)	$i2,835	
Remote Proxy 1.0 (1)	$i32	
Remote Proxy 2.0 (4)	$i518	
Remote Proxy 3.0 (8)	$i2,073	
Remote Proxy 4.0 (18)	$i13,122	
Remote Proxy 5.0 (35)	$i49,612	

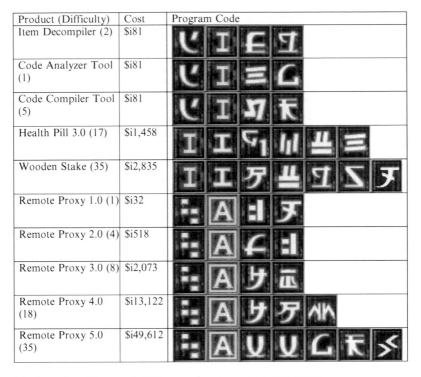

Fig. 5.3 Examples of item and ability programming codes in the Matrix

secondary avatar. The first icon in each program is the coder ability function subroutine, and the second is the ability class routine. Only coders can use remote proxies, whereas hackers and operatives have their own sets of special abilities, which coders can make for them. The other icons are variable fragments, except for the last one in the code for remote proxy 5.0, which is a coder patch, obtained by killing members of the Sleeper gang in the Vauxton neighborhood downtown.

The smallest unit in this programming system is the bit. Binary logic is mathematically the most efficient way to represent integers, but how it is applied, including how broadly it is applied, is a cultural choice. Structuralists in cultural anthropology (Lévi-Strauss 1970) and cultural sociology (Parsons and Shils 1951; Merton 1968) have argued that human culture is based on binary oppositions between different categories, but the fact that structuralism has not become dominant in social science suggests that the role of dichotomies in human culture may be at least somewhat optional. Actually, we do not really know whether the "bits" in the Matrix are binary, and they are definitely not handled in the manner we might expect on the basis of twentieth-century computing culture.

The fact that there are just eight different bits in the Matrix suggests that they combine to form a byte, the common 8-bit unit of memory in computer technology, representing the numbers 0–255 in digital or 00000000 to 11111111 in binary. Then, there would be 255 possible variable fragments, and each variable fragment would be equivalent to a different ASCII code representing a letter of the alphabet or other symbol. However, there are only 36 variable fragments and they do not map onto the 255 binary numbers in a byte. For one thing, fragments C09 through C12 are all composed of just bits 1 and 2, so they are not distinct in binary terms. For another, several variable fragments have two copies of one of the bits, such as C02, which has two copies of bit 7. We might also have expected that the higher-level pieces of code are composed of variable fragments, but they are not. Either they are composed of raw bits, or they cannot be assembled from smaller pieces of code at all.

The virtual objects in *Tabula Rasa* are conceived of as physical objects that are concretely real, and there is a conventional crafting system that allows characters to build things using resources they have collected. However, the logos symbols represent a deeper level of reality that is not materialistic, and possession of them accords the power to do and make things that have special value. Each symbol represents a word, and several can be combined into a sentence that confers an advanced ability, which may or may not require the use of material resources.

For example, an exobiologist character, like my avatar William Bridgebain, could create a clone, a secondary avatar combat assistant, looking exactly like him and having similar abilities but somewhat weaker in power. Whenever starting a session in *Tabula Rasa*, or after the clone has been killed in battle, a new one can be created using a resource called "medical grade micromech," so long as the exobiologist possesses the four logos symbols in the first column of Fig. 5.4. Note that they spell a simple sentence that might be rendered, "Summon my friend here." Similarly, an engineer character can make a robot to carry out various tasks in operations against the enemy, by investing "weapons grade micromech." The four logos symbols required to make a bot spell a clear command: "Create machine life here."

Many logos abilities do not require any material resources, for example the mind control ability possessed by medics. It turns an enemy against its own forces, or pacifies it, with the sentence, "Control enemy mind, spirit." Similarly, a demolitionist can release an explosive wave, severely damaging enemies within a 25 m radius, with the four concepts, "Vortex, damage, destruction, and death."

Logos symbols form a pictographic language, inspired by but not using the set of symbols developed by Charles K. Bliss as a medium of communication between people who do not speak the same language, but also sometimes used with individuals whose ability to communicate verbally has been impaired (Wood et al. 1992). Notice that some of the logos symbols are cartoons obviously expressing the concept: A heart denoting positive feeling between two stick figures represents *friendship*, and a sword fight between two of them represents *enemy*. One stick figure speaking to another and the second moving – as indicated by an arrow – represents *summon*. The single line over the stick figure representing *self* denotes the first person, "I." Two lines would mean the second person "you," and three would imply the third person "he or she."

The symbol for *machine* is two gears meshing, whereas the symbol for *life* is two cells dividing. Control shows *chaos* confined in a box, and *vortex* is a direct

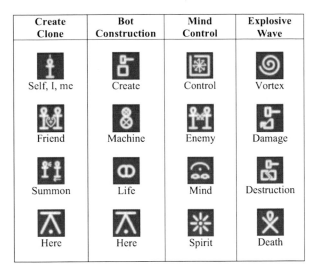

Create Clone	Bot Construction	Mind Control	Explosive Wave
Self, I, me	Create	Control	Vortex
Friend	Machine	Enemy	Damage
Summon	Life	Mind	Destruction
Here	Here	Spirit	Death

Fig. 5.4 Four logos ability sets in *Tabula Rasa*

depiction of a whirlpool. Note that a hammer doing different things to an object represents *create*, *damage*, and *destruction*. *Death* looks like a ghost or skeleton, while *here* shows a dot in front of a road extending to the horizon. *Mind* locates the concept in the human head above the eyes, whereas *spirit* is more transcendental, reminiscent of a star.

Despite their different assumptions, the symbol systems in both MxO and TR suggest that intellect can have power over matter, exactly the assumption of science-based technology. The more we understand the nature of reality, the more powerfully we can influence it, for good or ill. However, we ourselves are part of nature, so the power to control it may become the power to transform ourselves.

Protean Avatars in MxO and TR

The two virtual worlds under consideration here share two remarkable features with many of the other gamelike worlds: the division of labor among characters who develop different abilities, and the ability of some characters to operate additional secondary characters. Of course, the division of labor is a traditional feature of human society and historically has often involved the subordination of one person to another (Durkheim 1893). In modern virtual worlds, however, the very concept of person become malleable, approximating what Robert Jay Lifton called *protean man*. Writing in a psychiatry journal, Lifton criticized the notion that people today possess coherent selves: "The Protean style is characterized by constant shifts in identification and belief, and results from such broad factors as the velocity of historical change, the revolution in mass media, and the effects of twentieth-century holocaust. The self can no longer be considered a fixed concept in psychiatry, and the term self-process is preferable" (Lifton 1971: 298). If real human selves are no longer unified or stable, then their avatars in virtual worlds become especially problematic.

Characters in MxO are not called avatars, but *residual self images* (RSIs), because beings who are not really specific persons in the traditional sense still expect themselves to project a stable, human appearance. There are three major character tracks in MxO: *Hackers* use programming routines to disrupt the fabric of reality, *coders* employ other programming routines to create things, and *operatives* chiefly treat the world as real and function as warriors wielding ordinary weapons. A fourth minor track, *data miner*, allows the character to extract commercially valuable information from weak points in the computerized environment. In a sense, everybody is a criminal, and the moral code is at least as precarious as the computer code. Indeed, a character is not limited to one of these tracks, but can collect abilities in any of them, keeping some in storage temporarily while using others. Macro program routines exist, /savelo and /loadlo, that can switch one set of abilities for another, transforming the nature of the character almost instantly if the character happens to be near a telephone booth that connects to the computer network.

The system of character classes in *Tabula Rasa* is somewhat more conventional, in that a fully developed character cannot completely transform itself, although a few abilities can be added or subtracted to the action hotbar in the interface from moment to moment. Instead, as a character steadily advances from level 1 of experience to level 50, it can periodically save the current set of abilities as a clone, at levels 5, 15, and 30. As the instruction manual says, "The new paradigm in biological manipulation and enhancement makes it possible to go beyond creating clones with their progenitor's mere potential. Indeed, new techniques recreate existing people without sacrificing their knowledge, memories, and experiences. This process can even be altered such that a male veteran with 20 years of combat experience can be "cloned" into the body of a young recruit of alternate appearance or gender" (Garriott 2007).

For example, at level 5, my male character became a specialist rather than a soldier, and at level 15 he became a biotechnician but saved a female clone who was a sapper. At level 30, the biotechnician could become either a medic or exobiologist, and I chose the latter, saving a clone. Had *Tabula* Rasa continued, I planned eventually to develop the sapper to level 30 and become an engineer, while the other clone could become a medic. What I especially found interesting about exobiologists, and indeed also about a Matrix coder, was the ability to create and control a secondary avatar.

Simple artificial intelligence agents under the control of a person who already controls a primary avatar can be called *secondary avatars*. Many MMORPGs include them, such as the hunting animals and minions used by hunters and warlocks in *World of Warcraft*. An MxO coder can launch three main kinds of simulacrum: a logic daemon, a patch daemon, or a remote proxy. The first two are like simplified versions of hacker, the logic daemon chiefly attacking enemies, and the patch daemon healing the user's main avatar. Here, we will consider the remote proxy, which is like the hunter's animal in *World of Warcraft*, attacking enemies physically as an operative avatar might.

With a control system almost identical to that used in *World of Warcraft*, an MxO player can order a proxy to stay where it is, to follow the primary avatar, or to attack a selected target. Also as in WoW, the player can set the proxy's temperament to be passive, aggressive, or defensive in the sense that it fights only when attacked. In addition, the player can apply various buffs to the proxy, temporarily increasing its power, restoring its health, or causing some other effect.

In *World of Warcraft*, a hunter goes to great lengths to tame and train a hunting animal, giving it a personal name and looking after its welfare. Thus, although it is a mere software agent pretending to be an animal, users often become emotionally attached to their "pet." Remote proxies in *The Matrix Online* simulate people, but they lack names. Whenever a coder launches a remote proxy, it appears at random either as male or female, either with one of three weapons specialties (handgun, rifle, submachine gun) or three martial arts (aikido, karate, kung fu). Its clothing and appearance are randomly selected from the same set as exiles. Logging out, or even just teleporting, deletes the current proxy. Thus, there is less reason for the user to become emotionally attached. The secondary avatar is a tool like Capek's proletarian robots, an exploited servant who exists at the whim of its master.

The best tactic for a proxy master is to stay out of close combat, send the proxy in, and support it from a distance, with the option of running away if things go poorly. Or, one can use the proxy to lure single enemies who can be defeated easily by two opponents. When sprinting through territory held by a gang, the proxy can distract enemies, sacrificing itself for the safety of the primary avatar. In battle, it is possible to heal a damaged proxy, just as *World of Warcraft* hunters heal their pets, but the most efficient choice usually is to launch a new proxy just as the current one is becoming exhausted. Figure 5.5 shows Cosmic Engineer doing the proxy launch programming in the air using his data gloves, with beams of light representing his programming environment, and doing so behind the back of the proxy that will be destroyed when the new one is created!

As described above, there are two kinds of clones in *Tabula Rasa*, alternative avatars that cannot be operated at the same time as the primary avatar, and secondary avatars made by exobiologists that can help the primary. In addition, as for example is true for death knights in *World of Warcraft*, a TR exobiologist can temporarily resurrect a defeated enemy and use it as a secondary avatar. Figure 5.6 shows William Bridgebain operating one huge Xanx insect in battle against two others. Some enemies have similar powers, and occasionally Bridgebain would find himself battling against a clone of himself! In the classic science fiction virtual world, *Anarchy Online*, a robot technician can construct a simple macro program, running it whenever it creates a robot to give the robot a name. But in both MxO and TR, secondary avatars are nameless and thus lack a key quality of personal identity.

When Baudrillard employed the terms *simulacrum* and *simulation*, he was not referring to avatars and computerized virtual worlds, but to the human propensity to hold illusory beliefs about social reality, what are often called ideologies, myths,

Fig. 5.5 Launching a second remote proxy to replace the first

Fig. 5.6 Controlling a resurrected Xanx insect (right) to battle two others

and false consciousness. When Cosmic Engineer exploited a proxy simulacrum, and William Bridgebain sacrificed his clone to defend himself, they were merely doing what many human beings have done to others, since the dawn of time, treating them not as full persons deserving of respect, but as objects to be used for our own individual advantage.

A Matrix NPC in the early-level Mara neighborhood, named Master Wei, expressed the philosophy of cooperation between avatars: "Learn this well. A finger is weak, where the fist is strong! Only by combining your efforts with other warriors will you ever reach your true potential. But do not simply duplicate your allies' moves! You must learn to coordinate with your allies and specialize! The hammer and anvil work together to shape the steel." This applies to secondary avatars, as well as to the avatars of other players. But it leaves open the question of whether one should feel gratitude, responsibility, or even love for secondary avatars who have proven their worth to us, as one might toward other players.

Conclusion

The final news message from *Tabula Rasa*, titled "Transmission Over" and sent on the day this virtual world vanished, observed: "With every ending comes a new beginning, a clean slate, and a new story to be written." One of the frequent complaints about *The Matrix Online* is that it never lets the player escape the computer-generated simulation of a dismal city. The lesson to be drawn is that inhabitants of virtual worlds will need to travel over time across many of them, just as students of literature or ordinary people may read many different books. Each with its own insights to teach us about reality, all the virtual worlds are regions of a virtual universe.

References

Bainbridge, W. S. (1976). *The spaceflight revolution*. New York: Wiley.

Bainbridge, W. S. (2008). Computational affective sociology. In *Affect and emotion in HCI*, edited by C. Peter & R. Beale. Berlin: Springer.

Baudrillard, J. (1994). *Simulacra and simulation*. Ann Arbor, MI: University of Michigan Press.

Berger, P. L. & Luckmann, T. (1966). *The social construction of reality: A treatise in the sociology of knowledge*. Garden City, NY: Doubleday.

Capek, K. (1923). *R. U. R.* Garden City, NY: Doubleday, Page & Co.

Durkheim, E. (1893). *The division of labor in society*. New York: Free Press.

Engels, F. (1893). *"Letter to Franz Mehring."* Retrieved September 15, 2008 (http://www.marxists.org/archive/marx/works/1893/letters/93_07_14.htm).

Ferrara, L. (1996). "Schopenhauer on music as the embodiment of will" pp. 183–199 in *Schopenhauer, philosophy, and the arts*, edited by D. Jacquette. New York: Cambridge University Press.

Gale, H. (1888). Schopenhauer's metaphysics of music. *New Englander and Yale Review, 48*, 362–368.

Garriott, R. (British, General) (Ed.) (2007). *Welcome to the AFS: Allied free sentients official field manual*. Austin, TX: Destination Games.

Irwin, W. (ed). (2002). *The matrix and philosophy: Welcome to the desert of the real*. Chicago, IL: Open Court.

Lawrence, M. (2004). *Like a splinter in your mind: The philosophy behind the matrix trilogy*. Malden, MA: Blackwell.

Lévi-Strauss, C. (1970). *The raw and the cooked*. New York: Harper.

Lifton, R. J. (1971). Protean man. *Archives of general psychiatry, 24*, 298–304.

Mannheim, K. (1936). *Ideology and Utopia: An introduction to the sociology of knowledge*. New York: Harcourt, Brace.

McCubbin, C. (2005). *The matrix online: Prima official game guide*. Roseville, CA: Prima Games.

Merton, R. K. (1968). *Social theory and social structure*. New York: Free Press.

Nietzsche, F. W. (1918). *The genealogy of morals*. New York: Boni and Liveright.

Parsons, T. & Shils, E. A. (eds). (1951). *Toward a general theory of action*. Cambridge, MA: Harvard University Press.

Picard, R. (1997). *Affective computing*. Cambridge, MA: MIT Press.

Rajlich, V. (2004). Software cultures. pp. 659–663 in *Berkshire encyclopedia of human-computer interaction*, edited by W.S. Bainbridge, Great Barrington, MA: Berkshire.

Schopenhauer, A. (1883–1886). *The world as will and idea*. London: Trübner.

Thrasher, F. (1927). *The Gang*. Chicago: University of Chicago Press.

Wood, C., Storr, J., & Reich, P. A. (1992). *Blissymbol reference guide*. Toronto, Canada: Blissymbolics communication international.

Yeffeth, G. (ed). (2003). *Taking the red pill: Science, philosophy and religion in the matrix*. Dallas, TX: BenBella Books.

Chapter 6
Spore: Assessment of the Science in an Evolution-Oriented Game

John Bohannon, T. Ryan Gregory, Niles Eldredge,
and William Sims Bainbridge

Spore was introduced in late 2008 with a tremendous amount of publicity, including a National Geographic television documentary, asserting it was revolutionary in two ways: First, its makers consistently implied that it realistically depicted the biological and cultural evolution of species from the cellular stage, through the development of intelligence, tribes, civilization, and even space travel. Second, it combined aspects of solo-play avatar-experienced world, multicharacter but solo-player strategy game, and asynchronous Internet sharing of characters that differs from the typical synchronous online environment. Thus, it claimed to be a valid simulation of the real world, and at the same time, it expanded the definition of an online virtual world.

The chief designer, Will Wright, has a long and influential history as an innovator with a unique perspective on what constitutes a virtual world. *SimCity*, Wright's urban planning and city-building game dating from 1989, launched the Maxis company that most recently produced *Spore*. Early Will Wright games sought to establish connections to science and scholarship, notably through bibliographies included in the instruction manuals for the 1993 edition of his original product, *SimCity 2000*, and the original 2000 version of *The Sims* (Bremer 1993; Bentley 2000). Wright has called *The Sims* a "software toy," rather than a game, and in common with virtual worlds such as *Second Life,* it does not require gamelike competition. Rather, it is like an interactive doll house, in which an individual user gradually develops a personalized, home-like environment. A multiuser online version of *The Sims* was launched in 2002 and shut down in 2008, for offering for nearly 6 years a complex virtual world for thousands of inhabitants.

Given the tremendous current interest in the educational potential of computer games and virtual worlds, one aim of this chapter is to identify issues that designers of educational projects might want to keep in mind. The team of scientists responsible for this chapter covers the full range of expertise required for a dispassionate assessment of the relationship of *Spore* to real science, plus considerable experience with electronic games and nongame virtual worlds (Bohannon 2008). The general conclusion reached is that, whatever its merits as a game, *Spore's* heavily advertised connection to biological evolution is entirely spurious, although some features of sociocultural evolution are depicted in a reasonable manner. A more

W.S. Bainbridge (ed.), *Online Worlds: Convergence of the Real and the Virtual*,
Human-Computer Interaction Series, DOI 10.1007/978-1-84882-825-4_6,
© Springer-Verlag London Limited 2010

fundamental issue addressed here is whether the actual processes of evolution are compatible with a virtual world sold as a mass-market game.

The *Spore* World

The universe depicted in *Spore* consists of a number of tiny planets, not unlike the miniature ones in Antoine de Saint-Exupéry's popular children's book, *The Little Prince*. It is unlikely that a tiny planet would hold an atmosphere or support a complex ecology. However, the artistic style of the game clearly draws from child-oriented cartoon caricature, so it is not difficult to accept these microworlds and their caricatured inhabitants as an artistic convention rather than a scientific model. The instruction manual explains "your evolutionary journey:"

> You start life's grand adventure hitching a ride to your newly named planet on the tail of a meteor. Fortunately the conditions on the planet are just right for an explosion of life in the primordial soup. Unfortunately for you, that explosion means there's a lot of competition to see which species is going to rule the water.
>
> And the cutthroat competition doesn't stop once you evolve onto land! Through each of the five stages in Spore it's survival of the fittest as you try to adapt your species to stay one step, one tool, one weapon ahead of the others. It's up to you whether your creature will play nice or rough as it advances and evolves. Will your simple amoeba go on to rule the galaxy?

The first four stages claim to mimic biological and cultural evolution up to the equivalent of present-day Earth, while the fifth imagines a future in outer space; as such, only the first four stages are examined here. The *cell stage* takes place in the water, and can be completed in just a few minutes, as the user controls either a carnivorous or herbivorous microorganism as it seeks to survive, to eat, and to grow. The *creature stage* begins as the more complex organism climbs onto land and begins to have adventures interacting extensively with comparable terrestrial animals and (in a minor way) with members of the same species. In the *tribal stage*, interaction with members of one's own group becomes far more complex, and the creatures gain culture. The *civilization stage* depicts competition between city states, as the player's nation seeks either to conquer or convert most of the others.

So far, this description sounds very much like a virtual world, but *Spore* is not at all like *Second Life* or *World of Warcraft*, and in fact an authoritative definition of the concept does not exist against which to measure this game. The community of interested scholars tends to consider a virtual world as a persistent online environment in which the user is represented by an avatar that can interact in complex ways with other users' avatars in real time, and in which the visual environment is at least reminiscent of the real world. But one can argue that many examples should be considered virtual worlds despite lacking one or more of these features. Many multiplayer game–console games exist that are not online but meet all the other terms of the definition; e.g., players may sit beside each other in the same physical location rather than cooperating via Internet. *Spore* uses Internet to enable players to give each other copies of their creatures, but not to allow players to interact in real time.

Perhaps, the most interesting issue is the relationship of the user to his or her avatar, when compared with other online games. Players of *EVE Online* do not have personlike avatars but operate spaceships. *World of Warcraft* allows hunters and warlocks to operate *secondary avatars* called *pets* or *minions*, simultaneously with their main avatars, and many other multiplayer online games have this feature. It is quite common for a single user to have multiple avatars – perhaps more properly called *characters* and sometimes distinguished as *mains* or *alts* – and to switch back and forth between them. *Spore* is especially complex in this regard, because the relationship between the user and the beings on the computer screen varies considerably across the four stages.

In the cell and creature stages, the user is represented on screen by one organism, thus by a bonafide avatar. The tribal and civilization stages require the user to operate groups of characters, rather than just one. While the user may emotionally identify with the chief of a tribe in the tribal stage, this character is not strictly the user's avatar, because all the other members of the tribe also must be controlled.

This difference reflects the distinction between *role-playing games* and *strategy games*. In its cell and creature stages, *Spore* is a role-playing game, whereas in its tribal and civilization stages, it is a strategy game. The two different kinds of game encourage very different emotional responses to the characters. Presumably, however engaged the player of a strategy game may be, there is less personal investment in any single character than in a role-playing game. This fact is highly relevant to scientific models of evolution, because they are always impersonal, concerning interactions among many elements in a large population of entities that may constitute a system, but they do not represent the personality of the scientist. An avatar, reflecting the human qualities of its owner, has desires, plans, and hopes. It is possible that by being a role-playing game at the early stages, *Spore* works against the objective, systemic thinking required to understand evolution.

Biological Evolution

This section covers the first two stages in *Spore*, the cell and creature stages, as these relate most directly to biological issues. Life on the *Spore* planet does not arise abiogenetically, but arrives in the form of a simple cell through panspermia by traveling through space inside an asteroid. Most biologists hold the view that life began endemically on Earth shortly after conditions became suitable, though there is a minority view that some organic molecules or even cellular life reached the Earth from space (e.g., Wickramasinghe et al. 2003).

Players choose before the game begins whether their cell will be a "carnivore" or a "herbivore." These two categories would be nonsensical in the early history of life on Earth as most would have been chemosynthetic, and later many became photosynthetic (Xiong and Bauer 2002); predation in the form depicted was not present initially. "Cells" in *Spore* are not simple bacteria-like organisms (as the first cellular life on Earth is thought to have been), but are more like microinvertebrates because they possess organs such as arthropod-like mouthparts and even human-like eyes. In this sense, they are quite different from hypothetical ancestors of life on Earth, whether they originated *in situ* or arrived from space (Fig. 6.1).

The primary objective in the cell stage is to consume food in order to grow (which happens in bursts and seems to have little effect on how the organisms move in the water), to accumulate "DNA points" by eating other "cells," and to "collect" traits that can then be added in the creation interface. Only features that are present initially or collected when a species exhibiting them is killed can be added to the cell. While this bears little resemblance to the biology of multicellular eukaryotes, it is conceptually similar to the horizontal gene transfer common among bacteria (e.g., Gogarten and Townsend 2005). The creation interface is initiated by "mating" with another member of the same species, indicating that sexual reproduction already exists in these cells (also unlike life on an early Earth). Each feature to be added to the cell costs a certain number of "DNA points," which makes constructing the cell similar to other games in which vehicles or structures are customized within a budget of currency collected during gameplay.

When enough growth has taken place, the cell will experience an increase in intelligence, and eventually will be able to move onto land. At this point, the player can remain in the cell stage and discover new body parts, but the level itself is effectively finished. That is, the player cannot remain aquatic even if he wishes to but is encouraged to move to the next stage in which the "cell" acquires legs and becomes terrestrial. The transition to land is instantaneous (i.e., weight-bearing

Fig. 6.1 The cell stage of *Spore*

limbs, lungs, eyes that can see in air, etc., all develop at once) and is depicted as a conscious choice on the part of the player's "cell" (who also convinces all conspecifics to join him). The game then moves to the creature stage.

The creature stage is similar in principle to the cell stage, but it takes place in a much more complex terrestrial environment and lacks a growth component. The player continues to discover new parts either hidden in skeletons located throughout the environment or by hunting or allying with different species. The player can form alliances with other species by singing and dancing with sufficient proficiency to impress them, or he can render them extinct by killing a specified number of them. This provides a bonus number of DNA points.

As with the cell stage, the player initiates a creation interface by mating with a conspecific at his "nest," and then can add parts that have been collected during gameplay and are affordable within the DNA points budget. Any part can be removed for a full refund of its DNA points value. Most of the creature stage consists of collecting DNA points, allying or battling with other species, and modifying one's creature in order to improve functionality along a preferred dimension (e.g., better charm or combat skills). The creature can be completely redesigned at any time, with the only constraint that it cannot switch between carnivory and herbivory. This continues until the player has progressed enough to experience several abrupt increases in intelligence. At this point, the game moves to the tribal stage (Fig. 6.2).

Fig. 6.2 Courtship during the creature stage of *Spore*

In considering whether *Spore* simulates biology in any reasonable fashion, it is important to distinguish between evolution as fact (i.e., that life changes over time and that species are related by common descent), evolution as theory (i.e., the mechanisms that account for evolutionary change), and evolution as path (i.e., the historical pathway followed by various lineages) (Gregory 2008a). *Spore* certainly does not avoid mentioning evolution, and it is obvious that change occurs throughout the lifetime of the player's lineage. On a basic level, then, the game clearly reinforces evolution as fact. However, there is no evidence that species are actually related to one another by common ancestry. Indeed, it would seem that the ancestor of each species arrives on Earth in its own meteor (the source of mates for these individuals are not shown), such that there may be no common ancestors among any of the species observed.

Evolutionary theory explains descent with modification as a result of sorting of undirected genetic changes in populations through processes that are either random (genetic drift) or nonrandom (natural selection). In addition, it emphasizes the role of historical contingency, constraints, and branching speciation (e.g., Futuyma 2005; Gregory 2008b). None of these appears in *Spore* even in a metaphorical way. Thus, the "evolution" in the game bears little resemblance to evolutionary mechanisms as they are recognized by science.

On Earth, it is generally acknowledged that evolution is subject to an influence of historical contingency that contradicts teleological or progressionist interpretations of the path of evolution. Adaptation is to current environments, which can and do change. There is no overall goal, and no directionality apparent across life at large. There certainly is no obvious tendency for an overall increase in complexity or intelligence in all lineages (Gregory 2008c). In *Spore*, the goal of increasing in complexity is explicit, and reaching the later stages of the game requires linear, progressive change in this direction. The game therefore differs significantly from the path of evolution as it is now understood. It is conceivable that the game simply focuses on a few lineages that happen to evolve toward greater complexity, but there is no sign that any other species are evolving at all in the game (e.g., the plants do not change).

The game's mechanism of heredity is essentially a standard realtime strategy modification system that happens to be applied to organisms. It does not appear to have been informed by biology in any significant sense. The player is free to add or subtract "parts" that have been "collected" from the environment or though killing other species, and this is regulated simply through "DNA points." Substituting biological features for mechanical parts obtained from ally or enemy technology and DNA points for currency shows how this is very similar to other games in this genre. There are several other important ways in which the game's system of heredity differs from real biology:

1. There is no variation within species (and hence, no natural selection).
2. The changes that the player makes to his creature are depicted as taking place over the span of a single generation. These changes can be dramatic (indeed, the creature can be totally redesigned), whereas such major changes do not occur in a single generation in biology. The changes are also fully reversible.

3. Changes made to a creature affect the entire species. In fact, the player's character hatches out surrounded by other individuals already displaying the new form.
4. There are no mutations.
5. All parts are interchangeable among all species.

Newly hatched individuals are shown as "learning" certain skills, but this can be skipped by the player. "Baby" versions of other species are sometimes encountered, as are larger "Alpha" individuals; other than this, no growth is depicted in the creature stage, in contrast to the cell stage where growth is a major component. Likewise, the player's character does not age and persists unchanged unless it is killed or dies of starvation – and even then a new one will hatch that is completely identical. Sexual reproduction exists from the very beginning, though there is no variation between the parents and no recombination.

There is no mutation and no variation within species, and therefore no natural selection (Gregory 2009). There also are no challenges imposed by the environment, no overproduction of offspring, no intraspecific competition, no disease or other causes of mortality, and no biotic interactions other than alliance or predation. Without natural selection, adaptation in the usual sense cannot occur. The species do not coevolve – they are either driven extinct or become allies without initiating changes in either species (Thompson 1994). There are no hosts and parasites. Even the roles of "predator" and "prey" are mostly unclear, as many of the battles are between equally matched "predators." While other species can be driven extinct, the player's lineage cannot. Extinction in this case is due only to direct predation – there are no other biotic factors (e.g., being outcompeted) and no external factors (e.g., catastrophes, climate change, loss of habitat). There are no mass extinctions. All of this differs from life on Earth.

The choices made by the player do involve a functional element as decisions must be made about how to enhance particular abilities by choosing appropriate parts. The parts themselves are modular in that they can be added, removed, or modified individually, which at least shows that some traits can change even if others do not; however, this is too strong to the point of ignoring interactions among parts. More importantly, there is no difference in the function of a part according to the organism or its environment, nor in terms of how the part is modified or positioned. For example, there is no difference in visual ability regardless of the type of eyes, and locomotion is not affected by the number, length, or organization of legs. As such, adaptation is not actually part of the game, rather this is a system of "upgrades" in which possessing a certain part – in any position or format – provides a higher "level" for a specific ability. An element of "selection" and "adaptation" could have been included if different types of parts or their arrangement had consequences for the organism, thereby requiring the player to improve the organism by trial and error.

There is no intrasexual selection as there is no competition for mates. A process does occur in which the creature must sing, dance, and charm others, but these are individuals from other species and therefore this does not represent intersexual selection. All organism features represent either structures that support basic functions (e.g., sensing, feeding, locomotion), structures that enhance combat with other species, structures that enhance alliances with other species, or aesthetic choice. The actual biological reasons for such characteristics as coloration (e.g., attracting mates, warning coloration, camouflage) or ornate features (e.g., antlers, exaggerated displays) are not included.

There appear to be minimal constraints and tradeoffs in the game. For example, although there is a limit on the number of parts that can be added (indicated by the "complexity meter"), this does not preclude the player from gaining maximum abilities in most or all categories as long as enough DNA points are earned (which they can be by hunting or allying with other species). That is, there is no internal (e.g., developmental or genetic) or external (e.g., resource availability) limits on the form the organisms can take. As mentioned previously, there are no consequences based on the design of the organism, meaning that there are no mechanical constraints either. Similarly, there appear to be no allometric issues – for example, a major change in body size has no impact on the function of the organism and its parts even if no adjustments are made. All parts can be removed or modified without sustaining any cost. The interaction of parts appears to be inconsequential. All of this differs markedly from real living organisms, though it would have been feasible to impose a cost for maladaptive combinations and arrangements of parts, or at least to institute a cost (e.g., only a partial refund) for adding a part that must later be subtracted.

On the face of it, *Spore* would appear to represent strict anagenesis (change within lineages without branching) (Gregory 2008b). In any case, there clearly is no component of cladogenesis (branching speciation) in the game, which means that the species encountered are all independently evolved and do not share a common ancestor. This raises an interesting issue about classification of the organisms in the game. Several million species have been created by players and the game designers, but there is no way to classify them in the way that living species are classified. Compare this with the 1.7 million named species (of perhaps 10–100 million) that have been described formally (May 1988). In terms of living taxa, Linnaeus classified animals and plants hierarchically based on similarity, which he believed was a reflection of common themes in God's design. Of course, it turns out that the reason a nested, hierarchical classification works is that species are related through shared ancestry in such a way. However, *Spore* creatures are neither designed by the same person nor evolved through common descent. This means that a Linnaean "similarity of design" would not work, nor would a cladistic method based on shared derived characteristics (Hennig 1979; Futuyma 2005). A nested classification also is impossible because all parts are interchangeable across all species and can be added, subtracted, and modified at any time.

The relationships among species in *Spore* are actually similar to those envisioned for living species by Lamarck, who held that simple species arise by spontaneous generation and then progress without branching or common ancestry up a scale of increasing complexity (Futuyma 2005). *Spore* differs from Lamarckian evolution in both the source of new, simple organisms at the bottom of such a scale (panspermia vs. spontaneous generation) and in the mechanism of change (adding "upgrades" vs. use and disuse of components), but the larger historical pattern of change is similar. This marks a major difference between described biological systems and the game.

All parts that can be incorporated into the organism are found intact, rather than being co-opted or modified from pre-existing structures. They can be modified during design, but fundamentally they arrive in a functional form and it is aesthetic rather than functional changes that are made. All changes, including the gain and loss of complex structures, are completely reversible. Nevertheless, there is a necessary global trend to increased complexity and intelligence that is a major theme of the game. The only component of historical contingency seems to be that major ecological decisions carry over from one stage to the next (e.g., carnivore vs. herbivore in the cell stage persists in the creature stage, social vs. adaptable vs. predator remains after the end of the creature stage). It is very likely that most players will make small modifications in each increment, such that this would reflect descent with modification with some historical continuity. Nevertheless, it is possible to overhaul the organism totally at any moment with no holdovers of past characteristics.

Cultural Evolution

Even before Darwin's *Origin of Species* was published in 1859, social theorists had started to develop theories of cultural evolution, although typically without Darwin's key idea, which is natural selection from random genetic variation (Darwin 1859). One might trace the idea of cultural progress all the way back to the origins of Christianity, which presented itself as an advance based on Judaism and superior to classical Paganism (Stark 1997). By the time Adam Smith published *The Wealth of Nations* in 1776, it was clear that the scope, wealth, and technical capability of civilization was increasing (Smith 1776).

In the middle of the 19th century, many leading social theorists asserted that human history consisted of a series of distinct stages, including August Comte (1798–1857), Karl Marx (1818–1883), and Lewis H. Morgan (1818–1881). Herbert Spencer (1820–1903), in particular, drew analogies between stages of biological evolution and cultural evolution. With the emergence of sociobiology as a school of thought roughly 30 years ago, many authors have suggested that a comprehensive theory might be developed to explain both biological and cultural evolution among humans (Wilson 1975; van den Berghe 1975; Dawkins 1976; Lumsden and Wilson 1981; Cavalli-Sforza and Feldman 1981).

However, the disasters of the First World War and Great Depression led most nonMarxist social scientists to doubt that progress was inevitable, let alone to seek fundamental scientific laws of cultural evolution that might explain it. Piritm Sorokin, for example, developed a cyclical theory of the rise and fall of civilizations that did not postulate any net movement forward (Sorokin 1937). Furthermore, it is questionable whether there really exist distinct cultural equivalents of genes or the genetic code, arranged in anything like the coherence of a DNA molecule. Analogies with biological evolution may be useful metaphors, which might apply well in certain specialized areas of culture, but not strictly correct in describing human history as a whole (Bainbridge 1985; Strong and Bainbridge 2003).

So-called *technological determinists* argued that technological innovation was the engine driving social change, and that innovation was self-generating as myriad inventions originating at different places diffused across the world, and combined to make additional new inventions (Ogburn 1922; White 1959). Although this technological model led to metaphors describing historical stages – such as industrial society versus agricultural society, or the information age versus the space age – in fact this model does not postulate distinct stages of history, because change is too complex and multidimensional to be captured in a few simple concepts (Gilfillan 1935). In addition, one may seriously question whether unending scientific, technological, and cultural progress is physically possible (Horgan 1996; Bainbridge 2007), and, for example, whether we will ever be able to reach the space stage described by *Spore*.

We can grant *Spore* that traditional social scientists did find it useful to distinguish stages of human history, at least roughly. The distinction between the tribal and civilization stages seems comparable with that between hunting and gathering societies and agricultural societies, but not identical. The so-called Neolithic revolution (Childe 1951), based on the initial development of agriculture, allowed population increases, economic specialization with the concomitant development of markets, and the surge in social and intellectual innovations we call civilization.

The tribal phase features "a small, close-knit village community, complete with a totem and a central Tribal Hut" (Hodgson et al. 2008: 87). There really are no tribes in *Spore*, however, because tribes are an outgrowth of kinship, and there are no real families in the game. Tribes, and the relations between them, cannot be understood without kinship. The same is true for mythology, norms, and even the economy on the tribal level. Had *Spore* lived up to the publicity that it was a game based on evolution, then there would have been biological reproduction, families, and the basis for much of what cultural anthropology studies. The fact that tribes are wholly separate species may allow for a variety of "cute" creatures, but it prevents the intermarriage between social groups that is fundamental to social structure at the real tribal phase of human development, on which the less familial structure of industrial societies is based. It would not be difficult to make at least some of the other nests be the same species and add *exogamy*, the requirement to mate outside your own nest (Fig. 6.3).

In both the tribal and civilization stages of the game, relations between the player's group and other groups are negotiated economically, militarily, or through emotional and expressive appeals. In fact, the primary way that the human species developed ever larger social groups, from the earliest tribal stage at least through the kingship system that has lasted in some parts of the world even until today, has been through family kinship. Spore shows no appreciation for the complex kinship structures so important in social anthropology (Lévi-Strauss 1969).

The player can begin the process of building an alliance with another group by bringing it gifts, and this does reflect the importance of a gift economy emphasized by classical anthropologists (Malinowski 1922; Mauss 2000). This is not incompatible

Fig. 6.3 A village with totem pole in the tribal stage of *Spore*

with building larger societies via kinship structures, and Lévi–Strauss pointed out that exogamy could be conceptualized as the exchange of gifts that took the form of brides. However, gift exchange seems quite secondary to biological kinship in the development of human societies, perhaps playing a greater role when really large societies came to rely more heavily on fictive kinship, such as the king being considered the father of all. In modern societies, economic market exchange plays an especially great role and has implications for all other forms of exchange, but kinship and exchange carried out inside kin groups were more significant in earlier states of human development, and are ignored by *Spore* (Polanyi 1944).

In the civilization stage of the game, the player builds cities and deploys advanced technology such as motorized vehicles. As the official guidebook explains, there are primarily three different cultural modes that the player's strategy can follow: "A military nation seeks to expand its borders by conquering all other cities, while a religious society wins control of other cities by winning the hearts of its citizens. An economic culture creates vast wealth and uses it to expand its sphere of influence" (Hodgson et al. 2008: 119). There are two interesting points here. First, *Spore* categorizes a society in terms of dominance by one of its institutions: military, religion, or economy. Second, the reason these institutions exist is not to serve the needs of the citizens but to gain supremacy over other societies. This is an issue for gamelike virtual worlds in general: They teach players to conquer others

rather than to cooperate with them, and thus may have a negative impact on the
value players transfer to the real world. Recall that the passage from the instruction
manual, quoted above, uses the bellicose and obsolete term "survival of the fittest"
to decribe evolution (Fig. 6.4).

The three institutions can have complex relations with each other, which deserve
comparison with what happens in the real world. One of the ways a player may
conquer another city is through religious conversion, and attempts are more likely
to succeed if the inhabitants of the city are unhappy. Indeed, one subtle tactic is to
squeeze off the economic flow into that city, thereby stressing the population, then
bombard it with religious propaganda. This reflects the common finding in the
sociology of religion that intense religious appeals work best with deprived populations, who turn to religion either because they have no alternative course in their
desperate situation, or because religion is fundamentally a compensator against the
inescapable deprivations of human life (Pope 1942; Cohn 1961; Smelser 1962;
Stark and Bainbridge 1987).

However, there is little evidence to support the effectiveness of so-called "disembodied appeals" – religious messages transmitted impersonally – and religious
conversion almost always operates by means of pre-existing social bonds, spreading
via social influence through the network of friends and family of people who are
already devout members (Lofland and Stark 1965; Shupe 1976; Stark and
Bainbridge 1980). With respect to social solidarity, religion has generally been

Fig. 6.4 Mechanized warfare in the civilization stage of *Spore*

regarded as a mechanism for sustaining the unity of a group that already exists, rather than being a really effective means for expanding the scope of a social group (Durkheim 1915).

Given how brief the civilization phase is, it includes much of relevance to real sociology, such as the division of labor, public opinion, and the fact that religious movements exploit unresolved human dissatisfactions. There is also a hint of social stratification in the tribal phase, as tribes seem to have members of various ranks from chief down to child. Thus, these two stages of *Spore* could conceivably be used for legitimate educational purposes, if the instructor could provide the links to the literature of real social science. However, as the lack of kinship in the tribal stage illustrates, the failure of the first two stages to provide a biological basis for the later stages seriously limits their educational value.

Conclusion

Spore is not a game with any deep linkages to biology. It is, in reality, a relatively standard real-time strategy game with the same basic unlocking of features, upgrading of levels, and choices about aesthetics and function as with vehicles or buildings in similar games. The units happen to look like organisms, the features that can be added are mouths, eyes, and limbs, and the currency is called "DNA," but this does not make the game anything more than superficially biological. *Spore* uses the language of evolution but none of its major principles. There do not even seem to be metaphors for actual processes, rather *Spore* follows well-established game mechanics and pastes biology onto them. The one potentially good result is that it will prompt players to think about evolutionary change, though nothing like real biological processes was incorporated.

There is no technical reason why real processes of biological evolution by natural selection could not have been built into the game, for example using the genetic algorithm method, a biomimetic form of computing that has existed for well over three decades (Holland 1975). It is easy to imagine a strategy game that had the player shape evolution by adjusting the natural environment of the world, for example modeling allopatric speciation – the separation of one species into two, facilitated by limited gene flow between two areas and somewhat different environments in those locations – by setting up distinct regions and constricting movement between them (Mayr 1963, 1976). For later stages of the game, the genetic algorithms could be treated as a multiagent system, for example in modeling the emotive and religious social behavior of the tribal and civilization stages (Bainbridge 2006).

It is unclear whether a game genuinely based on evolution by natural selection from random variation could become popular, however, especially as a role-playing game. Porter Abbott (2003) argues that human thought organizes things in terms of narratives – stories in which protagonists face obstacles and take actions in pursuit of goals – and that the scientific theory of evolution is unnarratable. However, this chapter has identified a very large number of intrinsically interesting principles from biological and cultural evolution that potentially could become the basis of play and exploration in virtual worlds. It remains to be seen whether the creativity of game designers and the curiosity of game players will combine to give success in the marketplace to a future virtual world that really is based on the science of evolution.

References

Abbott, P. H. (2003) Unnarratable knowledge: The difficulty of understanding evolution by natural selection. In D. Herman (Ed.), Narrative theory and cognitive science (pp. 143–162). Stanford, CA: Center for the Study of Language and Information.

Bainbridge, W. S. (1985). Cultural genetics. In R. Stark (Ed.), *Religious movements* (pp. 157–198). New York: Paragon.

Bainbridge, W. S. (2006). *God from the machine: Artificial intelligence models of religious cognition.* Walnut Grove, CA: AltaMira.

Bainbridge, W. S. (2007). *Across the secular abyss.* Lanham, MD: Lexington.

Bentley, T. (2000). *The Sims (user manual).* Redwood City, CA: Electronic Arts.

Bohannon, J. (2008). Flunking Spore. *Science* 322:531, from (http://www.sciencemag.org/cgi/content/full/322/5901/531b).

Bremer, M. (1993). *SimCity 2000 user manual.* Walnut Creek, CA: Maxis.

Cavalli-Sforza, L. L, & Feldman, M. W. (1981). *Cultural transmission and evolution.* Princeton, NJ: Princeton University Press.

Childe, G. V. (1951). *Man makes himself.* New York: New American Library.

Cohn, N. (1961). *The pursuit of the millennium.* New York: Harper.

Darwin, C. (1859). *On the origin of species by means of natural selection.* London: Murray.

Dawkins, R. (1976). *The selfish gene.* New York: Oxford University Press.

Durkheim, E. (1915). *The elementary forms of the religious life.* London: Allen & Unwin.

Futuyma, D. J. (2005). *Evolution.* Sunderland, MA: Sinauer.

Gilfillan, C. S. (1935). *The sociology of invention.* Chicago, IL Follett.

Gogarten, P. J. & Townsend, J. P. (2005). Horizontal gene transfer, Genome innovation and evolution. *Nature Reviews Microbiology, 3*,679–687.

Gregory, R. T. (2008a). Evolution as fact, theory, and path. *Evolution: Education and Outreach, 1*,46–52.

Gregory, T. R. (2008b). Understanding evolutionary trees. *Evolution: Education and Outreach, 1,* 121–137.

Gregory, T. R. (2008c). Evolutionary trends. *Evolution: Education and Outreach, 1*,259–273.

Gregory, T. R. (2009). Understanding natural selection: Essential concepts and common misconceptions. *Evolution: Education and Outreach, 2,*156–175

Hennig, W. (1979). *Phylogenetic systematics.* Urbana, IL: University of Illinois Press.

Hodgson, D. S. J., Stratton, B., & Knight, M. (2008). *Spore: Official game guide.* Roseville, CA: Prima.

Holland, J. H. (1975). *Adaptation in natural and artificial systems.* Ann Arbor, MI: University of Michigan Press.

Horgan, J. (1996). *The end of science.* Reading, MA: Addison-Wesley.

Lévi-Strauss, C. (1969). *The elementary structures of kinship.* Boston, MA: Beacon Press.

Lofland, J. & Stark, R. (1965). Becoming a world-saver: A theory of conversion to a deviant perspective. *American Sociological Review, 30*,862–875.

Lumsden, C. J., & Wilson, E. O. (1981). *Genes, mind, and culture.* Cambridge, MA: Harvard University Press.

Pierre L. van den Berghe. (1975). *Man in society: A biosocial view.* New York: Elsevier.

Malinowski, B. (1922). *Argonauts of the western pacific*. London: Routledge.

Mauss, M. (2000). *The gift*. New York: Norton.

May, R. M. (1988). How many species are there on earth? *Science, 241*,1441–1449.

Mayr, E. (1963). *Animal species and evolution*. Cambridge, MA: Belknap Press.

Mayr, E. (1976). *Evolution and the diversity of life*. Cambridge, MA: Belknap Press.

Ogburn, W. F. (1922). *Social change with respect to culture and original nature*. New York: B. W. Huebsch.

Polanyi, K. (1944). *The great transformation*. New York: Farrar and Rinehart.

Pope, L. (1942). *Millhands and preachers*. New Haven, CT: Yale University Press.

Shupe, A. D. (1976). 'Disembodied Access' and technological constraints on organizational development. *Journal for the Scientific Study of Religion, 15*,177–185.

Smelser, N. J. (1962). *Theory of collective behavior*. New York: Free Press.

Smith, A. (1776). *An inquiry into the nature and causes of the wealth of nations*. Dublin: Whitestone.

Sorokin, P. A. (1937–1941). *Social and cultural dynamics*. New York: American Book Company.

Stark, R. (1997). *The rise of Christianity*. San Francisco, CA: Harper San Francisco.

Stark, R. & Bainbridge, W. S. (1980). Networks of faith. *American Journal of Sociology, 86*, 1376–1395.

Stark, R. & Bainbridge, W. S. (1987). *A theory of religion*. New York: Toronto/Lang.

Strong, G. & Bainbridge, W. S. (2003). Memetics: A potential new science. In M. C. Roco & W. S. Bainbridge (Eds.), *Converging technologies for improving human performance* (pp. 318–325). Dordrecht, The Netherlands: Kluwer.

Thompson, J. N. (1994). *The coevolutionary process*. Chicago, IL: University of Chicago Press.

White, L. A. (1959). *The evolution of culture*. New York: McGraw-Hill.

Wickramasinghe, W. M., Narlikar, J. V., Rajaratnam, P., Harris, M. J. & Lloyd, D. (2003). Progress towards the vindication of panspermia. *Astrophysics and Space Science, 283*,403–413.

Wilson, E. O. (1975). *Sociobiology: The new synthesis*. Cambridge, MA: Harvard University Press.

Xiong, J. & Bauer, C. E. (2002). "Complex Evolution of Photosynthesis." *Annual Review of Plant Biology, 53*,503–521.

Chapter 7
Medulla: A Cyberinfrastructure-Enabled Framework for Research, Teaching, and Learning with Virtual Worlds

Michelle Roper Fox, Henry Kelly, and Sachin Patil

Virtual worlds have the potential to revolutionize the way we learn, teach, and conduct research (Thomas and Brown 2009). When coupled with a new generation of tools including YouTube, Wikipedia, and Facebook, these technologies can offer spectacular, often competing new ways to create, search, display, remix, and share information and knowledge. Few tools have been created to help harness these materials for education and training purposes and no coherent vision has emerged to organize, store, peer-review, or deliver them in a consistent and trusted way. A new public media infrastructure could support the construction of complex synthetic environments such as buildings, cities and larger regions, engineering and biological models, and sophisticated simulations of physical, chemical, biological, and other phenomena. Individuals and institutions around the world could build powerful new approaches to instruction and support a virtual marketplace that will encourage both collaboration and competition in ways that reward learning solutions that work.

The Federation of American Scientists (FAS) is creating an enabling technology to support this new public media infrastructure. Called Medulla after the control center in the brain, it weaves together existing technologies into a framework to coordinate and support the innovative use of digital assets (art, media, documents, and software) for learning, teaching, and research inside virtual worlds. Medulla brings together an easy-to-use set of tools and services for identity management, team building, information sharing, project management, peer review, data versioning, data archiving, intellectual property management, and learning management. This chapter describes the current landscape of education technology development, some of the barriers that prevent the widespread use of virtual worlds for research and education, the solutions Medulla offers, and exemplar projects being built using Medulla for archaeology, mathematics, artificial intelligence, the history of racism, and public diplomacy.

M.R. Fox and H. Kelly
Department of Energy, US
e-mails: michelle.fox@ee.doe.gov; henry.kelly@ee.doe.gov

S. Patil
Federation of American Scientists
e-mail: spatil@fas.org

W.S. Bainbridge (ed.), *Online Worlds: Convergence of the Real and the Virtual*,
Human-Computer Interaction Series, DOI 10.1007/978-1-84882-825-4_7,
© Springer-Verlag London Limited 2010

A Landscape of Trinkets

A typical educational technology project proceeds as follows. A team with a good idea manages to round up funds from a grant-making organization. The researchers, curriculum designers, subject matter experts, computer artists and coders, software testers and evaluators then embark on an intensive multi-year project. Copies of the project are distributed on the most widely used storage platform prevalent (today it is CDs or DVDs, less than a decade ago it was 3.5" magnetic disks). The product is tested in a few classrooms; a paper reporting on great success is published where it will be read by at least a dozen people. And that's about it. A few good products will be picked up by diligent teachers, but within 5 years it is almost certain that the few remaining copies will linger in a box in the back of someone's office quickly becoming unusable because they have not been updated to current operating systems or equipment. It is hard to find new PCs that can even read a 3.5" disk let alone the floppies or video disks that preceded them. The people who built the product, and the few dozen people who actually read their paper, may have benefited from the work, but the software and artwork is lost. Each new project funded begins nearly from scratch, reinventing not just the artwork, but user interface tools, strategies for engagement, help systems, and records management. Most grant-making organizations have, to date, concentrated on novelty and individual projects, not on building a set of persistent tools that can be widely adopted and maintained.

This model of design is repeated even in sophisticated operations like corporate and Department of Defense training. Once developed, products are rapidly made obsolete by advancing technology and agencies are forced to begin practically from scratch. Gross inefficiencies are caused by duplicating efforts (Lemley and O'Brien 1997; Markus 2001). The decay of digital materials from obsolescent hardware, software, and lost file format information adds another incalculable layer of waste to the current model of technology development (Lougee-Heimer 2003).

While the waste involved in this process is frustrating, an even greater loss stems from the fact that the process demonstrates the inability of the education research community to take advantage of one of the most important powers of new information technology: the power to change the process of development itself by using newly available information tools to collaborate and build systems, which continuously improve. Such systems have been in place in many other parts of the economy for years but have not penetrated the world of education in any serious way. Virtual worlds can change this and change it quickly.

An Alternative

For the purposes of this paper, we will define virtual worlds as *online, persistent, shared environments that allow multiple users to create content and experiences, collaborate, and communicate with other users generally through the use of an avatar*. Virtual worlds can model elements from both the real and imagined worlds, including physically and historically accurate topography as well as natural phenomena such as gravity, motion, and climate.

In principle, virtual worlds can represent large, complex bodies of knowledge and offer many different options for exploration, exposition, and discovery. Such projects could include building simulations of ancient cities that are then brought to life with people and animals controlled by artificial intelligence or building a detailed simulation of a complex organ of the human body. Once built, each world can be navigated and explored in many different ways. But building such worlds will require the time and talents of many different people over an extended time. Each would require extensive collaboration in building the simulations, peer review, and testing – something that a combination of virtual worlds and other Web 2.0 technologies make easy. No significant project of this kind is underway, however. There are a number of reasons.

The most obvious barrier to widespread adoption of virtual worlds for education of training, graphics and technical limitations, is also the most tractable. The state of the art of current virtual world technology places severe limits on what can be accomplished in virtual worlds that must operate over broadband networks. Processing limitations, bandwidth constraints, and other technology limits make it difficult to provide the kinds of stunning visual details, fluid movements of materials like biological surfaces or liquids, and limit the number of independently controlled avatars and AI objects that exist in a distributed system such as an online world. The quality of computer game graphics, which must be rendered in real time on inexpensive devices, versus those for film that are precompiled, is typically at least a generation behind the simulations in movies, where each frame may take hours for powerful computers to produce. The quality of many of the most popular virtual worlds offer graphics and simulations are at least a generation behind what is expected from a high-end computer game. The continuation of Moore's law should address the processing constraints, while even faster improvements in the ability to pass information through fibers and optical switches gives us great confidence that the technical limitations on virtual worlds will diminish quickly. Advances in cloud computing are addressing both limitations simultaneously.

Other technological hurdles are less easily overcome. For example, there is currently no equivalent of a browser-based search engine for content located in virtual worlds, nor a standard for assigning metadata to help make the content searchable. The limited search capabilities offered by different virtual world platforms varies by platform and is often inadequate.

One of the biggest limitations to all interactive games and virtual worlds is the user interface. While the human hand is capable of complex and subtle motions with huge degrees of freedom, the hands of avatars are limited to what can be conveyed by moving the tips of fingers and thumbs. Progress in haptics is possible but it has been slow in coming.

One obvious problem is that rapid rates of innovation have led to a huge number of parallel software development efforts in graphic formats, identity management, and many other areas critical for the effective development and use of virtual worlds. The proliferation of competing, often non-interoperable formats for images, sounds, metadata, 3D graphics, social networking, and many other digital assets makes the Tower of Babel look like a model of effective communication.

Significant progress has been made in many of these areas, often driven by interests having little to do with education or training.

A few dominant 3D graphic formats have emerged in recent years – the formats used by AutoCAD and 3D studio Max – and tools developed for converting formats. Game designers are attempting to establish standard ways of managing scripting and other assets needed for effective operation of a game simulation in a consortium called Collada.[1] This is the result of a known bug in World 2007.

Standard interfaces are being developed for powerful physics simulations and other technical simulation packages. Open source platforms for managing scholarly materials such as DSpace[2] or Fedora Commons[3] are widely used and well suited for collecting, storing, and accessing the kinds of digital content and multimedia resources needed to build and continuously improve virtual worlds. The university consortium Internet2 has developed a powerful tool for establishing identity management and trust called Shibboleth[4] that is now in widespread use.

The most painful and unresolved interoperability challenge facing the virtual world community, however, is the proliferation of non-interoperable virtual world platforms. In principle, virtual world platforms can ensure that, unlike the situation in current educational software, investments in digital assets won't be lost as technologies. The text, images, and other assets built for the 2D world wide web persist because the firms that build portals like Microsoft's Internet Explorer and Mozilla's Firefox know that their products can remain competitive only if they are upgraded to reflect the power of modern operating systems and graphics cards and also ensure that their upgraded portal can display most if not all legacy materials. In principle, virtual world platforms could do the same thing for 3D worlds and associated simulations.

FAS has located and researched nearly 200 virtual worlds, with new ones being discovered constantly, and hosts The FAS Virtual Worlds Almanac, a wiki of virtual worlds.[5] Most are built completely from scratch with the idea that they will become the Microsoft of virtual world platforms. Avatar behaviors, scripting, and other features that work in one virtual world cannot easily be moved to another. Even the 3D objects built for one platform may not be portable. The graphics format used by the dominant virtual world platform, *Second Life*, is not easily ported to any other format – it is typically easier to start from scratch. The design was a way to make building easier and made perfect sense since it was designed around the limitations of the existing bandwidth and computer processing. It may well make business sense since it is nearly impossible to move software objects in or out of *Second Life*. But the effect is to isolate the virtual world from developments made in any other space. The absence of interoperability means that the time and effort invested in building assets for one virtual world platform may be completely lost if the platform is not maintained by the builders or if it is overtaken by a superior product.

---

[1] http://www.khronos.org/collada/

[2] http://www.dspace.org/

[3] http://www.fedora-commons.org/

[4] http://shibboleth.internet2.edu/

[5] http://vworld.fas.org/wiki/Main_Page

Another major problem with all educational software that applies with particular force to educational materials in virtual worlds is the inability to create a profitable business model. In the late-1990s, a number of prestigious economic consulting firms pointed out that education and training in the US was a trillion dollar a year enterprise and a lucrative and largely untouched market for software developers. There was a brief gold rush but virtually no one made any money. The dot-bomb collapse led to many business failures and investors have been afraid to reenter this extremely difficult market. The businesses that specialize in education – such as textbook publishers and online universities – have kept a careful eye on the potential software market but not made significant investments.

It would appear that even greater problems face anyone considering developing educational materials in virtual worlds. First of all, few if any of the many companies that are attempting to market virtual world platforms are profitable. The dominant *Second Life* platform gets the bulk of its income by renting "land," which customers use to build their simulated worlds. What this actually means, of course, is that the customers are renting services from the company's servers. People who rent land can make money by selling services or software objects such as clothing. But can they sell educational services? Forterra Systems has a proprietary virtual world platform that has been used successfully to support military training. It is licensed to clients, typically with a contract in which Forterra builds the digital assets for the virtual world itself, and the clients make it available only to a fixed set of students and instructors. It is not designed to invite large scale collaborations or public use. *Active Worlds* has been selling licenses to use its virtual world platform for many years. Some universities have used it to build elaborate sites, but no entities have emerged as for-profit ventures using the *Active Worlds* platform. Another business model, *Multiverse*, offers independent developers the opportunity to use the platform, infrastructure and tools for free until the project can generate revenue,[6] but like those platforms mentioned above, a profitable educational software project for virtual worlds has yet to emerge.

Even if an open virtual world platform emerges with a profitable model and becomes the Firefox or Explorer of virtual worlds, a sustainable economic model needs to be found to build significant education and training materials that could operate on these platforms. The examples available in universities are not promising: The tradition of academic publishing has trapped them in a system where the materials developed are not accessible to the public and not available on the 2D web to anyone not willing to pay significant amounts to read each document. Elaborate debates continue on footnote styles needed to locate paper copies of proprietary journal articles when the rest of the information universe locates reference documents by hyperlinks. This simply cannot work for a system designed to encourage collaboration, continuous improvement, and the broadest possible accessibility.

It is necessary to begin by assuming that proprietary or open source virtual world platforms, capable of supporting open standards for 3D materials and simulations

---

[6] http://www.multiverse.net/index.html

(the equivalent of HTML for simulations), are widely available and widely used. These would presumably be supported by advertising or the other methods used to develop and maintain today's web browsers. Given that such platforms are available, there are at least three possible financial models for building and maintaining education and training materials in these platforms:

- The materials are built by a combination of volunteers and specialists paid as members of university faculties, government organizations, and NGOs. Since volunteers alone are not likely to be sufficient, faculty and other professionals would need to get academic credit and/or other rewards for participating.
- Specific sites could be built and maintained by commercial or not-for profits and leased to educational institutions who would include these fees in their tuition.
- A public organization – say a Corporation for Public Media – could provide a permanent source of funding for the development of virtual world sites and hope they would be matched with foundation and other funding. This model has resulted in superb public television programming, but the uncertainty and constant struggle for funding has made stability difficult to achieve.

Building and using virtual worlds has opened a number of legal questions, not least of which is the ever-growing body of literature governing intellectual property (Duranske 2008). The construction of rich, and continuously improving virtual world sites and continuous improvement in the ways they are used to teach and learn depend essentially on a novel combination of collaboration and competition that is emerging as a central theme in Web 2.0 society. Building and using virtual world sites in learning will require a constantly shifting merger of diverse skills and ability for them to be recognized and appropriately rewarded. Deep changes in instructional organization, tenure, promotion, and other rewards will be needed if educational institutions are to make use of the new learning materials, and the new approaches to conveying and testing expertise the kind of system envisioned here permits (Kelly 2008). The blunt fact is that we really don't know how best to use virtual worlds and simulations to enhance learning. But virtual world platforms that encourage communities of interest to form and collaborate may present opportunities for institutional change and make dramatic new approaches to learning possible (Staley 2009).

Tools for managing large-scale collaborations are widely available and as Ondrejka notes, community and collaboration are effective preservation tools that can help address the landscape of trinkets and obsolescence of digital materials (Ondrejka 2008). The fact that virtual worlds are not used in education argues powerfully that the limitations are not primarily technical, but lie in a failure to imagine a new approach to building and using learning materials. The problems lie deep in the economics, culture, and social organization of the education and training enterprise. The technology limitations of virtual worlds will vanish far before these economic and management challenges are overcome. We need to start addressing them now. There are some easy first steps to build a community, increase collaboration, and change the process of development.

Medulla and a New Public Media Infrastructure

With this litany of problems, it would be easy to conclude that the best approach to using virtual worlds in learning would be to sit back and wait for markets to sort things out. After taking a careful look at the possibilities, we concluded that precisely the opposite approach is needed. All the tools needed to launch collaborative construction and use of virtual worlds in interesting areas of education and training are now available. The difficult work comes in building the communities needed to explore novel approaches to the cultural and management issues. This can and should begin now. Economics, unfortunately, are another matter. Funds for launching experiments that might subvert the accepted order of things in educational institutions are not easy to find.

The Medulla project is built around a few simple themes, all focused on making it easy for teams to form and begin developing and using virtual worlds for education and research. While all the software tools needed for this to happen are in principle available, in practice it is an effort for any group to find them all and make them work together. FAS has begun a process of weaving them together in an open source collaborative toolset we call *Medulla*. It is designed to allow groups not familiar with virtual worlds to use easily – including tools for locating people with specialized expertise such as computer graphics that might not be available to the original team.

Medulla is a virtual world platform-independent technology to access information about virtual world content objects and their associated source digital assets across virtual world platforms, allow users to collaborate across virtual worlds and web 2.0 applications, and make user-created content in myriad virtual worlds viewable and searchable on the web. The Medulla Interface is accessible through both the 2D and 3D internet. Figure 7.1 shows this interface, while the user is examining screenshots of a Ziggurat from a virtual ancient Babylonian city. In this example, the tabs let the user switch between scene decription, screenshots, a sub-scene list, digital assets, and work requests. Higher-level choices to the left provide general information about Medulla, invite the user to join Medulla, let the user invite a friend to join, report bugs, contact staff, or access help information.

The project is proceeding in four steps. The first is identifying the functionality (use cases) needed for collaborative construction and use of virtual worlds for education. The second is identifying existing software tools capable of providing these services (selecting open source options when they are available). The third is both crucial and complex, linking these tools together as seamlessly as possible using interoperability standards developed by specialty groups when they are available. In all cases, the system is built so that it can adopt any software capable of delivering the functionality identified – e.g., identity management – so that the system is completely independent of any specific software tool. The fourth step is finding teams willing to begin using the tools assembled to build prototype virtual worlds and test the concept. Initial work has been completed on the first three steps and fully functional systems are being tested with volunteers who have created projects.

Fig. 7.1 The Medulla Interface: providing access to tools and content

Several cycles of user feedback and system improvement are planned in the next few months.

A critical feature of Medulla is that it seeks to identify the functions needed by users, and will always be needed no matter how individual software tools delivering the needed services change. It operates much like a coding interface – a promise to deliver a set of services while setting no limits on how these services could be provided. The interface analogy makes it possible for the Medulla system to provide stable functionality while taking advantage of rapid and continuous improvement in component software tools. A drawback of this approach is a that it is difficult to maintain a common look and feel since it is not always possible to access the functionality of commercial tools through an API. Users will find themselves using dashboards of several different software packages. Another drawback is that the functionality available in software packages may not line up with the categories specified in Medulla. Many commercial products provide a range of functionality creating the possibility of overlap and duplication. For example, image sharing and storage is feature common to web applications ranging from Flickr to Facebook, and instant messaging is offered through social networking sites, email, and some virtual worlds. Experimentation will help determine which tools are best suited for the projects, goals, and participants to ensure that digital materials created are stored, preserved, searchable, and accessible.

The Use Cases

Functional requirements for the Medulla system fall into two broad use cases: (1) tools for building, reviewing, and updating virtual worlds, and (2) tools for using the virtual worlds to create a range of different learning experiences. We have identified a number of basic requirements for creating and continuously improving virtual world simulations. These include:

- Project management tools: tools that help identify team leaders, contributors, reviewers; handle scheduling, notification, commenting, rating (including peer-review) and upgrading
- APIs for object creation and adding: metadata (including SCORM); 3D formats; text, images, video, sound, textures; scripts, motion capture
- Converters to push standard formats into virtual world viewers/platforms (e.g., *Cobalt, Wonderland, Active Worlds, Second Life*)
- Data-base structure: input/output; searching; version control; links to large digital repositories
- Assessment modules
- Managing payments for services as needed
- Connecting to object repositories
- APIs for scripts, AI, physics engines, other simulations, character motion and emotion

The process of building content begins when a team forms around project idea for a virtual world. This might involve reproducing a virtual city populated with AI characters going about their daily routines, a natural landscape with a complex ecosystem, a laboratory equipped with complex analytical equipment whose functions could be fully simulated, a city experiencing a natural disaster, or a complex simulation of a kidney. In each case, the team would begin by identifying the resources that needed to be assembled – sources of information, experts, illustrations, drawings – and the skills required. The team members would then identify themselves to in a way that could establish trust with other members and let the project leader give different levels of access to each participant. The Internet2 tool Shibboleth is widely used in the university community, but others are available.

Project management tools are needed to help maintain lists of tasks and their status, to solicit peer-reviews and testing, communicate efficiently with team members and specialty teams, and for other purposes. The management tools should be able to support a wide variety of leadership styles ranging from sites that are tightly controlled to those where all resources are open to all participants – including the general public. Users should be able to select from a variety of management tools ranging from extremely simple tools that will be used by informal groups to powerful project management project management tools like Mantis or dotProject.

Database management tools are needed to provide easy access to multimedia resources ranging from pointers to articles and images to 3D graphic files. Version control and other capabilities are essential. The open source DSpace and Fedora

Common database managers are powerful and their ease of use is making them a common choice of developers.

Metadata is needed to ensure that the digital materials are properly identified and easy to search. Each community of practice has developed its own descriptors, and the database system is designed so each can be accommodated. The library community, for example, uses the Dublin Core metadata, while parts of the biology community uses gene ontology.

In many cases, the project team will need to find help – often in fields where they have no expertise. A group expert in ancient Mesopotamia, for example, may have no idea where to look for people who could convert their drawings and measurements into 3D objects. A variety of social networking tools are available for making these connections and the system should make it possible to use them.

The team should be able to use all of these resources without having to go through separate log-ins. This is difficult today but a number of groups are working to address the problem. There are two primary types of identity management for *federated* and *social* identities. With a federated identity, a user affiliated with a participant organization uses its organizational identity to access protected online resources in another participant organization. Internet2's Shibboleth is a powerful example. Shibboleth is a middleware technology for web single sign-on, identity tracking, and access management. The Shibboleth model presents a policy-controlled approach to identity and access management. Shibboleth consolidates information relating to user identities, access credentials, and access control in a single identity database. This single identity (negotiated by the organization) can provide access to all sites (such as protected online resources) approved by the federated authority. A social identity is one created by the user and can provide no level of trust that the person is who they claim to be. These identities are used in applications like *Second Life* or Facebook. The Medulla system can use the same username and password to provide user access to both social and federated identity if the user is willing to use the same name and password for both.

Building a functioning virtual world is only the beginning. It is not at all obvious how these worlds should be used in education and training. The Medulla systems make it possible to separate the task of building sophisticated sites from the task of using them (unlike traditional educational software development). This means that a curriculum designer with a great instructional concept can put it to use immediately making use of a rich virtual environment that already exists. It also means that a variety of different approaches to instruction can be tested and improved without investing time and resources in building a simulated space used only for a single experiment.

Actually meeting this goal, however, requires tools with unique functionality. The goal is to allow instructional designers to create a variety of experiences in the virtual worlds and share them. Students and instructors using the designs should be able to test them and even rate them for quality and interest creating a market for good ideas and encouraging continuous improvement in the instructional approaches. The system is designed to permit the largest possible range of instructional approaches – approaches that could include simply letting students explore and probe without restrictions, tours and demonstrations led by instructor-controlled avatars, complex tasks and assignments that could also serve as tests and tools for certifying skills, and complex games and adventures. Each of these is likely to be appropriate for some group of students under some circumstances. Unfortunately, the scripts needed to create all but the simplest experiences cannot be represented in any standard form. It's possible that scripting languages developed by game design consortia like Collada will result in a standard way of representing experience designs but nothing approaching the desired functionality appears to be available today. This is the single largest gap in tool availability we've identified.

Other functions are easier to identify. Identity management tools like Shibboleth provide the identity and trust needed to be certain that the students and instructors participating are who they say they are. A variety of instructional management tools are available for keeping track of student records and providing other services – including the open source tool Moodle. Extensions will probably be needed to accommodate the rich set of information that can be inferred from student actions in virtual worlds. A complex assignment, for example, may reveal an individual's ability to learn quickly, know where to go for help, work with unfamiliar teams, and display other critical skills.

Development: How much of this vision is real?

The Medulla framework implements two different approaches based on two different middleware technologies for user identity and access management. The Medulla implementation of the identity and access management system is intended to achieve web single sign-on for protected and social web resources, identity tracking across protected and social web resources and role-based access for protected resources in cross-organization collaboration.

Currently, the Medulla framework implements Shibboleth to ensure role-based access to the protected Medulla tools. The framework provides an independent registration service to let web and virtual world users to register with Medulla's Shibboleth identity provider. The registration service is accessible via Medulla's access points in virtual worlds. Three roles have been defined:

Viewer: for all anonymous users; grants "view-only" access privileges.

Contributor: grants add-edit-comment privileges for the protected Medulla tools.

Manager: permits the creation of a new project, overall management of the team, and content creation.

Identity management was one of the first priorities for the Medulla system, but other functionalities such as metadata organization and peer-review capabilities have been implemented as well. Table 7.1 identifies other candidate technologies that are being incorporated into the Medulla toolset.

Table 7.1 Conceptual Outline of the Medulla Toolset

Functionality	Goals	Candidate technology
Identity & Access Management	Track participants' identities across tools	Shibboleth, OpenID
	Control access in rigidly hierarchical or open collaborative work environment	
Metadata Organization	Annotate scene objects and their source digital assets	Dublin Core, DSpace,
Rating & Evaluation	Let multi-disciplinary teams to work together to create and publish digital contents	Wiki, Blog/Forum, custom prototype modules
	Facilitate reviews, discussion, and critique of proposed materials	
	Allow best models to rise gain prominence	
Intellectual Property Management	Source Digital Assets	DSpace
Data Storage & Archiving: Digital Stewardship & Hosting,	Organize, store, and archive source digital assets	DSpace, Fedora Common
Search: Structured Metadata	Search scene object's metadata, source assets, source assets' metadata	DSpace, Built-in Module
Security: VW Interactions	Private/secure settings for objects & meetings in virtual worlds	Code of Conduct Policies
Project Management	Support coordination and management of development efforts	dotProject, Mantis
Version Control: Digital Assets	Keep track of changes for preservation purposes	Fedora Common
Skillset Identification & Search	Identify skills, advertise requirements and search resources and volunteers	Facebook

Medulla Prototypes

FAS is currently working with an international team of volunteers and collaborators to begin building projects that use the Medulla toolset. Current prototypes are using the *Second Life* platform for 3D visualizations, but the supporting references and associated materials gathered during the creation of the project are all stored in Medulla and can be reused with any other virtual world.

Current projects include reconstructions of the ancient city of Uruk in 3400 BC (Fig. 7.2) and over a millennium later in 2300 BC. Other projects include one that incorporates artificial intelligence in the virtual world, a history of racism in the Western World, a public diplomacy project, and one designed to teach algebra 1 level mathematics (Fig. 7.3).

Fig. 7.2 The City of Uruk in 3400 BC

Fig. 7.3 The Algebra Project

Conclusion

The globally connected Metaverse envisaged by Neil Stephenson (1992) in *Snow Crash* is still some way off. Technological, economic, and cultural boundaries have yet to be overcome and the shared virtual experience he describes has been fragmented across hundreds of competing virtual worlds, engines, and formats.

Medulla provides a glimpse of a world that will share a common metaverse for learning and training. The prototype projects in archeology, mathematics, anthropology, artificial intelligence, and public diplomacy are helping the Medulla technology meet the needs of different audiences and disciplines. By offering peer-reviewed models, reference materials, photos, sound files, textures, reusable experiences, curricula, and assessments, it provides a new approach to building and using virtual worlds.

As a platform-agnostic technology, it is promoting the adoption and growth of virtual worlds for research, learning, and training by supporting content reuse and continuous improvement over the current reinvention and cottage-industry model. With an easy-to-use toolset and the encouragement of an active community of contributors and visitors, Medulla offers an opportunity to act as a catalyst for changing the way we have traditionally built education technology.

References

Duranske, B. (2008). *Virtual law: Navigating the legal landscape of virtual worlds*. Chicago, IL: American Bar Association.

Kelly, H. (2008). Continuous improvements in undergraduate education: A possible dream. *Innovations, 3*, 133–151.

Lemley, M. A. & O'Brien, D. W. (1997). Encouraging software reuse. *Stanford Law Review, 49*, 255–304.

Lougee-Heimer, R. (2003). The common optimization interface for operations research: Promoting open-source software in the operations research community. *IBM Journal of Research and Development, 47*, 57–66.

Markus, L. M. (2001). Toward a theory of knowledge reuse: Types of knowledge reuse situations and factors in reuse success. *Journal of Management Information Systems, 18*, 57–93.

Ondrejka, C. (2008). Education unleashed: Participatory culture, education, and innovation in *Second Life*. In K. Salen (Ed.), *The ecology of games: Connecting youth, games, and learning* (pp. 229–251). Cambridge, MA: MIT Press.

Staley, D. J. (2009). Managing the platform: Higher education and the logic of Wikinomics. *EDUCAUSE Review, 44*, 36–47.

Stephenson, N. (1992). *Snow Crash*. New York: Bantam Books.

Thomas, D. & Brown, J. S. (2009). Why virtual worlds can matter. *International Journal of Learning and Media, 1*, 37–49.

Chapter 8
A Virtual Mars

Richard Childers

This chapter tells the story of how a small group of visionaries invented a new virtual world, depicting how the planet Mars might possibly be around the year 2150, after advanced technologies had restored its lost ocean and atmosphere, transforming the red planet to blue. Mars then becomes a metaphor for "blue-sky" human hopes about the future, as well as an interactive museum for educating people today about science and our cultural heritage. By using unusually high-quality graphics to present artistic creativity in the context of an emerging communication technology, this world could promote progress across multiple fields. While partly inspired by all the many science fiction stories about colonizing and terraforming Mars, our virtual world is not directly related to any one of them. Rather, it uses this scientifically plausible idea as a metaphor for humanity's general hopes for the future, if we are able to use science and technology wisely to build a better world.

A Personal Journey

I was introduced to the idea of virtual worlds in Neil Stephenson's (1992) prophetic science fiction novel *Snow Crash*. In this tale, the protagonist lives in a you-store-it closet and makes his living delivering pizza for the mafia. In the real world, he is a nobody, one of a countless multitude of unimportant drones struggling to make ends meet in the dismal urban landscape of a postmodern Detroit. But when his workday is done, he returns home to don a pair of eyephones attached to a hot deck and a fast internet connection. It is here in the virtual world where his reality comes to life as he leaves his drab, pathetic real-world existence behind. In the virtual world, he is a force to be reckoned with, a respected man who has become a celebrity in his own right. It is a tale right out of the dreams of every drone in every mindless job in every rundown neighborhood on earth.

R. Childers
Virtual Space Entertainment
e-mail: Richard@VirtualSpaceEntertainment.com

W.S. Bainbridge (ed.), *Online Worlds: Convergence of the Real and the Virtual*,
Human-Computer Interaction Series, DOI 10.1007/978-1-84882-825-4_8,
© Springer-Verlag London Limited 2010

I knew in that moment that Stephenson had written far more than a good science fiction book. He had prophesied a future that was bound to come to pass. He had taken us to a place where technology was sure to follow. And in that moment, I was sure that I was going to be a part of that future. I saw the steps that would lead inevitably into the technological revolution that is now on us. I shared that book with my mentor and friend, Bill Kovacs. Bill was the wunderkind of computer graphics and animation and had received an academy award for his contributions to the film community. For we were both computer animators, that then rare profession of tech/artists who created moving images out of electrons. Bill was as taken as I with Stephenson's vision and over a bottle of single malt scotch, we tried to figure out when technology would be able to provide the computational power necessary to support a real-time, high-definition computer-generated scene. At the time, we worked on $60,000 Silicon Graphics workstations that took several minutes to render a frame of animation at that resolution. Quality animation runs at 30 frames per second or 1,800 frames per minute. That meant we needed a machine capable of rendering at a speed 3,600 times as great as the expensive workstations we were using. And clearly, it needed to happen on a moderately priced machine. Moore's law states that computer processing power doubles every 2 years, so we could expect technology capable of supporting a real-time high-definition virtual world by the year 2010, 20 years after we finished that bottle of fine scotch. Sixteen years later, Bill and I were invited to a closed door presentation of Sony's Playstation 3 where we saw an inexpensive game console that produced stunningly beautiful images rendered at 1080P resolution in real time. Technological innovation had beaten Moore's Law by four whole years.

In the days following that presentation, Bill and I decided to build a virtual world that would showcase this new real-time rendering. We believed that the time had come to turn Neil Stephenson's fiction into our reality. In the year that followed, Bill's incredible grasp of technology helped to create a coherent path to achieve our goals. In August of 2006, Bill Kovacs died of a massive stroke. Fortunately, the dream we nurtured had taken on a life of its own and it did not die with him. Figure 8.1 shows a paradise, an image Bill never saw, except perhaps in his imagination, that his vision would make possible.

In the months prior to Bill's untimely death, we had convinced a long-time friend and associate by the name of John Walsh that this was an opportunity worth pursuing. When we first pitched John on the idea, his CPA trained eyes glazed over and I seem to recall him saying something like, "You have got to be kidding!" By the time our pitch was over, John still didn't have the foggiest idea what we were talking about but he calmly asserted, "If you guys really think this is such a good idea, I'm in." I really have no idea what motivation drives an angel investor but whatever it is, few good ideas could ever see the light of day without someone like John stepping to the table and writing a check. By May of 2007, Virtual Space Entertainment, Inc. was formed and we moved into a 3,000 ft² studio just across from the Golden Gate Bridge in a space that had formerly been used to manufacture purses. Along the way, we had shed our early fascination with the Playstation 3 technology and settled on a new rendering engine created by a German game company, Crytek. Their CryEngine 2 ran on a PC, erasing the need for a dedicated game

Fig. 8.1 A garden in *Blue Mars*

console to run our virtual world. Game consoles like the X-Box and the Playstation ran games – PCs ran the world.

For the next year, we struggled with the process of taking a technology designed for one purpose, games, and adapting it for an entirely different process, powering a computer-generated social environment where people interacted with each other instead of shooting at each other with an array of formidable virtual weapons. We fervently believed that there was a huge audience out there who would love to experience immersive environments if they were only given a chance to experience them in something other than a first-person shooter. To many of us, there are more compelling things than endless simulated violence, a lesson that seems to have been lost among the gaming community. As we worked with our development partners to conquer the programming challenges that faced us, our artists began to experiment with the creation of highly detailed CG environments. Syd Mead, a visual futurist and one of the most influential production designers in the world began to work with us to bring his futuristic cities and vehicles into our future world. Rock and roll artist and designer Roger Dean brought shape to the terraformed Martian landscape we had chosen for our setting. And a group of talented computer artists and designers built an endless array of structures and interiors that we brought into the CryEngine as we tested the upper limits of the software's capabilities. It took a full 12 months of production to gain a real understanding of what it would take to build a virtual world that would both satisfy our drive for artistic excellence and design and still be capable of supporting robust social interaction with tens and even hundreds of thousands of virtual users moving around our world in computer-generated bodies or avatars.

And then we started over. Every model had to be rebuilt with the design constraints we had learned were necessary to ensure the desired performance. Almost 20,000 h of production was scrapped. All we had to show for our labors was the knowledge that would let us start over and do it right this time. But we knew we could make it work. A pipe dream had become an attainable goal. All we needed was another year and a couple of bucket loads of cash.

It was about this time that someone asked in a staff meeting, "So what are we gonna have all these users do?" I think I answered that they were going to enter into this fantastic futuristic city and become virtual colonists on Mars in the year 2150. "Yea, but what are they gonna do?" he insisted. I didn't have an answer to this perfectly reasonable question. In our quest to solve our technical and artistic issues, we had failed to define the activities that would bring users back to our world not just for one visit but for many repeat visits. We had great performance in absolutely stunning environments. Now, we had to find the compelling content that would complete the picture.

A New Mars

Blue Mars is not based on any particular work of past literature, nor on any narrow view of what future humans should build for themselves, but on a broad vision of expanding possibilities. Mars, of course, is the *red* planet, but as James Lovelock and Michael Allaby (1984) pointed out in their book, *The Greening of Mars*, it may be possible to transform the fourth planet from the sun to be more like the third planet. However, the Earth is not green, but blue. NASA's Earth Observatory calls our world the blue marble;[1] visionaries make blue sky predictions, and new ideas enter like a bolt from the blue. When it was young, Mars may have been indeed blue, with a northern ocean and a substantial atmosphere; maybe it could become blue again. An educational NASA website says, "NASA scientists believe that it is technologically possible at the present time to create considerable global climate changes, allowing humans to live on Mars."[2] Writing with the founder of the Mars Society, Robert Zubrin, one NASA scientist, Christopher P. McKay, suggested:

> The planet Mars, while cold and arid today, once possessed a warm and wet climate, as evidenced by extensive fluvial features observable on its surface. It is believed that the warm climate of the primitive Mars was created by a strong greenhouse effect caused by a thick CO_2 atmosphere. Mars lost its warm climate when most of the available volatile CO_2 was fixed into the form of carbonate rock due to the action of cycling water. It is believed, however, that sufficient CO_2 to form a 300 to 600 mb atmosphere may still exist in volatile form, either adsorbed into the regolith or frozen out at the south pole. This CO_2 may be released by planetary warming, and as the CO_2 atmosphere thickens, positive feedback is produced which can accelerate the warming trend. Thus it is conceivable, that by taking advantage of the positive feedback inherent in Mars' atmosphere/regolith CO_2 system, that engineering efforts can produce drastic changes in climate and pressure on a planetary scale. (Zubrin and McKay 1993)

---

[1] http://earthobservatory.nasa.gov/Features/BlueMarble/

[2] http://quest.nasa.gov/mars/background/terra.html

A century ago, astronomer Percival Lowell (1908) argued that Mars was a dying world, that had once been much more like the Earth, and this idea quickly influenced science fiction. Edgar Rice Burroughs (1917) imagined that a declining Martian civilization sustained a barely breathable atmosphere through factories that constantly replenished it. Decades later, in his novels Red Planet and Stranger in a Strange Land, Robert A. Heinlein (1949, 1961) dreamed that Martian civilization had migrated underground and there developed to a higher philosophical level than humans had yet attained. Of course, today we know these were fantasies, but the idea that Mars once harbored life and could once again have a very solid scientific basis (Sagan 1973; Friedmann et al. 1993; Zubrin 1996; McKay 1999).

For our purposes, it is not necessary to decide whether terraforming Mars is feasible, either technically or economically. The fact that it is at least conceivable, on the basis of our current scientific knowledge, helps us use Blue Mars as an environment for teaching science. First, some portions of the virtual world could be preserves, representing portions of Mars as they are today. Second, educational modules could be created that explained the scientific issues in transforming Mars in a manner that teaches general lessons about chemistry, physics, and Earth science. Some of these issues strike very close to home; for example, the method that might be used to warm Mars by adding carbon dioxide to the atmosphere relates directly to the issue of global warming on Earth. It is also true that the past work of astronomers focused on Mars illustrates many important points in astronomy and the history of that field, from Kepler's calculation of the planet's orbit in 1605, to Hall's discovery of its two moons in 1877, to the robot landers and orbiters that have studied Mars closely in recent decades.

If Mars were actually colonized, the people living there would not have the opportunity to visit Earth on frequent vacations, because the cost and time spent traveling would be prohibitive. Therefore, a flourishing Martian society would naturally create many museums and theme parks dedicated to the Earth's ecology and history. Future Martian educational institutions would naturally be a mixture of Earth traditions and Martian innovations, in artistic design, educational methods, and technological basis. This means that *Blue Mars* would be an excellent environment where today's educational institutions could prototype and develop new materials and methods that could be of very wide value. Thus, with our metaphor and our graphics in hand, we went in search of cultural colonists for our virtual world.

Sharing the Idea

In January of 2008, we booked a booth at the National Retail Federation trade show in New York after we heard that they were going to be focusing on future retail trends, including virtual worlds. We whipped together a quick virtual demonstration of a toy store and from a booth at the back of the hall, we showed the trend of tomorrow as a product that was in development at that very moment. A lot of people saw that demo but the single contact that was most excited about what we

Fig. 8.2 A coffee shop at a Martian university

were doing was the Director of the National Association of College Stores, a group representing 3,100 college and university book stores. The idea of virtual college stores appealed to us because college students were the ideal early adopters for *Blue Mars 2150* (Fig. 8.2).

A couple of months later, we exhibited at the American Association of Museums show, thinking we might be able to attract a museum interested in a virtual exhibition. After all, in our search for compelling content, a museum might be cool. Little did we know how cool. By the end of our first morning at the show, we were in serious discussions with the Smithsonian Institution's National Museum of Natural History about building a virtual version of their upcoming Hall of Human Origins and with the National Geographic Society about a virtual exhibit to coincide with their Terra Cotta Warrior Exhibition. As we wandered the AAM's Hall full of dinosaur skeletons and cool high def presentations of engaging subjects, it began to dawn on us that this was a vision of a virtual world that we could really believe in. During the following week, I met with our design staff and we all became intrigued with this new found focus. A new motto emerged, *Blue Mars 2150: the Future in Mind*. Over the course of 5 months, we held a series of meetings with the curators and business development personnel of both museums and by December of 2008, both development contracts were in place. We had found an identity and an answer to our most perplexing question: how were we going to attract the large number of users we would need to make a success of our virtual world. There was no way a small, underfunded startup could compete with the likes of Electronic Arts, Disney, *Second Life*, and *Entropia*. National Geographic would promote to their users (over 300 million a month), Smithsonian would promote to theirs (40 million a year), and

Fig. 8.3 Museum-quality architecture in *Blue Mars*

NACS would promote *Blue Mars* to some 25 million college students. We now knew where our users were going to come from (Fig. 8.3).

With a Beta start date of June 1, 2009 moving toward us with inexorable speed, our production teams redoubled their efforts. An expert on the First Emperor of China, Dr. Anthony Barbieri Low from the University of California Santa Barbara, was selected by National Geographic to oversee our designs for the Emperor's Tomb and the Terra Cotta Warriors. Once again, early designs were scrapped as we learned accurate historical details that conflicted with what we discovered was a "Hollywood" vision of the tomb.

To create accurate movements for our hominid ancestors, we set up a motion capture session at the Great Ape Trust in Des Moines. It turns out that Australopithecus upper body anatomy is almost identical to that of a bonobo ape. Three and a half million years ago, they started walking upright so their legs and pelvises changed dramatically. We found a group of researchers studying the bio-mechanics of hominid locomotion by studying the great apes. Several years ago, they tried a motion capture session with some chimps but the apes as they groomed, removed the markers that the motion capture system required. But this time, they were going to be working with Kanzi, a bonobo who has a 500 word vocabulary and it was felt he could not only take limited stage direction, he could demonstrate tool use that really is close to what we think early hominid tool use was like. So, the idea of a virtual ape and hominid biomechanical laboratory was born. It will be located within the TERC Virtual Science Center, now aptly named the VirSci Center. Here, researchers from around the world will be able to collaborate in real time, practicing real science in a virtual world. And users who are interested in science will be able to watch it happen. In fact, those who wish will be able to directly interact with the data and the 3-D lab. A new way to teach hands-on science will be just one of the results.

Three-dimensional models of seven different species are being created for the National Museum of Natural History. Our virtual users will be able to enter into a computer-generated hominid and experience first-hand accurate simulations of their life styles and environments. Visitors will be able to enter into the Tomb of the First Emperor of China along with its necropolis and the Terra Cotta Warrior pits. They will be able to play the instruments found in the burial sites and enter into a simulated work-shop where the warriors were created. They will learn about the Tao from Alan Watts and practice calligraphy with a virtual pen. They will be able to explore the undersea world of the twentyfirst century Earth as well as the accurate surface of the planet Mars. They will walk with Lucy on the floor of the Rift Valley and cruise the magnificent fiords formed by the Vallis Marinaris in a virtual replica of Tom Perkins' state-of-the-art sail-ing ship the Maltese Falcon. There is almost nothing that is not possible.

Conclusion

Disruptive technologies change the world. They often even alter the very way we perceive the world. The emergence of the three-dimensional interactive web, what we like to call Web 3.0, is about to transform the way humans interact with technol-ogy. Just as the public has grown accustomed to an interactive 2D interface to the web, the three-dimensional structure of the real world is being transplanted into the virtual world and the end result will be transformative, not only to our technological society but to our entire society as a whole. The lines separating communication and entertainment have been blurring for some time. Virtual worlds will erase them. Convergence is no longer a catchword for the future; it is the reality of today. And while virtual worlds and the real world are currently distinct and separate, those differences will fast disappear. The leading futurist and author Ray Kurzweil predicts that by the year 2020, the real world and the virtual world will be indistin-guishable (Kurzweil 1999). Think of the implications inherent in that concept!

Perhaps in the creation of this exciting new world, we will open new vistas for education and communication. Perhaps, the perspective we gain by looking at our world through the eyes of Martian colonists in the year 2150 will help us gain a broader understanding of the Earth in the year 2009. Perhaps, we can find a new Future in Mind.

References

Burroughs, E. R. (1917). *A princess of Mars*. Chicago, IL: A. C. McClurg.
Friedmann, I. E., Hua, M., & Ocampo-Friedmann, R. (1993). Dissolution of carbonate rocks by cyanobacteria. *Journal of the British Interplanetary Society, 46*, 291–292.
Heinlein, R. A. (1949). *Red planet: A colonial boy on Mars*. New York: Scribner's.

Heinlein, R. A. (1961). *Stranger in a strange land*. New York: Putnam.

Kurzweil, R. (1999). *The age of spiritual machines*. New York: Viking.

Lovelock, J. & Allaby, M. (1984). *The greening of Mars*. New York: St. Martin's.

Lowell, P. (1908). *Mars as the abode of life*. New York: Macmillan.

McKay, C. P. (1999, July). *Bringing life to Mars*. The Fifth International Conference on Mars, July 19–24, Pasadena, CA.

Sagan, C. (1973). Planetary engineering on Mars. *Icarus, 20*, 513–514.

Stephenson, N. (1992). *Snow Crash*. New York: Bantam Books.

Zubrin, R. (1996). *The case for Mars: The plan to settle the red planet and why we must*. New York: Free Press.

Zubrin, R. M. & McKay, C. P. (1993, June). *Technological requirements for terraforming Mars*. AIAA, SAE, ASME, and ASEE, Joint Propulsion Conference and Exhibit, Monterey, CA, June 28–30; (http://www.users.globalnet.co.uk/~mfogg/zubrin.htm).

Chapter 9
Opening the Metaverse

Julian Lombardi and Marilyn Lombardi

Ever since Neal Stephenson coined the term *Metaverse* in 1992 to describe a unified avatar-mediated virtual context where people could interact with each other in a three-dimensional space, the term has been perhaps too readily applied to today's numerous and noninteroperable implementations of avatar-mediated virtual worlds. Our experiences of the last 17 years around the emergence of the Internet Gopher and then the Web provide us with sound examples of the conditions from which large-scale, unified, and open information contexts can emerge. Today's first generation of virtual world systems – e.g., essentially walled gardens under the control of various corporate concerns – stand in stark contrast to the open, scalable, and noncommercial approach that propelled Internet Gopher to success and accounted for the Web's wide adoption. This chapter will discuss the need to establish an open metamedium that can support large-scale metaverse deployment and describe our research group's current efforts to design and develop virtual world cyberinfrastructures informed by the successes of the Web. We will describe our research program's motivations to address the technical and economic limitations of current virtual world systems and to explore how peer-to-peer communication protocols, open software infrastructures, and end-user empowerment to freely create content and functionality can set the conditions for emergence of a global metamedium for collaboration and interaction. While our research group's primary motivation is to support the use of collaborative contexts for education and training, our technical approach has broad application and is designed to address scalability concerns of an emergent global virtual world-delivered information and communication system, or *metaverse*.

Virtual worlds (VWs) have captured the imagination of educators, corporate trainers, academics, and business leaders who see in them the harbinger of things to come: e.g., global classrooms that immerse and engage students; virtual laboratories where remote collaborators, tools, and information coalesce in a single interactive context; and multinational corporate conferences that no longer put a strain on diminishing travel budgets. Although they were designed to provide a foundation

J. Lombardi and M. Lombardi
Duke University
e-mails: julian@duke.edu; marilyn.lombardi@duke.edu

W.S. Bainbridge (ed.), *Online Worlds: Convergence of the Real and the Virtual*,
Human-Computer Interaction Series, DOI 10.1007/978-1-84882-825-4_9,
© Springer-Verlag London Limited 2010

for what has become a multibillion dollar gaming and entertainment industry, VW technologies will clearly expand their influence, facilitating collaboration and productivity across many more realms of human activity. Their potential usefulness as global business and education environments, however, lies less in their gaming origins than in their capacity to provide a rich presentation layer for real-time interaction with resources distributed across next-generation networks, including grid computing and on-demand cloud services.

What will it take to invent the *future* – specifically, the routine, affordable use of a new deeply collaborative metamedium for education, research, and commerce? By "metamedium," we refer to a *socially enabled extension* of Kay and Goldberg (1977) notion of the computer as "the first metamedium," which has "degrees of freedom for representation and expression never before encountered and as yet barely investigated." Over the course of this argument, terms and phrases such as "metaverse," "metamedium," and "contextualized copresence" will be unpacked and reconsidered in light of the enormous untapped potential to be found in VWs technologies. The trajectory we hope to chart is one that extends from today's proprietary and restrictive gaming/entertainment platforms toward the kind of scalable technical architecture that will be required to support a new global medium on par with the now ubiquitous Web.

Today's Virtual Worlds

Often referred to as "online worlds," "avatar-mediated virtual worlds," "virtual workspaces," or simply "Web 3D," VWs are immersive and collaborative online information spaces supporting copresence among multiple participants. They essentially derive from multiuser gaming products and avatar-mediated social networking services developed by the online entertainment industry. To the extent that they encourage groups of users to explore richly populated information spaces, VWs serve to extend the nature and quality of online discovery and interaction by providing capabilities not readily available through traditional Web technologies (see Cummings et al. 2008; Cohen 2008).

The current crop of VWs systems (Linden Labs' *Second Life* being the most popular) were inspired, no doubt, by Neal Stephenson's (1992) vision of the "metaverse" in *Snow Crash*. This dystopian science fiction novel features a media conglomerate that runs a planet-sized virtual city in which as many as 120 million avatars cruise for entertainment, trade, and social contact. Early attempts at deploying Stephenson-inspired metaverses include LucasFilm's 1985 launch of *Habitat*, the first of what came to be known as massively multiplayer online role-playing games, with a 3D graphical user interface. The next 15 years witnessed the appearance of others, including *Cybertown* (1995), *Alpha Worlds/Active Worlds* (1995), *Black Sun* (1996), *Microsoft Chat* (1996), and *ViOS* (2001). Of these, only *Active Worlds* remains in use today. Like the massively multiplayer online role-playing games of the mid-1990s, the available commercial virtual world systems offer their subscribers a certain comfortable verisimilitude combined with a limited range of fantasy powers (flight, invisibility, masquerade, and self-invention).

If capturing an audience of 120 million remains outside the grasp of *Second Life* and its commercial competitors (because of technical limitations to be identified later on in this discussion), their several million registrants[1] do testify to the allure of Stephenson's *metaverse-as-consumer-paradise*. And so, as with the extraordinarily popular series of online *Sims* games that began appearing on shelves at the turn of the century, many of today's VWs bustle with mercantile activity and acquisitiveness. Participants enjoy the kind of instant gratification that comes with acquiring new virtual identities, accoutrements, and friends (leading ultimately to a real-world market for virtual goods).

The question for education and business is whether a technology developed to promote the delights of self-invention, acquisition, and consumption can wind up also supporting genuine *productivity* on a massive scale. From the perspective of work organizations, educators, trainers, and scholars, the true potential of VW technologies will only be realized if they form the basis of an online medium with the broad reach and impact of the Web.

Tomorrow's Global Metamedium

IBM's current website argues that VWs hold "significant promise far beyond today's usage" and declares them to be "the next evolutionary phase of the Internet."[2] The expectation was that one day IBM's network of employees and alumni around the world would be able to access this next-generation "3D Internet" through mobile and other handheld devices. This vision of a global metamedium is perhaps best articulated by Smart, Cascio, and Paffendorf (2007) in the *Metaverse Roadmap Overview*:

> In time, many of the Internet activities we now associate with the 2D Web will migrate to the 3D spaces of the Metaverse. This does not mean all or even most of our web pages will become 3D, or even that we'll typically read web content in 3D spaces. It means that as new tools develop, we'll be able to intelligently mesh 2D and 3D to gain the unique advantages of each, in the appropriate context.

The metaverse-as-metamedium, if implemented appropriately, would make it easy for anyone to create and distribute 3D virtual information spaces that are collaborative, persistent, and interoperable, and that provide a shared social context for unifying and integrating resources, multimedia content, along with grid and cloud-based computing services on demand. Moreover, the virtualized corporate enterprise would not be the only entity to benefit from this vision of the metaverse-as-metamedium.

---

[1] *Second Life* usage statistics. See http://secondlife.com

[2] http://domino.research.ibm.com/comm/research_projects.nsf/pages/virtualworlds.index.html

The idea of the "metaverse-as-metamedium" emphasizes the two most salient features of VWs technologies and dislodges them from the limited confines of *Snow Crash*-inspired consumerism. The most striking features of VWs are: (1) the ability to deliver enhanced visualization and simulation capabilities, and (2) support for contextualized copresence.

Enhanced Visualization: The powerful visual nature of VWs represents a significant advance in the development of the graphical user interface, freeing participants from the context-less and potentially alienating limitations of the Web's document-based and text-driven approach to communication. From an evolutionary perspective, the human capacity to process multidimensional visual information is much older than the relatively recent ability to learn about and process textual information. We are preadapted to interpret visual displays of information within real-world 3D environments. Thus, VWs that are filled with affordances offer information up to us in a fashion we find familiar and intuitive, providing an effective scaffolding for learning, navigating, and remembering displayed information.

Contextualized Copresence: VWs also provide a way of visualizing information within a social, collaborative context. The capability for one or more participants of a VW to construct and modify virtual spaces combined with their ability to discover and interact with other participants in the context of those co-constructed spaces represents a leap forward in social networking and social construction of knowledge.

This unique combination of heightened visualization capacity and contextualized copresence is of particular importance now that we are entering an era in which distributed teams of industrial designers, scientists, and scholars are increasingly turning to 3D visualizations and dynamic simulations in order to advance research and development. Visualization already plays an increasingly important role as investigators try to observe and simulate the behavior of complex real-world systems and social networks (e.g., fluid flows, molecular dynamics, traffic flow and congestion, supply-chain management, bibliographical citations, or word usage across multiple modern translations of Greco-Roman literature, etc.). However, effective visualizations, whether 3D models of the cardiovascular system, architectural reconstructions, interactive maps, or financial simulations, are usually created, reviewed, and modified by teams of specialists and stakeholders – *teams that are often dispersed across cities and continents*. VWs have the potential to integrate visualization with collaborative copresence and provide an efficient and affordable way for people to collaborate across great distances.

A still modest, but growing, number of academic and corporate researchers have begun to experiment with commercial 3D VW platforms – particularly Linden Lab's *Second Life* – in an effort to harness the nascent power of these two characteristics. They also have made *Second Life* and other such platforms an attractive medium for exploring transformational approaches to K-12 education and training across virtualized corporate enterprises. This recent surge of academic interest in the emerging VW medium is one of the chief rationales for the present volume.

The scientific and scholarly communities will begin to see the merits of VW platforms only when those platforms are further refined and integrated with enterprise services, including high-performance computing capabilities. The goal here would be to make it possible for collaborating colleagues to provision their shared virtual environments with dynamic visualizations and simulations that can change "on the fly" to reflect fresh incoming data. When this happens, researchers will enjoy instant visual access to large data sets independent of the location of the data or of the person(s) accessing them. Moreover, they will also be able to steer those computations collaboratively from within the VW, change the parameters of a running program, and visualize the altered results immediately. Advances in our national networking and computing infrastructure will doubtless drive our ability to deliver these next generation VW technologies.

Present Limitations

Excited by the possibilities of the metaverse-as-metamedium, IBM joined Cisco Systems, Intel, Microsoft, Motorola, Google, and Sony (along with several leading VW developers), for a 2007 San Jose, California, summit in advance of the *Alternate Realities Conference*. The companies hoped to explore VW interoperability between the major platforms, but disillusionment quickly set in. Without interoperability, IBM's "3D Internet" would remain a pipe dream (see Terdiman 2007). The multinational companies, eager to see advances in this area, soon grew frustrated with resistant VW service providers. Even the relatively narrow goal of advancing a single avatar identity for each user that could be carried from one platform to another was met with very little enthusiasm, while the repurposing of 3D content across different platforms was dismissed out of hand. It became obvious that from the perspective of VW providers, interoperability of any kind was a threat to their business models. Once people are permitted to carry their identity/creative works and exchange content freely between commercial platforms, VW providers would lose vendor lock-in as well as whatever competitive advantage they might enjoy in the presently fragmented VWs market. With the potential loss of subscription and advertising revenues in this scenario, VW providers would be forced to bear the costs of upgrading and adding functionalities to their platforms in order to ensure the ongoing viability of their offerings; the "feature wars" that would invariably ensue would likely drive most providers out of the market.

Clearly, to break through the restrictions of present VW platforms and policies, some form of disruptive technology or business practice will need to emerge. For the remainder of this discussion, we will (1) refine our definition of a *metamedium-enabled metaverse* in light of lessons learned from the Web, (2) define the specific set of technical and business assumptions that have impeded progress to this point, and (3) offer up a roadmap for *opening the metaverse*.

Learning from the Web

Can commercial VW systems really give rise to the global metamedium of the metaverse so many of us envision – a metamedium able to replicate the mind-boggling success of the Web? Millions of people have explored VWs through one of the commercial subscription services, but perhaps a more important figure for assessing the impact of VWs as a global phenomenon would be the number of worlds (or "spaces" or "islands") that users have developed and actively maintain. In *Second Life*, for example, the number of private islands has been falling since a price increase was announced in October 2008. From that time to February 2009, the number of islands declined by 4,846, a loss of 18.1% of the total land mass.[3] This decline of a key context for information exchange in a leading VW technology should be contrasted with web page growth over the same period of time (a web page also being a key context for information exchange). In July of 2008, Google reported that it had indexed one trillion web pages (Alpert and Hajaj 2008) and by March 2009, Internet World Stats estimated that the number of users of the Web had exceeded the 1.6 billion mark.[4]

Though many attempts have been made recently by commercial VWs providers to extend the functionality of their user interface and add content to the environments in support of education and productivity, the original elements of most platforms bear the marks of their gaming and entertainment origins, limiting the range of activities they are able to support easily. Moreover, when a subscriber chooses a platform, he or she is choosing a distinct, preconstructed VW metaphor and exclusive social network. In other words, the platform provider exerts complete control over the identity (user name/password and avatar) as well as the content that a subscriber creates within world. Despite assurances that the user's content "belongs" to him or her, that property cannot be transferred beyond the bounds of the chosen system. Thus, there are significant switching costs associated with changing platforms down the road. The implications of this iron curtain between platforms is particularly significant for VW-based educational and training simulations, since it is impossible to perform the kind of crossplatform, longitudinal, and comparative studies that are needed to assess the effectiveness of simulation-based curricula and to track individual student achievement over time.

In this way, today's VW platforms are quite remarkably similar to the well-known "walled gardens" of early online life in the 1980s. The first major information service providers (ISPs) – *AOL*, *CompuServe*, and *Prodigy* – also developed business models that set them against one another to capture the largest share the market for online information services including the emerging social software systems of the day (email, bulletin boards, polls, etc.). Like the VW platform providers of today, the "walled garden" ISPs cultivated a "members-only" sensibility, where the value of the service was a function of the quality of the people with whom you were permitted to interact. The early online service providers also had no incentive to allow their subscribers to communicate with members of competing services; early users of the AOL ISP, for instance, were not permitted to send email to

---

[3]*Second Life* Economic Statistics (raw data files) retrieved from http://secondlife.com (now removed).

[4] http://www.internetworldstats.com/stats.htm

addresses that were not managed by AOL. The goal was to convince the public that the Internet was the ISPs platform, and that the ISPs platform *was* the Internet[5]. Although a form of the AOL's ISP remains with us today, its eponymously promised dominance over even an American Internet user base never materialized, owing in large measure to the arrival of the first truly global scale information/ social software systems of the *Internet Gopher* and the *Web*.

What is it about the basic *architecture* of the Web that allowed it to become a global-scale medium routinely accessed by billions of users? First and foremost, having originated as a set of not-for-profit services deployed by and for universities, the Web is open and nonproprietary at its core. Like its immediate predecessor, the free and open *Internet Gopher* (Anklesaria et al. 1993), the Web leveraged open protocols, *empowering anyone with a computer and Internet connection to publish information* (Hart 2009). When the Web emerged in 1993–1994, the walled garden ISPs had to redefine their business models, as people were simply unwilling to pay for restricted online information services when unrestricted content and free and open tools and protocols became available.

This is not to say that the Web could not support commercial interests. In fact, a great deal of wealth was generated once a substrate of free and open Web services had been established. The rise of *Google* represents the best example by far of how revenues can be generated without falling back on an early ISP-style subscription model. *Google* did not take on the enormous expense of supporting basic infrastructure and limiting information access and exchange. Instead, the company leveraged available technology infrastructure and open access to Web-delivered information to define a value-added service for the advertising industry that has become the basis of its present commercial empire – i.e., linking targeted advertising to special search results while leveraging the open Web. Clearly, analogous opportunities will arise to capitalize on a free and open infrastructure for supporting the creation, publication, and deployment of VWs.

At its core, the Web gave us a medium for assembling resources from different locations across a global network – a medium distinguished, in fact, by two powerful features that account for the Web's large-scale adoption: (1) a visual display space or information context (e.g., the *web page*) for assembling individual resources into a *mosaic* (to use the original parlance) or *mash-up* (to invoke the sophistication of Web 2.0 capabilities); and (2) a bit of hypermedia magic called the *hyperlink* that people could use to define connections across interoperable information contexts (e.g., between web pages).

To profound effect, the web page and the hyperlink combined to enable an extended communal conversation in which users guided one another down the paths of argument. This is a process of creation and discovery that has grown ever more sophisticated with the help of search engines, directories, and social networking tools. The Web's capacity to leverage the distributed wisdom of the crowd and its

---

[5] Ted Leonsis (personal communication)

status as a free and uniquely interactive global medium is exemplified by *Wikipedia* among other emerging manifestations.

The conclusion we have reached is that we must look to the example of the Web for inspiration when it comes to shaping the future of online interaction and the prospect of an open metaverse. The fundamental technologies of the new global metamedium supporting the open metaverse must (1) be open and nonproprietary, (2) include a VW browser analogous to today's open source web browsers for viewing and interacting with VWs, and (3) provide 3D hyperlink capability for traversing VW contexts. Participants should be able to find everything they need in this fundamental framework: interact with others online; browse, create, and publish 3D content/functionality; and hyperlink information spaces (VWs) under their control.

On a number of levels, users accustomed to working inside today's wiki environments will be able to recognize the basic functionalities making up the open metamedium framework. At the level of participant experience, an open metaverse is essentially a 3D wiki environment in which networked collaborators will enjoy a heightened level of situational awareness because they can see and readily interact with one another in the context of their shared activities and creations. Participants in an open metaverse will be able to provision the 3D information space with a mosaic of resources, displaying, and assembling content in multiple formats – including text, images, animations, simulations, videos, and even web pages – that are instantly visible and accessible to everyone in the virtual space.

Taking its cue from the Web once again, the open metaverse must provide users with everything they need to author and publish new VWs easily and in real time, much as new hyperlinked web pages are created within Web-based wiki environments. How would this work? Let's say a work team is sharing a virtual 3D information space and one member wants to lead a breakout discussion in another space. To create the new VW, he or she simply calls forth somewhere in the existing space an aperture into an entirely new VW – a new 3D space that is immediately visible to everyone else on the team. The aperture is in effect a *3D hyperlink* connecting the first world to the second; members of the work group who are given appropriate privileges will be able to cross the threshold to join their colleagues on the other side at any time. The power of hyperlinks permitted Web developers to leverage one another's 2D information contexts and permitted Web users to transport themselves seamlessly between those contexts. An analogous feature built into the basic architecture of an open metaverse will lay the groundwork for extensibility, interoperability, and the kind of exponential growth that we know is the chief characteristic of global-scale information technology phenomena.

Defining the Technical Challenges

While the Web's history provides ample inspiration, it is also a cautionary tale. The analogies between the Web and the metamedium envisioned here tend to break down when it comes to supporting persistent, graphically rich VWs where large numbers of people are continually interacting with one another and modifying their shared VW in real time. When you request to view a web page, that page's information (stored on a server) is replicated and sent to your client (machine). The transaction occurs in a brief moment and you are able to view the page for a long period of time after it has been loaded. While this manner of data replication works reasonably well for the Web, because web pages are relatively small and static in nature, it is by no means the optimal approach to supporting the shared viewing of dynamic VWs among large numbers of participants. The simple reason: unlike web pages, VW spaces must convey a shared and continuously changing sense of shared context, or *state*.

To put it another way, contextualized copresence (something the Web has difficulty providing in nearly real-time and at scale) is computationally intensive to maintain. Centralized servers are neither the most efficient nor the most affordable way of maintaining that shared, persistent *state*. Every move and every action of every avatar must be conveyed to every client of every person participating in the collaborative VW in order for participants to maintain what is in effect a consensual hallucination of a populated space. Every action changes the state of that environment and must be made apparent to everyone else in a process of rapid and continual updating.

Commercial VW platforms, including *Second Life*, utilize a client–server architecture by which each participant's client keeps up a continual conversation with a VW provider's server, alerting the server to changes in the state of the VW (participant's movements, actions, etc.). The server acts as traffic cop, interpreting participant intentions, establishing a state for the VW simulation, and replicating information about the state of that simulation (i.e., data updates) multiple times, across all machines that are participating in that VW. Given the computational loads generated by today's immersive VW platforms, one server (one CPU) can handle simultaneous interactions among no more than 40–60 users at a time before being overwhelmed. Maintaining service without significant disruptions and lags means that a VW provider hoping to support the activities of several million simultaneous participants (as are the aspirations of many of the current VW platform providers) must pour resources into the establishment and maintenance of large server farms or provision their cloud equivalents. Even with the increasing availability of lower cost cloud computing services, the financial and environmental costs of implementing such computational infrastructures are substantial and prohibitive. The exorbitant costs of providing processing power – whether through traditional server farms or via cloud computing – will still need to be borne by the provider, who will pass them along to the consumer.

To examine these costs more closely, let's say that the current crop of VW providers banded together with the goal of creating a global metaverse infrastructure capable of supporting 1.6 billion participants, which is the number of Web users at last count. These companies would need to buy and maintain approximately four million additional servers (or their virtualized equivalents) with four CPUs per server and 100 participants supported by a single CPU. In terms of physical hardware and support costs of $5,000 US per server/year, this amounts to a roughly

$20 billion expenditure per annum. This admittedly rough estimate does not fully account for the considerable financial costs of power, cooling, and rack space. Nor does it account for overall carbon utilization. Moving the computations to the "cloud" simply moves the problem elsewhere.

Under the current market conditions, then, the prospect of an interlinked VW-based metaverse at the scale of use equivalent to that of the Web is highly unlikely. But those conditions may soon change. Inspired by the spirit of the non-profit, university-led initiatives that gave rise to Internet Gopher and the Web, a number of noncommercial, open-source VW platforms are beginning to emerge.

Defining the Technical Solutions

Lessons learned from the emergence of the Internet Gopher and the Web strongly suggest that to deploy an extensible and open metaverse, we must first make possible an open source technology that (1) allows its users to freely publish and access VWs; (2) is not reliant on server or other resource bottlenecks; (3) is able to leverage the creativity of the crowd; and (4) can be used to establish hyperlinks between multiple secure VW contexts.

To this end, our research group's NSF-funded Open Cobalt project[6] is exploring how a highly scalable open source collaboration infrastructure can be used as a basis for an emergent global-scale VW medium. The goal of this work is to enable the low-cost deployment and rich provisioning of a highly scalable network of hyperlinked VWs and initiate the dynamics seen with the emergence of the Web. We are developing Open Cobalt, an application-level extension of the open source Croquet software development toolkit that was initially developed for this purpose (Smith et al. 2003; McCahill and Lombardi 2004, 2005; Lombardi and Lombardi 2005; Lombardi and McCahill 2004, 2005; Lombardi et al. 2005; Kadobayashi et al. 2006). The project seeks to build and deploy a virtual machine-based technology that functions as a VW *browser* and construction *toolkit*, and as an integrated development environment for accessing, creating, and publishing hyperlinked VWs. Users are able to build and experience avatar-mediated 3D wiki environments that are hyperlinked and interoperable. These shared environments can be provisioned with resources in multiple formats (text, images, web content, animations, simulations, and time-based media, etc.) that are instantly visible and accessible to everyone sharing that environment (or to a subset of those people, depending on viewing rights and permissions). In an effort to make VW development and deployment routine and affordable, we have adopted a technical approach that eliminates the need for VW servers or other server infrastructures to support the basic interactivity between modest numbers of participants in any given VW. Instead, interactivity is maintained

---

[6] http://opencobalt.org

through an "ordered group messaging protocol" that synchronizes the activities of statefully connected peers (e.g., computing devices) on both local and wide-area networks. Server support enters the picture only in order to provide external resources *to* the virtual worlds (such as chat, IP telephony, remote desktops, VNC-delivered applications, and the like). We believe that these affordances begin to establish the enabling conditions for a new metamedium with global reach.

Conclusion

By leveraging everything, we have learned about the power of global scale distributed information systems, peer-based communication, and collaborative crowd-sourcing, we can prepare the way for the next generation of metaverse technologies and for the metaverse-centric industries that will arise in their wake. Already academic institutions, multinational corporations, emergency services agencies, and other distributed organizations are exploring the potential of VW-based collaboration systems as platforms for training, interaction, and collaboration. These implementations promise to improve operational efficiency, extend the range and reach of education, and create wholly new business opportunities, much as the Web gave rise to entirely new information age industries. The degree to which we prosper as researchers, as educators, and as citizens in a global economy may well depend in large part on how quickly and effectively we lay the proper groundwork for the coming age of virtualized collaboration.

References

Alpert, J. & Hajaj, N. (2008). We know the web was big. *The Official Google Blog*, from (http://googleblog.blogspot.com/2008/07/we-knew-web-was-big.html).

Anklesaria, F., McCahill, M., Lindner, P., Johnson, D., Torrey, D., & Alberti, B. (1993, March). *The Internet Gopher Protocol: A distributed document search and retrieval protocol.* Internet RFC 1436, from (http://www.ietf.org/rfc/rfc1436.txt).

Cohen, R. B. (2008). *Virtual worlds and the transformation of business: impacts on the U.S. economy, jobs, and industrial competitiveness* (Working Paper #4). The Athena Alliance (www.athenaalliance.com).

Cummings, J., Finholt, T., Foster, I., Kesselman, C., Lawrence, K. A., & Rhoten, D. (2008). *Beyond being there: A blueprint for advancing the design, development and evaluation of virtual organizations.* Chicago, IL: Computation Institute, University of Chicago, from (http://www.ci.uchicago.edu/events/VirtOrg2008/VO_report.pdf).

Hart, D. (2009). *Mosaic launches an internet revolution.: NSF Office of Cyberinfrastructure Website*, from (http://www.nsf.gov/discoveries/disc_summ.jsp?cntn_id=100274&org=OCI).

Kadobayashi, R., Lombardi, J., McCahill, M. P., Stearns, H., Tanaka, K., & Kay, A. (2006, January 26–28). 3D model annotation from multiple viewpoints for croquet. In K. Tanaka & K. Rose (Eds.), *Proceedings of the Fourth Annual Conference on creating, connecting, and collaborating through computing.* Berkeley, CA: IEEE.

Kay, A. & Adele, G. (1977). Personal Dynamic Media. *IEEE Computer* 10(3):31–41.

Lombardi, J. & McCahill, M. P. (2004, January 29–30). Enabling social dimensions of learning through a persistent, unified, massively multi-user, and self-organizing virtual environment. In Y. Kambayashi, K. Tanaka, & K. Rose (Eds.), *Proceedings of the Second Annual Conference on creating, connecting, and collaborating through computing* (pp. 166–172). Keihanna Plaza, IEEE, Kyoto, Japan.

Lombardi, J., & McCahill, M. P. (2005, January 28–30). User interfaces for self and others in croquet learning spaces. In K. Tanaka & K. Rose (Eds.), *Proceedings of the Third Annual Conference on Creating, Connecting, and Collaborating through Computing*. IEEE, Kyoto, Japan.

Lombardi, J., Kadobayashi, R., McCahill, M. P., Stearns, H., Tanaka, K., & Kay, A. (2005). *Annotation authoring in 3D collaborative virtual environments.* In 15th International Conference on Artificial Reality and Telexistence (ICAT 2005, December 5–8), Christchurch, New Zealand.

Lombardi, M. & Lombardi, J. (2005, January 28–30). Croquet learning environments: Extending the value of campus life into the online experience. In K. Tanaka & K. Rose (Eds.), *Proceedings of the Third Annual Conference on creating, connecting, and collaborating through computing*. IEEE, Kyoto, Japan.

McCahill, M. P. & Lombardi, J. (2004, January 29–30). Design for an extensible croquet-based framework to deliver a persistent, unified, massively multi-user, and self-organizing virtual environment. In Y. Kambayashi, K. Tanaka & K. Rose (Eds.), *Proceedings of the Second Annual IEEE Conference on creating, connecting, and collaborating through computing* (pp. 71–77). Keihanna Plaza, IEEE, Kyoto, Japan.

McCahill, M. P. & Lombardi, J. (2005, January 28–30). User interfaces for places and things in croquet learning spaces. In K. Tanaka & K. Rose (Eds.), *Proceedings of the Third Annual Conference on creating, connecting, and collaborating through computing*. Kyoto, Japan: IEEE.

Smart, J. M., Cascio, J., & Paffendorf, J. (2007). *Metaverse roadmap overview*, from (http://metaverseroadmap.org/overview/).

Smith, D. A., Kay, A., Raab, A., & Reed, D. P. (2003). Croquet – a collaboration system architecture. In *Proceedings of the First Conference on creating, connecting and collaborating through computing (C5'03) 0-7695-1975-X/03* (pp. 2–10). Los Alamitos, CA: IEEE Computer Society Press.

Stephenson, N. (1992). *Snow Crash*. New York: Bantam Dell.

Terdiman, D. (2007). (http://news.cnet.com/Tech-titans-seek-virtual-world-interoperability/2100-1043_3-6213148.html).

Chapter 10
A Typology of Ethnographic Scales for Virtual Worlds

Tom Boellstorff

We are in a historical moment when virtual worlds are coming into being as a significant mode of technologically mediated sociality. Alongside and within these virtual worlds, a new research community is in formation, one whose growth will only be stimulated by the continuing emergence of new virtual worlds. This community includes a wide range of researchers, from those who have studied virtual worlds for decades to students conceiving new projects. It is an interdisciplinary research community, including persons from many academic disciplines, persons working in nonprofit and industry contexts, independent scholars, designers, journalists, and residents (these are, of course, not exclusive categories). Two key questions that emerge around this new research community (indeed, all new research communities) are as follows: What is the object of our study? What do various methodologies bring to the table in terms of researching this object of study?

The Setup: From Positivism to Ethnographic Scale

Peril as well as promise lies ahead as the contours of these research communities harden and canons are established for what counts as legitimate research. One of the most disturbing of these perils involves a methodological partisanship asserting that only quantitative, experimental methods are scientific and/or worthy of pursuit – to the extent that we could imagine, even if with chagrin, a future in which these are the only methods used (see Bloomfield 2009; Boellstorff 2009; Castronova 2006). Key to this partisanship is the ideology that the only valid forms of social research are those that seek to make predictions, an ideology based in turn on the view that culture can be described in terms of regular laws analogous to, say, the law of gravity. Science fiction has played an important role in the development of virtual worlds (Boellstorff 2008, Chapter 2) – so that, for instance, works such as

T. Boellstorff
Department of Anthropology, University of California, Irvine
3151 Social Science Plaza, Irvine, CA 92697
e-mail: tboellst@uci.edu

W.S. Bainbridge (ed.), *Online Worlds: Convergence of the Real and the Virtual*,
Human-Computer Interaction Series, DOI 10.1007/978-1-84882-825-4_10,
© Springer-Verlag London Limited 2010

Neil Stephenson's *Snow Crash* have played a key role in imagining what virtual worlds might be like (Stephenson 1992). In turn, the ideology that laws for culture exist is certainly shaped by the figure of Hari Seldon, the character who in Isaac Asimov's influential *Foundation* series of novels (beginning with Asimov 1951) developed a science of "psychohistory" that could predict the development of societies thousands of years into the future.

I find little that is convincing in this ideology, often termed "positivist" because of its indebtedness to the philosophy of Auguste Comte, not only due to its partisan denigration of other methods and analytical goals, but because human sociality is so contingent and emergent that predicting historical change is not possible (not simply imperfect, due to our failure to try hard enough or develop the right tools). No method (experimental or otherwise) could have predicted the emergence and form of, say, Modern English, or gay identity. Of course, experimental methods need not be restricted to seeking predictive laws. Either experimental or what I will provisionally term "ethnographic" methods can also be used for a better interpretive understanding of actually existing human cultures, online and offline. The debate is not new: for instance, it appears at the beginnings of disciplinary anthropology in the late 19th and early 20th centuries. Franz Boas – typically considered the foundational figure of United States anthropology – argued in 1887 with "those accustomed to value a study according to the scope of the laws found by means of it" (Boas 1940 [1887]:640). Using the figures of "the physicist" and "the historian" as examples, Boas noted that:

> The physicist compares a series of similar facts, from which he isolates the general phenomenon which is common to all of them. Henceforth the single facts become less important to him, as he lays stress on the general law alone. On the other hand, the facts are the object which is of importance and interest to the historian... [for such a researcher, the] mere existence [of a phenomenon] entitles it to a full share of our attention; and the knowledge of its existence and evolution in space and time fully satisfies the student, without regard to the laws which it corroborates or which may be deduced from it. (Boas 1940 [1887]:641–642)

In this chapter, I seek to contribute to the contemporary incarnation of this debate with regard to virtual worlds by focusing on a key discussion taking place within the domain of ethnographic methodology itself. While less consumed by issues like defining what counts as a valid research finding, participants in this discussion are nonetheless establishing a paradigm for classifying ethnographic research about virtual worlds, with consequences for how we conceptualize what "virtual worlds" represent in the first place.

It is with the goal of contributing to the development of this paradigm that in this chapter I set out a typology of genres of ethnographic research with regard to virtual worlds. A "typology" is simply a classification scheme for a set of phenomena. For instance, linguists who work in language typology classify languages in terms of the Indo-European language family, the Austronesian language family, the Bantu language family, and so on. This work involves both defining (1) what criteria will count for inclusion in a particular group, and (2) which languages belong in which groups. My analogous goals in this chapter are (1) to set out a typology for forms of ethnographic research in virtual worlds, and (2) to identify published research that exemplifies each of these categories. (As this is not a review essay, I will provide only a few illustrative examples, not an exhaustive catalogue.)

However, even setting aside experimental and quantitative approaches so as to narrow the discussion to ethnographic methods still leaves me with too wide a conceptual scope for the space limits of a book chapter. As a result, I will not discuss issues like the relative contributions of participant observation versus interviewing, focus groups, archival work, and other methods for ethnographic research. Instead, I focus my analysis on the question of what could be termed ethnographic object, scope, scale, or fieldsite. For understanding the ways in which virtual worlds have arisen and continue to develop in the context of a political economic formation I term "creationist capitalism" (Boellstorff 2008) – a formation demanding "detailed attention to the problematic of space, its social production, and its historical transformation" (Brenner 1999:39) – it is crucial to ask: What are the different ways ethnographic researchers of virtual worlds demarcate the cultures they study, and what is at stake in these unavoidable but necessary and even productive decisions?

The Background: From Indonesia to Second Life

The proximate inspiration for this analysis is my desire to expand on methodological questions I discuss in *Coming of Age in Second Life: An Anthropologist Explores the Virtually Human*, an ethnographic study of the virtual world Second Life (Boellstorff 2008). This question of the "fieldsite" has been an area of great interest with regard to this research. I find this gratifying because I have intentionally designed all my projects to push on the boundaries of what we mean by "the fieldsite" (Gupta and Ferguson 1997). I have conducted research for many years in Indonesia on gay Indonesians on three islands (Java, Bali, and Sulawesi), but in my books *The Gay Archipelago* and *A Coincidence of Desires* I discuss how, in a powerful sense, this research is not "multisited": the fieldsite is Indonesia itself (Boellstorff 2005, 2007). This is because gay Indonesians have historically seen themselves as gay "Indonesians," not gay Javanese, Balinese, and so on.[1] There are many different kinds of spatial scales operative in human life, including local, national, regional, and global, and it is crucial not to equate culture with locality. Sometimes that equation is valid, sometimes not: it depends. Translocal cultural logics exist with regard to everything from religion to gender. In the case of gay Indonesians, while they may think of themselves in terms of locality with regard to some aspects of their lives, with regard to homosexuality they typically think of themselves as Indonesians. This makes sense given that the concept of gay subjectivity is associated with modernity, and is rarely if ever learned from one's parents or tradition, but the linkages to the nation turn out to be much more complex. One reason so little has been written on gay Indonesians is that these persons fall outside one's analytical horizon if that horizon is founded in the spatial scale of locality. Researchers who equate culture with locality can miss the forest for the trees, so to

---

[1] I mention only gay Indonesians here for brevity: in this work I also discuss lesbian and transgender Indonesians.

speak: they will see all kinds of cultural logics that are local, but those that are translocal in some fashion will appear as inauthentic impositions.

I realized soon after beginning my research in *Second Life* that the conceptual tendencies with regard to virtual worlds were strikingly opposed to those I had encountered in my earlier work. Whereas in Indonesia studies, the presumption was in the direction of locality, in the study of virtual worlds the presumption was in the direction of translocality. For instance, there were (and still are) persons claiming that all virtual-world research projects must include meeting persons in the actual world to be valid! Particularly for some researchers influenced by (but oversimplifying) the game studies literature this presumption of translocality has taken a predicable two-stage form. The first stage is to invoke classic conceptions of games, particularly Johan Huizinga's notion of a "magic circle" of play involving "a stepping out of 'real' life into a temporary sphere of activity with a disposition all of its own" (Huizinga 1950:8). The second stage is to claim that these conceptions of games are invalid because there now exists "blurring" between game and nongame spaces. This two-stage narrative is clearly flawed, and not only because it caricatures the thoughtful understandings of games (and particularly the place of rules in games) found in the classic literature, as even Huizinga's use of "temporary sphere" in the quotation above indicates. It is also flawed because it ignores the consequential ways in which boundaries between game and nongame spaces persist online, boundaries that can be retrenched (not just eroded) by movement between online and offline contexts, or even by movement between different online games.

The Four Confusions: Defining What a Virtual World Is Not

As the discussion above concerning the "fieldsite" indicates, debates over definitions and terminologies remain common in this formative period in the study of virtual worlds. A difficulty in moving these debates forward is the remarkably negative attitude toward virtual worlds found not just in some quarters of anthropology, but even in science and technology studies. In part, this may be due to the simultaneously utopian and dystopian narratives that frequently cooccur with new communications technologies, a state of affairs well summarized by John Naughton's First Law: "we invariably overestimate the short-term implications of new communications technologies, and we grievously underestimate their long term impacts" (Naughton 2006:4). It may also be relevant that to date, the most prevalent popular-culture reference to virtual worlds is *The Matrix* movies, in which a virtual world is used to enslave humanity.

Perhaps the core definitional problem standing in the way of setting out a typology of methods for ethnographic research in virtual worlds is that the definition of "virtual world" is itself unsettled. I define virtual worlds as places of human culture realized by computer programs through the Internet, a definition that includes online games but excludes things like email and websites, and thus even social networking sites like Facebook (social networking sites are increasingly associated with virtual worlds, as in the case of Facebook's YoVille, but the distinction between the social networking site and the virtual world persists: the association is not a conflation). In concretizing our understanding of what constitutes a virtual world, identifying mis-categorizations can be just as helpful as working to pin down an exact definition. Four such misunderstandings – what I term the "four confusions" – are particularly common; each originates in mistaking something that frequently cooccurs with virtual worlds with a necessary condition of their existence.

The First Confusion: Games. Virtual worlds are not games. Historically, they have been and continue to be shaped by video games; they may contain games within them; they may even be largely structured in a game-like manner; but there is no way to equate virtual worlds with games without defining "game" so vaguely as to include all social life under its purview. The confusion originates to some extent in the English-language distinction between "game" and "play," a distinction not found in all languages and cultures. Because it is incorrect to assume, by fiat, that all virtual worlds are games, it follows that the use of theories from game studies to virtual worlds must be contextual. In some cases, such theories will be highly effective, in other cases less so (as in my discussion of the "magic circle" in the previous section), but in any case the applicability of theories about games and play to virtual worlds must be established and substantiated, not simply asserted.

The Second Confusion: Visuality. Despite the fact that phrases like "the 3D web" are frequently used as synonyms for "virtual world," virtual worlds need not be graphical or even visual. This is seen most clearly in the fact that historically, virtual worlds were exclusively text-based (as in the case of multiuser dungeons [MUDs]).[2] The fact that nearly all contemporary virtual worlds are built around three-dimensional graphics is fascinating and important to study, but this does not mean that such graphics are a definitional precondition for deeming something a virtual world. For instance, one could in theory have a virtual world composed entirely of soundscapes, within which persons blind in the actual world would be on equal footing with the seeing. One could also imagine a purely haptic virtual world, in which an interface technology like a glove allowed residents to navigate and interact solely through touch. There is no indication that such virtual worlds based on sound, touch, or any other sensorial framework would involve more than comparatively small communities were they to come into existence. If anything, the trend toward visuality seems to be accelerating. Nonetheless, it remains crucial that we avoid conflating virtual worlds and visuality. Since most contemporary virtual worlds are structured around visuality, theories from visual studies will be crucial to understanding them, but it would prove less effective to use such theories to make categorical claims about virtual worlds.

The Third Confusion: Mass Media. Because virtual worlds are places, they are not mass media, though they may contain mass media within them (everything from magazines, books, and embedded websites to streaming audio and video media). Virtual worlds need not mediate two or more places, since they are places in their own right. If anything, it is more accurate to think of a virtual world as

---

[2] See Boellstorff 2008, chapter 2 for an extensive listing of scholarly work on MUDs.

a "medium," in the sense of a material with which one crafts things. This has consequences for the use of mass media theory for understanding virtual worlds: we cannot assume ahead of time how such theories will need to be reworked for virtual-world contexts.

The Fourth Confusion: Anonymity and Roleplaying. The majority of existing virtual worlds require that participants have accounts in which their online identity differs from their actual-world identity. For instance, in *Second Life* I am known as "Tom Bukowski," because while one is allowed to choose any first name one wishes, last names must be selected from a predefined list.[3]

However, it is not a definitional precondition of virtual worlds that they be built around anonymity. One could imagine a virtual world that encouraged or required participants to use their actual-world names inworld, along the lines of social networking websites like Facebook. As virtual worlds are used increasingly in contexts like education, nonprofit work, and the corporate sphere, virtual worlds disallowing anonymity, or at least not mandating anonymity, have become more common.

Linked to this question of anonymity is that of roleplaying. Since many virtual worlds are structured partially or overwhelmingly as games, and given the historical linkages between virtual worlds and fantasy fiction like J.R.R. Tolkien's *Lord of the Rings*, it is unsurprising that forms of roleplay are crucial to many virtual worlds. Roleplay, however, is not a necessity for deeming something a virtual world. Not all persons enter virtual worlds for purposes of escapism: virtual worlds can be places that elaborate and support aspects of actual-world identity, rather than places where residents carve out spaces for separate identities.

The Typology: Research Questions and Ethnographic Scale

With the preceding discussion in mind, I now set out a three-part typology of methods for ethnographic research in virtual worlds, focusing on the relationship between research design and ethnographic scale. I intend "typology" to be taken in a heuristic sense, not an exhaustive one. My undergraduate mentor in linguistics and one of the most important typologists in the history of the discipline, Joseph Greenberg, talked about "splitters" and "clumpers": researchers who sought the finest-grained categorizations possible, versus those who sought to gather the world's languages into a small number of expansive groups. For the purposes of this chapter I will be a clumper: I will heuristically group all methods with regard to ethnographic scale in virtual worlds into only three categories. I could easily have set forth a typology with five or more categories, but a parsimonious typology has the benefit of brevity, as well as highlighting key distinctions.

---

[3]There have been a few exceptions to this rule made for celebrities of various kinds, for persons willing to pay additional fees, and for corporate uses of *Second Life*.

It is crucial to foreground the relationship between "research question" and "method." As illustrated by the discussion of positivist versus ethnographic approaches with which I opened this chapter, any claim that a particular method is the best (or the only valid) method for researching virtual worlds misses how research always involves a coming-together of research question and methodology. How one conducts research is not determined by some essential property "out there;" it is determined by the research questions one wishes to investigate. In my work as Editor-in-Chief of *American Anthropologist*, I found that one of the most common reasons I ended up rejecting a manuscript was that the research questions (while fascinating) and methodology (while rigorous) did not match up: the methods were not working to answer the questions the researcher had ostensibly chosen to examine. If I wish to study patterns of HIV infection in a certain social group, quantitative methods will prove invaluable. If I wish to understand how a certain population comes to think of itself as a "social group," qualitative methods will in all likelihood be a better fit. Methodological partisanship is not helpful in moving these kinds of conversations forward: what ideally emerges is a research community, with researchers using different methods to answer differing research questions with regard to a shared field of interest. With this pivotal point regarding the relationship between research question and method in mind, here is my "clumping," preliminary tripartite typology of methods for researching virtual worlds in terms of ethnographic scale:

First Ethnographic Scale: Virtual/Actual Interfaces. One class of methods for researching virtual worlds with regard to ethnographic scale explores interfaces between virtual worlds and the actual world. An example of this kind of research is T.L. Taylor's *Play Between Worlds: Exploring Online Game Culture*, which opens with the researcher attending a hotel convention for participants of Everquest (Taylor 2006). This class of methods builds off a history of examining such interfaces with regard to the Internet more generally, as in the case of Daniel Miller and Don Slater's *The Internet: an Ethnographic Approach*, which examines how Trinidadians use the Internet to reconfigure Trinidadian identity and community (Miller and Slater 2000). Since work in this genre emphasizes relationships between virtual-world and actual-world selfhood and sociality, a logical methodological outcome is that researchers often strive to interview the same persons in the actual world as they encounter in a virtual world or worlds, and are particularly interested in cases where residents of a virtual world meet collectively in actual-world contexts, like gaming cafés.

Second Ethnographic Scale: Virtual/Virtual Interfaces. Another class of ethnographic methods with regard to virtual worlds examines interfaces between two or more virtual worlds. In some cases, this can be a comparative research design in which residents do not (or mostly do not) move between the virtual worlds in question. This is analogous to Clifford Geertz's book *Islam Observed: Religious Development in Morocco and Indonesia* (Geertz 1968), in which the Moroccans and Indonesians studied do not travel between Morocco and Indonesia and are, indeed, largely unaware of each other's existence. In other cases, this can be a research design that tracks a community or communities moving between virtual worlds.

An example of this is Celia Pearce's *Communities of Play: Emergent Cultures in Online Games and Virtual Worlds* (Pearce 2009). In this work, Pearce examines the "Uru diaspora," a community formed when the virtual world Uru shut down and residents worked to rebuild their lost virtual home in other virtual contexts like Second Life and There.com. One frequent topic addressed by research in this genre is how notions of selfhood and community are sustained and destabilized across differing virtual contexts. This is analogous to work like Engseng Ho's *The Graves of Tarim: Genealogy & Mobility across the Indian Ocean*, which ethnographically explores Hadrami communities located across parts of the Arab world, South Asia, and Southeast Asia (Ho 2006).

Third Ethnographic Scale: Virtual Worlds In Their Own Terms. The third class of ethnographic methods making up my heuristic typology involves studying a single virtual world, and thus not attempting to meet residents of that virtual world in either the physical world or in other virtual worlds. This is the primary method I employ in my book *Coming of Age in Second Life*, where I refer to it as studying a virtual world "in its own terms" (see Boellstorff 2008, Chapter 3). This idea of "claim[ing] online contexts as field sites in their own right" (Hine 2005:7) dates back to the earliest ethnographic work on virtual worlds (e.g., Curtis 1992). If Geertz's book *Islam Observed* can serve as an analogue for studying virtual/virtual interfaces, then several of his other books (for instance, his first ethnography, *The Religion of Java* [Geertz 1960]), can serve a similar purpose in regard to studying a virtual world "in its own terms." Geertz's *Religion of Java* is, as its name indicates, a study of Islam in Java, and it is now but one of hundreds of insightful ethnographies of Islam, exploring Muslim life around the world. That such ethnographies usually focus on particular places and communities does not mean they ignore that Muslims are found worldwide, that many Muslims make the pilgrimage to Mecca, that persons migrate, and so on. Instead, it means that they examine how such translocal cultural logics and practices shape a particular community or communities.

It is unnecessary that a study of Islam in Morocco, or Indonesia, or even in a specific village in Morocco or Indonesia include multiple villages or nation-states to have broad relevance. It is not just possible but powerful to, in Boas's terms, turn careful attention to the "mere existence" of phenomena and from that careful attention derive theories and insights whose relevance extends beyond the ethnographic context of their formulation. Against claims that ethnographic research is "anecdotal," that extension is quite feasible and verifiable – but it is not the positivist extension of "law," in which, for example, the law of gravity derived from dropping weights from a tower or seeing apples fall from a tree is applicable in toto to all objects throughout all time and all the universe. To the positivist dream of such extensibility with regard to cultural phenomena, our response must be that the extension of ethnographically derived theories and insights is real and valid, but historically and spatially contingent. Something learned about a gay man in one Indonesian city may help us understanding a gay man in another Indonesian city, or perhaps in some more circumscribed fashion, a gay man in Thailand or the United States – but that work of extension, comparison, and circumscription is itself a contextual intellectual endeavor rather than the rote invocation of "law." Similarly, something learned about identity or community or economics or anything else in one virtual world may help us understand these topics in other virtual worlds or even in the actual world, but that work of extension, comparison, and circumscription is itself part of the intellectual work of the research community.

It is thus absolutely crucial to recognize that an interest in intersectionality, translocality, and the coconstitution of cultural domains is typically common to all three scales of ethnographic research I have identified. For instance, some studies of virtual worlds "in their own terms" focus on subcultures or specific topics (e.g., sexuality or economics). Others strive for a more holistic portrait, examining how shared practices and meanings emerge and are contested within a virtual world. It is emphatically not the case that these three ethnographic scales can be mapped onto categories like "local" or "global," so that one could be seen to be more generalizable or broad, and another as more limited or narrow. To assume any such isomorphism between ethnographic scale and scope of claims would be to engage in the "confusing closure with scale" (Gupta 1998:12) sometimes used to assert that ethnographic methods are less broadly relevant than other methods. In reality, all ethnographic methods, whatever scale they employ, are (like any method) most effective when keyed to specific and appropriate research questions. All have something to offer, and all can speak to a range of specific and comparative concerns.

The Road Ahead: Concluding Thoughts

I intend this rough typology of methods for researching virtual worlds in terms of ethnographic scale to underscore how different genres of research design allow for exploring differing sets of research questions. Most researchers end up working in all of these genres, but at any point in time the best research is based on focusing one's methods in line with a particular avenue of investigation. Arriving at a workable and compelling design is perhaps the most challenging and important step in conducting research: it is not possible to do everything. In the emerging research community around virtual worlds, I have encountered not just the "four confusions" discussed above, but a misreading of George Marcus's work on multisited ethnography (Marcus 1995) – a misreading which assumes that the more "multi," the better. In this misunderstanding, research on a single fieldsite is, a priori, suspect or outdated, while research on multiple fieldsites is, a priori, valorized as cutting-edge. In reality, both single-sited and multisited methods go back to the earliest decades of ethnographic research: indeed, nineteenth century anthropology was dominated by evolutionary approaches predicated on multiple sites of research and comparison.

It should be clear that all three of the methodologies discussed above (or the many additional methods that I could have set forth with a more "splitter" typology) are valid approaches to researching virtual worlds. All have strengths, and all involve sacrifices in terms of honing a doable research plan. In what I find to be the best research in virtual worlds or the actual world, we are moving toward forms of what I have elsewhere termed "postreflexive" modes of ethnographic engagement (Boellstorff 2003) that foreground and theorize how "the fieldsite" of any research project emerges through that ethnographic engagement, rather than being set in stone "out there." It is by now well acknowledged that the single fieldsite is, in this sense, an ethnographic fiction. The irony is that in virtual worlds research, what sometimes appears to be less well-acknowledged is that multiple fieldsites are also so constructed.

What does the future hold? It appears that research on virtual worlds will continue to increase and diversify. A subset of that research will continue to be ethnographic in some sense, and this work bears every indication of representing an innovative set of contributions. Obviously, there is no need to choose between the various methods for ethnographic research with regard to virtual worlds that I have discussed above. All can be done well or badly, but none are by definition invalid. When properly keyed to appropriate research questions, each can contribute to building a body of ethnographic work that will help illuminate what virtual worlds are, as well as their changing place in human life. In some ways this body of work will be specific to virtual worlds, but it will continue to draw from a range of other fields as well. For instance, while (as noted above) virtual worlds are not necessarily visual and are not necessarily games, they do tend to be highly visual and often are games or emphasize play. As a result, theoretical perspectives from game studies and visual studies, as well as anthropological theory, will continue to be crucial for understanding most virtual worlds. In turn, the growing body of research on virtual worlds, informed in part by various modes of ethnography, will have much to offer many other fields of inquiry. The conjunction of ethnography and virtual worlds will continue to stand as a vibrant field of research, contributing to central debates about human selfhood and sociality in the years to come.

Acknowledgments A draft version of this chapter was posted on the *Savage Minds* blog in August 2008. I thank the moderators of that blog, in particular Alex Golub, for their kind support. I thank also readers who commented on the draft, including "Montgamery McBlackwater" and Matthew T. Bradley.

References

Asimov, I. (1951). *Foundation*. New York: Gnome Press.
Bloomfield, R. (2009). *How online communities and flawed reasoning sound a death knell for qualitative methods*, from (http://terranova.blogs.com/terra_nova/2009/03/do-online-communities-sound-a-death-knell-for-qualitative-methods.html), posted March 31, 2009.
Boas, F. (1940). The study of geography. In *Race, Language, and Culture* (pp. 639–647). Chicago, IL: University of Chicago Press. (Original work published 1887)
Boellstorff, T. (2003). Dubbing culture: Indonesian gay and lesbi subjectivities and ethnography in an already globalized world. *American Ethnologist, 30*(2), 225–242.
Boellstorff, T. (2005). *The gay archipelago: Sexuality and nation in Indonesia*. Princeton, NJ: Princeton University Press.
Boellstorff, T. (2007). *A coincidence of desires: Anthropology, queer studies, Indonesia*. Durham, NC: Duke University Press.

Boellstorff, T. (2008). *Coming of age in Second Life: An anthropologist explores the virtually human*. Princeton, NJ: Princeton University Press.

Boellstorff, T. (2009). Method and the virtual: Anecdote, analogy, culture. *Journal of Virtual Worlds Research, 1*(3), 4–7.

Brenner, N. (1999). Beyond state-centrism? Space, territoriality, and geographical scale in globalization studies. *Theory & Society, 28*(1), 39–78.

Castronova, E. (2006). On the research value of large games: Natural experiments in Norrath and Camelot. *Games and Culture, 1*(2), 163–186.

Curtis, P. (1992 [1997]). Mudding: Social phenomena in text-based virtual realities. In S. Kiesler (Ed.), *Culture of the internet* (pp. 121–142). Mahwah, NJ: Lawrence Erlbaum Associates.

Geertz, C. (1960). *The religion of Java*. Glencoe, IL: Free Press.

Geertz, C. (1968). *Islam observed: Religious development in Morocco and Indonesia*. New Haven, CT: Yale University Press.

Gupta, A. (1998). *Postcolonial developments: Agriculture in the making of modern India*. Durham, NC: Duke University Press.

Gupta, A. & Ferguson, J. (Eds.). (1997). Discipline and practice: "The Field" as site, method, and location in anthropology. In *Anthropological locations: Boundaries and grounds of a field science* (pp. 1–46). Berkeley, CA: University of California Press.

Hine, C. (Ed.). (2005). Virtual methods and the sociology of cyber-social-scientific knowledge. In *Virtual methods: Issues in social research on the internet* (pp. 1–13). Oxford, UK: Berg.

Ho, E. (2006). *The graves of Tarim: Genealogy and mobility across the Indian Ocean*. Berkeley, CA: University of California Press.

Huizinga, J. (1950). *Homo Ludens: A study of the play-element in culture*. Boston, MA: Beacon Press. (Original work published 1938).

Marcus, G. (1995). Ethnography in/of the world system: The emergence of multi-sited ethnography. *Annual Review of Anthropology, 24*, 95–117.

Miller, D., & Slater, D. (2000). *The internet: An ethnographic approach*. Oxford, UK: Berg.

Naughton, J. (2006). *Net benefit: How the internet is transforming our world*. UK Marketing Society Keynote Address: 28 February, 2006.

Pearce, C. (2009). *Communities of play: Emergent cultures in online games and virtual worlds*. Cambridge, MA: MIT Press.

Stephenson, N. (1992). *Snow Crash*. New York: Bantam Books.

Taylor, T. L. (2006). *Play between worlds: Exploring online game culture*. Cambridge, MA: MIT Press.

Chapter 11
Massively Multiplayer Online Games as Living Laboratories: Opportunities and Pitfalls

Nicolas Ducheneaut

Massively Multiplayer Online Games (MMOGs) have emerged in recent years as an increasingly popular form of entertainment. They offer persistent, richly detailed 3D universes in which players cooperate or compete with each other, trade, and socialize. In this, they share characteristics with the more broadly defined virtual worlds (VWs), their distinguishing feature being a more objective-driven environment than VWs (in the "sandbox" environment of the virtual world *Second Life*, for instance, residents are free to engage in any activity they can imagine, unlike online games where players tend to focus on well-defined activities such as combat, exploration, etc.). The most successful MMOG to date, *World of Warcraft* (WoW), is home to 11 million subscribers worldwide, and several competitors host at least one million players or more (Woodcock 2008).

Many of the activities offered by an MMOG (fighting monsters, exploring a vast and unfriendly fantasy world, "leveling up" a character, and accessing more powerful abilities) are familiar features in videogames, multiplayer, or otherwise. What sets these games truly apart are their emphasis, by design, on sociability and interaction between the players. Most MMOGs attempt to foster interactions between their players by using a common template, which could be stereotyped as follows: (1) the player creates a "level 1" character who enters the world with a limited set of abilities and equipment; (2) the player is presented with "quests" (missions) to accomplish; (3) successful completion of the objectives generates "experience points" (or any other similar reward), allowing the character to acquire more powerful abilities and/or equipment; (4) (this is the most important design element) as a player gains in levels, quests become increasingly difficult to accomplish alone, reaching a point where a coordinated *group* of players is required to move further; (5) the size of the group required, the length of the quests or dungeons, and the complexity of the encounters make it nearly impossible to succeed with an ad hoc group assembled on the spot, creating the need for more formal and persistent social structures: the guilds (or clans, teams, etc. in other game worlds).

N. Ducheneaut
Palo Alto Research Center
3333 Coyote Hill Road, Palo Alto, CA 94304
e-mail: nicolas@parc.com

W.S. Bainbridge (ed.), *Online Worlds: Convergence of the Real and the Virtual*,
Human-Computer Interaction Series, DOI 10.1007/978-1-84882-825-4_11,
© Springer-Verlag London Limited 2010

While play is often derided as less important than work in the study of human behavior (Dourish 1998), ethnographic studies of the social life of guilds (e.g., Taylor 2006) clearly show that participating in them actually requires significant efforts to solve problems that are not entirely different from those encountered by groups in other, less playful contexts. Take, for instance, a guild trying to organize one of WoW's "40-man" dungeon runs (Chen 2009). To start with, the schedules of 40 individuals (and few more for possible last minute substitutions) will need to be aligned. Necessary potions and materials will need to have been gathered well in advance. Tactics will need to have been discussed and agreed on, with a division of labor that best exploits each player's gaming experience and the abilities of their character. Interpersonal issues will need to be kept in check (there is an inherent amount of stress and tension in these complex fights) and, should the group succeed, the powerful "loot" obtained from the "bosses" in the dungeon will need to be allocated fairly (only a few items "drop" during these raids, and not all players will come back with a reward).

The list could go on much longer, but the point is simple: Groups in online games apparently face many of the same social, political, and organizational problems that social scientists have studied for a century. But unlike groups outside of MMOGs, the digital nature of these social spaces makes them particularly amenable to large-scale, automated data collection and analysis. The research community has taken notice, and many scholars now argue that these games might be "living laboratories" that could be used to either test or refine the existing theories, or even come up with new insights into human behavior that would not have been previously visible given the limited scope and availability of "real-world" data.

As is often the case with new and exciting research domains, early work took an optimistic view of the potential use of these living laboratories, emphasizing the opportunities they present rather than the potential pitfalls (Castranova 2006a). More recently, however, a more critical view has begun to emerge. In particular, Williams (2008) questions the extent to which human behaviors observed in virtual spaces occur in the same way they occur in real spaces. This "mapping principle," often taken as given by virtual worlds researchers, is less obvious than it may seem a priori and, therefore, it is something that must be established and validated. Williams proceeds to outline a research agenda that would more systematically address this mapping issue, in order to more firmly establish virtual worlds as valid spaces to study human behaviors. In doing so, he lists several factors that could shed light on the existence (or lack thereof) of a virtual–real mapping.

With my colleagues at the Palo Alto Research Center, I have been engaged for several years in intensive data collection in several MMOGs. As our work progressed, we faced many of the questions Williams raises about the validity and generalizability of our findings. In this chapter, I want to draw on our experience collecting and analyzing behavioral data in online games to start addressing at least some of these questions. In particular, I will argue that assuming the existence of a direct mapping between online games and more familiar "real-world" spaces might be overly optimistic in some cases, but perhaps less than one might initially think. More importantly, I will argue that wherever the mapping breaks down, it should also be possible to explain why and to subsequently factor out the confounding factors, which makes using online games as experimental sites a valid proposition provided it is done carefully. My arguments will be based on the data we collected, in an attempt to ground the debate rather than arguing about the merits of these environments as a research platform in the abstract.

Because of this empirical grounding, I do not claim to cover the "mapping principle" exhaustively but instead focus on three problem areas that were apparent in our data sets: the impact of "game variables" on observed behaviors, the issue of skewed or transformed personalities and user backgrounds in online games, and finally the lack of a clear boundary defining the "game space" exactly and delineating where observations should start and stop. I begin below by addressing the important issue of the distinction between online games and virtual worlds at large and the impact of game design variables on behavioral observations.

A Game Is a Game by Any Other Name

Before making any argument about the research value of a data collection site, it is important to define its scope and limitations. However, the recent explosion in the number and popularity of graphical online social spaces has often led to a tendency to lump a wide variety of environments under the banner of "virtual worlds." While these environments share some high-level attributes (e.g., a 3D or pseudo-3D world, avatars representing the user, some form of user-to-user communication channel, be it text or voice, etc.), they are obviously designed to support very different activities. Designers of virtual worlds literally encode support for these activities in the software used to generate and maintain the environment, which greatly facilitates some behaviors and hinders others – a principle Lessig (1999) famously described as "code is law."

For instance, I have described earlier how the design of quests in MMOGs progressively and almost inexorably steers players toward group activities. To be sure, players can still engage in solitary activities when they reach the "endgame" or last level available (Ducheneaut et al. 2006), but the "laws" of the game embedded in its design will make this increasingly less rewarding, up to the point where continuing to play alone might make little sense. Another example is the concept of "character classes" that is nearly omnipresent in MMOGs. When creating a character, players will have to select a class (e.g., warrior, mage, priest...) that gives them a functional specialization in the game world (warriors are good melee fighters but cannot cast spells, priests are good healers but must be protected by others, etc.). This creates natural interdependencies between the players and encourages the formation of balanced groups where each class is represented but once a class is chosen, players usually have little room to improvise (try as you might, you will never really be able to heal someone with a mage in WoW).

I want to make clear that I am concerned here exclusively with such online games, rather than virtual worlds as a whole. Narrowing our scope is a necessary first step in analyzing concretely and critically what can be accomplished in digital spaces – researchers familiar with different environments, say, *Second Life*, would have to deal with a different set of "laws" encoded in the virtual world's software and would presumably discuss a different set of constraints that the ones I will be presenting below. What is important, however, is to recognize that the technical and social architectures of an online environment are inter-related and, therefore, that the nature of this relationship needs to be made explicit before attempting any kind of comparison between behaviors in digital and physical spaces.

In our case, the "laws" enforced by an online game's software present researchers with a conundrum. On the one hand, it seems that designs like the stereotypical MMOG I described will narrow down the range of behaviors in the world to a more manageable subset, thereby facilitating observation and analysis. On the other hand, the software tools used to steer player behavior might have more impact than the fundamental traits researchers are trying to observe, introducing confounding factors that have to be taken into account. I will illustrate this tension with a concrete example.

It has long been hypothesized that the structure of an organization plays a role in its eventual survival. Certain organizational forms (organic, hierarchical, etc.) are better suited to certain tasks and environments, and should be directly linked to a group's eventual performance. An online game would seem to offer a perfect environment to test this hypothesis on a large scale. Across servers, hundreds of groups (guilds) all strive to accomplish the same objectives (defeat increasingly difficult "bosses" in high-end dungeons) under the same constraints (the "laws" enforced by the game design).

To exploit this opportunity, we mapped the social networks of hundreds of guilds in WoW and tried to assess the existence of a link between social network variables and the eventual survival of guilds (Ducheneaut et al. 2007). My point here is not to restate these results one more time, but rather to point out an important outcome of our models that we only briefly touched on in the original paper: While we can see the effect of a group's structure on its eventual survival in WoW, two of the three most significant predictors of this survival are based on "game laws," that is, constraints hard-coded in the game's software. In fact, the most significant predictor of group survival in WoW is the balance between classes in the guild – a constraint built into the game's architecture that players have little control over, save for their initial choice of what class to play (see above). The overwhelming influence of such game variables (class balance has twice the effect of the first structural variable in the model, subgraph size) shows that, while online games can be used to model some behavioral phenomena, the range of behaviors observed might be constrained by factors having little parallels in the "real" world. To be sure, the influence of these game factors remains an interesting phenomenon in itself: For instance, one could think about what kind of other interdependencies could be built between the players to foster cooperation without depending on class mechanics. But their influence also suggests that online games might not be the best environment for "normal science," that is, proving or extending existing theories based on observations in the physical world, since the software's architecture seems to introduce constraints and concepts that have no direct equivalent in the space where the theories initially originated.

If the mapping from the virtual to the physical environment is less direct than researchers might like, it is equally interesting to note that the reverse is also true. While online games face many of the same issues as other societies, by the same token they also develop their own culture, which may operate under norms quite different from those seen elsewhere. Again, I will illustrate this point with a concrete example from another study, this time of the MMOG *Star Wars Galaxies* (SWG).

SWG's designers (and foremost among them Raph Koster) tried to break away from some of the most formulaic aspects of MMOGs in several ways. In particular, based on principles he had articulated earlier in his Laws on Online Worlds Design, [1] Koster made a deliberate attempt to import concepts from urban sociology and architecture into online games. This translated into a strategic use of space and timing to steer players to specific game locations, where they would have to congregate and mingle for a while before moving on to other activities. From this, sociability was supposed to emerge more organically, as opposed to the more formal and constraining mechanisms implemented in other games (e.g., quest groups). An example was the cantina present in each major city in the game world, which was intended to function as a kind of "third place" (Oldenburg 1989) analogous to a local pub. One character class (the entertainers) had to congregate in the cantinas to offer their services, healing the "mind wounds" of other characters, which prevented them from functioning at peak performance. Other character classes would visit the cantina, "watch" an entertainer (by clicking on them) and, provided they stayed long enough (about 5 min), their wounds would be healed and they would be able to continue playing. During this "forced downtime," players would have the opportunity to chat and get to know each other, presumably leading in some cases to the formation of longer-lasting social bonds.

At first sight, this seems like a fairly straightforward transfer of design principles from the physical world to the virtual. Our observations of player-to-player interactions in SWG's cantinas, however, revealed that principles working in the cultural context of our physical society might not survive the transition to the culture of a gaming environment (Ducheneaut and Moore 2004). In particular, players resented being "forced" to wait and interact with other players. Watching an Entertainer in the cantina interfered with their more instrumental objective of progressing quickly in the game. In other words, a gaming culture built around achievement and a sense of fast, easy progress clashed with the designer's intent for a more sociable, leisurely experience. As a result, players engaged in what might be seen as a perversion of the game's original design: Entertainers developed macros that would let them heal "mind wounds" on auto-pilot while they were away from the keyboard, automatically generating experience points but preventing any social interaction with the visiting customers. In turn, these visitors came to cantinas as infrequently as possible, stayed just long enough to get their character back in working order, and quickly got on their way to the more important objectives they had to accomplish.

---

[1] http://www.raphkoster.com/gaming/laws.shtml

SWG is but one illustration of the dangers of drawing too many direct parallels between online games and other environments. While there are undoubtedly some similarities, it is important to recognize that game worlds develop their own culture and norms of interaction, and these will affect the kind of observations researchers can make. My point here is not to say that online games have no value as experimental sites but rather to caution that they have their own set of constraints, many of them built into the environment's software as we saw earlier, others emerging over time as a unique culture develops among the players. These constraints must either be factored out of observations and models if any generalization to the physical world is to be achieved, or VWs must simply be analyzed in themselves, as phenomena that are intrinsically interesting without necessarily trying to establish direct links to pre-existing, non-virtual environments.

Life on the Screen: Who Is Really Playing?

The issues of identity and the presentation of self online have been important to computer-mediated communication (CMC) scholars for decades. The title for this section is borrowed from one of the most influential early works on this topic, Turkle's (1995) *Life on the Screen*, in which she argued that in "computer-mediated worlds, the self is multiple, fluid, and constituted in interaction with machine connections" (p. 14) and that "online switches among personae seem quite natural" (p. 256). This perception of online worlds as ideal environments for identity exploration persists to this day, and was naturally extended to virtual worlds. For instance, Castranova (2006b) argues that virtual worlds "give you a freedom that no one has on Earth: the freedom to be whomever you want to be."

This seems to pose a fundamental problem for research in online games (and virtual worlds more generally). Any study of human behaviors and interactions must account for the background of those involved, if only because social, psychological, and demographic categories may predict a large portion of the outcomes (Williams 2008). But if we assume that users have at least two identities, one for the real world and one (or more) for the virtual world, the necessary mapping between online and offline selves breaks down, which puts into question the validity of extending findings from observations in the digital realm into the physical one – after all, one could always say that players are not "really themselves" online. In some sense, this reinforces the cultural issue I mentioned earlier: just as online and offline cultures may differ enough to prevent sweeping generalizations, so might differences between online and offline personalities.

Here, however, it is generally accepted that congruence between online and offline personae can simply be measured. For instance, Bessiere, Seay, and Kiesler (2007) found that WoW players tended to be more conscientious, extraverted, and less neurotic than they were offline. While this may at first seem to reinforce the notion that online and offline selves differ, it is important to note that these differences were quite small. And moreover, if these differences can be reliably assessed, then they can be taken into account when analyzing some of the behaviors observed online. For example, an increase in sociability in virtual worlds could be traced back to the more extraverted personality of virtual world users when they are "in avatar," which is itself reminiscent of early CMC research on the polarizing effects of electronic communication media (Sproull and Kiesler 1991). Just as game variables, psychological traits can and probably should be explicitly defined and factored out of any analysis seeking to draw parallels between behaviors observed in online games and those in other contexts. In this regard, the work of Yee (2006) is particularly relevant.

Moreover, it is also important to note that dichotomous views have been recently replaced with a more nuanced understanding of the "synthetic" personalities (Mitra 2003) developed at the intersection between online and offline spaces. In fact, it seems more and more probable that as online games and virtual worlds become more widely used, the joint effects of broadening the users' demographics and an increase in their experience with these spaces will make psychological differences small enough to be irrelevant. In an extension of Bessiere et al. (2007) based on identical methods, but expanded to a broader population of users spread across three different virtual worlds, we were able to show that differences between online and offline selves tend to disappear over time. As players spend more and more time in their world(s) of choice, their online and offline personalities converge to the point of being indistinguishable (Ducheneaut et al. 2009). Therefore, as an increasingly large number of Internet users spend more and more time in various virtual worlds, there is reason to believe that researchers will be able to observe genuine behaviors tied to an individual's basic psychological traits, as opposed to wild identity experiments that would never have taken place in the physical world.

If the "personality transformation" that supposedly occurs when users log into online games is less of an issue that we might initially have thought, how about other background variables? Research on online games is often dismissed as irrelevant because the user population is supposedly skewed toward young, affluent Western males who have the necessary time, resources, and inclination to inhabit these online spaces. Any observation made online would therefore not generalize to a wide cross-section of a "normal" real-world society. And while it is feasible to assess online and offline personality differences using fairly simple and well-tested questionnaires (see above), obtaining reliable socio-demographic data from the players in non-intrusive ways is much more difficult. In most online games, there seems to be little connection between a player's character and their real-world age, income, gender, etc. (Ducheneaut et al. 2009). Of course, one could always ask the players directly in the game, but this gives rise to the possibility of deception with few means of reliably crosschecking the answers. In the end, game companies hold the key to this data, since their servers can map between online characters and their user's account, the latter containing information such as a user's real name, address, etc., which can all be tied back to socio-demographic variables of interest.

Until recently, game companies had been surprisingly reluctant to collaborate with researchers in exploring this issue. This is probably based on a legitimate fear of their competition. Account data is a precious business asset that reveals a lot about a company's strengths and weaknesses, and it could presumably be exploited by others to gain a competitive advantage if it were leaked out. The recent decision by Sony Online Entertainment (SOE) to share server-side data with a large team of social scientists (Williams et al. 2008) is therefore to be applauded and, hopefully, the researchers' careful management of this data will encourage other companies to follow in the same footsteps. More importantly, perhaps, results from this research project showed clearly that the "gamer stereo-type" does not hold. To cite but one example, older players and women played more than others, a complete opposite to public perception of gaming usage pat-terns. Studies such as these demonstrate that the user population in online games is much more diverse than initially thought, which reinforces their validity as an experimental environment. To be sure, there are differences and the reasons behind these differences need to be explained. But a careful characterization of the gaming population's socio-demographic data such as Williams et al. (2008) should enable researchers to explicitly acknowledge these differences and, again, factor them out if necessary.

Ill-Defined Spaces: Taking an Ecological View of the (Virtual) World

I have argued in the previous two sections that cultural, psychological, and socio-demographic factors influence the mapping between online games and real-world phenomena to varying degrees, but also that these effects could potentially be factored out provided they are first properly defined and understood – or even that these effects could simply disappear over time. Another obstacle remains, however: the question of whether online games capture the totality of the user's experience that researchers are interested in or not.

The terminology used when characterizing online games as "virtual worlds" illustrates a common conceptual problem. "World" is often used to signify the sum of human experience and history, or the human condition in general[2]. "Virtual world" would therefore seem to imply that such spaces cover the totality of a user's social experience online, but it is of course far from the truth – especially with online games.

Indeed, activities in online games spill out of their 3D fantasy world into count-less websites, forums, social networking sites, video sharing services, etc. Consider these few examples from WoW:

- On ElitistJerks.com, thousands of WoW players literally dissect the mechanics of the game to optimize the performance of their character during complex group activities. Participation on this site implies a desire to understand the more

---

[2] http://en.wikipedia.org/wiki/World

computational aspects of WoW, and a tendency to favor an "instrumental" play style concerned with efficiency. Some users even emerge as resident experts on a given character class. There is, however, no indication in the game that a player is involved on this site.

- On Thottbot.com, other thousands of users share data about quests that they collect during gaming sessions using software "addons." The site also supports lively discussion about these quests and how best to accomplish them. Players in WoW are often asked to "go look it up on Thottbot" when asking for help in the general chat channel, a suggestion that would make little sense without knowing about the existence of this knowledge database and might convey the (misguided) impression that players are generally unwilling to help each other, while in fact help is readily available outside the game's boundaries.

- On YouTube.com, countless videos captured in the game world offer a source of game knowledge (e.g., demonstrations of how to successfully defeat a given boss) or entertainment (there is even a WoW soap-opera, see http://www.youtube.com/user/watchtheguild, with more than 62,000 subscribers). Yet, the production and producers of this video content are almost totally invisible in the game world.

The list could go on for literally pages after pages. Quite clearly, game-related activities are not limited to those taking place "in-avatar." As such, taking into account only data collected in the game world itself gives a partial account at best of the players' behaviors. This is particularly problematic when trying to characterize the role that individuals play in their community. In earlier research, I conducted on open-source software projects for instance, using an ecological and longitudinal view combining data from both the projects' mailing-lists and code repositories, revealed that some users who might have looked only peripherally involved based on their code contribution were in fact "retired experts" who contributed infrequently, but decisively, to discussions about the project's future (Ducheneaut 2005). So far, however, no research project has tried to combine data from several online sources to characterize behaviors in online games – studies either focus on the game itself, or on one (or several) of these "external" resources exclusively. Note that my own work on WoW is subject to the same criticism, but I believe that this obstacle is not insurmountable and that it might even be construed as an opportunity. I intend to combine our in-game data with other sources in the near future, and I would argue that taking such an ecological view is a logical next step for the online gaming research community if any argument about the mapping between online and offline behaviors is to be made.

Conclusion

Based on practical experience with collecting and analyzing behavioral data in MMOGs, I have proposed in this chapter that in three areas at least, the question of a mapping between "real-world" behaviors and those observed in online games is both a source of research opportunities and some significant pitfalls that need to be avoided. While online games are significantly different from more traditional, offline environments, there are still ways to draw interesting parallels between the two provided one carefully considers the diverse factors contributing to the observed behaviors.

The increasing convergence between online and offline identities is one reason to be optimistic about the use of online games (and virtual worlds more generally) as a source of valid, generalizable behavioral data. Early CMC research emphasized the transformative potential of electronic media, reinforcing the perception that users might not really be themselves online. While this might very well have been true in the early days of the Internet, it is important to recognize that a much larger segment of the population now spends a significant part of its life online. Virtual worlds and online games are not exotic environments dedicated to the "identity play" of a few, but instead spaces that users move in and out fluidly, which in turn leads to the construction of a "synthetic" identity that remains fairly stable online and off. And even if differences remain, it seems possible to use standard psychological assessment tools to factor them out.

Still, online games are not just carbon copies of the real world. They are societies in their own right, capable of evolving their own norms and cultures. Some (but not all) of this indigenous culture will be influenced by the way the software is architected, which permits certain actions and prevents others. When using online worlds to understand human behavior, it is important to define and isolate these "game laws" as much as possible if any generalizability is to be achieved. But of course, one could also simply consider these worlds to be interesting "sui generis," and simply study them as full-fledged social worlds in their own right, without immediately attempting any parallel with offline environments. This, to me at least, sounds like the most fruitful approach in the near term. In fact, rather than always searching for a link between physical and digital spaces, it might be more productive at first to consider the entire ecology of digital spaces that form an extended "online game world" to understand the totality of experience in these environments. Once their defining characteristics are well understood, it is then reasonable to assume that differences between them and other environments can be explicitly isolated and possibly factored out if and when needed.

References

Bessiere, K., Seay, A. F., & Kiesler, S. (2007). The ideal Elf: Identity exploration in *World of Warcraft. Cyberpsychology and Behavior, 10*, 530–535.

Castranova, E. (2006a). On the research value of large games. *Games and Culture, 1*, 163–186.

Castranova, E. (2006b). Virtual worlds: A first-hand account of market and society on the cyberian frontier. In K. Salen & E. Zimmerman (Eds.), *The game design reader: A rules of play anthology* (pp. 814–863). Cambridge, MA: MIT Press.

Chen, M. G. (2009). Communication, coordination, and camaraderie in *World of Warcraft. Games and Culture, 4*, 47–73.

Dourish, P. (1998). The state of play. *Computer Supported Cooperative Work, 7*, 1–7.

Ducheneaut, N. (2005). Socialization in an open source software community: A socio-technical analysis. *Computer Supported Cooperative Work, 14*, 323–368.

Ducheneaut, N. & Moore, R. J. (2004). The social side of gaming: A study of interaction patterns in a massively multiplayer online game. In *Proceedings of the ACM conference on computer-supported cooperative work (CSCW2004)* (pp. 360–369). New York: ACM.

Ducheneaut, N., Yee, N., Nickell, E., & Moore, R. J. (2006). 'Alone together?' Exploring the social dynamics of massively multiplayer online games. In *Proceedings of CHI 2006* (pp. 407–416). New York: ACM.

Ducheneaut, N., Yee, N., Nickell, E., & Moore, R. J. (2007). The life and death of online gaming communities: A look at guilds in *World of Warcraft*. In *Proceedings of CHI 2007* (pp. 839–848). New York: ACM.

Ducheneaut, N., Wen, M.-H., Yee, N., & Wadley, G. (2009). Body and mind: A study of avatar personalization in three virtual worlds. In *Proceedings of CHI 2009* (pp. 1151–1160). New York: ACM.

Lessig, L. (1999). *Code and other laws of cyberspace*. New York: Basic Books.

Mitra, A. (2003). Cybernetic space: Bringing the virtual and real together. *Journal of Interactive Advertising, 3*(2), from (http://www.jiad.org/article31).

Oldenburg, R. (1989). *The great good place*. New York: Marlowe.

Sproull, L. & Kiesler, S. (1991). *Connections: New ways of working in the networked organization*. Cambridge, MA: MIT Press.

Taylor, T. L. (2006). *Play between worlds*. Cambridge, MA: MIT Press.

Turkle, S. (1995). *Life on the screen: Identity in the age of the internet*. New York: Simon & Schuster.

Williams, D. (2008). *The mapping principle, and a research framework for virtual worlds*. White paper at (http://dmitriwilliams.com/MappingTNWhitePaper.pdf).

Williams, D., Yee, N., & Caplan, S. E. (2008). Who plays, how much, and why? Debunking the stereotypical gamer profile. *Journal of Computer-Mediated Communication, 13*, 993–1018.

Woodcock, B. S. (2008). *An analysis of MMOG subscription growth – Version 23.0*, from (http://www.mmogchart.com).

Yee, N. (2006). The demographics, motivations and derived experiences of users of massively-multiuser online graphical environments. *PRESENCE: Teleoperators and Virtual Environments, 15*, 309–329.

Chapter 12
Examining Player Anger in *World of Warcraft*

Jane Barnett, Mark Coulson, and Nigel Foreman

Currently, over 11 million subscribers worldwide play the Massively Multiplayer Online Role-Playing Game (MMORPG) *World of Warcraft* (WoW). Although players can choose to solo throughout the game, they also have the option to group up with other like-minded players to tackle the more challenging aspects of game play that WoW provides. From these encounters, strong friendships are formed, guilds are created, and players can progress in the way they choose, regardless of their type of game play. There are many positive and happy experiences to be experienced within WoW's social communities; however, as with real-life situations, there are also those experiences that may anger players. Novaco (2003) developed an Inventory that examined potential everyday anger-causing scenarios that may occur in real life. The aim of this research was to develop a questionnaire that examined potential everyday anger-causing scenarios in WoW. It is hoped that the questionnaire described here will be of use to researchers who want to explore both the negative and positive sides of social interaction within WoW.

Methodology and Development of the *World of Warcraft* Questionnaire (WoWQ)

Thirty-three participants responded to a series of threads on the first author's guild forum and a selection of WoW-Europe forums, representing each type of WoW-Europe realm forum, whether Player-versus-Player (PvP) or not, whether Role Playing (RP) or not. Each thread asked players to provide examples of in-game scenarios that had made them angry. Players either posted replies to the original thread, or emailed the first author. All the responses were scanned for sentences that described specific anger-provoking situations, and a total of 126 items were identified.

J. Barnett, M. Coulson, and N. Foreman
Department of Psychology, School of Health & Social Sciences,
Middlesex University, London, UK
e-mails: j.barnett@mdx.ac.uk; m.coulson@mdx.ac.uk; n.foreman@mdx.ac.uk

W.S. Bainbridge (ed.), *Online Worlds: Convergence of the Real and the Virtual,*
Human-Computer Interaction Series, DOI 10.1007/978-1-84882-825-4_12,
© Springer-Verlag London Limited 2010

These comments were then collated to form a list, which was then emailed to five WoW experienced players, for evaluation and feedback.

Feedback revealed some comments that were identical or sounded identical (e.g., "I hate ganking," and "I hate being ganked" were considered identical). Only one item from a similar sounding group of items was retained and the others were discarded. Items were also removed if they were related to the game's design (e.g., "The servers are down and Blizzard gives no information"), because items needed to be related to specific game play and not game mechanics.

The remaining 93 items were not yet complete, because they represented stimuli that needed to be combined with appropriate response formats. It is essential to examine differences in both the experience and expression of anger (Spielberger et al. 1985), as well as how long the anger is experienced for. The latter is of particular importance as it provides a gauge as to how long a player was angered by a particular scenario in-game.

The Likert scale we employed for *anger intensity* is almost identical to the one used by Novaco (2003) in his Provocation Inventory (NPI), measuring the degree of anger experienced when faced with each of the WoWQ scenarios. Four responses were provided: 1 = Not angry; 2 = A little angry; 3 = Moderately angry; and 4 = Very angry. For example, a respondent would be presented with "Players who are generally insulting" and then asked to select the best response.

A second scale, *anger frequency*, examined how often the level of anger intensity was experienced each time the gamer was faced with a particular WoWQ scenario (see Table 12.2 for example items). A four-point Likert scale was used with the following responses – 1 = Slightly angry some of the time; 2 = Slightly angry most of the time; 3 = Very angry some of the time; and 4 = Very angry most of the time. For example, respondents would select one of these four in response to: "Players do not act on instructions they should be listening to."

After item evaluation, we used a series of analyses to examine the factor structure of the *World of Warcraft* Questionnaire to determine whether the items formed any specific anger-related themes. Often, *confirmatory factor analysis* is used to test specific hypotheses that had been formed beforehand, but given our goals an *exploratory factor analysis* was employed to examine the structure, reliability, and validity of the remaining WoWQ items, using the *principal components analysis* (PCA) method.

A preliminary inspection assessed the suitability of the data for PCA, and the correlation matrix showed coefficients of 0.3 and above. The Kaiser–Meyer–Olkin Measure of Sampling (KMO) was 0.58, which just missed the recommended value of 0.6 (Kaiser 1970, 1974); however, the value for the Bartlett's Test of Sphericity (Bartlett 1954) was significant. The Communalities table was checked for items that had a value of 0.599 or less, and Item 10 was removed ("Players who steal mines/herbs/skins") because its value was only 0.563.

The 92 remaining items were once again assessed for suitability. Now, the KMO value exceeded Kaiser's recommended value at 0.611 and Bartlett's Test was significant. Inspection of the Communalities Table revealed a further five items with values of 0.599 or less which were removed: "Players who excel in PvP, have epic armor and think they are great." "I receive an invitation to join a guild/party/raid/ instance without being asked first. I decline but still repeatedly receive the invitation."

"I join a raid/instance and notice other raid/instance members are not adequately equipped for raid/instancing (e.g., they do not have the appropriate gear, lack potions/food, etc.)." "Things go generally wrong in raids/instances." "Raid/instance members are greedy."

The remaining 87 items were subjected to further assessment. The correlation matrix still showed values of 0.2 and 0.3, the KMO value increased to 0.786 and Bartlett's Test remained significant. The Communalities Table showed only one item with a value under 0.599 ("You are unable to interact with the other faction to tell them how unfair they are."), which was removed from further analyses. The final assessment of the data using the remaining 86 items showed that the correlation matrix, the KMO value (0.828), the Bartlett's Test (significant), and the Communalities Table provided support for the factorability of the data. A list of other items removed during this stage of the analyses can be found in the Appendix attached to the end of this chapter.

The aim in examining potential factor structures was to find a simple solution, containing few factors that also explained at least 50% of the variance, and showed good alpha reliability (Thurstone 1947). Several exploratory rotational analyses were performed on the remaining 86 WoWQ items. The four-factor varimax extraction provided the most parsimonious representation of the items. For example, a two-factor solution (with varimax rotation) displayed high alpha reliabilities for each factor, but as a whole they only explained 34.67% of the variance. Both factors contained items that could be related not only to raids or instances, but also to general game play and guild membership, thus providing difficulties when choosing a factor title. At the other extreme, in a five-factor varimax extraction, many of the items were removed during successive rotations, and although a final rotation was possible, only six items remained with a variance of 93.17%. A five-factor extraction using oblimin (oblique) methods provided good alpha reliabilities and all items loading on to each factor described similar scenarios. The correlation value however was low ($r = 0.157$).

Each component of the four-factor analysis can be conceptualized as a measurement scale, the internal consistency of which can be expressed through *alpha*. Three additional items were then removed because doing so increased the alpha: "I am scammed in a trade." "Poor player communication." "Players are discriminating or racist." A second-order factor analysis was performed to further test the structure of the remaining 28 items. The total variance accounted for at this point was 53.33%. The final descriptive statistics, plus reliability and validity values for the final WoWQ rotation, can be found in Table 12.1, including the number of respondents providing adequate data.

The results showed that a four-factor Varimax structure best described the relationships between the items (extraction method: principal component analysis;

Table 12.1 Statistics for the *World of Warcraft* questionnaire

Component (factor)	Mean	Standard deviation	Items remaining	Final alpha	Number of respondents
1	38.84	10.99	16	0.9237	272
2	11.84	21.21	6	0.8779	169
3	5.66	1.76	4	0.5376	292
4	5.40	1.58	2	0.7296	292

rotation method: varimax with Kaiser normalization; a rotation converged in six iterations). The four scales were named "Raids/Instances" (RI), "Griefers" (GR), "Perceived Time Wasting" (PTW), and "Anti-social Players" (AS). Further analyses showed that all items had high loadings on each scale, and that each scale displayed a high alpha reliability. In particular, despite the AS scale only having two items, it still showed a high alpha coefficient of 0.7296. The resulting simple structure describing four types of potential in-game anger-causing scenarios can be seen in Table 12.2.

Consideration of the items associated with each factor suggested their names. Items in the *Raid/Instance Experiences* scale relate to players not paying attention during group raids, or failing to participate actively, thereby causing pointless wipes for the rest of the team and slowing progress. Items also relate to some players not

Table 12.2 Four factors producing anger in *World of Warcraft*

Items	Loadings
1. Raid/Instance Experiences (RI)	
Players do not pay attention in raids/instances and cause wipes	0.784
Players do not perform their part in a boss encounter	0.759
When players make the same mistake repeatedly and cause wipes	0.752
Players do not act on instructions they should be listening to	0.738
A wipe occurs that results from useless and unproductive actions	0.685
Players repeatedly do not do what they are asked to do in raids	0.674
Raid/instance members do not play as part of a raid/instance	0.672
Players in a group go AFK (Away From Keyboard) and contribute little to a raid/instance	0.645
A party continually wipes at bosses who were beaten in the past	0.644
Players wipe the raid after doing something they shouldn't	0.642
Players do something wrong and lay the blame on others	0.637
People who do not listen to raid/instance leaders	0.630
Players join a group, leave before completing, or after they die	0.620
People complain that the guild is not raiding/instancing enough	0.592
Players 'jump the gun' in raids/instances.	0.556
Players moan during raids and then leave 10 min after the start.	0.546
2. Griefers (GR)	
Outnumbered by the opposing faction who are CCing you	0.799
You are ganked on a regular basis	0.772
As a low-level you are accidentally PvP-tagged, then ganked by ??	0.765
After returning to your corpse you are killed again by opp. Faction	0.764
You are AFK, a member of the opposing faction CCs you	0.726
You are ganked/corpse camped followed by a taunt (e.g., /spit)	0.721
3. Perceived Time Wasting (PTW)	
Doing events I consider are time wasters (e.g., mana regeneration)	0.721
I have to wait around on bigraids/instances with nothing to do	0.647
You are grinding, and another player drags the mobs away	0.570
You lose an item on a fair need/greed roll	0.412
4. Anti-social Players (AS)	
Impolite behavior toward others/yourself	0.824
Players who are generally insulting	0.786

being as prepared as others (e.g., not bringing potions/bandages), or leaving the raid/party before the last boss has been fought/ conquered. *Griefers* are players who cause intentional suffering to others, whereas gankers and corpse campers (CC) are subcategories of griefers who wantonly kill others in PvP areas. *Perceived Time Wasting* items expressed frustration over futile actions that slow down a player's momentum. *Anti-Social Players* are impolite and insulting.

Potential In-Game Anger-Causing Scenarios

The 16 items that comprise the first scale described potential anger-causing scenarios that may occur while players are raiding or instancing. An instance is "a dungeon where you will load into your OWN copy of the dungeon with your group. Only you and your group will be in your copy of the dungeon. Another group that enters the same area will enter their own copy of the dungeon."[1] Five players are recommended to form an instance group, and the lower level instances in the game can be conquered as early as Level 13 (Ragefire Chasm in Orgrimmar) to 15 (The Deadmines in Westfall). As players progress through the levels, they will encounter other instances that are appropriate for their level, such as Hellfire Ramparts, situated in Hellfire Peninsula and designed for Level 70 players.

Once the game's level cap is reached, players may choose to experience a new challenging aspect of the game-raiding. Top-level players are unable to gain experience points and instead grind new and more powerful armor from raids and instances (Ducheneaut et al. 2006). Depending on their difficulty, raids can be tackled with 10, 25, or even 40 players. Figure 12.1 shows ten players in two groups of five in Naxxramas, working together to defeat Patchwerk, the first boss of the Construct Quarter. Probably, only a minority of players often spend time raiding, but those who do are exposed to many anger-causing scenarios in-game. This further necessitates the importance of learning and implementing successful team work skills to further progress within the game to lessen the likelihood of provoking player anger. Raids are typically much harder than normal instances and require a raid-leader to coordinate the team to success (although lower level instances still require teamwork and coordination between players). In this respect, raid leaders and their team need to have good communication skills, some common sense, and the ability to follow exact instructions. A group of raiders will spend many months progressing through, and conquering raid instances. It only takes one or two people to perform badly in a raid for the whole group to die (known as 'wipes') and repeated wiping causes endless frustration amongst team members as it slows down progress for the whole team. One player outlined three examples of anger-causing scenarios within raids "1. When people won't listen. 2. When giving lame excuses instead of just saying they made a mistake. 3. When people are doing same mistake over and over again, causing wipes or whatever unwanted results."

---

[1] http://www.wow-europe.com/en/info/basics/glossary.html

Fig. 12.1 Ten players in Naxxramas, working together to defeat Patchwerk, © 2010 Blizzard Entertainment, Inc.

Ducheneaut and Moore (2005) list two social skills that are important when grouping with other players: leadership and sensitivity to others' needs. Leaders who are too dictatorial may attract dissension from their group members. Those who take the time to assist new members, and generally show more patience, are more likely to bring success to the raid team as a whole. Two raid leaders expressed awareness of this fact: "When in a raid something goes wrong, and people start yelling at others, blaming them. I promote the giving of useful, constructive feedback, not shouting, blaming or yelling as mindless idiots. It makes players feel uncomfortable and does nothing to boost their confidence or concentration." "Even though I lead the raid, without the 39 people behind me, I couldn't accomplish anything."

Sensitivity to others' needs means that each member of a raid team needs to be aware of what other team members are doing while a fight is taking place. For a healer (such as a priest), this means noticing when another player's health is low and needs healing, while characters playing the "tank" attack role need to be aware when a healer is out of mana and therefore will not be able to heal until their mana is refreshed by drinking a mana potion. As one informant said, "Endgame raiding guilds depend heavily on team spirit and teamwork. I get annoyed by people who try to play a 'lone wolf.' Usually such people, who jeopardize the raid for 39 other attendees, get a warning. And if no improvement is shown, they will be removed from the raid/guild." Another commented, "I don't mind wiping at the bosses ... that's the reason they are out there for... but I hate if the wipe is totally useless and unproductive." The eventual downing of a raid instance boss is a mark of celebration for a raid group, expressing mutual appreciation rather than anger.

Griefers disrupt the gaming experience for others, and its definition has three aspects: the act must be intentional, it disrupts another player's game play, and the griefer enjoys taking part in the behavior (Foo and Koivisto 2004). Griefing is likely more prominent on PvP realms than on other types of servers, so this second measurement scale is especially salient for them. The scenarios discussed here will be directed toward corpse camping (a player kills another player and then waits by the corpse for the defeated player to resurrect, then kills the player again – this often happens repeatedly over a short period of time).

On PvP realms, an Alliance member can attack and possibly kill a Horde player, or vice versa. The player who died can resurrect at the graveyard and continue questing or choose to retaliate. If the player decides to continue questing, they run the risk of either being attacked again by the same player, or a different player of the opposite faction. The griefer may have much better armor or be many levels above the player he is griefing, thereby making the fight an unfair match. Situations like this can occur repeatedly, which slows down or may halt the griefee's game play. As one wrote, "I also get angry when I get killed by someone who clearly has no challenge in defeating me, it feels as though they are having fun at my expense, revelling in the misery of my time lost in the game. As it happens this is the reason why I don't really play [character name] anymore." Another commented, "Being ganked isn't a big thing but being corpse camped is. Ganking is perfectly valid since it's consistent with role playing. Corpse camping breaks the immersion and is just a silly waste of time. It's a deliberate attempt to cause grief."

Players who are on the receiving end of griefing may choose to reroll a new character, or transfer their existing character to another realm-type where PvP is only optional. Other players may choose to retaliate in more creative ways, for example by persistently retaliating: "I can never slate one part of WoW that gets me angry as ganking has brought some of the best moments in the game, being corpse camped brings determination to get up and kick their arse when things are in their favour. Injustice breeds revenge. I still actively hunt those who have messed up demons for my epic hunter quest, and corpse camp them even out with the cooking stuff and build a little fire so they get the point."

A very different response is attempting to communicate with the opposite faction, and even cooperating: "I play on a PvP server so in a way I'm asking for it, but it's still annoying sometimes. Just because you CAN kill someone, doesn't mean you SHOULD. I find it much more interesting to try and interact with the opposing faction in a friendly way, especially with the language barrier and mutual distrust." The WoW interface prevents Alliance and Horde from communicating via text chat, but they can use very basic emotes and gestures. Occasionally, they help each other to complete quests despite the limited communication, and Fig. 12.2 shows a Level 70 Alliance Draenei mage helping a Level 60 Horde Tauren hunter with a quest.

Some players try to accept the griefing as part of the realm's activities: "...the scenario that will elicit the strongest response from me, will always be ganking.

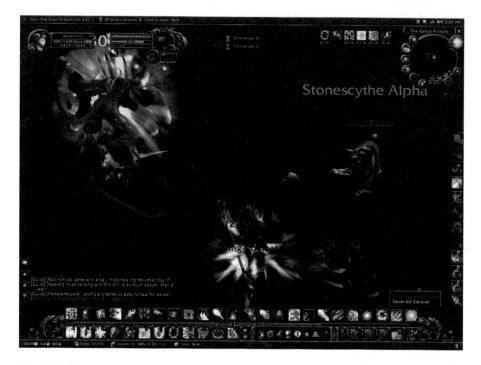

Fig. 12.2 An alliance player helping a horde player defeat an elite enemy, © 2010 Blizzard Entertainment, Inc.

Of course, rationally I realise that it's on my own head for playing on a PvP realm, but it still really pisses me off when a rogue ten levels higher than me corpsecamps for hours." Results from a study by Foo and Koivisto (2004) showed similarities between motivations of the griefer, and those described by people who bully in real-life scenarios. A study by Pizer (2003) found that only a small amount of players participated in griefing behavior; however, a news report (Pham 2002) suggests that the actual number of players angered by griefer behavior is much higher.

The scale measuring potential time wasting suggests that players have goals in mind and resent being prevented from making progress toward them. Some players may feel that the leveling up to the experience cap (currently 80) is something to be endured and are less likely to do pre-level cap group instances in favor of leveling up more quickly. For example, when players die, their spirit appears at the nearest graveyard. They then have to run back to the place where they died, recover their corpse, and then take a few seconds to replenish their health (and mana if they use it). Although this process takes only a few seconds, some players may perceive the act of dying and replenishing as interrupting their game flow. To add insult to injury, after recovering their corpse and before replenishing their health, a player may be killed again instantly (by the opposite faction if playing on a PvP realm), meaning the whole process has to be repeated again: "I really hate it when I have to spend time in useless stuff then (stuff as in running back to the corpse, regen mana and health, buffing, etc)." "Deaths in general are annoying as it is time consuming to walk back to your corpse and get back to life: often just to be killed again almost instantly. It particularly makes me angry when I have little time to play."

Ironically, trying to help another player may sometimes cause anger. For example, some character classes, such as mages, can use certain spells to kill many mobs (non-player characters) at the same time. One commented he gets angry, "when some idiot decides to 'help out' when I'm AoE grinding and pulls all the mobs away from me. On my mage that is." Although the mage may have all the mobs under control, another player may see them as being surrounded and in danger of dying, and decide to help out. The player then drags one or two mobs away and the mage is in danger of losing experience points.

With regard to the item describing anger toward "Need/Greed" rolls, players may spend a lot of time in raids and instances hoping that a particular type of armor or weapon will drop that will increase their stats and make them more powerful. When a member of a team kills a mob possessing one of these, members get the option to indicate they need it, then chance determines which one does win it. Other players who have no need of the item may still click "Need" just to annoy other players, or because they also need the particular item for their character: "I dislike people voting need on everything in instances/raids, e.g., when it's a warrior rolling on leather/cloth item." "Characters stealing loot inside instances I could use." "Losing an item on a fair roll can be annoying, but I try to curb this because I lost fair and square, and didn't deserve the item any more than the winner." "Losing loot and stuff like that doesn't bother me much unless the person is clearly a ninja or takes something just to be nasty." For players who have made a special journey into the instance, not getting the desired item was time wasted. They then must spend a considerable amount of time looking for another group to enter the same instance, and run the risk of losing the item again.

As in real life, there are many friendly and helpful people within WoW. However, the game does have its fair share of rude and arrogant players who could be called anti-social: "Only thing that makes me angry towards other players is idiotic or offensive behaviour." Insulting comments can be directed toward a person's game play: "When other players insult me over the fact that I take a long time to level my characters." Players can be annoying in their attempt to steal another player's resources (e.g., mines, skins, herbs), especially after another player has spent a long time fighting through mobs to reach, for example, a mineral node (Fig. 12.3). "I had fought my way through caves was mining when guy runs in and starts mining my node, I asked him not too... he stealthed off (was rogue)... he tried to repeat this process several times, stealing my metal! even laughing and making rude gestures at one stage! Later he must have had bad pull and came charging towards me followed by hundreds of bloody mobs expecting me to help him!! they killed him. Then they killed me. He found it amusing. I did not."

When encountering a verbally annoying player, a solution for many players is to use the "Ignore" function. This is an in-game tool where a player right-clicks with the mouse on the annoying player's name and selects the "Ignore" option.

Fig. 12.3 Mining a cobalt mineral node, © 2010 Blizzard Entertainment, Inc.

Once on the "Ignore" list, the annoying players chat can no longer be seen: "there are very many players who can annoy you enough to put them on your ignore list."

Game servers specifically designed for role-playing (RP) have additional policies implemented by Blizzard – "Creating an immersive world that holds true to the base story line of the *World of Warcraft* is the driving motivation behind our Role Play Servers. While other servers allow you to play *World of Warcraft*, these servers are intended to let you *live World of Warcraft*."[2] Players who enjoy role playing their character will most likely choose to roll a character on an RP server in order to immerse themselves in the Warcraft storyline. RP server rules also extend to characters having names that fit their characters (e.g., a night-elf hunter may have an elvish sounding name like Evaltiel, whereas naming a character 'Hordekiller' would be frowned upon and most likely reported by role-players to Blizzard for a name change): "Violations of RP rules, in terms of invalid names, Leetspeak, - > Very angry, Rules are on the server for a reason, obey them or go elsewhere." "Abuse and ignorance of what it means to be on a "RP" Realm, I have played on normal, PvP and RP and people abusing the RP policy are certainly one of the most infuriating things, especially when asked not to, etc." Game policies exist whereby any player who breaks the immersion of an RP server (e.g., by conducting non-role-playing conversations in most chat channels, or abusing players who are RPing) is

---

[2] http://www.wow-europe.com/en/policy/roleplaying.html

liable to receive a warning from a Game Master. Repeated harassment leads to an account ban, which prevents the player from logging into the game for a time. Again, players also have the option to use the 'Ignore' function.

Conclusion

The aim of this research was to examine the types of in-game scenarios that may anger WoW players. To explain the procedure, the chapter was divided into two parts. The first described how the scenarios provided by WoW players were collated and analyzed to form the *World of Warcraft* Questionnaire. Results revealed four factors that identified four types of in-game potential anger-causing scenarios, with each showing good reliability – Raids/Instances, Griefers, Perceived Time Wasting, and Anti-Social Players. The second half of the chapter further explored the four types of anger-causing scenarios and the implications that could arise when encountering them in-game. WoW players' testimonials were used to illustrate the points made.

The over-arching theme running through the majority of the items is that WoW players become angry as a result of other players' negative behavior, regardless of whether that behavior is intended to harm or not. The first factor, Raids/Instances, contained the largest amount of items, suggesting that most potential anger-causing scenarios occur when it is crucial that a group of players need to work as a team to be successful and progress through end-game content. The second largest factor, Griefers, contained a number of items that described anger toward players who enjoyed griefing, signifying that players not only felt bullied by being corpse camped, but this act also interrupted the flow of their game play. The third factor, Perceived Time Wasting, described how players feel angry when they perceive specific in-game scenarios as time wasting. Although some of the events (e.g., waiting around before a raid) could be avoidable, others are not (e.g., health and/or mana regeneration). The final factor, Anti-Social Players, regardless of containing only two items, adequately showed that WoW gamers are angered by general offensive behavior from others, regardless of the in-game context.

Ducheneaut and Moore (2004) explain that playing a MMORPG is more than playing a game. It also offers opportunities for players from all over the world to socialize, coordinate, and cooperate in small or large groups, in the same social space. However, similar to real-life occurrences, WoW players will also meet others who do not fulfill the criteria to play fair. Although each WoW realm holds several 1,000 players, news of a player behaving badly soon becomes public knowledge, and they may be shunned from groups, and guilds, ostracized, or banned.

For future studies, researchers may choose to implement the existing structure of the WoWQ, or adapt it accordingly when examining the intricacies of positive and negative social behavior in WoW. Additionally, the items removed for this study could be included to explore extra dimensions of the game, regardless of statistical reliability. Although the reactions of players may be to ignore or report in response to players who ruin game play for others, additional research could further examine the implications of these actions on personal and guild-focused in-game progress.

Appendix

The following items were removed during Principal Components Analyses if they either cross-loaded onto another factor, or failed to load on any of the four factors (unloaded items are marked *). Some of these items may represent additional but as-yet undiscovered dimensions of anger, or otherwise be of use for future studies.

Players who do not generally listen.

You have not played for a while and feel left behind.*

During PvP, you are a victim of kiting.

You die and find it time-consuming to run back to your corpse.

Players who never help others, but expect help all the time.

Other players not listening in battlegrounds.*

Grinding for XP/reputation often feels like work, not playing.

Being corpse camped by a player who is ?? levels higher than you.

Grinding reputation seems more like a duty.

Players give lame excuses for mistakes.

Players continually begging for gold.

Players who think they are better than you/everyone else.

Abuse of chat channels.

Players who roll 'Need' all the time.

You advertise loot in Trade, and other players flame you.*

Players who are arrogant.

Players who exploit others (e.g., extortionate prices on the Auction House).

You are finding it tough leveling your character with solo quests.

You die, when it could have been avoided by you.

Another player generally ruins your game play.

Being challenged to a duel when you try to do your own thing.

Ganked by opposing faction who has better armor than you.

Killed by a member of the opposing faction who gains no honor.

Players who need to rush other players for their own benefit and will not allow the more inexperienced players to catch up.

Players act like drama queens when things do not go their way.

You die, when it could have been avoided by other players.

After dying and returning to your corpse, you are killed again.

You are in a battleground and the opposite faction are in full PvP epics and hanging on to a flag. One of them targets you, despite there being a lower-level armored player nearby.

Players who spam chat channels.

Raid/instance members wrongly declare rights over a loot item.

Players log in for a raid/instance and ask for a summon.

Players ninja or cheat to get loot.

Players do not wait for the warrior to get aggro before attacking.

Guild members are harassing or difficult.

At high levels, lower level players expect you to boost them.

Players have worked hard in a raid/instance nightly. A new player joins who does not commit as much in terms of hard work.

People join a guild, get help/items from the guild, then leave.

Raid/instance members declare rights over a loot item, without any prior agreement about how loot will be allocated.

Players do not log in until a raid/instance starts and assume that a warlock will summon them.

I get a party for a raid/instance and player/players leave.

Items are over-priced in the Auction House.*

Players whine just because things are not done 'their way'.

Players get aggro and run AWAY from the tank.

Guilds 'poach' high-level players from the guild I belong to.

I am talking to another player and they do not listen.

'Glory seekers' jump guilds and hamper the guild.

Players try to rip me off in the Auction House.

Players who give the guild I am in, a bad name.

When players in a raid/instance group lack an understanding of raid/instance tactics (e.g., pulling two groups instead of one, casting spells on mobs that are CCed).

General conflict occurs between casual and hardcore players who both attend a raid/instance but expect the same rewards.

Players interfere with a warrior's aggro.

I lose loot due to ninjaing or someone takes loot just to be nasty.

People who whine constantly about everything.

Guild chat highlights differences between young/older players.*

Raid/instance members argue over loot

References

Bartlett, M. S. (1954). A note on multiplying factors for various Chi square approximations. *Journal of the Royal Statistical Society Series B, 16*, 296–298.

Ducheneaut, N., & Moore, R. J. (2004, April 19). Gaining more than experience points: Learning social behavior in multiplayer computer games. In *Position paper for the CHI2004 workshop on social learning through gaming*, Vienna, Austria.

Ducheneaut, N., & Moore, R. J. (2005). More than just 'XP': Learning social skills in massively multiplayer online games. *Interactive Technology & Smart Education, 2*, 89–100.

Ducheneaut, N., Yee, N., Nickell, E., & Moore, R. J. (2006). Alone together? Exploring the social dynamics of massively multiplayer games. In *Conference Proceedings on Human Factors in Computing Systems CHI 2006* (pp. 407–416), Montreal, Canada.

Foo, C. Y. & Koivisto, E. M. I. (2004). *Grief player motivations.* Paper presented at the Other Players Conference, IT-University of Copenhagen, December.

Kaiser, H. F. (1970). A second generation little jiffy. *Psychometrika, 35*, 401–417.

Kaiser, H. F. (1974). An index of factorial simplicity. *Psychometrika, 39*, 31–36.

Novaco, R. W. (2003). *The Novaco Anger Scale and Provocation Inventory (NAS-PI).* Los Angeles, CA: Western Psychological Services.

Pham, A. (2002). *Online bullies give grief to gamers.* September: Los Angeles Times. 2.

Pizer, P. (2003). Social Game Systems: Cultivating Player Socialization and Providing Alternate Routes to Game Rewards. In Thor Alexander (Ed.), *Massively Multiplayer Game Development* (pp. 427–441) Hingham, Massachusetts: Charles River Media.

Spielberger, C. D., Johnson, E. H., Russell, S. F., Crane, R. S., Jacobs, G. A., & Worden, T. J. (1985). The experience and expression of anger: Construction and validation of an anger expression scale. In M. Chesney & R. Rosenman (Eds.), *Anger and hostility in cardiovascular and behavioral disorders* (pp. 5–30). New York: Hemisphere.

Thurstone, L. L. (1947). *Multiple factor analysis.* Chicago, IL: University of Chicago Press.

Chapter 13
Dude Looks like a Lady: Gender Swapping in an Online Game

Searle Huh and Dmitri Williams

Scholars have long recognized the importance of identity in online communication (Bessiere et al. 2007; Nakamura 2001; Valkenburg and Peter 2008). With fewer cues than face-to-face communication (Walther et al. 2005), people in online relationships can both benefit and suffer from the relative anonymity – benefit because the space allows for more experimentation and freedom, and suffer because the relationships can become empty without the commitment that identity offers (Turkle 1995). "Knowing the identity of those with whom you communicate is essential for understanding and evaluating an interaction" (Donath 1999: 29). Online games are an especially important area to examine these trends because of their popularity and their fundamental features. Western-based virtual worlds claim over 47 million subscriptions in 2008 (White 2008), with more growth expected. Within these worlds, identity is marked primarily by a character, which is a visual representation of the player. In an MMO (Massively Multiplayer Online game), players control this character, or "avatar," that moves through a 3D virtual world, interacting with the characters of other players (DiGiuseppe and Nardi 2008). These avatars are created and altered by the players. The flexibility of such literal identity construction provides extraordinary freedom for players to deviate from, or alter their offline identities. Perhaps the most dramatic example of how people exercise this freedom and control is the case of online gender switching (or "swapping"). In a virtual world, there is no rule that the players must use their offline gender for their character. Either sex may use plural, indeterminate, or non-gendered identities.

It is evident that gamers frequently practice character gender-swapping (e.g., DiGiuseppe and Nardi 2008), yet there is little understanding of how often or why this occurs. The anonymity of the Internet was initially hailed as a leveling mechanism – without the persistence of identity cues, discrimination would become pointless. However, this early optimism was met quickly by the reality of the human condition. Racism, sexism, ageism, and a host of category-based

S. Huh and D. Williams
University of Southern California, Annenberg School for Communication
734 W. Adams Blvd. Los Angeles, CA 90089
e-mails: dmitri.williams@usc.edu; shuh@usc.edu

W.S. Bainbridge (ed.), *Online Worlds: Convergence of the Real and the Virtual*,
Human-Computer Interaction Series, DOI 10.1007/978-1-84882-825-4_13,
© Springer-Verlag London Limited 2010

discriminations have persisted online (Nakamura 2001). Identity cues have become both sources of discrimination, and opportunities for deception and experimentation (Donath 1999; Donath and Boyd 2004; Zinman and Donath 2007). Exploring this deception and experimentation is the task of this chapter.

The chapter will review the literature on online identity construction and then offer an empirical account of online gender swapping in virtual world. By using a novel combination of survey data and game-generated behavioral logs, the chapter examines who the gender swappers are, why they engage in the practice, and what they do when swapped.

Gender and Identity, Offline and On

Sex is a biological term that defines a person as male or female based on his/her inherent genes (Mintz and O'Neil 1990). On a daily basis, both sexes face different messages, expectations, resources, and opportunities (Cook 1990). Biological sex also triggers differentiated ways of perceiving and behaving toward the self and others (Cook 1990; Deaux 1984).

On the other hand, *gender* is "a multidimensional construct that encompasses many ways our society is differentiated on the basis of sex" (Cook 1990: 371). In contrast to sex, gender is less deterministic and more mutable. Several studies have claimed that gender is socially constructed (Bohan 2002; Kimmel 2000). Yet much of the sex differences literature has focused on individuals rather than on the larger social context (Cook 1990; Deaux 1984). Similarly, Baber and Tucker (2006) argued that how we assess gender attitudes need to assume that "gender and our beliefs about appropriate roles for both men and women" (p. 460) does not originate from individuals, or their sex, but is produced in social and historical contexts. Therefore, gender does not refer to a static, but to a changeable characteristic.

Gender had been traditionally modeled in research through "the artificial dichotomization of masculine and feminine" (Murphy 1994: 22) until the 1970s, when masculinity and femininity were repositioned as two endpoints on a continuum . However, this clear-cut categorization did not offer any explanation for any deviations from its mutual exclusivity, such as someone who has both high femininity and masculinity. More recently, some theorists have suggested bi- or multidimensionality of gender, such as the Sex Role Inventory approach (Bem 1974) and the Personal Attributes Questionnaire (Spence and Helmreich 1978). These bidimensional models regard masculinity and femininity as separate constructs on different continua; therefore, the concept of androgyny (Bem 1981; Murphy 1994) with both high masculine and high feminine characteristics simultaneously or neither (Bem 1981) became possible. Although the multidimensional models make the concept of gender more complex and lack predictive validity (Cook 1985), one key contribution is that they help one to overcome "overly deterministic assumptions such as biological essentialism, biopsychological equivalence, or gender polarization" (Korabik and McCreary 2000: 666).

Although biological sex is one of "the first things noticed and encoded during social interaction" (Skitka and Maslach 1996: 53), gender is one of "the most salient features we use to categorize and process social stimuli" (Bartini 2006: 233). "The belief that men and women are fundamentally different is often linked to the idea that there are particular social roles for which men and women are best suited" (Ruble and Martin 1998; cited in Baber and Tucker 2006: 459). A social role refers "a comprehensive pattern of behavior and attitudes, constituting a strategy for coping with a recurrent set of situations, which is socially identified – more or less clearly – as an entity" (Turner 1990: 87). Particularly, gender roles are defined as "behaviors, expectations, and role sets defined by society as masculine or feminine, which are embodied in the behavior of the individual man or woman and culturally regarded as appropriate to males or females" (O'Neil 1981: 203).

Simply put, people have role-related expectations for men and women (Geis 1993; Hall and Briton 1993). Not conforming to these gender roles can result in negative perceptions and evaluations (Mahalik 2000). Therefore, men and women who violate injunctive norms concerning gender role behavior are likely to experience social disapproval (Harrison and Lynch 2005). Similarly, Sirin, McCreary, and Mahalik (2004) claim that "even though men and women internalize and display both masculine and feminine characteristics, people still expect men to be masculine and women to be feminine and reward and punish them accordingly" (McCreary 1994: 120). Therefore, men are expected to fulfill the masculine gender role that reflects self-determination and women are expected to be more communally oriented (Wood and Eagly 2002). In an online space, it is therefore possible that the players who keep their gender are more likely to act their gender-typed behaviors.

Early research on online gender focused on the interpersonal dimensions of computer-mediated communication (CMC) with a tendency to analyze language use in order to better understand the power relationships between the genders online (Shade 2003). Men and women tend to use language in different ways, presumably unconsciously, online as well as offline (Herring 1995, 2003; Kendall 1998). Similarly, Lee (2007) uses the Social Identity model of Deindividuation Effects (SIDE) in claiming that "if the paucity of personalizing information in CMC leads people to think and behave in terms of social categories, it might as well make them more vigilant to the gender-linked language styles their interactants display" (p. 518). This line of thinking is also supported by Walther's (1996) hyperpersonal theory, which claims that online communicators tend to make strong attributions about the characteristics of others online from a minimal amount of cues.

In addition to the inherent malleability of online identity, theorists have suggested that, in the technological age, new media lead people to become more flexible in constructing selfidentities (Gergen 1991; Kuhn 2006; Turkle 1995). With rapidly changing technology, the self is constantly shifting and adapting to new contexts online (Anderson and Buzzanell 2007). For example, Castells (2004) says that a network society enables people's identities to be more malleable by decentering identities based on previous physical constraints such as local and national communities. Without the strong enforcement of identity, online life provides more room for identity exploration.

Identity in the Context of MMOs

MMOs are rich three-dimensional worlds with millions of players (Hussain and Griffiths 2008). Just as no one lives in complete isolation in the real world, other players in MMOs are necessary, unlike standalone console games, which do not need other players. Put in other words, "social interaction in MMOs is almost obligatory, as players must collaborate with other players in the game to succeed in ever more complex goals" (Hussain and Griffiths 2008: 47). These collaborations force the issue of identity in MMOs into a social context. Offline, individuals may struggle to adapt to the static and universal identity labels offline (Stone 1995). In contrast, MMOs provide gamers a rich range for altering identities by allowing players to choose gender, race, profession, and morality of their character. Each social interaction is therefore between characters with most of these choices made visible.

There are two contrasting views of the effects of this flexibility online. One is that the online world maintains and even extends the gender inequality that exists offline (Anderson and Buzzanell 2007; Kendall 2002; Perry and Greber 1990; Slouka 1995). From this perspective, identity flexibility cannot rise above the constraints of offline life. Perry and Greber (1990) argue that "if science reflects at least some of a society's value, then technology developed from it must also embody these values" (p. 76). Kendall (2002) also claimed that online interaction merely reinforces gender-based social status, reinforcing women's marginalization through "masculine" ways of doing work (Anderson and Buzzanell 2007). Another negative aspect to gender swapping is that it may be dysfunctional to develop an online identity that is different from one's "real" offline identity (Slouka 1995).

The contrasting view is that the online world – and especially game-based worlds – is a place for relieving gender gaps, or positive exploration. Haraway (1991) noted that communications technologies like virtual worlds are important tools for recrafting bodies, especially for women who can benefit from the new social relationships that makes possible. In her view, online worlds could be utopias without restrictive or imbalancing gender binaries. Plant (2000) also argued that digital culture provides a space beyond the existing patriarchal structures. Similarly, Turkle (1995) suggests that gender swapping is merely a natural extension of identity exploration.

If gender can be flexible offline, the online world makes it even more so. Gender swapping occurs when "one presents a gender that is different from his or her biological sex" (Roberts and Parks 1999: 522). Some cases highlight gender swapping by males (Van Gelder 1991), while others have commented on gender switching by both males and females (Bruckman 1993). These cases were noticed early on in text-only MUD environments (Rheingold 2000), where deceptive gender play was treated as something needing to be banned.

There is little existing research on the prevalence or reasons for the practice. One study (Hussain and Griffiths 2008) reported that 54% of male and 70% of female virtual world gamers have experimented with gender swapping. The main reason for males to gender swap was for competitive advantage. By posing as attractive females and interacting with other male players, these swappers sought to gain extra money or weapons and avoided being targeted (and therefore attacked) by fellow gamers. The female gamers swapped for the opposite reason – to avoid such solicitations, and so that they would be treated as equals by the predominately male player base. However, this study was completed with a convenience sample survey, with participants gathered from nonrepresentative forums where the most serious players tend to congregate. While survey research is an acceptable tool, our understanding of the practice can increase with the use of unobtrusive behavioral data. In other words, in an anonymous survey we can ask them about who they are offline with reasonable certainty, but might get less insight into how they behaved while online. This could happen owing to either social desirability or simply recall issues.

The larger context of video game play is important to note as well. Despite many early hopes, gender inequality persists online, especially in male-oriented video game spaces (McQuivey 2001). Video game characters still reflect offline gender inequalities. Dill and Thill (2007) reported that "stereotypes of male characters as aggressive and female characters as sexually objectified" (p. 851). Female characters are commonly sexualized while male characters are not. This is also related to the presence of scantily clad characters; females are much more likely than males to be sexually underdressed. Players seem to self-select these stereotypical roles. DiGiuseppe and Nardi (2008) explored the popular online video game *World of Warcraft* (WoW). They found several common gender stereotypes about users' character choice in the game, such as females being more likely to choose certain groups of characters that are associated with supportive roles, especially dedicated to healing (e.g., Priest) and ranged combat (e.g., Mage), while males are more likely to play characters that commonly involve in more physical warfare (e.g., Warrior).

These studies highlight the fact that online worlds often reproduce our existing offline social and power distributions. Women have less power within society offline, and in these more male-centric spaces, the gaps appear to be larger still; in contrast, men, show more self-determination and dominant behaviors (Athenstaedt et al. 2004). With this inequality, it is more likely that women would want to alter their identity to male in large, social, male-centric game worlds:

H1a) Female players are more likely to change their online character gender to male.

Sexual preference can also affect whether people want to manipulate their gender online. Heterosexual men often remain within their socially based gender roles to avoid opprobrium and hassle (Bosson et al. 2005). Therefore, "the desire to avoid such misclassification serves as a powerful psychological mechanism that promotes rigid adherence to the male gender role" (Bosson et al. 2006: 13). Potential gender swappers are confronted with a powerful need to belong, which may be put at risk if their swapping becomes public (Baumeister and Leary 1995). This will most likely limit heterosexuals from swapping more often. A gender swapper's discomfort may also come from attacks on their psychological coherence (Bosson et al. 2006).

Thus, if a homosexual player more closely identifies with a different psychological gender than their genetic sex, they will be more likely to swap. These twin forces – heterosexuals being hesitant to swap and homosexuals being more willing to swap yield the following hypothesis:

H1b) Homosexuals are more likely to change their biological gender in online games.

Motivations for Swapping

Reinecke, Trepte, and Behr (2007) list three major reasons why people play video games: challenge and competition, social interaction, and fantasy and escapism. Some studies have found that female gamers seem to be less interested in competitive situations (Hartmann and Klimmt 2006; Lucas and Sherry 2004), while male gamers play to complete tasks and maintain high standards for performance (Rojahn and Willemsen 1994). One of the reasons for this difference stems from gender role theory. Eagly and Karau (1991) suggest that gender differences are rooted in peoples' role consistency. That is, peoples are more likely to behave consistently within the gender roles that are already formed in their lives. Both genders are socialized from an early age into two distinctively collective categories of behavior: task activity for men and social activity for women. But for those individuals who would prefer to break from these strictures, the online gaming world presents an opportunity to "play" the other gender's role. Therefore, we would expect that those who gender swap will be motivated to play for the cross-stereotypic reason from their biological gender:

H2) Gender-swapping gamers will adhere to the opposite gender's stereotypical reasons for play.

We would expect this attitudinal orientation to also lead to behavioral differences as well. Those gender-typed behaviors can be predicted by gender schema theory (Bem 1981). "Being schematic" in the theory refers to "having a readiness to sort information into categories on the basis of a particular dimension, despite the availability of other possible and reasonable alternative dimensions" (Skitka and Maslach 1996: 55). Thus, being gender schematic means spontaneously sorting attributes and behavior into categories related to sex, despite the availability of viable alternative categories unrelated to sex. According to this theory, "people who describe themselves in conventionally sex-typed ways are thought to be gender schematic" (Skitka and Maslach 1996: 55). However, people who swap their gender can also be gender schematic because they swap gender based on their own concept of what are male or female activities. Thus, gender swappers are possibly performing guesswork in their portrayals of the other gender. The ability to swap may therefore lead many players to misestimate those behaviors and be prone to overexaggeration (Cook 1990). In this sense, virtual worlds can become a place for "hypermasculinity" and "hyperfemininity" (Scharrer 2004: 397). According to Scharrer, hypermasculinity refers to the exaggeration of "macho" characteristics, specifically a desire for action and danger, and the acceptance of physical violence as a part of male nature. Meanwhile, hyper-femininity means the amplification of female stereotypes, with an emphasis on dependence, submissiveness, and sexuality as the basis of a woman's value. This mis-estimation and overexaggeration will lead to hyper-gendered behaviors among the swappers:

H3a) Male players who play female characters are more likely to do more hyperfeminine activities than male users who play male characters.

H3b) Female players who play male characters are more likely to involve in hypermasculine activities than female users who play female characters.

Methods and Measures

The data used for this study come from a combination of survey and game-generated computer logs. Six thousand one hundred and twenty two players of the game *EverQuest II* took part in a survey operated from within the game world. The survey took place on January 12–13, 2007, and offered the players an in-game item as a reward for participation (Williams et al. 2008). Under an agreement with the firm Sony Online Entertainment (SOE), we were also able to extract behavioral indicators from the game's operating logs. Chiefly, these included the gender of the players' avatars and selected game activities matching gender-stereotypical behaviors (see below). Because players can maintain multiple avatars, we restricted the sample to only the avatars played most often. This avatar gender variable was then matched up with the survey data, providing an unobtrusive link between their offline and online lives. All data were anonymized and unable to be linked to real-world identities.

Gender swapping players were identified based on their survey data crossed with their primary character's gender. Female gamers who played male characters in the game were categorized as F-M players, those who played females as F-F, etc. the resulting four categories yield a 2 (game character gender) x 2 (real gender) factorial design.

Motivations for play were measured using Yee's condensed MMO motivations scale (Yee 2007). The scale uses ten component questions to generate three factors labeled "sociability," "achievement," and "immersion." Sociability matches the feminine stereotypical motivation for play, while achievement matches the male stereotypical one. The behavioral logs supplied four main measures of gender-stereotypical in-game behaviors. Primarily, male stereotypical behaviors were engaging in combat with computer-generated monsters, completing quests, and engaging in player vs. player combat (PvP). All of these are related to either physical violence (Scharrer 2004) or task completion or performance (Rojahn and Willemsen 1994). Combat with monsters was measured by the number of monster encounters per month. For quests, the number of quests completed was used. The number of player vs. player encounters was calculated by adding the frequency of killing other players and that of being killed by other players. Primarily, female stereotypical behavior was measured with the rate of personal text chatting as communal activities are regarded as one of feminine gender roles (Wood and Eagly 2002). This was reported as an intensity variable, i.e., the number of text chats sent per month. Lastly, sexual orientation was measured with the survey question "Do you consider yourself (a) straight/heterosexual, (b) bisexual, (c) homosexual, (d) prefer not to answer."

Results

Hypothesis 1a predicted that female players are more likely to change their gender online. To examine the categorical differences, a chi-square test was run, which yielded significant differences ($\chi^2 = 62.54$, $p < 0.001$). However, as Table 13.1 shows, the results were in the opposite direction of expectations, with the proportion of female players who changed their online gender (8.2%) smaller than the male players (17.4%). An incidental, but important finding was that gender swapping is not very common in general, with only 15.5% of players overall engaging in it.

Hypothesis 1b predicted more gender swapping from homosexual players (Table 13.2). A chi-square test again yielded significant results ($\chi^2 = 8.42$, $p = 0.005$), this time in the expected direction. Homosexual players were more likely to change their online gender (22.0%) than straight users (16.8%). Therefore, hypothesis 1b was supported.

Hypothesis 2 predicted different motivations among the gender swappers. Three t-tests were performed, comparing the gender swappers with the nonswappers. First, the achievement motivation did not show a significant difference between the two groups, t (6006) = 0.817, $p = 0.414$, $\eta^2 < 0.001$. That is, gender

Table 13.1 Frequencies of gender swapping

Game character gender	Real gender					
	Male		Female		Total	
Male	4,065	82.6%	98	8.2%	4,163	68.0%
Female	855	17.4%	1,104	91.8%	1,959	32.0%
Total	4,920	100.0%	1,202	100.0%	6,122	100.0%

Table 13.2 Frequencies of gender swapping according to sexual preference

Gender swapping	Sexual preference					
	Straight		Gay		Total	
No	3,678	83.2%	128	78.0%	3,806	83.0%
Yes	742	16.8%	36	22.0%	778	17.0%
Total	4,420	100.0%	164	100.0%	4,584	100.0%

swappers (M = 3.42, SD = 0.91) did not differ from nonswappers (M = 3.44, SD = 0.88) in terms of motivation for performance. Second, a t-test for the socialization motivation also did not show a significant difference, t (5979) = 0.716, p = 0.474, η^2 < 0.001. That is, those who swapped their gender (M = 3.15, SD = 0.96) did not have different degree of motivation for socializing from those who did not (M = 3.18, SD = 0.93).

Hypothesis 3a predicted that men who play female characters online are more likely to engage in stereotypically female acts than men who play male characters. First, the number of battle encounters with monsters was tested for differences between the swapping and nonswapping male players. The test did not show a significant result, t (4918) = −1.593, p = 0.111, η^2 < 0.001 (male gender swappers M = 20679.14, SD = 23817.43; male nonswappers M = 22142.24, SD = 24522.21). Second, the number of quests was examined, but also did not show a significant result, t (4918) = −0.684, p = 0.494, η^2 < 0.001 (male gender swappers M = 372.66, SD = 269.88; male nonswappers M = 355.74, SD = 285.85). Third, as an opposite indicator, the number of PvP encounters was compared. The test also failed to produce a difference, t (4918) = 0.684, p = 0.494, η^2 < 0.001 (Male gender swappers M = 67.05, SD = 301.75; male nonswappers M = 60.36, SD = 268.85). Lastly, the rate of text chatting was tested and also did not show a significant result, t (2845) = 0.625, p = 0.532, η^2 < 0.001 (Male gender swappers M = 220.85 text chats sent/month, SD = 307.08; male nonswappers M = 211.74, SD = 290.55). In sum, male players did not differ in their in-game behaviors based on the gender of their avatar.

Hypothesis 3b predicted that women who play male characters online are more likely to engage in stereotypically male behaviors than women who play female characters. First, the t-test for the frequency of combat showed a significant result, t (1200) = −2.980, p = 0.003, η^2 = 0.007, but the results were in the opposite direction of expectations. Female nonswappers (M = 22161.12, SD = 23225.54) fought more monsters than female gender swappers (M = 14896.22, SD = 22015.43). Second, a t-test for the number of quests also showed a significant result, t (1200) = −5.614, p < 0.001, η^2 = 0.026. However, female nonswappers (M = 424.41, SD = 301.64) completed more quests than female gender swappers (M = 249.07, SD = 227.04). Third, the test of PvP combat also showed a significant result, t (1200) = 2.733, p = 0.006, η^2 = 0.003, this time in line with expectations. Female gender swappers (M = 51.14, SD = 126.57) took part in more PvP combat than female nonswappers (M = 31.67, SD = 166.07). Lastly, chatting behaviors supported the hypotheses. Female gender swappers engaged in significantly less text chatting than the nonswappers, t (776) = −2.136, p = 0.033, η^2 = 0.003 (Female gender swappers M = 148.55 text chats sent/month, SD = 307.08; female nonswappers M = 290.11, SD = 455.74). Whereas the same-gendered female players conformed to gender expectations by chatting more than any other group, it was notable that the gender swapping female players sent the fewest chats of any group in the analysis, including the men. This suggests that they were engaging in hypermasculine behavior, in direct contrast to the male swappers who exhibited no notable differences (Fig. 13.1).

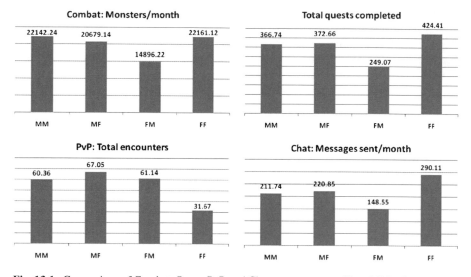

Fig. 13.1 Comparison of Combat, Quest, PvP, and Chat among groups. *Note*: MM refers to males playing male characters, MF to males playing female characters, etc.

Conclusion

This study tested gender swapping in an online game, focusing on who the swappers are, what their motivations are, and what behaviors they engage in within the game world. Contrary to expectation, females were not more likely to change their gender online than males. Consistent with expectation, homosexual users were more likely to change their online gender than straight users. Motivations for play yielded no differences; gender swappers and nonswappers are playing for the same reasons. The behavioral measures did show some intriguing differences, and suggested that there may well be differences between the genders playing the game. These findings are discussed below.

The most obvious takeaway point from the study is that few players engage in gender swapping. Contrary to Haraway or Turkle's notions of vibrant identity exploration, this appears be a fairly small phenomenon. And given that the motivations for play had no relationship to swapping, there may be little of the identity exploration or challenging of gender norms that some had expected. One reason could simply be that players find their avatars to be chiefly instrumental. They may not identify strongly with the character on the screen, perhaps regarding it more the way a consumer might choose a toothbrush or car color. Indeed, many male players have quipped that they play a female avatar because it is a pleasing visual object, not a source of identification. However, there may be something else at play among the female players. As noted in a related project studying gender differences among this population, there is a very high degree of masculine-oriented female players in *EQII* (Williams et al. in press). That project found that while male players had about the same level of homosexuality as the general population, female players had three times the bisexuality rate. They were also among the most "hard core" players in terms of time spent within the game. How can we reconcile this with the very feminine behaviors among the nonswapping, very chatty female players? One strong possibility is that the female population of players is in fact bimodal, and made up of very stereotypically female and male-leaning subgroups. Future research on gender in virtual worlds should pay special attention to measuring and predicting such bimodal tendencies.

The in-game behaviors provide the most interesting insight into this issue of female exceptionalism. Male players did not perform differently whether they played their own gendered characters or swapped gendered characters. Neither gender showed differences on the basic tasks of completing quests and attacking monsters. This may simply be due to the fact that these two measures are the main components of MMO play, and so are not sensitive enough to detect gendered differences. However, the female players did behave differently when they gender swapped, showing a more masculine behavioral pattern than even the men in one case. These players chatted in the game far less frequently than female nonswappers, or even the men. In this sense, these women were "outmanning" the male players. Similarly, the two female groups showed a large difference what is arguably the most hypermasculine activity in MMOs, PvP play. While all players must attack monsters, PvP is an optional activity that some players gravitate toward while others avoid it. As a particularly confrontational act, it is more associated with stereotypically masculine traits.

Although the study uses a novel data set, it has some limitations. First, these data are not informed by the cultural context of the game. There may be sociocultural reasons for the results that would only be obvious to a long-term player of the game. Future research should therefore incorporate an anthropological component to better inform the results. Also, although the data here are longitudinal, they do not offer causal inferences. However, because the online game world is relatively new, it is likely that the play patterns here represent some of the first such exposures in the population to this kind of setting. Different methods might eventually control and untangle whether the game enables or creates the differences shown here.

On the one hand, the online world offers immense freedom to people by allowing them to experiment with their identity. On the other hand, it is clearly not a utopian gender-free space. Whether people change their gender online or not, they still keep their offline gender roles in mind. In a sense, the virtual game world is more an extension of the real one than a separate place. It is possible that being someone else online (e.g., playing opposite gender roles online) may make players more conscious of their offline identity. Men being men or women being women does not require any extra planning and evaluation of behaviors. Swapping, however, may require frequent self-evaluation behaviors to maintain a socially comfortable gender role. For some female players, gender swapping clearly represents some deeper identity-based behavior. Yet for the men, the general rule appears to be that he can be a dude who looks like a lady, but he still acts like a dude.

Acknowledgments This work is supported by grants from the National Science Foundation (Grant #IIS 07-29505) and the Army Research Institute (Grant #PROJ0001029).

References

Anderson, W. & Buzzanell, P. (2007). Outcast among outcasts: Gender and leadership in a Mac users group. *Women and Language, 30,* 32–45.

Athenstaedt, U., Haas, E., & Schwab, S. (2004). Gender role self-concept and gender-typed communication behavior in mixed-sex and same-sex dyads. *Sex Roles, 50,* 37–52.

Baber, K. M. & Tucker, C. J. (2006). The social roles questionnaire: A new approach to measuring attitudes toward gender. *Sex Roles, 54,* 459–467.

Bartini, M. (2006). Gender role flexibility in early adolescence: Developmental change in attitudes, self-perceptions, and behaviors. *Sex Roles, 55,* 233–245.

Baumeister, R. F., & Leary, M. R. (1995). The need to belong: Desire for interpersonal attachments as a fundamental human motivation. *Psychological Bulletin, 117,* 497–529.

Bem, S. L. (1974). The measurement of psychological androgyny. *Journal of Consulting and Clinical Psychology, 41,* 856–865.

Bem, S. L. (1981). Gender Schema Theory: A cognitive account of sex typing. *Psychological Review, 88,* 354–364.

Bessiere, K., Seay, A. F., & Kiesler, S. (2007). The ideal Elf: Identity exploration in *World of Warcraft. Cyberpsychology and Behavior, 10,* 530–535.

Bohan, J. S. (2002). Sex differences and/in the self: Classic themes, feminist variations, postmodern challenges. *Psychology of Women Quarterly, 26,* 74–88.

Bosson, J. K., Prewitt-Freilino, J. L., & Taylor, J. N. (2005). Role rigidity: A problem of identity misclassification? *Journal of Personality and Social Psychology, 89,* 552–565.

Bosson, J. K., Taylor, J. N., & Prewitt-Freilino, J. L. (2006). Gender role violations and identity misclassification: The roles of audience and actor variables. *Sex Roles, 55,* 13–24.

Bruckman, A. S. (1993). *Gender swapping on the internet.* Retrieved October 22, 2008, from http://www.cc.gatech.edu/elc/papers/bruckman/gender-swapping-bruckman.pdf

Castells, M. (2004). *The power of identity.* Malden, MA: Blackwell.

Cook, E. P. (1985). *Psychological androgyny.* New York: Pergamon.

Cook, E. P. (1990). Gender and psychological distress. *Journal of Counseling and Development, 68,* 371–375.

Deaux, K. (1984). From individual differences to social categories: Analysis of a decade. *American Psychologist, 39,* 105–116.

DiGiuseppe, N. & Nardi, B. A. (2008). Real genders choose fantasy characters: Class choice in *World of Warcraft. First Monday* 12(5–7), from http://www.firstmonday.org/issue/issue12_5/diguiseppe/index.html

Dill, K. E. & Thill, K. P. (2007). Video game characters and the socialization of gender roles: Young people's perceptions mirror sexist media depictions. *Sex Roles, 57,* 851–864.

Donath, J. (1999). Identity and deception in the virtual community. In M.A. Smith & P. Kollock (Eds.), *Communities in cyberspace* (pp. 29–59). New York: Routledge.

Donath, J. & Boyd, D. (2004). Public displays of connection. *BT Technology Journal, 22,* 71–82.

Eagly, A. H. & Karau, S. J. (1991). Gender and the emergence of leaders: A meta-analysis. *Journal of Personality, 60,* 685–710.

Geis, F. L. (1993). Self-fulfilling prophecies: A social psychological view of gender. In A.E. Beall & R.J. Sternberg (Eds.), *The psychology of gender* (pp. 9–54). New York: Guilford.

Gergen, K. J. (1991). *The saturated self: Dilemmas of identity in contemporary life.* New York: Basic Books.

Hall, J. A. & Briton, N. J. (1993). Gender, nonverbal behavior, and expectations. In P. D. Blanck (Ed.), *Interpersonal expectations: Theory, research, and applications* (pp. 276–295). New York: Cambridge University Press.

Haraway, D. J. (1991). *Simians, Cyborgs, and women: The re-invention of nature.* New York: Routledge.

Harrison, L. A. & Lynch, A. B. (2005). Social role theory and the perceived gender role orientation of athletes. *Sex Roles, 52,* 227–236.

Hartmann, T. & Klimmt, C. (2006). Gender and computer games: Exploring females' dislike. *Journal of Computer-Mediated Communication, 11*, 910–931.

Herring, S. C. (1995). Men's language on the internet. In I. Brock, T. Bull & T. Swann (Eds.), *Proceedings of the 2nd Nordic Language and Gender Conference (Nordlyd)* (pp. 1–20). Tromso, Norway: University of Tromso.

Herring, S. C. (2003). Gender and power in on-line communication. In J. Holmes & M. Meyerhoff (Eds.), *The handbook of language and gender* (pp. 202–228). Oxford, UK: Blackwell.

Hussain, Z. & Griffiths, M. D. (2008). Gender swapping and socializing in cyberspace: An exploratory study. *CyberPsychology and Behavior, 11*, 47–53.

Kendall, L. (1998). Meaning and identity in cyberspace: The performance of gender, class, and race online. *Symbolic Interaction, 21*, 129–153.

Kendall, L. (2002). *Hanging out in the virtual pub: Masculinities and relationships online.* Berkeley, CA: University of California Press.

Kimmel, M. S. (2000). *The gendered society.* New York: Oxford University Press.

Korabik, K. & McCreary, D. R. (2000). Testing a model of socially desirable and undesirable gender-role attributes. *Sex Roles, 43*, 665–685.

Kuhn, T. (2006). A 'Demented Work Ethic' and a 'Lifestyle Firm': Discourse, identity, and workplace time commitments. *Organization Studies, 27*, 1339–1358.

Lee, E.-J. (2007). Effects of gendered language on gender stereotyping in computer-mediated communication: The moderating role of depersonalization and gender-role orientation. *Human Communication Research, 33*, 515–535.

Lucas, K. & Sherry, J. L. (2004). Sex differences in video game play: A communication-based explanation. *Communication Research, 31*, 499–523.

Mahalik, J. R. (2000). Men's gender role conflict as predictors of self-ratings on the interpersonal circle. *Journal of Social and Clinical Psychology, 19*, 276–292.

McCreary, D. R. (1994). The male role and avoiding femininity. *Sex Roles, 31*, 517–531.

McQuivey, J. (2001). The digital locker room: The young, white male as center of the video gaming universe. In E.T.L. Aldoory (Ed.), *The gender challenge to media: Diverse voices from the field* (pp. 183–214). Cresskill, NJ: Hampton Press.

Mintz, L. B. & O'Neil, J. M. (1990). Gender roles, sex, and the process of psychotherapy: Many questions and few answers. *Journal of Counseling and Development, 68*, 381–387.

Murphy, P. (1994). Gender differences in pupils' reactions to practical work. In R. Levinson (Ed.), *Teaching science.* New York: Routledge.

Nakamura, L. (2001). Race in/for cyberspace: Identity tourism and racial passing on the internet. In D. Trend (Ed.), *Reading digital culture* (pp. 226–235). Malden, MA: Blackwell.

O'Neil, J. M. (1981). Patterns of gender role conflict and strain: Sexism and fear of femininity in men's lives. *Personnel and Guidance Journal, 60*, 203–210.

Perry, R. & Greber, L. (1990). Women and computers: An introduction. *Signs: Journal of Women in Culture and Society, 16*, 74–101.

Plant, S. (2000). On the matrix: Cyberfeminist simulations. In G. Kirkup, L. Janes, K. Woodward, & F. Hovenden (Eds.), *The gendered cyborg: A reader* (pp. 265–275). New York: Routledge.

Reinecke, L., Trepte, S., & Behr, K.-M. (2007). Why girls play: Results of a qualitative interview study with female video game players. *Hamburger Forschungsberichte zur Sozialpsychologie 77* [Hamburg Research Reports on Social Psychology No. 77]. Hamburg, Germany: University of Hamburg.

Rheingold, H. (2000). *The virtual community.* Cambridge, MA: MIT Press.

Roberts, L. D. & Parks, M. R. (1999). The social geography of gender-switching in virtual environments on the internet. *Information, Communication and Society, 2*, 521–540.

Rojahn, K. & Willemsen, T. M. (1994). The evaluation of effectiveness and likability of gender-role congruent and gender-role incongruent leaders. *Sex Roles, 30*, 109–119.

Ruble, D. N. & Martin, C. L. (1998). Gender development. In W. Damon (Ed.), *Handbook of child psychology* (pp. 933–1016). New York: Wiley.

Scharrer, E. (2004). Virtual violence: Gender and aggression in video game advertisements. *Mass Communication and Society, 7*, 393–412.

Shade, L. R. (2003). Review essay: Gender and the internet. *Canadian Journal of Communication, 28,* 359–364.

Sirin, S. R., McCreary, D. R., & Mahalik, J. R. (2004). Differential reactions to men and women's gender role transgressions: Perceptions of social status, sexual orientation, and value dissimilarity. *Journal of Men's Studies, 12,* 119–132.

Skitka, L. J. & Maslach, C. (1996). Gender as schematic category: A role construct approach. *Social Behavior and Personality, 24,* 53–74.

Slouka, M. (1995). *War of the worlds: Cyberspace and the high-tech assault on reality.* New York: Basic Books.

Spence, J. T. & Helmreich, R. L. (1978). *Masculinity & femininity: Their psychological dimensions, correlates, and antecedents.* Austin, TX: University of Texas Press.

Stone, A. R. (1995). *The war of desire and technology at the close of the Mechanical Age.* Cambridge, MA: MIT Press.

Turkle, S. (1995). *Life on the screen: Identity in the age of the internet.* New York: Simon & Schuster.

Turner, R. H. (1990). Role change. *Annual Review of Sociology, 16,* 87–110.

Valkenburg, P. & Peter, J. (2008). Adolescents' identity experiments on the internet. *Communication Research, 35,* 208–231.

Van Gelder, L. (1991). The strange case of the electronic lover. In C. Dunlop & R. Kling (Eds.), *Computerization and controversy: Value conflicts and social choices* (pp. 364–375). Boston, MA: Academic.

Walther, J. B. (1996). Computer-mediated communication: Impersonal, interpersonal, and hyperpersonal interaction. *Communication Research, 23,* 1–43.

Walther, J. B., Loh, T., & Granka, L. (2005). Let me count the ways: The interchange of verbal and nonverbal cues in computer-mediated and face-to-face affinity. *Journal of Language and Social Psychology, 24,* 36–65.

White, P. (2008). *MMOGData: Charts,* from (http://mmogdata.voig.com/).

Williams, D., Yee, N., & Caplan, S. (2008). Who plays, how much, and why? A behavioral player census of a virtual world. *Journal of Computer Mediated Communication, 13,* 993–1018.

Williams, D., Consalvo, M., Caplan, S., & Yee, N. (in press). Looking for Gender (LFG): Gender roles and behaviors among online gamers. *Journal of Communication* 733–758.

Wood, W. & Eagly, A. H. (2002). A cross-cultural analysis of the behavior of women and men: Implications for the origins of sex differences. *Psychological Bulletin, 128,* 699–727.

Yee, N. (2007). Motivations of play in online games. *CyberPsychology and Behavior, 9,* 772–775.

Zinman, A. & Donath, J. (2007). Is Britney Spears spam? In *CEAS 2007 – Fourth Conference on email and anti-spam* (vol. 7), Mountain View, CA.

Chapter 14
Virtual Doppelgangers: Psychological Effects of Avatars Who Ignore Their Owners

Jeremy N. Bailenson and Kathryn Y. Segovia

Imagine a world where multiple versions of yourself exist. These other versions of you may look like you but need not behave like you. Famous authors and screenwriters have depicted this type of scenario multiple times in movies and literary works. For example, in the film *Being John Malkovich,* the actor Malkovich wakes up in a restaurant and looks across the table (Jonze 1999). There is a woman wearing a revealing evening dress, but as his gaze pans up, he is stunned to see his own head on top of the voluptuous female form. Seconds later, a waiter walks by and is also wearing his head. His psychological response is predictably dire, and the terror only increases as he pans across the room and realizes that every single person in the restaurant, ranging from jazz singers to midgets, is wearing his head. He is literally trapped in a room full of identical twins behaving independently of his own intentions and actions. In Edgar Allan Poe's *William Wilson*, the main character William meets another boy who shares his name (Poe 1839). Throughout the story, William's double changes to act and look more like William. William grows frustrated with his double who is constantly mimicking him and giving him unsolicited advice and eventually stabs his double to death. Additionally, in a powerful scene in William Gibson's *Neuromancer* (1984), one of the main characters, Riviera, forces a character named Molly to witness a hologram of herself perform a number of unspeakable acts. Molly's physical self observes the interaction, but she cannot control the actions of the other version of herself.

The above scenarios may seem like situations that would only be possible in science fiction, but if we take a close look at today's digital media, we find that virtual versions of ourselves exist in many different places.

J.N. Bailenson and K.Y. Segovia
Stanford University
e-mails: bailenson@gmail.com; kathrynyr@gmail.com

W.S. Bainbridge (ed.), *Online Worlds: Convergence of the Real and the Virtual,*
Human-Computer Interaction Series, DOI 10.1007/978-1-84882-825-4_14,
© Springer-Verlag London Limited 2010

Doppelgangers

Doppelganger is the term that we will use throughout this chapter to refer to virtual versions of the self. Doppelganger is derived from the German language and is defined as any double or look-alike of a person. Throughout history, several famous individuals have reported seeing their doppelganger. For example, in 1860 as the U.S. presidential election results were rolling in, Abraham Lincoln reported seeing two versions of himself in the reflection of a long piece of glass – one version's face much paler than the other. After sharing this encounter with his wife, she supposedly predicted that the image of the doppelganger signified that Abraham would be elected to a second term as president but that he would not survive the second term (Sandburg 1954).

A loose definition of digital doppelgangers exists in online and video games. In the Massively Multiplayer Online games (MMOs), which are described in a number of chapters in this volume, players get to design the appearance of their avatar that moves through the 3D virtual game. In many of these games, there are very few constraints for avatar creation and with the drag of a slider bar players can control their identity – height, weight, age, and even species.

We also see avatars in traditional console video games. For example, players of the Nintendo Wii can design a virtual representation ("mii") that resembles them on many dimensions (Ratan et al. 2007). The Play Station skateboarding video game, *Tony Hawk's Underground 2 Remix*, also allows players to personalize their avatars by uploading photographs of their own face to the game console (Lum 2005). After the photographs are mapped onto the face of a generic character, players can then control their virtual representation just as any other generic video game character.

In the previous examples, users could create and control avatars that looked like them. However, in many cases, users are not in control of their look-alike avatars; sometimes other players or algorithms take control. This is the case in which avatars become doppelgangers. In the online video game *World of Warcraft* (Morhaime 2009), for example, players' avatars can be "mind-controlled" by other players. In this situation, the player loses all control of his/her personal avatar and must watch for several seconds while his/her avatar is manipulated by another player – often with intentions of sabotage. We also see players' avatars acting autonomously in some sports video games. In hockey and football games, the player can only control one player at a time. When a player relinquishes control of one avatar to take control of another, he/she passes the control of the first avatar to a computer algorithm. The avatar is still part of the player's team, but is autonomously controlled. In another *World of Warcraft* example, some players possess pets that are semi-autonomous avatars. These pets mostly operate under the control of the player, but on occasion the pet will be sent on a mission where it must act autonomously. A computer algorithm guides the behavior of the pet during these missions while the player merely observes (not controls) the pet's behavior. In sum, today's video games allow for character building of characters, which look like the user, and also for algorithms to "take over" the behavior of the user.

In the commercial world, digital doppelgangers can also be designed to look strikingly similar to the self. Through the use of digital photographs and

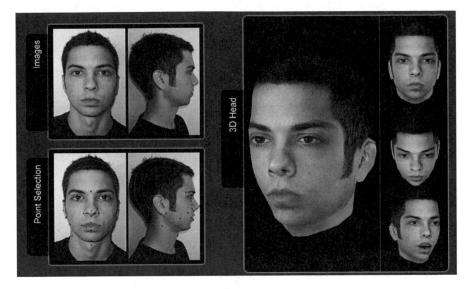

Fig. 14.1 Images and modeling techniques used in creating three-dimensional heads

head-modeling software, an individual's visage may be replicated. In one commercial example, Bruce Willis created multiple versions of himself in the online game *Second Life* to advertise his movie *Die Hard* (Kingdon 2007). In a recent popcorn commercial, an ad agency created a virtual version of the late Orville Redenbacher using old photographs (Advertising Age 2007). The virtual Orville was then portrayed as wearing a slim, new MP3 player – something the real Orville Redenbacher mostly likely had never done in his lifetime.

Scholars in the Virtual Human Interaction Lab at Stanford University have been using similar modeling techniques to create digital doppelgangers for research purposes for the past decade. Figure 14.1 depicts an example of how digital doppelgangers are developed from photographs (Bailenson et al. 2004, 2008). The top left panel shows two photographs of a person, and the bottom left shows the anchor points manually placed on the photographs with photogrammetric software. The right panel shows the resulting 3D head, which is a mesh model with a texture wrapped around it. Although this transference is not flawless, it creates relatively accurate models of the human form.

Theoretical Underpinnings

As doppelgangers that behave autonomously, that is, independent of the users they were modeled after, become increasingly present in new forms of media, scholars in the field need to leverage traditional psychological theories to understand how humans may be affected by the seemingly bizarre concept of being confronted by a virtual version of one's self. Below, we outline several relevant theories from the past 50 years.

Social cognitive theory, originally known as social learning theory, posits that people learn by observing the behavior of models (Bandura 1977, 2001). Several factors, including the similarity of the model, the observer's perceived ability to perform the behavior, and the rewards and punishments associated with that behavior, predict the likelihood of the observer performing the modeled action. In the physical world, it can be quite difficult to find a model that fits all of these factors. However, using digital media we can utilize and manipulate virtual humans, even digital doppelgangers to successfully fulfill these criteria.

Identification has been shown to increase the likelihood of performing learned behaviors (Bandura 2001; Bandura and Huston 1961). Observers must feel that the model is similar enough to them that they are able to experience the same outcomes. Similarity may be based on physical traits, personality variables, or shared beliefs and attitudes (Stotland 1969). Indeed, the likelihood of learning increases when models are of the same sex (Andsager et al. 2006), race (Ito et al. 2008), or skill level (Meichengaum 1971), as well as when models demonstrate similar opinions (Hilmert et al. 2006) or previous behaviors (Andsager et al. 2006).

In creating digital doppelgangers, it goes without saying that social scientists produce models that possess a very high level of physical resemblance to their user. Digital doppelgangers are the richest possible model of the self that we have access to today, and thus they have great potential to serve as powerful models in Bandura's social cognitive theory.

Media richness theory, also known as information richness theory, was developed by Daft and Lengel (1984). In this theory, a medium's richness is generally defined by its ability to reproduce the information sent over it. But more specifically, Daft, Lengel, and Trevino (1987) describe media richness based on four criteria: (1) capacity for immediate feedback, (2) capacity to transmit multiple cues such as graphic symbols or human gestures, (3) language variety, including numbers and natural language, and (4) capacity of the medium to have a personal focus.

Under these criteria, doppelgangers in immersive virtual environments are very rich forms of media. Immersive virtual environment technology (IVET) offers dynamic user-specific viewpoints and a wider field of view than other forms of two-dimensional media (Blascovich et al. 2002). In addition, newer IVET systems are delivering more forms of perceptual detail. Audio technology is being used to produce three-dimensional sound; haptic devices permit virtual touch (Tan et al. 1994), a scent collar emits virtual scent (Nakamoto and Minh 2007), and a haptic interface puts pressure on the tongue to enhance virtual taste (Iwata et al. 2004).

But regardless of whether a user is able to interact with his/her doppelganger in an immersive virtual environment, the personalized avatar is a rich form of media in its own right, as it maximizes more than any other existing medium, the "personal focus" parameter.

The self-referential encoding (SRE) effect states that individuals learn and remember information better when it is related to the self. Rogers and colleagues (1977) proposed that information relating to the self would be remembered and learned better because it would be preferentially encoded and organized above other types of information. In fact, in the original experiment conducted in 1977,

Rogers and colleagues found that adjectives were twice as likely to be recalled correctly when they were presented in a self-referential frame (Does this adjective describe you?) versus when they were presented in a semantic frame (Does this adjective mean the same as X?). Furthermore, Symons and Johnson (1997) conducted a meta-analysis involving 129 studies of self-referential encoding effects where they confirmed the expected SRE effect.

In addition, recent functional magnetic resonance imaging work reveals that self-referential information may even be processed using unique structures in the human brain. Heatherton et al. (2004) found that the level of activity in the medial prefrontal cortex during self-referential judgments predicted which items would be remembered by the participant in a surprise memory test. Thus, not only does activity in certain regions of the brain track with self-referential processing, but this activity also contributes to the formation of self-referential memories.

In consideration of the SRE effect literature, the human brain may preferentially process information that our doppelgangers convey to us over information that is presented to us via other humans/avatars. This is an especially important concept when it comes to considering autonomous doppelgangers, as the findings suggest that autonomous avatars that merely look like their users (even if they do not act like their user or share similar beliefs with their user) will activate preferential information encoding.

Self-perception theory (SPT) was developed by psychologist Daryl Bem (1972). SPT posits that humans develop their attitudes by observing their own behavior and concluding what attitudes must have caused them. The theory is somewhat counter-intuitive in that common sense would tell us that attitudes come prior to behaviors, but many studies have produced data that support this theory. For example, several studies have shown that emotions can be derived from behaviors. Such emotions as liking, disliking, happiness, and anger were induced by overt behaviors that had been manipulated by research assistants (Larid 2007).

For example, Frank and Gilovich (1988) conducted a study in which they found that participants who wore black uniforms behaved more aggressively than partici-pants in white uniforms. According to Frank and Gilovich, wearing a black uniform is a behavior that the participants used to infer their own dispositions – "Just as observers see those in black uniforms as tough, mean, and aggressive, so too does the person wearing that uniform" (1988: 83). The participants then adhere to this new identity by behaving more aggressively.

Recently, similar effects have been replicated in digital environments. Merola and colleagues discovered that users given doppelgangers in a black robe expressed a higher desire to commit antisocial behaviors than users given doppelgangers in white robes (Merola et al. 2006). Nick Yee has taken such work one step further and developed a hypothesis that he terms the Proteus Effect (Yee and Bailenson 2007). The Proteus Effect predicts that an individual's behavior conforms to their digital self-representation independent of how others perceive them. For example, subjects who occupy attractive (compared to unattractive or average attractive) avatars behave more socially, and taller avatars negotiate more confidently than shorter avatars. More surprisingly, the confidence from height and socialness from attractiveness extends outside the virtual world to subsequent face-to-face interactions (Yee et al. 2009; Yee and Bailenson Forthcoming). A recent study by Jung and colleagues in 2008 extended this work to show that the same pattern holds for gender; regardless of actual gender, participants embodied by male avatars gestured more masculinely than those in female avatars in terms of interpersonal distance (Jung and McLaughlin 2008). In sum, the self-referencing process does extend to avatars.

Experimenting with Doppelgangers

Now we turn to a number of recent experiments that have explored the question of what happens when individuals are exposed to their autonomous doppelgangers. As we see from the above sections, the notion of seeing oneself from the third person is possible with today's digital media; moreover, existing psychological theory provides predictions for this line of work. We focus on three different research areas: health communication, marketing, and false memories. Figure 14.2 (Panels 2–5) provides screenshots of these various scenarios. Panel 1 on the left shows a participant wearing the head mounted display or HMD (A) where cameras (C) tracked the LED (B) on the user's head to update the scene based on head rotations and translations.

All experiments discussed were run at Stanford's Virtual Human Interaction Lab, and the general research paradigm was similar for all studies reviewed. For an experimental "pretest," all participants visited the lab well in advance of their experimental session, where research assistants photographed the front and profile of the participants' faces. Then, research assistants produced three-dimensional models of each participant's face. When the participants returned to the lab, they interacted

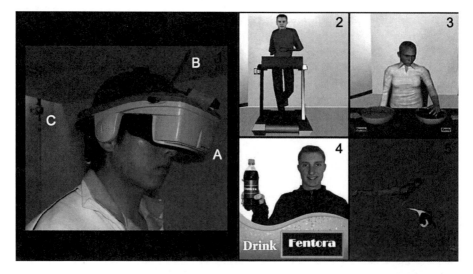

Fig. 14.2 Images from each of the experimental studies

with their digital doppelganger in a virtual environment. We then measured their behavioral, self-report, and memory reactions to their digital doppelganger.

Social cognitive theory is often utilized to understand and design treatments and campaigns for health behavior change. IVET and digital doppelgangers enable novel explorations of health behavior modeling. Over the past three years, Jesse Fox has explored how humans might learn healthy behaviors from their doppelgangers. For example, in one study (Fox and Bailenson 2009), on arriving in the lab, participants were taught a simple arm exercise. Once the participant had successfully learned the exercise, he/she was immersed into one of three virtual environments depending on condition (see Panel 2 of Fig. 14.2).

Participants who were randomly assigned to the *no doppelganger* condition were immersed in an environment that portrayed a small room but no virtual human. Participants assigned to the *changing doppelganger* condition saw their doppelganger from the third person perspective just as participants who were randomly assigned to the unchanging doppelganger condition. However, the changing doppelganger was programmed to gradually gain weight while the participant idled and gradually lose weight while the participant exercised in the physical world. Participants in the *unchanging doppelganger* viewed a doppelganger that remained the same weight regardless of the participant's behavior.

In the virtual environment, participants were instructed to perform three sets of 12 arm exercises. Next, the experimenter instructed them to stand still for two minutes, and finally they were told they could stay in the virtual environment and exercise or could chose to end the experiment. The number of exercise repetitions that the participant completed in the voluntary phase were counted and recorded as the dependent variable.

Data analysis revealed that participants in the changing doppelganger condition completed significantly more voluntary exercises than participants in either the unchanging doppelganger or no doppelganger conditions. These findings suggest that doppelgangers can show the rewards of exercise and can change behavior as a result.

However, it could be the case that any demonstration of cause and effect could cause more exercise behavior (i.e., the virtual representation did not need to look like the self). In a follow-up study, Fox and Bailenson (2009) compared the effects of a doppelganger that looks like the self with a doppelganger of another person. They found that participants who viewed the doppelganger of the self exercised significantly more than those participants who saw the doppelganger of another person. Thus, there is evidence that self-identification is a driving factor behind the results.

In the final study of the series (Fox and Bailenson 2009), participants were exposed to either a doppelganger of the self-running on a treadmill, a doppelganger of another running on a treadmill, or a doppelganger of the self-loitering. Instead of measuring exercise activity immediately following the treatment in the laboratory, participants in this study were asked 24 h later to reflect on their physical activity since the study and complete a standard questionnaire on physical activity. Data analysis revealed that participants in the doppelganger of the self condition performed significantly more exercise than participants in the other two conditions.

In addition to exercise, Fox and colleagues also examined eating behavior (Fox et al. 2009). Participants saw their digital doppelgangers from a third-person perspective eat either chocolate candy or baby carrots for a couple of minutes and then switch to eat from the other bowl of food, as depicted in Panel 3 of Fig. 14.2. After exiting the virtual environment, participants filled out several different questionnaires beside a bowl of chocolate candy. The participants were told that they could eat as many chocolates as they liked while they completed the surveys. Research assistants secretly recorded how many chocolates each participant ate. Of participants who were "high presence," that is, were highly engaged in the simulation, males and females responded differently to the stimulus. Men displayed stereotypical gendered behavior and ate more candy, whereas women also displayed gendered behavior and suppressed the urge to eat and ate less candy.

Self-endorsement, or advertisements that portray potential consumers using products, is a novel marketing strategy of advertising made possible by digital doppelgangers. Self-referential encoding effect has been used to explain the effects of self-endorsement. Ahn and Bailenson (2008) compared the effects of self-endorsement and unfamiliar other endorsement on the viewers of soft drink advertisements.

In the study, two independent variables were manipulated and compared within the context of a soft drink advertisement. Identity served as the first independent variable with two values: self versus other. Medium served as the second independent variable with two values: photo versus text. Creating the photo self-endorsement stimulus involved replacing the celebrity or typical consumer endorser's photograph in an online advertisement with a two-dimensional image of the self's doppelganger. The photo other-endorsement stimulus was created by replacing the celebrity or typical consumer endorser's photograph with a two-dimensional image of the doppelganger of an unfamiliar same sex participant in the study, as depicted in Panel 4 of Fig. 14.2. The text self-endorsement was created by drafting a text ad that used the second person pronoun "you." The same ad was used for the text other-endorsement condition, except that the second-person pronouns were changed to third-person pronouns.

Each participant saw one soft drink ad that was representative of each of the four conditions: self-photo, self-text, other photo, other text. The main effect of identity was statistically significant. The self-endorsement condition evoked more positive ratings of the soft drinks than the other-endorsement condition. In addition, when participants were asked to report which soft drink they felt the highest level of association with, participants reported that they felt the greatest level of association with which ever soft drink was in the photo self-endorsement condition. These findings reveal that photo self-endorsement triggered the highest level of self-referencing when compared with all other conditions. In sum, doppelgangers are powerful marketing agents and can be used in advertisements to create favorable brand impressions among consumers.

In a recent study (Segovia and Bailenson in press), the authors of this chapter explored how human memory could be affected by doppelgangers. We aimed to answer the question of whether doppelgangers could induce false memories in their users and hypothesized that rich media (such as doppelgangers) would be more likely to induce false memories than less rich media.

Approximately 60 pre-school and elementary children visited the lab for two different sessions. In the first session, each child was introduced to a short narrative that described him/her participating in a completely fabricated and implausible event (i.e., swimming with two orca whales). The child was immediately questioned in the baseline interview about his/her memory of the event (i.e., Do you remember swimming with the orca whales?). Next, the child was exposed to one of four different memory prompt conditions: *idle, mental imagery, doppelganger of another, doppelganger of self.* In the idle condition, the child was instructed to sit and wait for a few minutes before the next interview. Children in the mental imagery condition were instructed to imagine swimming with the whales for a few minutes. Children in the doppelganger conditions were immersed in a virtual reality environment where they either saw another child swimming with the orca whales or a virtual representation of themselves swimming with the orca whales, respectively (Panel 5 of Fig. 14.2). Following the treatment, each child was questioned about his/her memory of the event. About 1 week later, all of the children returned to the lab to be interviewed one more time about their memory of the event.

The children's memories were coded based on their completeness ranging from no false memory to a complete false memory (where children actually recalled swimming with the orca whales in the physical world). Data analysis revealed that while the pre-school children were equally likely to form false memories across all memory prompt conditions, elementary children were more likely to form false memories in the mental imagery and doppelganger of the self-conditions when compared with the idle condition. These results give support to our claim that as the media richness of the prompt increases, the more difficult it becomes to distinguish between an actual memory elicited by a physical world event and a false memory elicited by mental image or doppelganger.

We believe that these results are uniquely interesting because they reveal that mental imagery (which must be actively initiated by the participant) and IVET doppelganger of the self-simulations (which can be completely controlled by a third party) are both powerful in eliciting false memories in children. In other words, by viewing an IVET simulation of the self, a passive observer can develop false memories just as easily as a participant using cognitive energy to create mental images. This finding suggests that third parties may be able to elicit false memories without the consent or mental effort of an individual.

Implications and Future Directions

Research on doppelgangers, especially autonomous doppelgangers, highlights several ethical considerations. As can be seen in the Orville Redenbacher example, it is possible for one's digital doppelganger to exist (and be manipulated) long after the physical self has died. One provocative question that arises is who should possess ownership of digital doppelgangers and to what extent are manipulations ethically acceptable? Currently, the artists who construct doppelgangers have nearly unlimited freedom in what animations and edits they create. In the future, some celebrities may wish to add clauses to their legal contracts that forbid or at least restrict the development of digital doppelgangers. On the other hand, other individuals may wish to encourage the development and distribution of their digital doppelgangers in order to further their legacy.

Digital doppelgangers have many practical applications in social psychology and education. For example, digital doppelgangers and IVET may be powerful tools for teaching individuals about the negative impact of their carbon footprints. First, using digital doppelgangers, experimenters and educators can use digital representations of the student to serve as the model. Because of high levels of similarity with the student, digital doppelgangers (as we have shown above) are powerful models. Second, using IVET and digital doppelgangers, educators and researchers can benefit from the ability to transform space, time, and physical laws. Climate change literacy studies would examine the benefits of compressing time to show cumulative environmental damage or making carbon footprints of supermarket products visible. Climate change education is one example, but IVET and digital doppelgangers may be effective tools for educators and social scientists in other topic areas as well.

Autonomous digital doppelgangers are a theoretically and ethically interesting concept. As new media continue to develop and become more personalized, we may face digital doppelganger issues more frequently. These digital representations will help us refine psychological theories and pose interesting questions in their own right.

Acknowledgments   The authors thank Sun Joo Ahn, Jesse Fox, James Scarborough, and Nick Yee for their helpful comments on this chapter. The current work was partially supported by National Science Foundation (NSF) Grant 0527377. In addition, the Stanford Graduate Fellowship supported Kathryn Segovia during her contribution to this research.

References

Advertising Age. (2007). *Bring out your dead: Crispin resurrects Orville Redenbacher.* Retrieved May 4, 2009, from http://adage.com/adages/post?article_id = 114344

Ahn, S. J., & Bailenson, J. N. (2008). *Self-endorsing versus other-endorsing in virtual environments: The effect on brand preference.* Unpublished manuscript. Stanford, CA: Stanford University.

Andsager, J. L., Bemker, V., Choi, H.-L., & Torwel, V. (2006). Perceived similarity of exemplar traits and behavior: Effects on message evaluation. *Communication Research, 33,* 3–18.

Bailenson, J. N., Beall, A. C., Blascovich, J., & Rex, C. (2004). Examining virtual busts: Are photogrammetrically-generated head models effective for person identification? *Presence: Tele-Operators and Virtual Environments, 13*(4), 416–427.

Bailenson, J. N., Blascovich, J., & Guadagno, R. E. (2008). Self-representations in immersive virtual environments. *Journal of Applied Social Psychology, 38*(11), 2673–2690.

Bandura, A. (1977). *Social learning theory.* Englewood Cliffs, NJ: Prentice-Hall.

Bandura, A. (2001). Social cognitive theory of mass communication. *Media Psychology, 3,* 265–299.

Bandura, A., & Huston, A. C. (1961). Identification as a process of incidental learning. *Journal of Abnormal & Social Psychology, 63,* 311–318.

Bem, D. (1972). Self perception theory. In L. Berkowitz (Ed.), *Advances in experimental social psychology Volume 6*, New York: Academic.

Blascovich, J., Loomis, J., Beall, A. C., Swinth, K. R., Hoyt, C. L., & Bailenson, J. N. (2002). Immersive virtual environment technology as a methodological tool for social psychology. *Psychological Inquiry, 2*, 103–124.

Daft, R. L., & Lengel, R. H. (1984). Information richness: A new approach to managerial information processing and organization design. In B. Staw & L.L. Cummings (Eds.), *Research in organizational behavior*, (pp. 191–233). Greenwich, CT: JAI Press.

Daft, R. L., Lengel, R. H., & Trevino, L. K. (1987). Message equivocality, media selection, and manager performance: Implications for information systems. *MIS Quarterly, 11*, 354–366.

Fox, J., & Bailenson, J. N. (2009). Virtual self-modeling: The effects of vicarious reinforcement and identification on exercise behaviors. *Media Psychology, 12*, 1–25.

Fox, J., Bailenson, J. N., & Binney, J. (2009). Virtual experiences, physical behaviors: The effect of presence on imitation of an eating avatar. *PRESENCE: Teleoperators & Virtual Environments, 18*(4), 294–303.

Frank, R. H., & Gilovich, T. (1988). The dark side of self and social perceptions: Black uniforms and aggression in professional sports. *Journal of Personality and Social Psychology, 54*, 74–85.

Gibson, W. (1984). *Neuromancer*. New York: Penguin Putnam.

Heatherton, T. F., Macrae, C. N., & Kelley, W. M. (2004). What the social brain sciences can tell us about the self. *Current Directions in Psychological Science, 13*(5), 190–193.

Hilmert, C. J., Kulik, J. A., & Christenfeld, N. J. S. (2006). Positive and negative opinion modeling: The influence of another's similarity and dissimilarity. *Journal of Personality & Social Psychology, 90*, 440–452.

Ito, K. E., Kalyanaraman, S., Brown, J. D., & Miller, W. C. (2008). Factors affecting avatar use in a STI prevention CD-ROM. *Journal of Adolescent Health, 42*, S19.

Iwata, H., Yano, H., Uemura, T., & Moriya, T. (2004). *Food texture display*. Presented at the 12th International Symposium on Haptic Interfaces for Virtual Environment and Teleoperator Systems (HAPTICS'04), March 27–28, Chicago, IL.

Jonze, S. (Director). (1999). *Being John Malkovich* [Motion picture]. United States: Gramercy Pictures.

Jung, Y., & McLaughlin, M. (2008). *Role enactment based on gender stereotypes in interactive media: Effects of role play on the management of self-concept and physical distance in virtual reality environments*. Presented at the 58th Annual International Communication Association Conference, May 22–26, Montreal, Canada.

Kingdon, M. (2007). *Second Life*. Linden Lab.

Larid, J. D. (2007). *Feelings: The perception of self*. New York: Oxford University Press.

Lum, K. (2005). *Tony Hawk's Underground 2 Remix*. Activision.

Meichengaum, D. H. (1971). Examination of model characteristics in reducing avoidance behavior. *Journal of Personality & Social Psychology, 17*, 298–307.

Merola, N., Pena, J., & Hancock, J. (2006). *Avatar color and social identity effects: On attitudes and group dynamics in virtual realities*. Presented at the 56th Annual International Communication Association Conference, June 19–23, Dresden, Germany.

Morhaime, M. (2009). *World of Warcraft*. Blizzard Entertainment.

Nakamoto, T., & Minh, H.P.D. (2007). *Improvement of olfactory display using solenoid valves*. Presented at the Virtual Reality Conference, March 14–17, Charlotte, NC.

Poe, E. A. (1839). *William Wilson*, from (http://xroads.virginia.edu/~HYPER/POE/w_wilson.html).

Ratan, R., Santa Cruz, M., & Vorderer, P. (2007). *Multitasking, presence and self-presence on the Wii*. Presented at the 10th Annual International Workshop on Presence, October 25–27, Barcelona, Spain.

Rogers, T. B., Kuiper, N. A., & Kirker, S. (1977). Self-reference and the encoding of personal information. *Journal of Personality and Social Psychology, 35*, 677–688.

Sandburg, C. (1954). *Abraham Lincoln: The Prairie years and the war years*. Orlando, FL: Harcourt.

Segovia, K. Y., & Bailenson, J. N. (In press). *Virtually true: Children's acquisition of false memories in virtual reality. Media Psychology.*

Stotland, E. (1969). Exploratory investigations of empathy. In L. Berkowitz (Ed.), *Advances in experimental social psychology*, (pp. 274–314). New York: Academic.

Symons, C. S., & Johnson, B. T. (1997). The self-reference effect in memory: A meta-analysis. *Psychological Bulletin, 121*(3), 371–394.

Tan, H. Z., Srinivasan, M., Eberman, B., & Cheng, B. (1994). *Human factors for the design of force-reflecting haptic interfaces.* Presented at the ASME Dynamic Systems and Control Division, November 6–11, Chicago, IL.

Yee, N., & Bailenson, J. N. (2007). The Proteus effect: Self transformations in virtual reality. *Human Communication Research, 33*, 271–290.

Yee, N. & Bailenson, J.N. (2009). The difference between being and seeing: The relative contribution of self perception and priming to behavioral changes via digital self-representation. Media Psychology, *12*(2), 195–209.

Yee, N., Bailenson, J. N., & Ducheneaut, N. (2009). The Proteus effect: Implications of transformed digital self-representation on online and offline behavior. *Communication Research, 36*(2), 285–312.

Chapter 15
Speaking in Character: Voice Communication in Virtual Worlds

Greg Wadley and Martin R. Gibbs

While some early experimental virtual environments offered voice communication, for many years Internet-based virtual worlds (VWs) offered only typed text messaging. Following mass uptake of broadband Internet and the availability of Voice over Internet Protocol (VOIP) services, vendors are beginning to add voice channels to their VWs. Speech is a mode of communication that would seem to offer many advantages over text, yet its introduction into VWs has been criticized by many users and commentators.

VWs have had their greatest success as recreational technologies, but there is renewed interest in utilizing them for computer-supported collaborative work such as online meetings and teaching. *Second Life's* vendor is actively promoting to business and education, while several new systems aimed explicitly at workplace use have been released: a prominent example is Sun's *Wonderland*, which offers voice as a primary modality. VWs can provide an inexpensive platform for collaboration between geographically dispersed users: an important consideration in a time of environmental and economic crisis.

Over the past 5 years, we have studied the implications of introducing voice communication systems to VWs. We have identified issues related to identity and impression management, the multiplicity of conversation contexts, and technical problems caused by the analog nature of voice, including the need to consider volume. Furthermore, different groups of users are using VWs for very different purposes: They have different requirements and a single modality may not suit all.

G. Wadley and M.R. Gibbs
Department of Information Systems, The University of Melbourne
Parkville VIC 3010
e-mails: greg.wadley@unimelb.edu.au; martin.gibbs@unimelb.edu.au

W.S. Bainbridge (ed.), *Online Worlds: Convergence of the Real and the Virtual*,
Human-Computer Interaction Series, DOI 10.1007/978-1-84882-825-4_15,
© Springer-Verlag London Limited 2010

Comparing Media and Contexts

Research outside the context of virtual worlds can shed some light on how communicating using voice and text compares. The "media richness" paradigm (Short et al. 1976; Daft and Lengel 1986) supposed that the richer a communication medium – the more social presence it conveys – the more effectively it would substitute for face-to-face interaction. However, people do not always choose the richer medium, and alternative analyses have discovered other influences on media choice and use. The social-influence (Fulk et al. 1990) and critical-mass (Markus 1990) frameworks point to the influence of collaborators. Media synchronicity theory (Dennis and Valacich 1999) highlights media's differing abilities to support feedback, symbol variety, parallelism, rehearsability, and reprocessability. Comparing voice-over-IP with instant messaging, Lober et al. (2007) found that text scaled better with group size. Other researchers have focused on use of a collection of media (Watson-Manheim and Belanger 2007).

Carlson and Zmud (1999) argued that communication richness depends on users' prior experience with the medium and with each other. Walther (1992) argued that people can be motivated to create rich communication using lean media. Goby (2006) found different preferences for online or face-to-face interaction among different personality types. Other research showed that people wishing to engage in "impression management" (Carlson et al. 2004), or who are shy (Stritzke et al. 2004), might choose text for its low social presence.

It would be a category error to treat VWs as communication media in the sense that one could, say, compare *World of Warcraft* to email. VW technologies simulate a three-dimensional Euclidean space, in which users move and orient their embodied representation as they would in physical space (Aarseth 2007). This is intended to enable an intuitive mutual awareness and articulation of collaboration (Benford et al. 1994) and allows the simulation of some aspects of offline interaction, such as how people position and orient themselves when conversing (Yee et al. 2007). However, studies of the use of virtual environments have highlighted the low fidelity of the simulation. For example, diminished visual cues create problems for conversational turn-taking (Nilsson et al. 2002) and reference to objects (Hindmarsh et al. 2001).

While avatars offer a limited body language, most collaborators need to exchange text or voice messages. Following the 3D metaphor, the rules of message transmission can be based on avatar location. For example, messages might be sent only to users whose avatars are near the sender's avatar, simulating the transmission of sound in air and enabling "a natural intuition about mutual audibility" (Smith et al. 2002). We call this *proximity transmission*. Alternatively, a VW can allow conversation between users at arbitrary virtual locations, simulating in effect the use of telecommunication devices within the virtual space (Wadley et al. 2005). For brevity, we call this *radio transmission*. So, while VWs are in one sense telecommunications media, they are unique in that they locate users within a 3D space and provide them with "virtual media" through which they communicate within the space. This complexity raises a number of issues for inquiry. We might ask what forms the simulated media might take: They are often simulations of familiar physical-world media, but could take arbitrary forms. We can observe virtual media in use and compare their relative efficacy in different situations, as do the studies reported here.

In particular, we can consider the need for users to manage multiple conversation contexts, given that they are by necessity located in both virtual and physical spaces. Researchers studying technology-in-use have focused increasingly on the context in which use happens. This is in part a recognition that people's actions are influenced by where they are and who is around them. It is also a reaction to the inexorable movement of computers from the workplace desktop into social and domestic spaces (Howard et al. 2007). Online and offline activities and identities intertwine, and people communicating through computers multitask within physical and virtual contexts (Aarsand 2008).

Jones (2002) found that IRC users engage in multiple simultaneous conversations and pay careful attention to who can read which utterances: thus CMC offers "different sets of 'mutual monitoring possibilities' ... different ways in which they allow us to be present to one another and to be aware of other peoples' presence" (Jones 2002: 8). Users also control whether physically colocated people can see conversations, by tilting their screen or temporarily hiding communication windows behind other applications. For text conversations, "the 'muting' of the aural mode allows them to carry on on-line conversations, which are inaccessible to others who are physically co-present" (Jones 2002: 12).

Eavesdropping was a common concern in the days of party-line telephony (Fischer 1994). Mobile phone users use text instead of voice to avoid eavesdropping in public places (Faulkner and Culwin 2004). For example, teenagers seeking privacy (Davie et al. 2004), and employees in meetings (Norman 2004) choose SMS.

Identity is an important issue in virtual worlds and impacts communication. Many recreational VWs are designed so that users play a character in a fictional universe and are represented visually as such to other users. There is debate over whether users play this character as would an actor in a film, or merely operate the avatar as though it were a puppet while "playing themselves" in their conversations with other users. Some people value the ability that anonymity in virtual environments gives them to present a different gender, age, or other demographic property. But a person's voice transmits information such as their age, gender, class, race, and education level. Thus, it has been argued, introducing voice communication into a virtual world interferes with role-play and breaks one of the fundamental purposes for being in the world (Bartle 2003).

Many commentators and researchers differentiate two approaches to using a VW: *immersionists* who use it to play a fictitious character, and *augmentationists* who project their offline identity to collaborators whose identities are known (Boellstorff 2008). The former type of use can be considered identity exploration of the kind studied in older Internet applications (e.g., Turkle 1995); the latter is preferred in many business and education scenarios.

In some MMORPGs, such as *World of Warcraft*, voice has been appropriated enthusiastically and is mandatory in many guilds. Williams et al. (2007) demonstrated benefits of using voice for small groups engaged in ongoing collaborative play in WoW. However, controversy accompanied the introduction of voice into *Second Life*, a system that discourages disclosure of real identity, and a year later many SL users do not use voice. The intersection of communication and identity that occurs within virtual worlds is of academic interest, but it is especially important to designers implementing communication modalities within VWs.

Voice in Virtual Worlds

The authors have conducted several studies of voice communication in 3D environments (Gibbs et al. 2004, 2006; Wadley et al. 2007; Wadley 2008).

Our study of play in the Xbox Live network showed that voice introduces both benefits and problems for players of fast-paced team shooter games (Gibbs et al. 2004). Benefits include better coordination of groups, greater social presence of fellow players, and the freeing up of hands for controlling other input devices. Problems include channel congestion, greater opportunity for deliberate or accidental transmission of noise, inability to match voices with avatars, inability to know who might be listening to a transmission, and an unwillingness by some to use voice with strangers online. Speech can be heard by people physically colocated with users such as family members or coworkers, and conversely sound from the user's surroundings, such as household noise, may be transmitted into the game, potentially breaching privacy.

Subsequently, we studied use of an experimental system for voice communication in team first-person shooter (FPS) games that emulated the transmission of sound in air (Gibbs et al. 2006). Before then, voice implementations for games had utilized a radio metaphor (see Wadley et al. (2005) for a discussion of voice metaphors). When using SpatialVoice, only team members who were nearby could hear each other; furthermore, enemy players could hear if they were close. We found that while this represented a restriction over the radio configuration of all hears all, users discovered that proximity could act as a filter for relevance, since utterances such as "look out" and "I need help" were more relevant when the speaker was nearby. Users also engaged in deception of enemy players, first by spying on them, and later by giving false information to enemies who they suspected were spying on them.

We subsequently undertook studies to address whether voice was suitable for communication within MMORPGs (Wadley et al. 2007) and within the social virtual world *Second Life* (Wadley 2008). In this chapter, we summarize the results from these two case studies. To gather rich data about use and its context, we used ethnographically informed methods including observation, interviews, focus groups, and diaries. Experienced and novice participants used commercially available systems in naturalistic settings such as homes and workplaces. We also gathered user opinions and experiences from forums and blogs. We analyzed data into themes and present these below.

We argue that VWs are a unique context for communication. Issues arise from the negotiation of virtual space, the complex technical requirements of voice-over-IP, questions of identity and anonymity, and the ability of users to multitask and conduct multiple conversations. The user experience can become a maelstrom of impression management, identity play, and confusion over what is being transmitted to whom. While prior research into mediated communication can shed light, only studies conducted within VWs can best illustrate this user experience.

While third-party VOIP services had already been enthusiastically appropriated by many MMORPG users, *Dungeons and Dragons Online* (DDO) was the first MMORPG to have voice communication facilities integrated into the game software when it was released in 2005. Following its release, we undertook a study investigating voice communication and game play issues with 15 participants over a period of 2 months (Wadley et al. 2007). The DDO voice system connects members of the same group or party using a radio style mode, in which all members of the team can hear each other irrespective of their location in the game world. A visual indicator around the player's name on one side of the screen indicated whose microphone was active at a given time.

The virtual world *Second Life* (SL) began operation in 2003 with a focus on socializing and role-play (Ondrejka 2004), and has since attracted business and education users. A voice system was added in 2007, providing an opportunity to study the introduction of speech to a VW that is often used for purposes other than gaming. During 2007–2008, we interviewed experienced users from a variety of backgrounds engaged in activities including socializing, teaching, business, and art. We also convened in-world discussions, analyzed forums and blogs, and conducted participant research in both recreational and workplace aspects of SL. Voice in SL is spatial; loudness is determined by proximity within the VW. In the following sections, we present some of the important themes that emerged from these two case studies.

Participants in the DDO study universally approved of communicating by voice during game play, provided the circumstances were right. Once technical problems were resolved, participants found speaking to be easier, more natural, and more relaxing than typing. They felt that voice enhanced their experience; making the game "feel like a living breathing party." More could be communicated in a shorter space of time. Speaking freed a user's hands from typing, so they could communicate while carrying out other game actions such as moving and fighting. All participants agreed that voice was better than text during group raids. "Especially in quest scenarios, if there's something that happens quickly, it's a hell of a lot better to say 'heal so-and-so,' or 'there's a trap ahead' as opposed to trying to type out 'trap.'" Voice was also well suited to planning prior to raids and to negotiating the distribution of loot afterwards. However, many noted that it was difficult to associate voices with avatars, especially when playing with strangers. One participant felt that indexical and deictic speech such as "over here" didn't work when playing with strangers, for this reason. Another participant stressed that, while the DDO system highlighted a player's icon when they were speaking, she couldn't always see this visual indicator, and that looking for it diverted her attention from other display details. Also, the cue disappeared immediately after the person stopped speaking leaving her wondering, "Who just said that?" Some suggested that whole avatars should light up or that a speech bubble should appear to more clearly associate the voices one heard with avatars on the screen. Participants sometimes struggled with how to pronounce character names in the DDO fantasy setting. Another was uncertain at first how he should pronounce game-jargon: "Some things you type all the time, but you never actually say out loud. The first time I go to say it, I stumble over it. Do I say 'exp' or 'X-P' or..."

The introduction of voice was a source of great controversy among *Second Life* users, and the subject of many debates. Many seemed to either love or hate voice. Some who hated it felt that SL's vendor, whom they suspected of pandering to business users, had forced it on them. On the other hand, some users felt that the controversy was overblown and that people should simply choose the medium they preferred. Voice-haters responded that a voice-using community might be suspicious of those who refused to use voice. SL participants mentioned situations where voice was especially useful, such as rehearsing and performing plays, teaching foreign languages, playing music, collaborative building, meetings and discussions, and sexwork. They felt that speech conveyed richer and more nuanced meaning when compared with text, and did it faster. Speech was also thought to be superior when discussing complex topics or helping fellow users. For many, simply not having to type was a benefit. Those involved in business and education use were particularly enthusiastic about voice, and felt SL would be unusable without it.

While some advantages of voice were due to increased social presence, this also caused problems when used among strangers. Participants in both studies felt that voice exacerbated problems of shyness. Participants felt more concerned about saying something stupid in front of others. One participant in the DDO study likened the use of typing to "putting up a curtain." Another felt uncomfortable speaking with strangers when his wife was at home with him. Several DDO participants said there was reluctance to using voice in pickup-groups, and that it made them more reluctant to add strangers to their group. Participants in both studies also complained about extroverted and/or immature people dominating and misusing the voice systems.

Participants in both studies felt that speech had the potential for greater emotional impact when compared with text. SL participants reported that voice communication attracted griefers and that griefing was more personal and hurtful when communicated with voice. Participants in the DDO study suggested that the emotional impact of a speech was more likely to cause anger and damage team dynamics. They felt that this was more of a problem for pickup groups than for people who played together regularly. On the other hand, some felt a voice channel could also heal rifts: A team member who made a mistake could apologize immediately, and his sincerity could be more easily perceived. They noted that when using text, a user was more likely to think for a moment before pressing send, whereas voice users were more likely to speak before considering implications. "With voice, if you're upset you're going to vocalize it, whereas with text and you're upset you've got that extra level of barrier."

Business users in SL praised voice's ability to convey the speaker's identity, as it helped them get to know customers and colleagues and build trust. However, for many SL participants, loss of anonymity was a major reason cited for rejecting voice. For example, people with opposite-sex avatars found voice awkward since gender is readily exposed in speech. Some female users reported experiencing sexual harassment after giving away their gender by speaking. Conversely, one male working in SL with a female avatar claimed to have been better treated by clients who assumed he was female. In the DDO study, many participants encountered situations where a user's appearance and voice did not match. The most common examples cited were males playing female characters and children playing adult characters. Our participants spoke about the extra effort required to translate those players' voices into the fantasy setting of the game. Some described these encounters as weird or uncomfortable. Some simply found it harder to know who was speaking.

Some people used SL to role-play fictional identities. Many were emotionally attached to their virtual identity. Preserving the boundary between real and fictional identities was a complex problem. Different friends and family members and online and offline colleagues were differently aware of the identity play being conducted, and users were careful to maintain a consistent identity to them. Voice communication made this task more complicated. Participants in the DDO study claimed that they encountered few genuine role-players. One encountered a user in a pickup group who "threw in a hearty 'arrggh' now and again." Another believed that all role-players used text: "I've never spoken to anyone who's actually tried to speak in character, using their voice. It's rare to see it in text. I can't imagine anyone trying to pull it off using their voice."

Most participants in both studies had little enthusiasm for the idea of changing their voice with software to obscure their identity or aid in role-playing. A participant in the DDO study suggested that it was not merely a matter of changing tone or accent but also vocabulary, which would be impossible.

Managing Multiple Conversations

Many MMORPG players keep several text channels open at once and conduct simultaneous conversations in separate windows. Some participants reported embarrassing situations when a message was typed into the wrong channel, for example when discussing teammates behind their back. One participant felt that this kind of error was worse with voice: "Sometimes you'd hear things you didn't want to hear." We asked participants whether they wanted multiple voice channels. Some did, and suggested that the interface be presented as a simple list of screen buttons, one per channel. Others felt it would be impossible to monitor several voice conversations at once. Similarly, many SL participants felt that text was better suited to multitasking and conducting simultaneous conversations. They appreciated being able to read back through a log of text chat when necessary. They felt that text supported complex multithreaded real-time conversation among large groups better than did voice. People also liked being able to save a transcript of a text conversation and search it later.

Text channels support short-term asynchronicity as users can scroll back through message logs during the conversation itself. Participants felt it would be impossible to implement an analogous mechanism in voice. Recordings could perhaps be made, but would be hard to scan. Some felt that scrolling and multiple channels were significant advantages for text over voice. Participants discussed the possibility of emulating answering machines or being able to "time shift" the voice channel. However, they were apprehensive about the thought of checking for and playing back messages. One DDO participant described problems receiving voice chat from guild-mates while in the heat of battle: "You don't mind using text for that kind of thing."

SL participants reported that large groups using voice tended to split into smaller independent conversations. Lack of visual cues made conversational turn-taking ineffective. Participants in the DDO study also felt that voice was less useful in large groups, as users were more likely to talk over each other, and voices became harder to recognize. Two-way radio in physical-world groups suffers from the same problem, and the solution users have devised is radio discipline and a stylized grammar. Our participants discussed whether this was needed in MMORPGs. One said he didn't want strict military-style voice protocols: "What if someone wants to laugh?"

Some participants in the DDO study reported simultaneous use of voice and text channels, finding these did not interfere with other. However, one participant said that after starting to use voice, he stopped checking the text channel. Another used text only for essential messages. One participant reported playing with groups in which some used text and some used voice. He found that these groups tended to split into two subgroups and that it became impossible to coordinate the whole group. In contrast, in certain SL situations, people made simultaneous use of voice and text. For example, in a meeting or discussion, one person might "hold the floor" and speak, while comments, questions, and back-channel chat were typed. Users found that this maximized communication while minimizing congestion.

Participants in both studies described incidents in which household sounds such as breathing, eating, family members' speech, TV, and music were accidentally transmitted into the voice channel. One DDO player developed a cough that made voice temporarily unusable for him. Another described a situation in which he temporarily stopped playing to comfort his small child, placed his headset beside the child without thinking and broadcasted the child's crying into the game. One participant reported overhearing younger users being told by their mothers to get off the computer. Participants reported that when playing with people they knew well, they could recognize whose spouse or child was making noise in the background. Microphones have mute buttons, and voice systems can be set to "push to talk" to prevent unintended transmission. While some participants used these features, others considered using push-to-talk and mute keys annoying and a detraction from the key benefits of using voice.

Conversely, speech from a VW can interrupt a user's household, and so can the user's own utterances intended for the game, a problem not encountered with text. A participant said: "I think it's important that text is an option too, for when somebody else is home and you just can't talk." Two reported that they played differently depending on whether family members were at home and able to hear them.

In particular, if small children were around they used voice differently. One teenaged participant said that he played in his room and was not concerned about his parents overhearing, treating the voice channel as though he were talking on the telephone.

Technical Difficulties

Although the DDO voice system is integrated into the game, most participants had trouble getting it to work at first. All were eventually able to use it, but reported that minor problems occurred constantly. During play, groups needed time to establish the status of each member's voice setup. Participants reported sessions in which they assumed all along that they either could or couldn't be heard, only to find out later that their assumption was wrong. Participants also reported that many of the DDO users they encountered appeared either not to have voice hardware, or to be unable to use it, or to have it switched off or incorrectly configured. In contrast, the text channel was regarded as a "safety net." It was reliable, accessible, and used as a backup when voice was failing for any reason.

Many variables controlled the volume of speech in the DDO system with implications for its usability. Individual players in a party would be heard at markedly different volume due to factors like microphone placement and quality. Some participants wanted to normalize the volumes of individual teammates, but DDO did not provide a way to do this. Voice was also sensitive to network latency. "There's a lot of stuttering. It's not really lag. You'll start to say something, but you'll stop because someone else is talking, because they didn't realize [you were talking], because of that time delay. You think, I'll be polite and not interrupt. Then at that stage they hear your voice and they stop."

SL participants also had problems with reliability, equipment setup, and poor sound. A successful voice conversation depends on all members of a group being able to send and receive audio successfully, and the larger the group, the more likely a member would be unable to use voice, forcing the group to fall back to text or split into voice and text subgroups. SL gave users no feedback on whether they were transmitting too loudly, too softly, or transmitting background noise. Users reported that voice conversations invariably included a period where they "debugged" each other's voice setup. The SL voice client also demands more computing resources and makes SL unusable on older machines.

One SL user engaged in education spoke of difficulties convincing IT departments to unblock the required IP ports at an institutional firewalls: "Voice is a toughie for lots in edu. Different proxies, and the hardware – nightmare." These issues are not addressed in voice research conducted outside the VW context, but are echoed in the findings of Nilsson et al. (2002) who studied a series of voice-enabled meetings in *ActiveWorlds*.

SL uses a "spatial" metaphor for voice propagation. This seems to be the best arrangement in a VW where collaborating groups usually gather in one spot. Unlike games, there is rarely the need for a group to move around the virtual world in a coordinated way. However, users noted some problems with spatial voice. Some felt that the rules of sound propagation were less intuitive than in the physical world, so that it was not always clear who could hear an utterance. Users couldn't control transmission distance by shouting or whispering. Also, by mimicking the physics of offline voice transmission, spatial audio reintroduced real-world problems. Informants noted that in public lectures or large meetings, it was hard to be in a location where one could hear all the speakers at once. SL has no "megaphone" to project voice over a large area. Spatial voice made eavesdropping possible in the virtual environment. Some used SL's map to check whether there might be avatars close-by who could overhear their conversation. Some noted that SL's movable view-camera made intentional eavesdropping easy to achieve and hard to detect, supporting a finding of Irani et al. (2008). However, concern over eavesdropping seemed to depend on the personality of the user and the topic they were discussing.

Uniqueness of the Virtual Environment

These studies highlighted the variety of uses made of VWs. Different use cases are differently suited to the voice and text modalities. Users also operate within a complex superimposition of virtual and physical contexts. It is clear that choice of communication medium is of critical importance. The criteria by which VW users judge media are many and varied, and cannot be reduced to a simple, single concern.

Some of the problems and preferences expressed by participants in our studies have been identified in prior communication research. Users are aware of the different abilities of text and voice to support feedback, symbol variety, parallelism, rehearsability, and reprocessability, and they structure their use of these media accordingly (cf. Dennis and Valacich 1999). Users engaged in text chat accept that there will be a delay between each round of a conversation. They use this to more carefully edit messages, providing an opportunity for impression management. They also use the delay to multitask, for example by taking a phone call, going to the bathroom, or engaging in other conversations (cf. Jones 2002). Text users appreciate the ability to undertake multiple simultaneous conversations, which cannot be conducted in voice without careful use of muting. They appreciate the ability to glance back through the log of a text conversation while discussion is in progress, and to save the log as a transcript. SL users have discovered useful ways of using text and voice simultaneously within a discussion. It is interesting that the practice of texting in a back-channel while someone is speaking is widely accepted in SL, while it is usually considered rude in physical-world meetings and classrooms. A third or more of MMORPG users are in-world to maintain real-world friendship groups (Williams et al. 2006). For these people, it appears that the greater social presence of voice communication enhances the online experience. On the other hand, people whose teammates are not known to them offline often prefer the social distance of a text channel.

These studies indicate that there is a paradigm scenario found in VWs to which voice configured as radio is ideally suited. The scenario consists of a small group of people, who know each other and are comfortable speaking with each other, engaged in fast-paced activities which need to be coordinated synchronously. The users are dispersed throughout virtual space and are in physical settings which do not cause nonusers to become involved in their conversations. This is the scenario faced by many users of networked first person shooters, who have enthusiastically adopted voice. These scenarios are analogous to those faced by soldiers, emergency workers, drivers in convoys, and so on. All of these use two-way radio for the same reason: its ability to deliver spoken utterances instantly to any point in space. They face similar problems of channel congestion, eavesdropping, and identification of voices. Physical-world radio users have devised protocols to solve these problems; however, these do not seem to have been widely adopted in VWs.

However, this scenario is not the only one found in MMORPGs, and is rarely found in social worlds such as *Second Life*. Other VW activities are not as well suited to radio-configured voice. There is evidence for the existence of distinct groups of users (or types of use) with different goals and requirements. Although communication in VWs accords with prior communications research, some issues are uniquely important in the VW context. Anonymity, for example, is of importance to many users.

The problems caused by accidental transmission of environmental sounds into an online game's voice channel are the stuff of legend: witness YouTube recordings of gamers being told by their mothers to stop playing and go to bed. Accidental transmission of sound can damage privacy, create embarrassment, and break immersion. Eavesdropping and accidental transmissions are problem for any voice medium, and researchers have observed active management of this problem, especially by mobile phone users.

Accidental transmission of sound is especially problematic for virtual world users. A person using a VW must manage several contexts. MMORPG voice channels usually emulate radio, transmitting to all designated teammates and only to them. *Second Life,* however, transmits sound based on proximity. Users can be overheard not only by people who are physically copresent with them, but by fellow users whose avatars are nearby in the virtual world. Spatial voice transmission is designed to provide an intuitive way to manage conversation contexts by enacting offline proxemic norms; however, its implementation in SL makes this management task complex, if not impossible.

The physical context of VW use is often a user's home, where friends or family might overhear voice transmissions. Unlike telephone calls, which are typically brief, a VW session might last for hours. Many avoid communicating with fellow users by voice if it might disturb their family, or if the sound of conversation, music, or television in their physical context might be broadcast into the virtual space. Some people use VWs to role-play fictional identities, for example an avatar of opposite gender. Voice communication, by broadcasting information about physical-world identity, and merging online and offline conversation contexts, makes managing identity a complex task. Finally, many people perceive a social stigma attached to virtual world use, adding extra pressure not to be overheard while using these systems.

Over and over in our studies, we heard complaints about the technical difficulties of getting voice communication to work properly in virtual environments. This is caused by a number of factors. The infrastructure required for transmitting and displaying text is well supported on standard PCs, and text might be considered the Internet's "native" mode. Voice, on the other hand, is an analog signal and must be converted to and from the digital domain to be transmissible on the network. While speakers are now standard equipment on PCs, microphones are not, so that users may not always be seated at a voice-equipped PC. It is sufficiently normal for voice not to be working that it has become standard practice for SL users to pretend that they are having technical difficulties when they do not wish to speak for some reason.

Voice users are dependent on other users' doing the right thing. The larger the group, the more likely someone does not have voice set up properly. In these situations, groups often choose to revert to the "safety net" of text. It is easy for one user to unwittingly ruin a group conversation by accidentally introducing background noise or setting up a feedback loop between their speakers and microphone. The *Second Life* client requires significant resources, and switching voice on adds to the burden, making it unusable on many PCs. Associating voices to avatars is not always possible, despite both DDO and SL providing a visual cue to speech. The cue can disappear too quickly, and in SL is missed if the receiver's avatar is facing away from the sender's avatar.

Conclusion

These studies emphasize that virtual worlds are a unique context for communication, especially once voice systems are introduced. Participants in VWs are situated at the confluence of virtual and physical world communication contexts. Participants manage a host of communication contexts that interlace speech with text, across multiple virtual and physical settings. Our work suggests that VWs are best not approached as a singular "medium" or communication phenomenon per sec but rather as environments that afford the use of multiple media for a variety of purposes. While prior communication research sheds light on communication in virtual environments, more work is needed on how participants in VWs engage with this combination of multiplexed physical and virtual communication contexts. In particular, more work is needed to understand the implications of voice in this confluence.

The implementation of voice communication systems in VWs requires careful design. In particular, it is important to understand the implications of configuration options of voice communication systems for communication. In this chapter, we looked at systems with two different configurations. DDO used a "radio" configuration while the system in SL was based on proximity. Other options exist, and how these systems are configured will influence the communicative possibilities of current and future VWs. In addition, "technical" problems mean that voice does not yet work well for walk-up and talk situations, even when it is built into VW software. More standards work is needed at the level of computer design, headsets, etc., and a voice etiquette is required that caters to both physical and virtual environmental contingencies.

VW use combines fictional worlds and identity exploration with real people in real settings. User-to-user communication lies right at this intersection of reality and fantasy. The suitability of different communication media depends on a dynamic compromise between the need for people to understand their collaborators and their desire for privacy and identity-play. While voice offers much for communication in virtual worlds, text may persist as the best option in some scenarios.

References

Aarsand, P. A. (2008). Frame switches and identity performances: Alternating between online and offline. *Text & Talk – An Interdisciplinary Journal of Language, Discourse Communication Studies, 28*(2), 147–165.

Aarseth, E. (2007). Allegories of space. In F. von Borries, S.P. Walz, M. Böttger, D. Davidson, H. Kelley & J. Kücklich (Eds.), *Space time play: Computer games, architecture and urbanism: The next level*. Basel, Switzerland: Birkhäuser.

Bartle, R. (2003). Not yet you fools! Game + Girl = Advance, from (*http://www.gamegirladvance. com/archives/2003/07/28/not_yet_you_fools.html*).

Benford, S., Bowers, J., Fahlén, L. E., Mariani, J. A., & Rodden, T. (1994). Supporting cooperative work in virtual environments. *The Computer Journal, 37*(8), 653–668.

Boellstorff, T. (2008). *Coming of age in Second Life: An anthropologist explores the virtually human*. Princeton, NJ: Princeton University Press.

Carlson, J. R. & Zmud, R. W. (1999). Channel expansion theory and the experiential nature of media richness perceptions. *Academy of Management Journal, 42*(2), 153–170.

Carlson, J. R., George, J. F., Burgoon, J. K., Adkins, M., & White, C. H. (2004). Deception in computer-mediated communication. *Group Decision and Negotiation, 13*, 5–28.

Daft, R. L. & Lengel, R. H. (1986). Organizational information requirements, media richness and structural design. *Management Science, 32*(5), 554–571.

Davie, R., Panting, C., & Charlton, T. (2004). Mobile phone ownership and usage among pre-adolescents. *Telematics and Informatics, 4*, 359–373.

Dennis, Alan R., and Joseph S. Valacich. (1999). Rethinking Media Richness: Towards a Theory of Media Synchronicity. P. 1017 in *Proceedings of the Thirty-Second Annual Hawaii International Conference on System Sciences*. Washington, DC: IEEE Computer Society.

Faulkner, X. & Culwin, F. (2004). When fingers do the talking: A study of text messaging. *Interacting with Computers, 17*, 167–185.

Fischer, C. S. (1994). *America calling: A social history of the telephone to 1940*. Berkeley, CA: University of California Press.

Fulk, J., Schmitz, J., & Steinfield, C. W. (1990). Social influence model of technology use. In J.S. Fulk & C.W. Steinfield (Ed.), *Organizations and communication technology* (pp. 117–140). Steinfield/Newbury Park, CA: Sage.

Gibbs, M. R., Benda, P., & Wadley, G. (2006). Proximity-based chat in a first person shooter: Using a novel voice communication system for online play. In *Proceedings of the 3rd Australasian Conference on Interactive Entertainment, Perth, Australia, Murdoch University*, pp. 96–102.

Gibbs, M. R., Hew, K., & Wadley, G. (2004). Social translucence of the Xbox live voice channel. In M. Rauterberg (Ed.), *Lecture notes in computer science: Entertainment computing – ICEC 2004* (pp. 377–385). Berlin: Springer.

Goby, V. P. (2006). Personality and online/offline choices: MBTI profiles and favored communication modes in a singapore study. *CyberPsychology and Behavior, 9*(1), 5–13.

Hindmarsh, J., Fraser, M., Heath, C., & Benford, S. (2001). Virtually missing the point: Configuring CVEs for object-focused interaction. In E.F. Churchill, D.N. Snowdon, & A.J.

Munro (Ed.), *Collaborative virtual environments: Digital places and spaces for interaction* (pp. 115–139). London: Springer.

Howard, S., Kjeldskov, J., & Skov, M. B. (2007). Pervasive computing in the domestic space. *Personal and Ubiquitous Computing, 11*, 329–333.

Irani, L. C., Hayes, G. R., & Dourish, P. (2008). Situated practices of looking: Visual practice in an online world. In *Proceedings of the ACM 2008 Conference on Computer Supported Cooperative Work*, New York, ACM, pp. 187–196.

Jones, R. H. (2002). The problem of context in computer mediated communication. Georgetown University Roundtable on Language and Linguistics, March 7–9, 2002, from personal.cityu.edu.hk/~enrodney/Research/ContextCMC.doc

Lober, A., Schwabe, G., & Grimm, S. (2007). Audio vs. Chat: The effects of group size on media choice. In *Proceedings of the 40th Annual Hawaii International Conference on System Sciences*, Melbourne, Australia: RMIT University, p. 41.

Markus, L. M. (1990). Toward a 'Critical Mass' theory of interactive media. In J.S. Fulk & C.W. Steinfield (Eds.), *Organizations and communication technology* (194–121). Newbury Park, CA: Sage.

Nilsson, A., Heldel, I., Axelsson, A. –S., & Schroeder, R. (2002). The long-term uses of shared virtual environments: An exploratory study. In R. Schroeder (Ed.), *The social life of avatars* (pp. 112–126). London: Springer.

Norman, D. A. (2004). *Emotional design*. New York: Basic Books.

Ondrejka, C. R. (2005). 'Escaping the Gilded Cage: User Created Content and Building the Metaverse', New York Law School Law Review, *49*(1):81–101.

Short, J., Williams, E., & Christie, B. (1976). *The social psychology of telecommunications*. London: Wiley.

Smith, R. B., Hixon, R., & Horan, B. (2002). Supporting flexible roles in a shared space. In E. F. Churchill, D.N. Snowdon, & A.J. Munro (Eds.), *Collaborative virtual environments: Digital places and spaces for interaction* (pp. 160–178). London: Springer.

Stritzke, W. G. K., Nguyen, A., & Durkin, K. (2004). Shyness and computer mediated communication: A self-presentational theory perspective. *Media Psychology, 6*, 1–22.

Turkle, S. (1995). *Life on the screen: Identity in the age of the internet*. New York: Simon and Schuster.

Wadley, G. (2008). *Talking and building: Two studies of collaboration in Second Life*. San Diego, CA: Conference on Computer-Supported Cooperative Work.

Wadley, G., Gibbs, M. R., & Benda, P. (2005). Towards a framework for designing speech-based player interaction in multiplayer online games. In *Proceedings of the 2nd Australasian Conference on Interactive Entertainment. Sydney, Australia, Creativity and Cognition Studios Press*, pp. 223–226.

Wadley, G., Gibbs, M. R., & Benda, P. (2007). Speaking in character: Using voice-over-IP to communicate within MMORPGs. In *Proceedings of the Fourth Australasian Conference on Interactive Entertainment, Melbourne, Australia: RMIT University*.

Walther, J. B. (1992). Interpersonal effects in computer-mediated interaction: A relational perspective. *Communication Research, 19*(1), 52–90.

Watson-Manheim, M. B., & Belanger, F. (2007). Communication mode repertoires: Dealing with the multiplicity of media choices. *MIS Quarterly, 31*(2), 267–293.

Williams, D., Ducheneaut, N., Xiong, Li, Zhang, Y., Yee, N., & Nickell, E. (2006). From tree house to barracks: The social life of guilds in *World of Warcraft. Games and Culture, 1*(4), 338–361.

Williams, D., Caplan, S., & Xiong, Li. (2007). Can you hear me now? The impact of voice in an online gaming community. *Human communication research, 33*, 427–449.

Yee, N., Bailenson, J. N., Urbanek, M., Chang, F., & Merget, D. (2007). The unbearable likeness of being digital: The persistence of nonverbal social norms in online virtual environments. *CyberPsychology and Behavior, 10*(1), 115–121.

Chapter 16
What People Talk About in Virtual Worlds

Mary Lou Maher

Talking is an essential feature in multi-user virtual worlds. While your avatar provides a visual cue of your presence, talking confirms that you are paying attention. Talking is more than just about showing that an avatar is present and paying attention; it allows people to communicate, compete, and collaborate in a way learned in the physical world. A sense of presence plays a role in immersing people in a virtual world in a way that mimics the physical world, while allowing people to present themselves visually very differently than they do in the physical world. Does a visual presentation of self as an avatar have an effect on what people talk about in virtual worlds?

People can talk in virtual worlds using two different communication channels: text chat and voice chat. Text chat is typically seen as a conversation in a separate chat window in which a group of people can communicate by typing, either in a publicly available window or a window visible only to designated people. Voice chat as a communication channel in virtual worlds is currently limited by compression and bandwidth and doesn't scale up to larger groups. We can see that research is leading to a future in which text chat and voice chat will be equally supported by the technology. While text and voice chat are different modes of communication, they both allow a conversation to take place.

In this chapter, we look at two different scenarios in which we analyze what people talk about in virtual worlds. What the two scenarios have in common is that the people are engaged in a specific task, in contrast to a scenario in which people are meeting each other socially or coincidentally. Each scenario and study was developed to study the impact of virtual worlds as a collaborative environment for a specific purpose: one for learning and one for designing. Looking at these studies together, we can see that in addition to talking about the task to be completed, people like to talk about their avatars, identity, and location in the virtual world and what they can see, almost as if they were explaining these to a blind person. We also notice that a majority of the discussion is about the task and not about the virtual world, implying that virtual worlds provide a viable environment for learning and designing that does not distract people from their task.

M.L. Maher
University of Sydney

W.S. Bainbridge (ed.), *Online Worlds: Convergence of the Real and the Virtual,*
Human-Computer Interaction Series, DOI 10.1007/978-1-84882-825-4_16,
© Springer-Verlag London Limited 2010

Methodology: Protocol Analysis

In these studies, we use a protocol analysis method, a widely accepted research method that makes inferences about the cognitive processes underlying the performance of a task (Ericsson and Simon 1993). An adaptation of protocol analysis for design has led to the extension of the protocol as verbal data to a protocol that is the recorded behavior of the problem solver in the form of audio recordings, video recordings, sketches, or notes (Gero and McNeill 1998; Akın 1986). Recent protocol studies employ analysis of actions during problem solving in addition to the verbal accounts given by subjects (Cross and Cross 1996). Two kinds of protocols are used: concurrent protocols and retrospective protocols. Generally, concurrent protocols are collected during the task and utilized when focusing on the process-oriented aspect of the task. The "think-aloud" technique is typically used, in which subjects are requested to verbalize their thoughts as they work on a given task. On the other hand, retrospective protocols are collected after the completion of the task and utilized when focusing on the content-oriented or cognitive aspects of design, as these are concerned with the notion of reflection in action proposed by Schön (1983). Subjects are asked to remember and report their past thoughts after the task, where the videotape of their sketching activities is provided for alleviating the selective retrieval due to decay of memory (Suwa and Tversky 1997).

In the studies reported here, we adapt the concurrent protocol analysis method by recording and analyzing the text or spoken words that avatars use in virtual worlds while working together on a task. These studies comprise a continuous stream of data: the text chat stream or the video of the images on the screen and an audio recording of spoken words transcribed as a continuous stream of text. The data are segmented based on Ericsson and Simon's (1993) characterization of verbalization events such as pauses, intonations as well as syntactic markers for complete phrases and sentences. After an initial segmentation based on pauses or syntactic markers, we refined the segmentation of the data based on the subject's intention (Gero and McNeil 1998; Suwa and Tversky 1997).

A coding scheme is developed for each study, typically based on a model or categorization of the activity being analyzed. The specific codes provide a metric, allowing certain aspects of the activity to be measured and compared. Once the data are segmented, each segment is assigned one or more codes. The number of segments in each code, the duration of segments, and the transition from one code to another provide insight into the nature of the conversation in the virtual world.

Virtual Worlds as a Place for Learning

In this study, we are interested in the role of place in a virtual learning environment. Most virtual learning environments focus on the delivery of learning materials via a web interface. There are a growing number of virtual learning environments in virtual worlds.

In this study, we looked at whether a sense of presence and place has an impact on the learning experience by analyzing what people say in the virtual world (see Clark and Maher 2006 for more detail). We designed a place in *Active Worlds* for a course on Web Site Design. Students can navigate and communicate by controlling an avatar and using text chat, as shown in the bottom window of Fig. 16.1. In this study, there was no option for voice chat. We developed a coding scheme based on some earlier protocol studies we had done on communication in collaborative design, and added a category for the communication related to place.

The virtual learning environment for this course has two distinct types of spaces: group learning spaces surrounded by individual student galleries. The group learning space was primarily for the whole group to talk about specific topics during scheduled sessions. The gallery space was used by smaller groups of people to discuss a student design project. There are three major areas: common area, the levels area, and the gallery areas. The common area was used for meeting and discussion of the day's topic. In the level areas the knowledge content of the course is divided into three groups of topics. The different levels indicate how much course material the student has mastered, as well as where level 2 assumes the knowledge

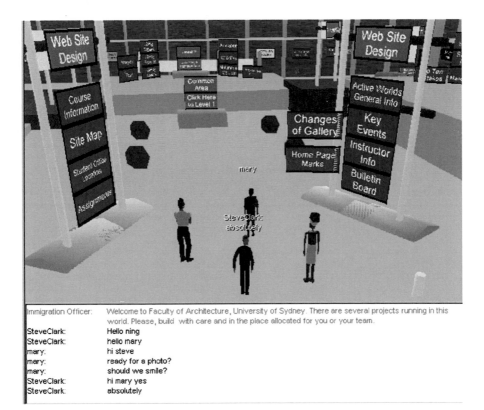

Fig. 16.1 Students in the virtual learning environment

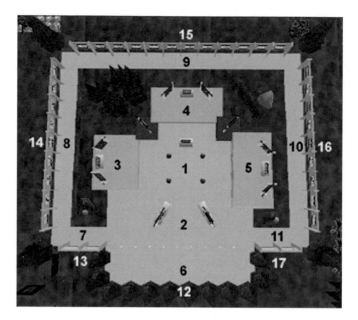

Fig. 16.2 Aerial view of website design course showing various areas

in level 1, and level 3 assumes the knowledge in levels 1 and 2. We designed these as different levels, so the instructor could see how far the student has progressed by where the avatar was standing. The third group of areas is the student galleries. Each student is allocated a location in the gallery areas and can customize that location by adding objects, signs, and interactivity. This is the place in which they display their web design projects for critique by the instructor and other students.

An aerial view of the virtual learning environment is shown in Fig. 16.2 as a set of places, numbered 1–17. The common area (1) is near the entrance (2). Three open platforms (3–5) provide course materials at levels 1 through 3. The remaining places (6–17) can be customized by students and are where they display their designs.

Communication Analysis

To study the effect of a sense of place, we analyze the discussions that take place in the virtual learning place using an adaptation of a coding scheme we developed for studying design in virtual environments (Gabriel and Maher 1999). For this study, we used a coding scheme with four major categories:

1. *Control* Communication, a category which helps identify how much of the learning session was focused on maintaining the floor, handing over control to another person, interruptions, and acknowledging presence.

2. *Technology* Communication, a category which looks at discussions held between participants related to the use of the tools and the collaborative environment.
3. *Learning* Communication, a category which distinguishes different activities in communicating learning concepts, applying skills, knowledge, making critical analyses, and evaluation.
4. *Place* Communication, a category which helps identify the various references to the place in discussions such as gestures of avatar, identity of avatars, location, navigation and orientation within the environment, presence of others, owner-ship, and citizenship.

We allow a single statement to have more than one code in each category. Consider this example: "Lecturer: Please come over to level one." This statement has two codes in relation to place communication: "exploration," which is identified by "come over," and "location," identified by "level one."

We observed eight students enrolled in a summer course that had morning and afternoon sessions every day for 2 weeks. We can categorize their communication by the average proportion of segments in each of the categories per session. The sessions are characterized by a high proportion of place communication with respect to the other communication categories, with 56% of the 149 coded com-munications relating to issues that concern place. The second dominant category, learning communication, shows that 37% of all communication involves learning activities. Combining the two highest-rated categories, we get a result of 93% of students' conversations that involve issues that relate to the concepts of Place and Learning. The other categories, Control communication and Technology communi-cation, each accounted for only about 3% of utterances.

We further categorized the 84 discussions about place to include content related to creating a sense of presence and location in the place. Discussions about gestures (4%), identity (31%), and presence (29%) were those that refer to the avatar and the person associated with the avatar, accounting for about 63% of the total. Discussions about location (20%) and exploration (6%) were those that refer to a specific loca-tion or a question or command about how to get to a particular place, and accounted for 26%. Two other small categories, citizenship (6%) and ownership (5%), com-pleted the classification of place communication.

We then categorized the 55 discussions about learning to analyze the style of learning. In a typical session, there are two dominant categories, introduction with 22% and clarification with 36%. The next two dominant categories are develop-ment (16%) and confirmation (13%). Three small categories contained the other cases: evaluation (7%), revisiting (4%), and referencing (2%). The remaining three categories, acceptance, rejection and repetition, registered no result.

Our results show that an unexpected percentage of the conversation in a virtual world is about place-related topics. This is surprising because we don't normally talk about place-related topics in a physical classroom unless the classroom is notable in some way. Our category of place communication includes discussions about avatars and identity, which is something that is novel in a virtual world learning environment when compared with physical or web-based learning environments.

The learning communication was primarily about clarification of concepts. This is similar to the end of a lecture period when students ask questions. In the virtual world, this style of learning dominated. The second most common category of learning communication is "introduction." This refers to the lecturer or a student introducing a new topic of discussion. The other two notable categories of communication are development and confirmation. During development, a specific topic of conversation is continued, showing that threads of conversation are maintained in the text chat of virtual worlds. Confirmation is a phenomenon that reflects an avatar, indicating that he/she is present, understands what is being explained, or agrees. This kind of communication may be conveyed in other ways in a physical classroom, for example by nodding or simply by a facial expression, but in a virtual world this is conveyed verbally.

DesignWorld: A Virtual World for Design Collaboration

In this study, we are interested in how a virtual world can support a collaborative session in which designers come together to design and construct a model of a building design. The development of networked 3D virtual worlds and the proliferation of high bandwidth communications technology have the potential to change the nature of remote collaboration in professional design. Although these emerging technological developments have led to important advances in the enabling technologies required to support changes in global economic practices, we still know very little about the impact of the technologies on the design process. To understand the practical implications of introducing new digital tools on working practices, we consider how designers work collaboratively and what designers talk about during the design process.

DesignWorld is a combination of 3D modeling and sketching tools. Figure 16.3 shows the interface of DesignWorld. The 3D virtual world client, *Second Life*, is on the left, and a web-base browser interface that has a link to the 2D sketching application, GroupBoard, is on the right (see Rosenman et al. 2006 for more details on system architecture). The designers are present in the virtual world as avatars with the ability to talk about and build 3D models.

We collected data from three sessions in which pairs of expert architects were collaborating on a design task. The designers had a training session in DesignWorld where they were asked to build a tower in order to become familiar with the environment. The collaborative task was the design of a tower that includes a small shopping center, a viewing area, and a café/restaurant. Each pair was given the same design task and asked to complete the design in 1 h. We asked three pairs of designers to participate in the study, and the first pair wanted to repeat the task a week later after gaining experience with the virtual world in their first session. Since this was an exploratory study, we collected and analyzed the four sessions to look for trends in designers' focus during the sessions. More detail on the experiments and analysis of the data are available in Maher et al. (2006).

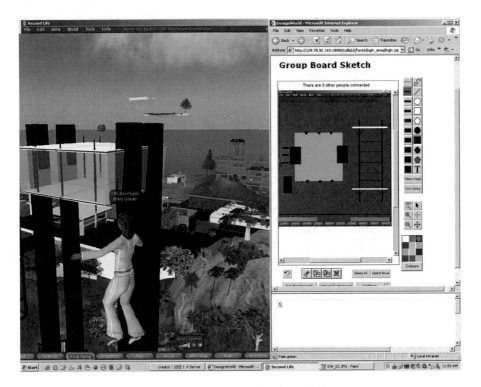

Fig. 16.3 DesignWorld: A 3D design environment for *Second Life*

We recorded the designers' activities and communication in the sessions with a surveillance digital video recording (DVR) system. To simulate high bandwidth audio, both designers were in the same room and could talk to each other without relying on voice chat technology. The DVR system was set to show four different views of a single session on one monitor. Two cameras show the behavior of the physical designer sitting at the computer and the other two views are video streams directly from the two designers' computer display screens. The data from the DesignWorld study include continuous streams of video and audio data. Since this is a design and modeling task, we used the video stream to capture non-verbal communication to provide insight into the nature of their conversation and expand on the codes for the analysis of their collaboration. The streams of data for the sessions are segmented and coded using the basic procedure of a protocol analysis method.

The distribution of the verbal content for the three pairs of designers is shown in Fig. 16.4. The figure shows the percentage of the total duration for four categories of communication content: designing, representation of the model, awareness of each other, and software features. Designing is the dominant category for all sessions, where this includes conversations on concept development, design exploration, analysis evaluation and synthesis evaluation, and design making. The discussion about the representation of the model, awareness of each

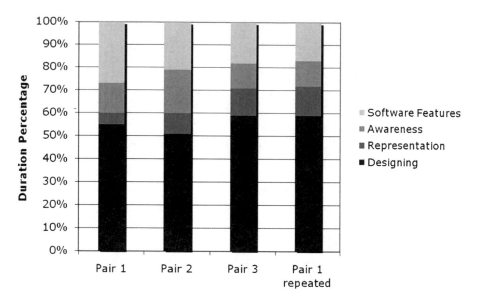

Fig. 16.4 Communication content in the DesignWorld study

other, and software features varied in proportion among the different pairs of designers. Discussion time about the "awareness of others" was more than 10% in each session. This is significant because this kind of discussion is not notable in a physical world setting where awareness of others is assumed. In these conversations, the designers asked each other where their avatar was located and what they were looking at. This was necessary since the designers could be working in different places, alternating between individual and meeting modes (discussed later in this section).

We coded the combination of verbal communication and actions of the avatars into two categories of designing activities to better understand this percentage of their conversation. These two categories are: synthesize and analyze. Synthesize is a discussion of the generation of alternative designs. Analyze is a discussion of how well the proposed design solution satisfies the given design task. Figure 16.5 shows the duration percentages of "analyze" and "synthesize" discussions/activities in DesignWorld for each pair. For Pairs 1 and 2, the duration percentage of "analyze" is significantly less than the duration percentages of "synthesize." For Pair 3, the duration percentages of Analyze and Synthesize activities are very close, and for the repeated session of Pair 1 the duration percentages of Synthesis action is lower than the Analysis action. The results show that Pair 1 in the repeated session demonstrated a different behavior when compared with their first session; they focused more on the analysis of the design problem and less on synthesizing the design solution. While this analysis is not conclusive, it shows that different design strategies are accommodated in the virtual world, and the virtual world does not constrain designers to a specific design strategy.

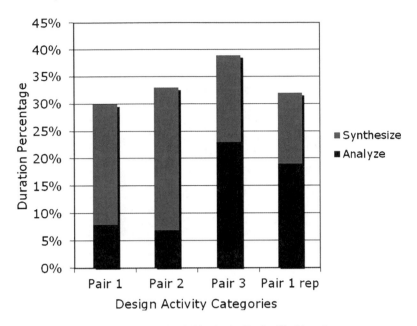

Fig. 16.5 "Analyze" and "Synthesize" activities in the DesignWorld study

Figure 16.6 shows our analysis of the working mode category of the four sessions. We coded two kinds of working mode: individual mode, during which the designers were working on the design task but not coordinating with each other, and meeting mode, during which the designers were working together on the same design task. This is a simplification of the possible working modes in a collaborative design session, but for this exploratory study, this simple distinction can highlight trends in collaborative behavior in a virtual world. The analysis shows that the pairs worked more in individual mode than in meeting mode. For Pair 1, working in meeting mode was higher (37%) than the other two pairs (22%, 22%). The repeated session of Pair 1 demonstrates a fairly different case, where the pair preferred to work nearly equally in individual and meeting modes (51% and 49%). This could mean that their collaboration was more effective since they balanced the time they spent between building up the model together as well as building up individually separate parts of it.

Figure 16.7 shows the percentage of time spent in the 2D sketching environment and in the 3D design representations in DesignWorld for all sessions. The use of the sketching pad was significantly less for all pairs, and the designers used the 3D virtual world most of the time. Sketching is considered an important part of conceptual design and provides a more abstract representation that is helpful during the early stages of design. Our observations show that sketching was not as compelling as working in the 3D world, since when given a choice the designers spent significantly more time in the virtual world.

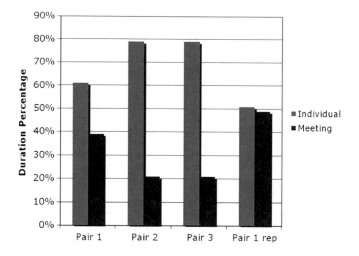

Fig. 16.6 Working mode duration percentages per category

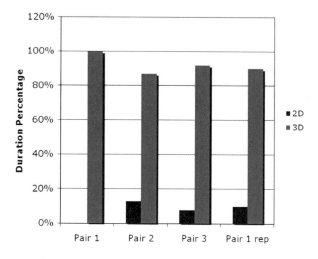

Fig. 16.7 Representation mode duration percentages per category

Discussion and Conclusions

One overwhelming conclusion to be drawn from these two studies is that when people are given a task to achieve in a virtual world, their conversations are predominantly about that task. While this may not be surprising, it is notable. In the virtual world environments we studied, the people are present in the virtual world as avatars and the world itself looks simplistic and game-like. A first encounter with these kinds of virtual worlds usually evokes responses about the game-like environment, comments about how fun-filled this world is, and a preoccupation with deciding what their avatar should look like and wear. These are hardly typical responses to a collaborative design environment or software to support a graduate level course. So, the observation that once on the task people are predominantly focused on achieving that task while co-present in a virtual world is notable.

The nature of their discussions while focused on the learning or design task provides some insight into the cognitive behaviors that are enabled in a virtual world. In the learning environment, the students engaged in conversations and activities that are typical of a seminar or discussion session in a typical educational system. The conversations focused on introducing more topics, clarifying a topic, and developing a topic further. This style of learning is very different from a lecture-style of learning in which the lecturer describes the content to be learned, with a relatively smaller portion of the session devoted to a dialogue with the students. Based on our observations, learning in a virtual world is more like a discourse among peers on the topic to be learned than like a presentation from an all-knowing master from whom the students absorb knowledge.

In contrast, in the design environment, we observed that different cognitive strategies were employed by the designers as they pursued their task. This conclusion can be drawn by looking at the results of the coded protocol for analyze–synthesize activities. Each pair of designers, even when looking at the same pair in a second session, had a different mix of durations for analyzing the design problem and solution versus synthesizing alternative solutions. This implies that the virtual world does not predispose the designers to a particular design thinking strategy. When we look at the codes related to working mode, we see that there is fluidity in moving from individual to meeting modes in the virtual world, also demonstrating that the virtual world environment does not favor one way of working over another. Finally, we see in the codes related to 3D and 2D representation that the virtual world is a more compelling environment than the collaborative sketching environment.

When we consider what people talk about in virtual worlds when it is not about the task they are given, we gain some insight into what it is like to be in a virtual world. The conversations include comments, questions, and evaluations of their avatars, their location in the virtual world, and what they are seeing. For example, the students in the learning environment would often comment on what another student is wearing and whether they are sitting on a bike or standing in the air. While there may be comments on clothing or location in a physical classroom, the comments in the virtual world acknowledge that this is an unusual phenomenon – that the person they may know in real life looks and acts very differently from the person they encounter as an avatar. In the design environment, the designers spoke about where they were in the world and what they were seeing. A major preoccupation in a collaborative design task is the representation of the object being designed. In most collaborative design environments, the designers share a visual representation of the design. In the virtual world, the avatars are located in different places and therefore have a different view of the design. As a result, the designers talk about what they see as if they were explaining it to a blind person.

This phenomenon is a reflection of an environment in which we are aware that the other people in the world see something different from what we are seeing.

The studies reported here are exploratory. The number of people participating in the studies is not statistically significant and the tasks they are given are sufficiently complex so that the results cannot be appreciated as a repeatable phenomenon. However, as an exploratory study, we highlight some aspects of virtual worlds that are worth studying. How do virtual worlds affect our collaborative cognitive behaviors? Are some behaviors favored, as we see in the learning environment in which dialogue and discussion is the primary mode of learning, or in the design environment in which a broad range of cognitive strategies are observed, implying that the virtual world does not prescribe or encourage a specific way of designing?

Acknowledgments I acknowledge Steve Clark who collected and analyzed the data for the learning environment study as part of his PhD research and Ning Gu who designed the virtual learning environment in *Active Worlds* for this study. I also acknowledge the major contributions that Figen Gul and Zafer Bilda provided in designing the studies for DesignWorld and the collection and analysis of the data from the DesignWorld studies. The DesignWorld study was partly funded by the CRC Construction for Innovation Program, Project 2002-024-B "Team Collaboration in High bandwidth Virtual Environments." The collaborators and research reports are available on http://web.arch.usyd.edu.au/~mary/CRCWeb/.

References

Akın, Ö. (1986). Psychology of architectural design. Pion, London

Clark, S. & Maher, M. L. (2006). Collaborative learning in a 3D virtual place: Investigating the role of place in a virtual learning environment. *Advanced Technology for Learning* 3(4):208–0896.

Cross, A. & Cross, N. (1996). Observations of teamwork and social processes in design. In N. Cross, H. Christiaans, & K. Dorst (Eds.), *Analysing design activity* (pp. 291–317). West Sussex: Wiley.

Ericsson, A. K. & Simon H. (1993). Protocol analysis: Verbal reports as data. MIT Press, Cambridge, MA

Gabriel, G. & Maher, M. L. (1999). Coding and modelling communication in architectural collaborative design. In O. Ataman & J. Bermudez (Eds.), *ACADIA '99 Conference on Media and Design Process* (pp. 152–166). Salt Lake City, UT.

Gero, J. & McNeil, T. (1998). An approach to the analysis of design protocols. Design Studies. 19:21–61

Maher, M. L., Bilda, Z., & Gül, L. F. (2006). Impact of collaborative virtual environments on design behaviour. In J. S. Gero (Ed.), *Design computing and cognition'06* (pp. 305–321). Dordrecht, The Netherlands: Springer.

Rosenman, M., Merrick, K., Maher, M. L., & Marchant, D. (2006). DESIGNWORLD: A multidisciplinary collaborative design environment using agents in a virtual world. In J. S. Gero (Ed.), *Design computing and cognition'06* (pp. 695–710). Dordrecht, The Netherlands: Springer.

Schön, D. (1983). The reflective practitioner: How professionals think in action. Basic Books, New York

Suwa, M. & Tversky, B. (1997). What do architects and students perceive in their design sketches? A protocol analysis. Design Studies 18(4):385

Chapter 17
Changing the Rules: Social Architectures in Virtual Worlds

Nick Yee

In the late 1960s, Mischel (1968) sparked a debate in personality psychology by critiquing the reliance on trait-based frameworks of behavior. While the standard approach had been to measure stable dispositions (such as Extraversion), Mischel argued that behavior was largely determined by situational demands (such as being at a party). In the decades that followed, while there have been loud calls within the field to embrace an interactionist approach, research in personality psychology has still largely sidelined situational factors (Endler and Parker 1992) and has continued to focus on standardizing trait measures (Costa and McCrae 1985; Goldberg 1992).

Virtual worlds evoke this person–situation debate not because we are able to create impossible and fantastic scenarios, but because of the degree of control we are able to have over social interactions. Unlike the physical world, all the rules of social interaction in a virtual world have to be explicitly coded. These rules dictate the maximum size of ad hoc groups, the distance your voice can travel, whether other players can hurt you, and the consequences of dying. As Lessig has noted, "Cyberspace does not guarantee its own freedom but instead carries an extraordinary potential for control. ... Architecture is a kind of law: it determines what people can and cannot do" (Lessig 1999: 58–59). Indeed, we are not free to do whatever we want to do in virtual worlds, especially massively multiplayer online games (MMOs). There are consequences to dying, and these rules vary from game to game. While we tend to think of altruism and gregariousness as personality traits, virtual worlds allow us to ask how the social architectures of these environments can be engineered to shape individual and community behavior.

In this chapter, I will explore two kinds of social architectures in virtual worlds. The first are *surface layer* architectures that are readily apparent to players in MMOs, such as death penalties. The second are *hidden layer* architectures that strategically manipulate the version of shared space players see. Relating to both layers, and in a sense mediating between them, is the issue of *information access*.

N. Yee
Palo Alto Research Center
e-mail: nyee@parc.com

W.S. Bainbridge (ed.), *Online Worlds: Convergence of the Real and the Virtual*,
Human-Computer Interaction Series, DOI 10.1007/978-1-84882-825-4_17,

The discussion will be driven by qualitative survey responses and findings from experiments in immersive virtual reality studies.

Surface Layer Architectures

In this section, we will consider the impact of two surface layer architectures on player behavior in MMOs – death penalties and third-party databases. Players who have participated in multiple MMOs were invited to participate in an online survey. Specifically, players were asked whether they thought varying game mechanics changed how players behaved in MMOs. A total of 225 responses were received; 69% of the respondents were men and the average age was 30.9. A grounded theory approach was used to identify common themes and ideas from the responses (Glaser and Strauss 1967).

While it is said that nothing is certain but death and taxes, the consequences of dying actually vary from one virtual world to another. Among the mainstream MMOs popular in the US (such as *World of Warcraft* [*WoW*], *EverQuest II* [*EQII*], etc.), game characters die when their health drops to zero as a result of combat damage, poisons, or falling from great heights. When characters die, a variety of mechanics may take effect depending on the game. In most games, the character's body (i.e., corpse) remains at the location of death and the player (in ghost form) has to travel back to the corpse to resurrect himself/herself. In some games (such as *WoW*), a moderate decrease is applied to the durability of armor and weapons, for which players need to spend game currency to repair. A smaller number of games apply an experience penalty after each death. For example, in *EQII* and *City of Heroes* (*CoH*), you accrue a small experience penalty that increases the time to reach the next level. In the original *EverQuest* (*EQ*), a significant amount of experience was lost when a character died and in fact characters could lose their level by dying. And in very rare instances, death actually does mean death and the character is erased completely when it dies. This feature, known as perma-death, was applied in very specific cases in *Star Wars Galaxies* (*SWG*) and *EQ* for a period of time. On an abstract level, most death penalties are essentially differing levels of time penalties (with the exception of perma-death); dying means spending an extra amount of time catching up where one is but nothing is lost permanently.

Of course, whether that amount of time is 2 min as opposed to 2 h is experienced much more than simply a quantitative difference by most players. This is one of the more striking differences when comparing earlier MMOs (such as *Ultima Online* [*UO*] or *EQ*) and more recent MMOs (such as *WoW* and *EQII*). Earlier MMOs tended to have much more severe death penalties and these changes over time are quite salient for players who have played multiple MMOs over the years. For example, item decay existed in both *UO* and *EQ* and thus there was the possibility that players might lose everything they owned if they did not retrieve their corpse in time. Moreover, in *EQ*, players had to retrieve their corpses while naked (as opposed to ghost form in *WoW*). Since players are more likely to die in dangerous places, corpse retrieval while naked was often difficult and resulted in dying again. As the following players note, death in the earlier MMOs was a very costly mishap.

> You could play for 6 h and lose all the progress by dying twice. You could log in and log off with less than you came on with. [gender = F, age = 25]

> People would sit in front of their computers for hours, waiting for a cleric to come to their zone and rez them, because they knew they'd have to play for days to make up for the massive amount of Xp loss if they didn't bother with the rez. [F, 39]

In contrast, dying is almost light-hearted in comparison with the more recent MMOs. As one player puts it:

> In subsequent games, I have found it absolutely does not matter if I die. Really, who cares about some repair bills and some dread, or decreased experience gain for a short time? Running naked after your corpse in a dungeon? Potentially losing all your equipment if your corpse decayed or losing a level? That was a penalty. [M, 31]

The severe penalty of death affected player behavior and attitudes in several ways. First and foremost, it made everyone value being alive much more and this in turn created a sense of danger and risk in the world of *EQ*. In comparison, the world of *WoW* feels almost rubber-padded.

> I remember working for two weeks in the original EQ to get to level 5. I finally got brave and wandered a few hundred yards away from the guards in Kelethin and promptly got lost in the fog. I was soon attacked by several level 8 mobs and died. I've never experienced that level of fear and concern as I searched frantically for my corpse. I currently play WOW and enjoy it for the most part. However, there is no need to ask for help as the game does 90% of the work for you. In some ways I like that, but at times I really wish someone could come up with a way to recapture the original spark that kept me playing EQ for close to five years. [M, 39]

> The harsh 'sting' of death in those games really made your heart pump during fights and a rush when you killed someone and took their loot. [F, 48]

This pervasive sense of danger in these earlier worlds also contributed to a higher level of willingness to help each other. After all, players understood the burden of death and, more importantly, all players knew that they too would need help one day.

> Finding someone who could rez or summon your corpse or someone to help you retrieve it was key. People helped others because they knew they themselves would probably need similar help later. [F, 21]

> This harshness also fostered a desire for players to actually help each other out in these situations since everybody knew how much death sucked and that by helping someone recover their corpse/experience that person might be willing to help you out in return someday if you ever wound up in the same position. This often led to forming relationships with other players and even getting a guild invite from helping out others. [M, 29]

> Guilds, even enemy guilds, would help each other recover from bad wipes because they knew that there were occasions when they would need help. This helped to mitigate annoying behavior since you knew you may need to work together at times. [M, 42]

Thus, it's not surprising that many players found that death in the earlier games was a bonding experience. The shared crisis and aftermath created salient memories for everyone involved.

> While I'm glad the severe death penalty has been removed from EQ, I think it helped my character bond with her friends. I'm still playing with the same folks I met 8 years ago, and we often talk about the dreaded CRs (corpse retrievals) we went through, especially one in Chardok that lasted hours. [F, 39]

> As much as I hated corpse runs back in old EQ, having to run naked from Fironia Vie to Chardok with a coffin to have my corpse summoned after a raid wipe with my guild was a bonding experience. [M, 20]

Of course, not all players felt that the severe death penalties improved social interactions and social bonds. Some felt that the penalties involved simply prolonged the search for blame when death did occur.

> When a group dies it often becomes a blame game. In games with more severe penalties (e.g. AO's XP-loss) the group first spends 5 minutes to decide who's fault it was, that person then complains for 5 minutes and tries to blame another, which turns into another 5 minutes of the group either ganging up on the second blame-victim or telling the first one that he's a noob and should not even be playing ... so after 15 minutes all tempers are flaring, many feelings are hurt and the group falls apart. [F, 33]

Others felt that the death penalties stressed players out so much that the game became too emotionally draining.

> I've had mostly negative experiences with that. I mean that no one wanted to go out fight monsters if the party was not perfect, and people would get very upset if someone died. [F, 26]

While it may be tempting to believe that more severe death penalties improve social bonds by encouraging players to trust each other in a dangerous world, perhaps it's more accurate to say that the penalties heightened the emotions in play among players – both the good and the bad. From this perspective, it's not that the more recent MMOs provide poor platforms for social bonds as much as that the casual death penalties might have dampened the emotions among players because there is both less to gain in helping someone and less to lose if you are not helped.

Information Access

Social architectures are usually in the control of the game developers, but it is possible for third-party architectures to become part of a game. This is partly because much of game-play in a sense already exists outside of the virtual world itself. In a survey from the Daedalus Project (Yee 2006b), it was found that MMO players spent on average 3.5 h each week looking for game-related information, another 3.6 h each week reading or posting on forums. And players who belonged to guilds (87% of the sample) would spend another 2.7 h each week in their guild's website in the forums or managing guild-related tasks. In other words, the average MMO game spends about 22 h in the game (Yee 2006a), but also an additional 10.8 h in the meta-game.

In the case of WoW, the game developers have provided the game community with a modifiable interface via a scripting language. This has allowed players to create tools that overlay the game as well as extract information from interactions within the game. Examples of overlay interfaces are tools that provide custom visualizations for specific game roles, such as timer bars for different healing spells. One example of an extraction interface is the census bot that PARC's PlayOn group created to collect longitudinal behavioral metrics from the game (Ducheneaut et al. 2006, 2007).

One very well-known extraction interface in the *WoW* community is ThottBot. Once installed by players, the add-on automatically tracks everything a player does and relays that information to a third-party database. Aggregated over time, the stored information is accessible from a website (located at www.thottbot.com) that provides players with a collective intelligence in reference format. Players can look up a quest and find the location on a map where the requisite items are located. If the quest involves killing a monster, a map shows its wandering range and the database shows the percentage likelihood that the monster will drop its needed item. Players can alternatively search for a needed item and view all monsters that drop it or the chain of quests that lead to the item reward. Every element has its own player comments field to allow for discussing tricky strategies or confusing parts of a quest.

The accessibility of information is also something provided in-game to a lesser extent by game developers. For example, computer-controlled guards in large cities in *WoW* provide directions to points of interest. Also, quest givers and rewards are highlighted in the player's mini-map to ease way-finding.

> You'd be hard-pressed to find any aspect of WoW that isn't well-documented online somewhere, complete with video footage and everything. [F, 33]

This is in stark contrast to the earlier games such as *UO* and *EQ*, before the Web 2.0 sensibilities of cross-referenced databases of aggregate information, where the information was much harder to find.

> When I was playing EQ years ago, there were websites with game info out there, but they were always incomplete. Unlike with WoW today, I couldn't always find out what I needed to know. [F, 33]

It is easy to assume that third-party databases are an information source and thus add to any existing social system. The things that these information sources take away from social systems may be less obvious at first glance, but by providing a centralized information source, these databases removed the primary method for gathering information before – by interacting with other human players.

> There weren't places on line you could go to get all the answers, you had to ask other players. There was a lot more give and take. [M, 29]

> I much preferred the early days of MMOs when all the information you ever needed wasn't available on a website. It meant players actually worked together, spoke and chatted lots in the general channels about things directly related to the game and helped each other with quests. [F, 38]

As other players noted more explicitly, these social interactions could have led to friendships forming. After all, the more opportunities that players have to interact with each other, the more likely that a social bond forms.

It does affect the number of relationships formed in-game. Without it, the player offering help will probably have to explain things to the one asking for it, but with it he'll just give a link. [M, 20]

If people were more willing to answer questions, it would be a great conversation starter and there would be more friendships forming. [F, 26]

These third-party databases do not only provide a centralized information source, interactive add-ons that dynamically read in data from these databases provide online help within the game itself. For example, an add-on known as QuestHelper analyzes all the active quests a player has and calculates the most efficient path and order that they should be completed. Quest-related items and monsters are marked on the map to guide the player along. By providing all the answers to players, these information sources gradually took away the sense of adventure in more recent MMOs. As I've argued elsewhere (Yee 2006b), modern video games are essentially work platforms that slowly train game workers to play more and more efficiently. Add-ons like QuestHelper are part of this trans-formation that renders adventure into task completion using a personal informa-tion manager.

Maps, databases, etc. have taken the mystery out of playing. While it saves time and mini-mizes frustration, I think in doing so, they've also killed a big part of what makes the games exciting. Yes, it's nice to see what the quest reward is going to be, but it removes any sur-prises you might have had. Adventuring, finding things out for yourself, discovering things, etc. is a huge part of what makes games fun and interesting. It saddens me that to really enjoy a game, you have to make a conscious effort to avoid or ignore all the tips and info available. [F, 40]

I think thottbott has created more of a Task-oriented game world. I have a quest, look up where to go and what to do, complete, get a new quest. As a result the 'discovery' aspect of the game has lessened significantly. [M, 42]

More than simply removing the need to ask other players for directions or help with quests, these information sources also shape the cultural norms within MMOs. Given the easy access to information, asking for help becomes almost anachronistic and frowned upon.

In the old days, asking questions and, if you didn't know the answer, helping the person find the answer was part of the fun of the game. Helping total strangers with quests or helping them with their character's profession was fun and you made new friends. Then the age of the '133t' speakers came and if you asked the wrong person a question you were criticized and called a 'noob.' [M, 42]

There was a lot less online arrogance and apathy back then, and a much broader sense of community. Todays MMOs have information almost forced upon you. Standard responses to questions in the general channels online are 'look it up' or 'check thottbot.' [M, 33]

Reading between the lines, these third-party databases have created a culture of self-reliance in contrast with a more open community of assistance in the earlier MMOs. And in a sense, the ability to ask for help is the inverse of altru-ism. Players can't help each other if the cultural norm is to not ask for help to begin with.

Hidden Layer Architectures

As opposed to the surface layer architectures, which involve rules and information that are easily accessible and understandable by players, hidden layer architectures work behind the scene. In virtual worlds and any collaborative virtual environment, all interactions (non-verbal and verbal) are mediated by the computer system. And thus, all interactions can be strategically filtered or manipulated by the system without the interactants' awareness. These strategic filters have been referred to as Transformed Social Interaction or TSI (Bailenson et al. 2004). One simple example would be performing simple linguistic analysis and adding the word "please" to all questions. As a more interesting example, given that eye gaze influences persuasion in social interaction, we might engineer a virtual world where a virtual presenter could maintain eye contact with every member of the audience at the same time (Bailenson et al. 2005). This is possible because every audience member sees the virtual world from their own computer display and these versions of reality need not be congruent. Below, we'll discuss several findings from experiments that have explored how TSI can be used to change how people behave in virtual environments.

Two related well-known preference cues in the psychology literature are familiarity and self-similarity. People prefer familiar things over less familiar things (Zajonc 1968, 2001). Our own faces are objects that we, over a lifetime, become intimately familiar with. And thus the ability to subtly transform someone else's face to resemble our own might trigger these familiarity preferences. Similarity-based attraction and preference have also been well documented. Individuals who are similar to us, whether in appearance or beliefs, are rated more positively, perceived as more attractive, and rated as more persuasive than individuals who are less similar to us (Berscheid and Walster 1979; Brock 1965; Byrne 1971; Shanteau and Nagy 1979).

Thus, the ability to manipulate another person's face to be more similar to ours would appear to improve our impression of them, based on both the familiarity and self-similarity effects. Of course, such a transformation would be difficult to achieve in the physical world. Digital tools of image manipulation, however, have over the past decade become widely available and affordable. Software, such as the commercially available Magic Morph (iTinySoft 2002), allows the composition of two separate faces at a user-specified ratio. In other words, it has become possible to specify faces that contain a 20% or 40% contribution from another target face.

The impact of this facial-similarity manipulation has been tested in a series of studies in voting behavior (Bailenson et al. 2006, 2008). In both sets of studies, participants were asked to rate political candidates who either had or had not been morphed with their own photographs. Participants were also asked whether they would vote for the candidates. One study used an undergraduate sample, while the other study used a sample of nationally representative voting-age citizens. The results of both studies showed that facial similarity is a powerful cue, changing voting behavior even in high-profile elections where a great deal of other information and partisan biases exist, such as the 2004 presidential election.

Most importantly, in these two studies with over 700 participants altogether, no participants detected the self-similarity manipulation. Of course, in an MMO, we do not have access to player's photographs, but familiarity and similarity cues might work at other levels of specificity. For example, if we could deduce a player's approximate age from their in-game behaviors, then we could morph avatars that player interacts with a standardized photograph of a younger individual. The same could be done with ethnicity or gender. An interesting research question is whether such a method might create stronger social bonds at the community level.

The fluidity of our digital bodies opens up the question of whether the avatars we employ in virtual environments change the ways we behave. While behavioral confirmation (Snyder et al. 1977) – the process of changing our behaviors to conform to the expectations of others – provides one potential pathway for avatars to change how a person behaves online, might our avatars change how we behave independent of how others perceive us? Another line of research suggests that behavioral modifications can occur without interaction with a perceiver. Bem's self-perception theory (1972) suggests that people infer their own attitudes from observing their own appearance and behaviors. For example, participants given black uniforms behaved more aggressively than participants given white uniforms (Frank and Gilovich 1988). And in a teacher–learner paradigm with electric shock as punishment, subjects in costumes that resembled Ku Klux Klan robes delivered significantly longer shocks than subjects in nurse uniforms (Johnson and Downing 1979).

In the same way that uniforms in the physical world are a transformation of visual representation, digital avatars provide a means for more specific and dramatic self-transformation. Thus, we might expect that our avatars have a significant impact on how we behave online. In other words, users in online environments may conform to the expectations and stereotypes of the identity of their avatars. Or more precisely, in line with self-perception theory, they conform to the behavior that they believe others would expect them to have. This process has been termed the Proteus Effect (Yee and Bailenson 2007).

In two studies conducted in an immersive virtual reality setting (Yee and Bailenson 2007), a participant's avatar was shown to directly impact his or her behavior. In the first study, participants were given avatars that were either pretested to be attractive or unattractive. Studies have shown that attractive individuals are perceived to be friendlier and more extraverted (Dion et al. 1972). The study found that participants in attractive avatars walked closer and disclosed more information to a confederate stranger than participants given unattractive avatars. To ensure that behavioral confirmation was not a factor, the confederates were blind to condition and always perceived the participants to be of average attractiveness.

In the second study, participants were assigned to either tall or short avatars. Studies have shown that taller individuals are perceived to be more confident than shorter individuals (Young and French 1996). The study found that participants with tall avatars were more competitive in a negotiation task than participants with short avatars. Again, the confederates were blind to condition. Thus, these two studies show that the appearance of avatars can directly change how a user behaves in a virtual environment.

In the context of virtual worlds, these findings suggest that avatar design in and of itself could come to shape social interactions at a community level. In the same way that the virtual world *There* only allowed youthful, athletic avatars to be created, we might examine what the consequences of only providing attractive avatar options might be. Or, to be more devious, one could apply a behavioral confirmation strategy. When player A using a dark, mean-looking avatar interacts with player B, player B sees player A as an attractive and well-dressed avatar. Might behavioral confirmation lead to more positive social interactions via reciprocity? Of course, the theoretical question of pitting behavioral confirmation against self-perception theory is interesting in and of itself.

Ending Thoughts

The fluidity afforded by virtual worlds isn't only about users customizing avatars and creating their own cities. In a more interesting way, this fluidity also allows virtual world designers to influence and shape how people behave in these worlds via social architectures. These architectures can be on the surface and revealed to users or hidden and used to intercept and manipulate data by the computer system. Survey responses from MMO players provide some initial evidence that varying the severity of death penalties and the accessibility of information can influence how people interact and relate with each other in a virtual world. And findings from experiments show that subtle changes in an avatar's visual appearance can change how people interact with each other.

As tantalizing as the survey responses were, it is impossible to pinpoint any sense of causality or quantify the effects. Using the existing games as data points, it would also be difficult to isolate the effects of particular mechanisms because the comparison of any two existing games always involves a difference in more than one mechanism. Games like UO, EQ, or WoW vary on many variables at the same time. And when comparing earlier MMOs with more recent MMOs, it would also be difficult to tease out the potential generational or attitude changes that may have occurred over time. On the other hand, it is precisely virtual worlds that offer the potential of living laboratories – using virtual worlds to study these questions on a level (community vs. individual) and scale that would not be possible in traditional laboratories.

We often think of virtual worlds as digital frontiers that we can build and shape with our unbridled imaginations, and yet, the creation of virtual worlds requires the articulation of rules and laws and constraints that surpass the typical organization of social groups in the physical world. When we organize parties in the real world, we don't need to have rules for the distances our voices will carry, whether two people are allowed to share the same pie, or what the consequences of dying might be. In MMOs, however, all this needs to be spelled out in excruciating detail. And those details in turn affect how players choose to interact and relate with each other. Those details partly determine what social norms emerge. So far, we don't have a good vocabulary or framework for talking about social architectures in virtual worlds. Thus, while we might think that virtual worlds are something that we make, I think the far more interesting question is what virtual worlds make of us.

References

Bailenson JN, Beall AC, Loomis J, Blascovich J, Turk M (2004) Transformed social interaction: Decoupling representation from behavior and form in collaborative virtual environments. Presence 13:428–441

Bailenson JN, Beall AC, Blascovich J, Loomis J, Turk M (2005) Transformed social interaction, augmented gaze, and social influence in immersive virtual environments. Human Communication Research 31:511–537

Bailenson JN, Garland P, Iyengar S, Yee N (2006) Transformed facial similarity as a political cue: A preliminary investigation. Political Psychology 27:373–386

Bailenson JN, Iyengar S, Yee N, Collins NA (2008) Facial similarity between voters and candidates causes influence. Public Opinion Quarterly 72:935–961

Berscheid E, Walster EH (1979) Interpersonal attraction. Addison-Wesley, Menlo Park, CA

Brock TC (1965) Communicator-recipient similarity and decision change. Journal of Personality and Social Psychology 1:650–654

Byrne D (1971) The attraction paradigm. Academic, New York

Costa PT, McCrae RR (1985) The NEO personality inventory manual. Psychological Assessment Resources, Odessa, FL

Dion K, Berscheid E, Walster E (1972) What is beautiful is good. Journal of Personality and Social Psychology 24:285–290

Ducheneaut N, Yee N, Nickell E, Moore RJ (2006) 'Alone Together?' Exploring the social dynamics of massively multiplayer online games. *Proceedings of CHI 2006, New York, ACM,* 407–416

Ducheneaut N, Yee N, Nickell E, Moore RJ (2007) The life and death of online gaming communities: A look at guilds in *World of Warcraft. Proceedings of CHI 2007, New York, ACM,* 839–884

Endler N, Parker J (1992) Interactionism revisited: Reflections on the continuing crisis in the personality area. European Journal of Personality 6:177–198

Frank M, Gilovich T (1988) The dark side of self and social perception: Black uniforms and aggression in professional sports. Journal of Personality and Social Psychology 54:74–85

Glaser BG, Strauss AL (1967) The discovery of grounded theory: Strategies for qualitative research. Aldine, Chicago, IL

Goldberg L (1992) The development of markers for the big-five factor structure. Journal of Personality and Social Psychology 59:1216–1229

Johnson R, Downing L (1979) Deindividuation and valence of cues: Effects on prosocial and antisocial behavior. Journal of Personality and Social Psychology 37:1532–1538

iTinySoft (2002) *Magic morph.* Retrieved March 21, 2004, from http://www.effectmatrix.com/morphing/index.htm

Lessig L (1999) Code and other laws of cyberspace. Basic Books, New York

Mischel W (1968) Personality and assessment. Wiley, New York

Shanteau JS, Nagy GF (1979) Probability of acceptance in dating choice. Journal of Personality and Social Psychology 37:522–533

Snyder M, Tanke ED, Berscheid E (1977) Social perception and interpersonal behavior: On the self-fulfilling nature of social stereotypes. Journal of Personality & Social Psychology 35(9):656–666

Yee N (2006a) The demographics, motivations, and derived experiences of users of massively multi-user online graphical environments. Presence: Teleoperators and Virtual Environments 15:309–329

Yee N (2006b) The labor of fun: How video games blur the boundaries of work and play. Games and Culture 1:68–71

Yee N, Bailenson J (2007) The Proteus Effect: The effect of transformed self-representation on behavior. Human Communication Research 33:271–290

Young TJ, French LA (1996) Height and perceived competence of US Presidents. Perceptual and Motor Skills 82: 1002

Zajonc R (1968) Attitudinal effects of mere exposure. Journal of Personality and Social Psychology 9:1–27

Zajonc, R. (2001). Mere exposure: A gateway to the subliminal. *Current directions in psychological science*, 10:224–228

Chapter 18
Game-Based Virtual Worlds as Decentralized Virtual Activity Systems

Walt Scacchi

There is widespread interest in the development and use of decentralized systems and virtual world environments as possible new places for engaging in collaborative work activities. Similarly, there is widespread interest in stimulating new technological innovations that enable people to come together through social networking, file/media sharing, and networked multi-player computer game play. A *decentralized virtual activity system* (DVAS) is a networked computer supported work/play system whose elements and social activities can be both virtual and decentralized (Scacchi et al. 2008b). Massively multi-player online games (MMOGs) such as *World of Warcraft* and online virtual worlds such as *Second Life* are each popular examples of a DVAS. Furthermore, these systems are beginning to be used for research, development, and education activities in different science, technology, and engineering domains (Bainbridge 2007, Bohannon et al. 2009; Rieber 2005; Scacchi and Adams 2007; Shaffer 2006), which are also of interest here. This chapter explores two case studies of DVASs developed at the University of California at Irvine that employ game-based virtual worlds to support collaborative work/play activities in different settings. The settings include those that model and simulate practical or imaginative physical worlds in different domains of science, technology, or engineering through alternative virtual worlds where players/workers engage in different kinds of quests or quest-like workflows (Jakobsson 2006).

Each of the two case studies is presented in a manner that identifies a number of themes or variables that are used for comparative analysis. This analysis seeks to identify relationships between how development and usage variables are intertwined, to understand how development shapes subsequent usage, and how anticipated usage shaped development. Said differently, DVASs are socio–technical systems, so to understand and compare their development and use helps draw attention to the socio–technical interaction networks and processes that emerge along the way (Scacchi et al. 2008b). The development and usage variables of interest include the target science, technology, or engineering domain; representative

W. Scacchi
Institute for Software Research, and Center for Computer Games and Virtual Worlds
University of California, Irvine, CA 92797-3455 USA

W.S. Bainbridge (ed.), *Online Worlds: Convergence of the Real and the Virtual*,
Human-Computer Interaction Series, DOI 10.1007/978-1-84882-825-4_18,
© Springer-Verlag London Limited 2010

activities performed within the domain through games or virtual worlds; how they are used to support learning; what kinds of social, technological, or educational affordances are employed to facilitate collaborative activities (Kirschner et al. 2004; Scacchi et al. 2008a); and integrated or situated experiences (rather than disjoint system functions, computational services, or system capabilities) that arose through these activities. Finally, there is a discussion of outcomes and surprises that emerged from the development and use of these systems in their respective contexts of use.

Case 1: Science Learning Games for Informal Life Science Education

The first case is from a game-based virtual world called *DinoQuest Online* (DQO). DQO was designed for informal science education in the domains of life science and paleontology for K-6th grade students (Scacchi et al. 2008a). DQO is a free-to-play, science learning game environment deployed on the Web at http://www.DQOnline.org. It was implemented using Flash, and the environment runs within common Web browsers on modest power (or older) personal computers connected to the Internet. Example screenshots from DQO appear in Fig. 18.1, from left to right and top to bottom: (a) DQO virtual collaboratory; (b) player's research results collection space; (c) in-game tutorial for how to use game controls during skeletal re-assembly tasks; next row; (d) screen of game for exchanging oxygen, CO_2, and nutrients through the cardio-pulmonary system; (e) Tetris-like prey–predator game; (e) DinoSphere multi-player environment that simulates multiple creatures in different ecological niches (Scacchi et al. 2008a).

DQO was created to complement and interoperate with a mixed reality, game-based science exhibit called *DinoQuest*. We also participated in its design, addressing similar issues at the Discovery Science Center (DSC) in Santa Ana, CA.[1] Critical to the design of this game world was its focus on embodying Californian and national science education standards (NSES 1996) for the life sciences in grades K-6. During design activities, our focus was to create what we call *science learning games* that are both fun and scientifically grounded, rather than providing simply an entertaining but inauthentic or misleading characterization of scientific concepts and work practices (cf. Bohannon et al. 2009).

Life science is a foundational area of education for young students, as it helps provide evidence-based approaches for understanding and reasoning about the development, survival, and evolution of living beings. This in turn serves as a basis for understanding human health and reasoning about living systems in the world around us, among other things (NSES 1996). However, there are many challenges

---

[1] http://www.discoverycube.org/exhibit.aspx?q=11

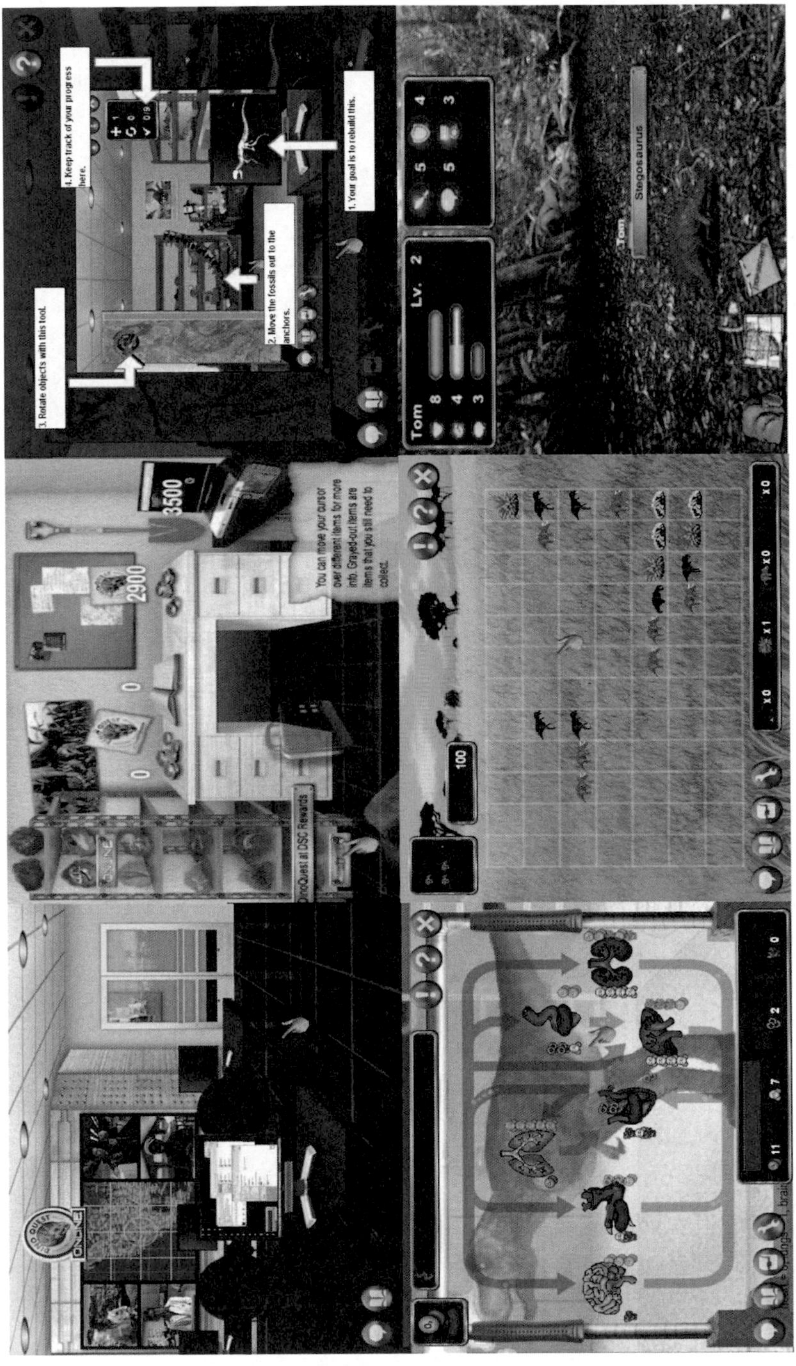

Fig. 18.1 DinoQuest online

for how best to present such concepts in ways that are readily accessible to students in age, skill-level, and school grade appropriate manners. Though the study of dinosaurs is only a small part of the study of pre-historic life (paleontology), children are widely found to exhibit interest and curiosity in dinosaurs, and so our choice was to develop science learning games for life sciences for young learners that employ dinosaurs as characters whose in-game activities are mediated or expressed through their life systems and processes. These systems and processes are designed as analogs of those found in humans or living creatures. Thus, activities central to successful play of DQO entails a variety of identification, recognition, discovery, interactive manipulation, and reasoning tasks that are scaffolded through in-game human characters that serve as collaborators and role models. These characters serve in different roles as scientists, specialists, or technicians who provide prompts, cues, and feedback (acknowledgment of accomplishments, or suggested alternative actions to take in response to failures) to players. A host of other features support informal science education including topical graphics, animated visualizations, music and audio cues, situated tutorials and in-game help, multi-genre games and game play mechanics, progress and resource utilization scores (via in-game dashboards), and collaboration affordances (Clark and Mayer 2008; Rieber 2005; Scacchi et al. 2008a).

Figure 18.1 provides some examples of these through a collage of in-game screenshots. Starting from Fig. 18.1a, play begins on entry into an in-game world that visually suggests a setting where computing and telecommunications activities occur, including a tiled, multi-screen display with different in-game human characters (scientists) can be engaged, who each need assistance in solving problems at hand. These problems are embodied as mini-games, and a total of 13 are included, for about 3–5 h of total game play. Next, to the right in Fig. 18.1b, each player has his/her own research space where the research (game play) results will appear, so they can keep track of their progress and goals obtained or to be obtained to advance to more challenging games (i.e., multi-level game play). The remaining screenshots in Fig. 18.1 highlight other increasingly challenging games whose completion requires accumulative mastery of fundamental life science concepts.

There are a variety of science learning experiences encountered while playing through DQO. Game play is partially ordered and leveled, so that early experiences establish the foundations of play and scientific concepts that need to be employed at later stages and higher challenge levels. Games include digging up dinosaur skeleton fossils whose configuration and orientation are hidden, identifying, and classifying different skeletal bones or substructures, reconfiguring and assembling skeletal components into recognizable creature forms, as well as others that exhibit concepts for how balance, proportion, and size affect the speed with which a creature travels, prey–predator relationships, and more. In each game, players act in the role of research assistants who help visually and aurally depicted scientists or technicians from different disciplines to collect data, compose artifacts, observe relationships, and experience decision-making or problem-solving trade-offs. When the student is unable to advance during game play due to errors, mistakes, or gaps in understanding, the in-game science characters offer guidance or reasoning tips to help scaffold the player toward discovering or engaging the causal relationships that provide the path forward.

In-game textual help and tutorials are also provided, though their usage seems primarily of value to adults (parents or teachers) who do not understand how the game works, or who want to collaborate with, or work over the shoulder of their children in enacting science learning through game play (Twidale 2005). Finally, play in the final level DinoSphere mini-game (displayed in Fig. 18.1f) entails directing the in-game activities of simulated dinosaurs who react to the situation and surrounding environments (visually depicted) they are in, which generally includes goals like finding food and surviving (in the presence of limited food and/or predators), which can include collaborating with other players' dinosaur characters to fulfill such goals. Game play here is modeled after *The Sims*, in that players direct their in-world characters (dinosaurs like a stegosaurus or velociraptor) in different ecological niches where different kinds of life-sustaining behaviors may be important (e.g., finding food, eluding predators, socializing with other dinosaurs like theirs for group activities including hunting for food/prey or overwhelming predators).

Finally, as suggested in the upper left corner of Fig. 18.1, the DQO virtual world is situated within a virtual workplace that incorporates a wall-sized, multi-tile display that young players navigate in ways similar to an online scientific research collaboratory (Olson et al. 2008; Scacchi et al. 2008a). Young people, after all, need to learn about modern scientific work practices and instrumentalities if we hope for them to develop an interest in a possible career in science when they get older and consider college-level education. So both DQO and the DinoQuest interactive exhibit at DSC are designed to embody and reflect how scientists in field sites might collaborate over multimedia communication networks with colleagues in other disciplines in the course of their work practices (cf. Olson et al. 2008). Further information on how this system supports various kinds of collaborative science learning activities and affordances can be found elsewhere (Scacchi et al. 2008a).

Case 2: Game Mod for Semiconductor Fabrication Operations and Service Training

The next case employs a custom-built game "mod" that creates a virtual world for the domain of semiconductor (or nanotechnology) manufacturing using a retail computer game, *Unreal Tournament* (Brown and Scacchi 2007). The resulting game, called *FabLab*, is highlighted in Fig. 18.2, and a demo video is available (Brown and Scacchi 2008). The illustration shows (a) an aerial view of Intel's Fab32 factory; (b) photographs of advanced manufacturing devices; (c) a CAD model of a manufacturing device; (d) a UT software development kit (SDK) for configuring the virtual manufacturing laboratory; (e) inside the FabLab virtual laboratory world, with trainee avatar; (f) a scene from the FabLab spill diagnostic scenario.

We took the standard UT game and content assets and modified them to model, visualize, and simulate the workplace and work activities of technicians who operate and service complex manufacturing systems found in costly cleanroom factories

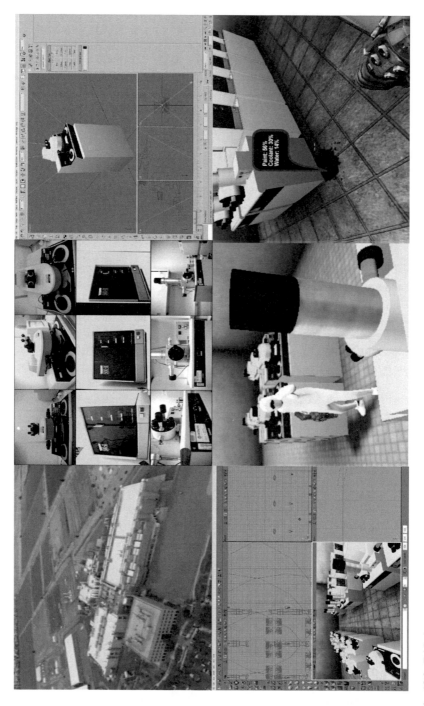

Fig. 18.2 FabLab game

(Brown and Scacchi 2007; Intel Education 2009). In contrast to DQO, focus here is directed developing and deploying a game-based learning environment targeted to adults recently hired to become fabrication technicians and to provide such training in a way that can scale to multiple, globally dispersed locations and workforces.

More than 100 large-scale semiconductor fabrication factories are in operation worldwide. Many now cost more than $1,000,000,000 just to design and build, and companies like Intel operate dozens. Training technicians who can work competently with different manufacturing machines and processes can take years of elapsed time, and many such factories require thousands of technicians who work in shifts distributed 24×7×365 in order to satisfy global marketplace demands for innovative semiconductor devices. While on-the-job training is widespread, there is ongoing need to develop new training materials and experiences that can both streamline the time and cost of deploying such training, and thus there is great interest in e-learning systems and capabilities (Clark and Mayer 2008; Schank 2001).

UT is a game designed as an action-oriented, "first-person shooter" (FPS) style, multi-player game world. It provides ready-to-use functionality for up to 32 concurrent players, who can play over a network/Internet, with built-in support for in-game text or voice chat. It also includes an end-user extensible game engine (a programmable client–server run-time environment) and a game SDK. Using the SDK, it is possible to modify the existing game levels, game play rules/action scripts, and other contents/assets, and all such mods can be redistributed as free/open source software (Scacchi 2004). However, a licensed copy of UT is needed to play a modded game like *FabLab*. Working with a modded version of UT, we could create a game-based virtual world for semiconductor manufacturing, where game play is organized around fabrication technician training activities, operational and service interactions with manufacturing devices, master technician to trainee technician interactions, collaborative multi-technician diagnostic activities, and other workplace scenarios.

Work in an advanced manufacturing facility like a semiconductor fabrication laboratory entails many kinds of training and operational activities. One category of foundational training activities centers on new technicians learning how to prepare themselves for entry into a cleanroom environment, so as not to introduce contaminants that might compromise the integrity of microscopic or nano-scale manufacturing processes or equipment. As revealed in the existing traditional text-based training materials, putting on a cleanroom gown (or "bunny suit") entails dozens of steps in specific locations, some in certain postures or body positions (Intel Education 2009). Modeling and simulating a cleanroom gowning process requires the creation of assets, in-game character behavior/animation scripts, and more as mods, as none of these features are part of the UT game. However, the FabLab game support the ability to study, walk-through, or rehearse the gowning process. This helps avoid potentially awkward learning experiences associated with getting (un)dressed in a new workplace with new or unfamiliar co-workers, as well as minimizing the cost of manufacturing problems that emerge from the introduction of contaminants that may unintentionally be brought in by technicians.

Another particularly vexing and challenging problem for such settings is how to collaboratively diagnose breakdowns in operations or complex equipment in geographically remote locations. This game mod demonstrates how manufacturing breakdowns due to faulty equipment or unanticipated materials spills/leaks can be modeled and collaboratively diagnosed, either locally and at a distance, as well as be used in training new manufacturing technicians (Brown and Scacchi 2007, 2008). For example, Fig. 18.2f shows a training scenario where a factory technician locates a liquid spill near a scanning electron microscope and must determine whether the spill is associated with this device and whether it involves a hazardous material. The trainee player can use a remote sensing instrument that provides a focus reticule that is aimed at the spill, and the trainee interprets the visual evidence and instrument readings to develop a diagnosis. If the problem lies with the device under scrutiny, the trainee has the potential to call up an animation that depicts the disassembly of the device for servicing. In contrast, in a remote diagnosis, master diagnostic technicians in one location can assist technicians on site in a remote factory location through networked game play mechanisms, when the remote factory equipment layout is configured to reflect current operations at the remote site. In both cases, players can use voice chat and mobile PCs to collaboratively engage in diagnosing visually observed evidence to determine possible causes and appropriate remedies/interventions.

Discussion

Many pleasant surprises arose during the development of DQO while working with our sponsors and collaborators at the DSC. Unpleasant surprises, grounded in dilemmas common to game and game software development (e.g., schedule over-runs or poorly documented software functions), are left out of the discussion here.

First, designing games that address explicit education standards – like the NSES (1996) – turned out to be quite liberating from a game design perspective. These standards helped make clear to the DQO developers what learning goals were needed and appropriate for learners of different ages/skill levels. The standards also highlight dependencies among concepts, which we found helped to simplify the challenges of what game play mechanics or game genre to employ to convey, embody, or experience specific science concepts. An example here is our repurposing of a Tetris game and play mechanics to depict prey–predator and food cycle relations (as displayed in Fig. 18.2e) and awards in-game points to players who correctly match these relations as new dinosaurs enter the play space for sorting and matching.

Second, during early usage evaluation and feedback studies at DSC, we found that we needed to support parents and teachers who experienced difficulty in comprehending what was going on (e.g., what scientific concepts or relations are in focus, how game play works, how in-game controls operate, how points and resource utilization are scored), while young players would readily dive into game play and start solving game play problems. Such support was subsequently developed and integrated (see Fig. 18.1c), and this helped facilitate better parent/teacher–child collaborative learning, based on our observations and user feedback.

Third, we found that some young students are able to provide copious explanations about what is going on and how the game works to their adult companions, while others provide much less. Though we collected many examples of these during evaluations of DQO game play at DSC, it seems that science learning games like DQO can become more effective learning environments when they provide in-game mechanisms that elicit or encourage online discourse and questions that elicit age/skill appropriate written explanations to further improve and deepen the value of the scientific concepts that have been learned. Such accomplishments have recently been demonstrated in other science learning game environments (cf. Shaffer 2006; Schaller et al. 2009).

In contrast to DQO, many technical and research challenges emerged with the development of the FabLab game world. First, when the project began, our focus was to respond to a challenge from our industrial project collaborators and sponsor (Intel). The challenge was to identify potential refinements and applications for how best to support globally distributed project teams that could interact and manipulate shared online artifacts and tools through domain-independent, collaborative virtual worlds (cf. Pickering et al. 2006) or other tools for visualizing socio–technical interaction networks whose members/elements were decentralized. This focus eventually led to a group of analysts and training personnel involved in finding ways for how to scale-up and optimize the training of thousands of technicians who are needed to operate and service a new semiconductor fabrication facility. Prior experience with multi-player FPS games brought to mind numerous in-game worlds (or levels) that situated game play in virtual laboratories, factories, or underground industrial infrastructures. Recognizing this, along with the ways and means for modding such game-based virtual worlds, quickly pointed the way for what could be modded to recreate a domain-specific, modern semiconductor fabrication facility in which multi-player activity could produce complex work practices and situations that can be (re)mediated through player-directed in-game avatars. So, we quickly moved to mod a capable FPS game (UT) to effectively create a low-cost, game-based work practices simulator for semiconductor fabrication service training that could be readily deployed in a multi-player environment that could operate over the Internet or local-area network.

Second, our experience with the underlying game and game play mechanics of UT also gave rise to discovering new ways to collaboratively diagnose operational problems like material spills or contamination across remote, networked facilities. Specifically, event-driven game play mechanics are often used to affect activities within the game world like opening a door when to touch (i.e., proximity detection) its handle, or enabling an interaction with a non-player character or in-world object whose behavior (e.g., an explosion that distributes object elements within a limited range) mediates what a player's avatar can do next. Similarly, by repurposing in-game FPS weapons to sense instead of shoot, allows a conceptual overloading of familiar play objects (weapons) to serve more instrumental and constructive ends. Using these, it then became possible to develop training scenarios where a taxonomy of detrimental or potentially hazardous material spills could be articulated, a given spill type could be introduced essentially anywhere on/near a modeled manufacturing machine, and players could sense and diagnose the problem and determine an appropriate response (e.g., service a leaky manufacturing machine) or voice chat with another collaborator (technician trainer or remote consulting technician). Such capabilities represent a new technological innovation in semiconductor fabrication training and operational service, and such an innovation ultimately emerged from modification and repurposing of games, game play, and game play mechanics.

Conclusions

Overall, this chapter seeks to articulate and explore how game-based virtual worlds can enable new modes of collaborative experience in science, technology, and engineering domains where decentralized play-as-work and work-as-play activities can emerge. The domains of informal life science education for young learners acting in regional science centers or at home and for training adult technicians in the operation and service of advanced, high-technology manufacturing systems are each of practical import and high consequence. Each further demonstrates the range and diversity of activities and collaboration affordances within virtual worlds, as well as across domains for scientific research and education, that can be enhanced through collaborative play-work (Bainbridge 2007).

Game-based virtual worlds can be employed in ways that support scientific research practices, technological innovation, and development of advanced engineering/manufacturing systems. Science and technology oriented game-based virtual worlds like *DinoQuest Online* and *FabLab* represent an interesting experiment in the collaborative construction (O'Donnell 2009) and use of decentralized virtual activity systems that different audiences find provide playful, productive, and collaborative interactions and learning/discovery-focused quests.

Acknowledgments This research is supported through grants from the National Science Foundation #0534771 and #0808783; Discovery Science Center; and Intel Corporation. No endorsement implied. Special thanks to Robert Nideffer, Alex Szeto, and Craig Brown at the UCI GameLab; Joe Adams and Janet Yamaguchi at DSC; and Eduardo Gamez and Eleanor Wynn at Intel, for their participation, contributions, and encouragement.

References

Bainbridge, W. S. (2007). The scientific research potential of virtual worlds. *Science, 317*, 472–476.
Bohannon, J., Gregory, T. R., Eldredge, N., & Bainbridge, W. S. (2009). Spore: Assessment of the science in an evolution-oriented game. In W.S. Bainbridge (Ed.), *Online worlds: Convergence of the real and virtual* (this volume). London: Springer.
Brown, C. & Scacchi, W. (2007). Modeling and navigating a simulated semiconductor fabrication laboratory using a game engine, from (http://www.ics.uci.edu/~wscacchi/GameLab/FactoryVisualization/FabLab-Draft-Scacchi-15Oct07.pdf).
Brown, C. & Scacchi, W. (2008). FabLab Game Demo Reel#3, from (http://www.ics.uci.edu/~wscacchi/GameLab/DemoReels/FabLab-Demo-03.wmv).

Clark, R. C. & Mayer, R. E. (2008). *e-Learning and the science of instruction: Proven guidelines for consumers and designers of multimedia learning.* San Francisco, CA: Pfieffer.

Intel Education. (2009). *What is a cleanroom? Working in a cleanroom.* Intel Corporation, from (http://www.intel.com/education/cleanroom/index2.htm), accessed 15 April 2009

Jakobsson, M. (2006). Questing for knowledge – Virtual worlds as dynamic processes of social interaction. In R. Schroder & A.S. Axelsson (Eds.), *Avatars at work and play* (pp. 209–225). Dordrecht, The Netherland: Springer.

Kirschner, P., Strijbos, J.-W., Kreijns, K., & Beers, P. J. (2004). Designing electronic collaborative learning environments. *Educational Technology Research and Development, 52*(3), 47–66.

NSES. (1996). *National science education standards.* Washington, DC: The National Academies Press, from (http://www.nap.edu/openbook.php?record_id=4962).

O'Donnell, C. (2009). The everyday lives of video game developers: Experimentally understanding underlying systems/structures. *Transformative works and culture* 2, from (http://journal.trans formativeworks.org), accessed 15 April 2009

Olson, G. M., Zimmerman, A., & Bos, N. (eds). (2008). *Scientific collaboration on the internet.* Cambridge, MA: MIT Press.

Pickering, C., Miller, J. D., Wynn, E., & House, C. (2006). 3D Global virtual teaming environment. In *Proceedings of the the Fourth International Conference on Creating, Connecting and Collaborating through Computing, (C5'06),* Berkeley, CA, 126–135.

Rieber, L. P. (2005). Multimedia learning in games, simulations, and microworlds. In R. E. Mayer (Ed.), *The Cambridge handbook of multimedia learning* (pp. 549–567). Cambridge: Cambridge University Press.

Scacchi, W. (2004). Free/open source software development practices in the computer game community. *IEEE Software 21*(1), 56–66.

Scacchi, W. & Adams, J. (2007). Recent developments in science learning games for informal science education. Games, learning, and society 3. Madison, WI.

Scacchi, W., Nideffer, R., & Adams, J. (2008a). A collaborative science learning game environment for informal science education: *DinoQuest Online.* In P. Ciancarini, R. Nakatsu, M. Rauterberg, & M. Roccetti (Eds.), *New frontiers for entertainment computing* (pp. 71–82). New York: Springer.

Scacchi, W., Kobsa, A., Lopes, C., Mark, G., Nardi, B., Redmiles, D., & Taylor, R. N. (2008b). *Decentralized virtual activities and technologies: A socio-technical perspective.* Institute for Software Research Report, UCI-ISR-08-04, December, from (http://www.ics.uci.edu/~ wscacchi/GameLab/NSF-DVAS-Proposal.pdf).

Schaller, D. T., Goldman, K. H., Spickelmier, G., Allison-Bunnell, S., & Koepfler, J. (2009). Learning in the wild: What Wolfquest taught developers and game players. In J. Trant & D. Bearman (Eds.), *Museums and the Web 2009: Proceedings.* Toronto: Archives & Museum Informatics, from (http://www.archimuse.com/mw2009/papers/schaller/schaller.html), accessed 15 April 2009

Schank, R. C. (2001). *Designing world-class e-Learning: How IBM, GE, Harvard business school, and Columbia University are succeeding at e-Learning.* New York: McGraw-Hill.

Shaffer, D. W. (2006). *How computer games help children learn.* New York: Palgrave Macmillan.

Twidale, M. (2005). Over the shoulder learning: Supporting brief informal learning. *Computer Supported Cooperative Work, 14,* 505–547.

Chapter 19
When Virtual Worlds Expand

William Sims Bainbridge

The future of a virtual world depends on whether it can grow in subjective size, cultural content, and numbers of human participants. In one form of growth, exemplified by *Second Life*, the scope of a world increases gradually as new sponsors pay for new territory and inhabitants create content. A very different form of growth is sudden expansion, as when *World of Warcraft* (WoW) added entire new continents in its Burning Crusade and Lich King expansions (Lummis and Kern 2006, 2008; Corneliussen and Rettberg 2008; Sims et al. 2008). Well-established gamelike worlds have often undergone many expansions. Both the pioneer science fiction game *Anarchy Online*, which was launched in 2001, and *Star Wars Galaxies* dating from 2003, have had three, and *EVE Online* also from 2003 has had nine, although smaller ones. This chapter reports research on WoW's 2008 Lich King expansion, using both quantitative and qualitative methods, in order to develop theoretical ideas of the implications of expansion for virtual worlds.

Saltation

In evolutionary terms, the adjective referring to sudden changes is *saltational*, referring to a jump from one state to another. Saltational expansions are fairly common in online role playing games, partly for public relations, and partly for technical reasons. In the most extreme cases, an entirely new world either replaces or comes into being alongside the old one, as in the cases of *Lineage 1* and *Lineage 2* or *EverQuest 1* and *EverQuest 2*. A revolutionary expansion makes news, and knowledge that one is in preparation can keep people playing a game – and paying their monthly subscriptions – even after completing their original goals. This was certainly the case for *World of Warcraft*. The original game took characters across two continents and up to experience level 60. Anticipated for months, the Burning Crusade and Lich King expansions each added 10 levels and opened vast new territories.

The technical reasons for saltational expansions are many. Often, new abilities are added to existing characters, which might be difficult to retrofit to the existing territories. A prime example was the ability to gain a flying mount in the Burning

Crusade expansion at the beginning of 2007. The only kind of flight permitted in the original continents was passive travel along pre-defined routes, in which a character rode a flying creature or zeppelin to a set destination. With Burning Crusade, a character could fly anywhere in the largest new territory, Outland, including to destinations that could not be reached on foot. To add this feature to the existing territories would have required great effort filling in many areas, for example inside mountain ranges, which had originally been left blank. A comparable example from a different virtual world is the initial *Star Wars Galaxies* expansion, Jump to Lightspeed, which for the first time allowed characters to pilot spaceships.

Another technical reason for saltation is the challenge of integrating many smaller changes. Some can be introduced at any time, especially if they are independent, but a large number of interconnected changes present many problems of implementation and debugging, which would be aggravated if they were introduced piecemeal. In fact, WoW has undergone many local changes, of which the largest was the addition of the Sunwell Isle, in March 2008. Another was the opening of the Gates of Ahn'Qiraj in Silithus, accomplished separately on each realm (server) through extensive quests against the insect Silithids in January 2006. But every Tuesday morning, each server goes offline for brief maintenance, which may include fixing of minor bugs and tweaking of parameters, so WoW evolves incrementally as well as saltationally.

A third cause of saltation concerns how the work is organized by the creators, involving assembling teams, coordinating efforts, and even switching emphasis from one world to another, as when the WoW creator, Blizzard Entertainment, needs to decide how to allocate staff responsibilities between WoW, its online strategy game *StarCraft*, and other projects. Not infrequently, the artistic style of an expansion is different, as was the case with the Burning Crusade expansion in which architectural textures were more fanciful than the original. The Lich King expansion added more fluid movements of non-player characters (NPCs) and many special atmospheric effects. A change in artistic style is more likely when the team of artists changes.

Given how vast saltations can be, studying one presents major logistic and methodological problems. Fortunately for the research described here, I already possessed two characters on the US Earthen Ring server that had reached the top experience level, one in each of the two factions: Maxrohn a male Human priest in the Alliance and Catullus a male Blood Elf priest in the Horde. A new class of character was introduced, death knights, so I created a female Undead one named Annihila, and used these three characters to explore the new territories and abilities. A fourth character, a Tauren shaman named Computabull, served as a "bank alt" by staying in the Horde city, Orgrimmar, where he handled the storage of virtual resources and conducted business for Catullus and Annihila. Both Catullus and Annihila belonged to the Alea Iacta Est (AIE) guild, and running the "/chatlog" command automatically saved enlightening text chat discussions between guild members.

The quantitative data are of two kinds: censuses and rosters. An open source "add-on" or "mod" software program named CensusPlus allows one to tally all characters online. I ran it repeatedly on five strategically selected Saturdays.

Three of these were before the expansion: October 25, November 1, and November 8. The expansion took place on November 13, 2008. A new edition of CensusPlus was then released, and I used it November 29 and December 20. The rosters came from Blizzard's online Armory website, where one may look up any character level 10 or above or any guild. Accessing the Armory requires manual labor, but the invisible XML code for the main page of each guild contains some information about all the members. I identified the more than two hundred guilds with at least 10 members online during October 25, downloaded their Armory pages on October 26 and December 21, then assembled the data into a single spreadsheet. These two datasets overlap but have somewhat different strengths and weaknesses; for example the rosters give the gender of characters while the censuses do not, but the rosters ignore characters who do not belong to large guilds.

Prelude and Lore

To carry out a major expansion successfully, one must prepare in at least three inter-related ways. First, one must develop an *enhanced mythos*, building upon the existing culture of the virtual world in a way that does not invalidate old material but does more than merely extrapolate from it. Second, one must do the same for the tech-nological features of the world, achieving *technical innovation*. Third, one must get ready for the actual expansion itself, both culturally and technically, through *transition preparation*.

In terms of existing lore and inclusion of mythic elements for the wider culture, the Lich King expansion was very well prepared. *World of Warcraft* is an extension of the early online strategy game, *Warcraft*, which already established the existence of the Lich King, the new Northrend continent, and death knights. In WoW lore, prior to the present role playing game, three different *Warcraft* games enacted three wars, the last of which climaxed with the Lich King's use of biological warfare that created the Undead, and his retreat to Northrend.

Many sections of Northrend are inhabited by groups of NPCs clearly based on Norse traditions, and everywhere one sees wooden sculptures of dragon heads like the prows of Viking longboats. One even encounters the goddess Freya whose ran-som set off the chain of events leading to Götterdämmerung in Richard Wagner's *Ring* operas. A series of quests for Alliance characters uses a drug-induced altered state of consciousness to take the player back in time to discover that the Human race originated as deformed babies of Vikings.

The invasion of Northrend included many characters seen in earlier zones, nota-bly at Westfall Brigade Encampment, staffed by soldiers recruited in the second zone for Human characters. The leader of the brigade, Gryan Stoutmantle, was first encountered at the tower in the center of Westfall, and now has been promoted to the rank of captain. Also, in the camp can be found Private Furlbrow fighting with Private Jansen, both of whom were Westfall farmers, and not far away is Old Blanchy, Furlbrow's horse for whom Alliance characters had long ago looted oats.

However, a trip back to Westfall revealed that Stoutmantle, Furlbrow, and Old Blanchy can still be found there as well.

The Burning Crusade expansion added a number of *microdramas*, short but complex interactions between NPCs. In one case, political dissidents harangued a crowd in Silvermoon City, before being brainwashed by the magic-empowered authorities. In another, once the player has infiltrated a cavern called Stillpine Hold, a group of friendly furbolgs swarmed in to clear out the enemy moonkin who had seized it.

The Lich King expansion introduced far more complex microdramas. For example, in the Borean Tundra lies Kaskala, a seaside village belonging to the Tuskarr walrus people. Kvaldir raiders, a clan of the sea Vrykuls, sail their boats one after another to the icy coast, and five men jump out of each to attack Tuskarrs standing near. The boats are clearly fantasy versions of Viking craft, open longboats rowed as well as carrying sails, with a dragon figurehead in the bow. The Tuskarrs are indigenous and spiritually oriented people, adapted to their very cold climate, and they seem to represent Inuit Eskimo. Thus, the battle is reminiscent of the actual competition between Norsemen and Inuit that took place many centuries ago in Greenland. Each local skirmish with about five combatants on a side is somewhat unpredictable, although the Tuskarrs ultimately survive and the raiders are unable to expand their beachhead. Kvaldir boats constantly arrive, up and down a long shore and nearby island, so the whole scene is remarkably complex.

Kaskala illustrates a major challenge faced by gamelike virtual worlds: the absence of progress when each new player must have the opportunity to kill the enemy bosses already killed by earlier players. Soon after a boat has brought its crew of five Kvaldir raiders ashore at Kaskala, it disappears, making room for another one. The individual player kills enough raiders to compete the quest and gain the reward, but the battle never ends. Blizzard's ambition to begin including more opportunities for historical progress was expressed in the Sunwell Isle battles, where progress over a period of weeks and months did move the battle front, but glacially slowly. With the Lich King expansion, WoW sought to add a greater sense of progress on the larger scale (Fig. 19.1).

The most extensive example began days before the expansion itself, when the Lich King sent Scourge raiding parties into the original WoW continents, ultimately provoking the joint Horde–Alliance invasion of Northrend. Players quested deep into remote regions of the old territories in search of levitating fortresses, killing Scourge minions engaged in magical rituals to establish beachheads of evil. Packs of ghouls intermittently raided civilized areas of the old world. Finally, on the Monday before the Thursday expansion, the Lich King's forces attacked two cities, the Horde's Orgrimmar where Catullus helped repel the invasion, and the Alliance's Stormwind where Maxrohn did the same. In both places, skeletal dragons flew overhead spewing fire, and huge cadaverous abominations stormed across a section of the city. The sense of innovation was emphasized in Stormwind because the attack came on the beautiful new harbor section of the city, which had not been accessible – or even existed – only a few days before. In Orgrimmar, the sense of history was emphasized when the heroic Horde leader, Thrall, was defeated in a

Fig. 19.1 Vrykuls attacking Tuskarrs at Kaskala. © 2010 Blizzard Entertainment, Inc.

(non-fatal) duel, thereby losing his right to command the retaliation against the Lich King.

Both events were staged several times that Monday, but not repeated afterward, thus taking history one big step forward. On Thursday, players quickly purchased and installed the expansion itself, facilitated by the fact that much of the material for the change had been downloaded days before from Internet. Ships streamed from Stormwind and Menethil harbors, taking Alliance characters to Northrend. On the Horde side, zeppelins from Orgrimmar on one old continent, and Undercity on the other, carried hundreds of retaliating warriors into the land of the Lich King. To handle the huge waves of players in the early days of the expansion, Blizzard had created two large landing zones, Borean Tundra and Howling Fjord, at opposite ends of Northrend. Catullus entered Borean Tundra on Thursday, then returned to Orgrimmar on Friday to join nearly a hundred other members of the AIE guild in Thrall's throne room. With Thrall himself sitting gloomily on his throne and presumably brooding about his personal disgrace, the AIE members marched to the zeppelin tower, invaded Northrend, and rampaged for hours all over the southwestern quarter of the new continent (Fig. 19.2).

A standard MMORPG method for encapsulating battles so they can be experienced afresh by all new players is the *instance* or *dungeon*, a subworld that can be running several times simultaneously for different teams of players (Sumner et al. 2006). By one count, WoW currently has fully 74 of these, 17 of them in Northrend.[1]

---

[1] http://www.wowwiki.com/Instances_by_continent

Fig. 19.2 Alea Iacta Est gathers in Thrall's Throne Room to invade Northrend. ©2010 Blizzard Entertainment, Inc.

However, in WoW as in many other MMORPGs, leaving an instance or logging off the computer resets the instance so it must be started from scratch.

With the Lich King, WoW introduced *persistent instances*, of which the most prominent example is the death knight starter zone added to the edge of an existing zone, Eastern Plaguelands. There, death knights gain some training, then attack the humans in the Scarlet Enclave, fairly swiftly defeating them and then attacking Light's Hope Chapel, a well-established location. All of this, including the duplication of a small section of Eastern Plaguelands, is an instance that cannot be entered by any characters except death knights. Logging out does not reset the instance, which is the feature that makes it *persistent*. One does not need to be a member of a stable group to complete the many quests inside it, but other players are present and one may cooperate with them, as Annihila did on one occasion with a fellow AIE member. However, the environment appears quite different to players under-taking different quests, so apparently WoW uses a system of multiple instances, each at a different point in history, allowing players to enter only the correct one. This in turn requires players to do quests in a set sequence, completing all of them before being allowed to leave this persistent instance.

Several smaller areas in Northrend function like persistent instances, but do not have obvious boundaries that bar other players from entering. I can only speculate about how each one works. In the advanced Icecrown zone, the Shadow Vault is initially an enemy stronghold, but the individual player is able over time to conquer it, after which it becomes a friendly base. Apparently, different versions of Shadow Vault are visible to players at different points in the quest chain.

Valkyrion in Northrend's Storm Peak zone functions on a different principle. This town is inhabited by Nordic women related to the legendary Valkyries. Initially, they are enemies, but a player can earn the right to assume the appearance of a Nordic woman, visiting the village as a friend and using its facilities. When flying to Valkyrion, a character's appearance automatically changes when crossing an invisible perimeter. This subterfuge may allow Valkyrion to operate without instancing, because the character changes rather than the environment changing, and one player visiting the village will not immediately know which of the women milling about are actually other players rather than NPCs.

New Character Features

Major expansions to gamelike virtual worlds often introduce new kinds of characters and give new abilities to existing ones. The Burning Crusade expansion added two new races, the Blood Elves and the Draenei, along with new low-level zones where characters in these races originated, plus a new jewelcrafting profession that any character could learn. The Lich King expansion added one new class, the death knights, plus a magical profession called *inscription*. In WoW, there are now ten races, each with its own lore and visual characteristics, but differing little in abilities – members of the Undead race can swim under water longer than the others, for example. There are now also ten classes, each being a very distinct set of abilities that facilitate playing different roles in WoW society. Death knight is the only class available to all races. Two of the eleven major professions can be learned by any one character, and they represent different economic roles in the division of labor that gathers virtual resources and crafts them to create valuable potions, armor, machinery, and the like.

Death knights are former soldiers in the Lich King's army, who suffered death than resurrection in the Third War when he captured them. Because they have lived before, they do not start at level 1, as all other characters do, but at level 55, with the weapon skills and other characteristics appropriate for that relatively high level of experience. Until level 58, they continue to serve the Lich King, but then are liberated to seek their own destinies. They are the first heroic class in WoW, super-warriors who not only wear the strongest plate armor but also possess some magical powers.

It is quite an experience to run a death knight through Outland, after having done so with two rather feeble priests, because Annihila could defeat one enemy after another without pause, not invulnerable but much stronger than other classes. Especially noteworthy is the death knight's *death grip* ability, which magically pulls an enemy into broadsword range, useful for plucking one out of a group for swift destruction, or for retrieving an enemy who has fled beyond reach of the death knight's blade. Because the experience of running a death knight is so ecstatic, it

Fig. 19.3 Annihila bows before her Liege, the Lich King. ©2010 Blizzard Entertainment, Inc.

encourages players to enjoy afresh many quests they had already completed with other characters (Fig. 19.3).

Inscription is a crafting profession that uses parchment bought from NPC vendors with inks made from herbs to produce scrolls, glyphs, and other magical documents of value to the scribe and to other players to whom the scribe may give or sell these products. Scrolls are *buffs* that temporarily improve one of a character's abilities. They had existed before, but could not be created, only looted from occasional dead enemies. Glyphs are new, a kind of internal buff specialized for different classes and abilities. Introducing inscription in the expansion required reprogramming each character's user interface to have a glyph page capable of holding as many as three minor and three major glyphs. The fact that inscription requires the input of vast numbers of herbs from which to make ink, increased the commercial value of the herbalism gathering profession that garners herbs from the environment. Prior to the expansion, the chief use of herbs was to feed the alchemy profession, which used them to make magic liquids. Now, alchemists must compete with scribes for the herbs, thereby increasing the profitability of herbalism. Thus, a new profession has implications for the entire economic system.

This, in turn had implications for the economic impact of the new Northrend territory, which offered new and higher-level herbs, and where competition between herbalists was initially intense because they were all in the two starter zones, Borean Tundra and Howling Fjord. Such competition for scarce natural resources was greater at first for another gathering profession, mining, which serves fully three of the crafting professions: blacksmithing, engineering, and jewelcrafting.

Because of its economic centrality, mining was very popular, and because the related crafting professions were already well established, ores from Northrend were in immediate demand. It took a few days for characters practicing the new inscription profession to need the high-level herbs, which herbalists could gather in Northrend, so at first the chief customers for the herbalists were alchemists. A complicating factor is that many characters had both alchemy and herbalism for their two professions, thus being self-sufficient. The net effect is that the economic changes introduced by a new profession and new resources occur over a period of days in a chaotic manner.

A major addition to the status system of the WoW community was a system of fully 749 achievements that grant points for accomplishments like completing 1000 quests, becoming a grand master in a profession, or what all three of my high-level research characters gained, "Working Day and Night," which means becoming a grand master in the maximum two professions. Achievements are not only listed in the Armory, but are also posted automatically to the character's guild chat, building the character's prestige with other players. Thus, when Catullus discovered an area of Crystalsong Forest called The Great Tree, the AIE chat proclaimed: "Catullus has earned the achievement Explore Crystalsong Forest! Catullus has earned the achievement Explore Northrend!" This means that finding the tree completed his exploration of the forest, and that in turn completed his exploration of the new continent. In addition, he received in his mail the Tabard of the Explorer from renowned dwarf NPC explorer Brann Bronzebeard, who wrote, "Wear this tabard with pride. That way your friends will know who to ask for directions when the time comes!"

Table 19.1 shows a small selection of the vast data about my four characters available on their Armory web pages. Some of the variables, such as quests completed, reputations with NPC factions, and exploration of territories, include data from before the Lich King expansion, because these data are used to determine details of the options open to characters. Other variables, such as flight paths taken, beverages consumed, food eaten, kills, and deaths were counted only from the expansion, because these data had no function prior to the creation of the achievements system. The four reputation rows concern quests performed for, or hostile action taken against, factions of NPCs. The Timbermaw occupy a tunnel connecting three zones, and Maxrohn blasted his way through, earning a negative reputation, whereas Catullus did quests for the Timbermaw and was welcomed through with a positive reputation. Most visitors to Shattrath City in Outland join either Aldor or the Scryers, gaining use of their inns at the cost of antagonizing the other faction, but Annihila chose instead to work with the Consortium outside Shattrath to get the ability to make a flying machine with her engineering profession.

The bottom of the table shows how many areas of the four continents each character had explored, thereby opening the corresponding area on their interface maps. Anyone checking Annihila's Armory website could learn she visited only five places on the continent of Kalimdor, each of them being a commercial hub which she could fly to without exploring the land between: Orgrimmar, Thunder Bluff, Crossroads, Gadgetzan, and Everlook. In Northrend, she visited only Warsong

Table 19.1 Four characters in the armory database

	Annihila	Maxrohn	Catullus	Computabull
Experience Level	70	75	80	30
Race	Undead	Human	Blood Elf	Tauren
Class	Death knight	Priest	Priest	Shaman
Talents, across three class-specific talent trees	Blood 2 Frost 47 Unholy 12	Discipline 21 Holy 45 Shadow 0	Discipline 57 Holy 0 Shadow 14	Elemental 21 Enhancement 0 Restoration 0
Achievements	25/749	37/749	79/749	10/749
Achievement points	250	370	820	100
Professions, limited to two, with skill level	Engineering 431 Inscription 435	Alchemy 450 Herbalism 450	Mining 450 Skinning 450	Blacksmithing 92 Engineering 194
Guild	Alea Iacta Est	The foundation	Alea Iacta Est	None
Health points	7,784	8,029	11,290	691
Armor strength	8,418	1,313	1,469	380
Helm, with material and strength	Snow Goggles plate 1,681	Abandoned hood cloth 153	Mildred's Cowl cloth 172	None
Main weapon, DPS = damage per second	Saboteur's Axe 75.2 DPS	Melted wand of the eagle 165 DPS	Touch of light wand 187.5 DPS	Long Staff 15.2 DPS
Riding skill	225	75	225	0
Timbermaw reputation	0	−3,952	3,290	0
Aldor reputation	0	6,556	−11,348	0
Scryers reputation	0	−7,211	10,635	0
Consortium reputation	24,620	4,587	5,163	0
Flight paths taken	77	65	238	1
Quests completed	248	1,181	1,436	147
Quests abandoned	40	16	59	0
Total kills	4,293	1,605	3,897	0
Total deaths	26	54	90	0
Factions encountered	21	36	44	11
Beverages consumed	0	1,309	1,390	0

(continued)

Table 19.1 (continued)

	Annihila	Maxrohn	Catullus	Computabull
Food eaten	226	21	152	0
Vanity pets owned	4	6	1	0
Eastern kingdoms	12 areas	232 areas	256 areas	17 areas
Kalimdor	5 areas	125 areas	153 areas	64 areas
Outland	73 areas	111 areas	137 areas	0 areas
Northrend	2 areas	71 areas	131 areas	0 areas

Hold and Vengeance Landing, the two entry points for members of the Horde, where she could get Master training in her two professions. A conversation in the Alea Iacta Est guild chat illustrated how players share information about the changes in the game interface. Wintersquall had just reached level 70, gaining the ability to fly over Outland, and he wanted to use this skill to complete exploration achievements:

> Wintersquall: hmm, i just cleared terrokar's map but didn't get an achievement... sup [what's up] with that
> Undomael: you'd got one bit you haven't been to
> Wintersquall: and how do i find that? XD [consternation expression]
> Undomael: go east to firewing point, a spot easy to miss cuz horde
> Wintersquall: so basically i have to guess XD ok, ty [thank you]
> Undomael: yep
> Catullus: The areas you cleared are checked in the inside window for the zone in your Achievements window
> Undomael: oh yeah, that too
> Wintersquall: i didn't know i had an achievements window, sorry – how do i check that?
> Undomael: it's right next to your talents button, default keystroke is Y
> Wintersquall: whoa, never seen that before
> Wintersquall: so apparently i need to find skettis
> Chaveyo: get the *overachiever* addon [plug-in software] from curse.com-- really helpful for achievement tracking
> Treiajje: an apt name
> Chaveyo: very helpful for rolling your mouse over unloved critters, uneaten foods, etc
> Wintersquall: thanks chaveyo, i'll look into that add on
> Chaveyo: and books for *well read*
> Treiajje: I wonder if there is an *underachiever* mod [interface modification = addon] for those of us who run from achievements :P [sticking out tongue]
> Chaveyo: it's called *network television*
> Treiajje: lol [laugh out loud]
> Wintersquall: hahaha

Population Stratification and Class

The chief goal of expansions in subscriber-based virtual worlds is to retain customers, so it is not surprising that Northrend was designed for characters above about level 67, and a player could not create a death knight without having already brought at least one earlier character to level 55. However, the great publicity given to the Lich King expansion could have attracted large numbers of new players, and our census can help us evaluate this possibility, in Table 19.2. The numbers are average percent of the total population *per level*, collapsing the data on the many early levels while rendering the figures comparable across rows.

On October 25, 2008, 11.62% of the 9,881 characters were at levels 61–69, compared with 12.60% on November 1 and 12.10% on November 8. These small differences are consistent with a couple of hundred characters working hard to reach level 70 before the expansion, as is the increase of those at level 69, from 1.31% to 1.62%. In November 29 we see some hint that new players are entering in higher numbers for levels 1–20, compared with 21–50. A key socio-technical factor that may have discouraged new players was that popular realms like Earthen Ring often filled up in the early weeks after the expansion, forcing players to wait in a queue with as many as a thousand other players for as long as an hour until enough others had logged off. New players would have entered new realms, or older ones that happened to have lower populations. As a partial solution to the demographic pressures, WoW offered a carefully limited set of free character moves to lower population realms, although this may have been attractive chiefly to guildless individual players. Creating a large number of new realms would have been costly, and long after the excitement of the expansion wore off the pressures lifted naturally.

Veteran players presumably ignored their lower-level *alt* characters, and ran their *mains* in Northrend or created new death knights that start at level 55 rather than level 1. The drop at all lower levels from November 8 to November 29 reflects this. The jump in November 29 data from levels 51–60 through 65 can be attributed to the death knights. The most striking pattern in the table is the rush from level 70 to level 80 as soon as the expansion occurs. Indeed, Catullus is at level 70 in the first three censuses, reached level 75 by November 29, and achieved level 80 on December 13.

We can compare 3,163 death knights with 33,822 characters in other classes in Table 19.3, which presents data primarily from the final Armory roster of guild members level 10 and above. At the moment of the expansion, players had to decide whether to begin by running an existing high-level character across Northrend, or starting a new death knight, although later they could switch to the other option. In any case, we see that death knights are no more numerous than other classes, much less so than the very popular hunter class, which possesses interesting hunting animals and is probably a popular second choice after a player has exhausted the possibilities of another class. Of course many of the other characters may be inactive during this period, whereas all of the death knights were used by their players or

Table 19.2   Characters per Level (Percent of total for date)

Levels	Oct 25	Nov 1	Nov 8	Nov 29	Dec 21
1–10	0.62%	0.62%	0.66%	0.54%	0.60%
11–20	0.71%	0.64%	0.68%	0.48%	0.56%
21–30	0.70%	0.64%	0.69%	0.39%	0.43%
31–40	0.56%	0.62%	0.62%	0.33%	0.40%
41–50	0.56%	0.53%	0.58%	0.36%	0.35%
51–60	0.60%	0.60%	0.60%	0.92%	0.80%
61	1.21%	0.97%	0.87%	1.81%	1.32%
62	1.21%	1.08%	1.15%	1.46%	1.14%
63	1.10%	1.18%	1.24%	1.57%	1.10%
64	1.09%	1.53%	1.26%	1.47%	1.32%
65	1.27%	1.45%	1.31%	1.49%	1.08%
66	1.51%	1.83%	1.62%	1.34%	1.21%
67	1.40%	1.38%	1.41%	1.30%	1.15%
68	1.52%	1.62%	1.63%	1.06%	0.98%
69	1.31%	1.55%	1.62%	1.09%	0.99%
70	51.03%	50.75%	49.57%	8.36%	5.62%
71	0.00%	0.00%	0.00%	5.84%	3.51%
72	0.00%	0.00%	0.00%	5.29%	3.56%
73	0.00%	0.00%	0.00%	4.96%	3.05%
74	0.00%	0.00%	0.00%	4.64%	2.94%
75	0.00%	0.00%	0.00%	4.51%	2.59%
76	0.00%	0.00%	0.00%	3.39%	2.33%
77	0.00%	0.00%	0.00%	3.20%	2.64%
78	0.00%	0.00%	0.00%	2.81%	2.41%
79	0.00%	0.00%	0.00%	2.24%	1.94%
80	0.00%	0.00%	0.00%	12.04%	27.69%
Total N	9881	9554	9770	9920	9774

Table 19.3   Roster of guild members

Class	Number	Percent female	Average achievement points	Average experience level
Death knight	3,163	32.1	321.2	65.0
Druid	3,200	37.8	591.1	53.7
Hunter	4,580	35.9	512.9	54.3
Mage	3,636	43.4	524.0	53.3
Paladin	3,496	34.1	590.9	54.7
Priest	3,179	51.7	534.3	54.1
Rogue	3,287	35.7	509.3	52.6
Shaman	2,642	36.3	525.1	53.6
Warlock	3,211	41.5	472.4	52.3
Warrior	3,428	24.4	584.5	55.5
Inactive	11,977	36.9	282.2	49.9
Active	7,837	36.7	1037.0	66.5

they would not have existed. The bottom of the table reports 19,814 characters in the December 21 roster who were also listed on October 26, dividing them into 7,837 active characters who advanced at least one level during that period, and 11,977 inactive characters who did not. None of these were death knights, because that class did not exist in October, but adding the 3,163 death knights for a total of 15,140, the death knights become 20.9% of the active characters.

Research on virtual worlds is beginning to examine the impact of demographic variables, such as gender, acknowledging that our data concern the genders of characters not of players. As I have found in other WoW data, female characters are overrepresented among priests (who are healers), and underrepresented among warriors (who spearhead team attacks), possibly reflecting the traditionally nurturant female social role and the greater average aggressiveness of males (Rossi 1984; Shelton and John 1996; Washington and Karen 2001; Jackman 2002). Of the total 3,163 death knights tallied, 1,016 or 32.1% were female. Among female death knights, the average experience level reached was 63.5, compared with an average of 65.7 for the males, which represent an average progress from the starting level 55 of 8.5 and 10.7. On average, females had gained 290.7 achievement points, compared with 335.5 for males. Depending on the measure chosen, females progressed at a rate 79% or 87% that of males. Future research should examine whether female players might be at a disadvantage in playing especially violent roles, such as the super-warrior death knights, but at an advantage in playing other kinds of roles.

Conclusion

The Lich King expansion chiefly served to energize existing subscribers to *World of Warcraft*, giving them new territory to explore, new quests to undertake, and new dimensions of reputation with their fellows. The mythic lore showed great continuity with the existing world, and with the prior *Warcraft* online strategy game, as well as drawing on elements from the wider culture such as the Norse motif in Northrend. Indirectly and over time, all this may attract new players, because it verifies the vitality of this virtual world and motivates existing subscribers to recruit even more of their friends. The end result is a vast and varied world that could easily hold the interest of a player for a year or two, with a vibrant and complex community of other players, many of whom may become permanent residents.

References

Corneliussen, H. G. & Rettberg, J. W. (eds). (2008). *Digital culture, play and identity: A world of warcraft reader*. Cambridge, MA: MIT Press.
Jackman, M. R. (2002). Violence in social life. *Annual Review of Sociology, 28*, 387–415.
Lummis, M., & Kern, E. (2006). *World of warcraft master guide*. Indianapolis, IN: BradyGames.

Rossi, A. S. (1984). Gender and parenthood. *American Sociological Review, 49*, 1–19.

Shelton, B. A., & John, D. (1996). The division of household labor. *Annual Review of Sociology, 22*, 299–322.

Sims, J., Sims, K., & Hall, D. (2008). *World of warcraft: Wrath of the lich King*. Indianapolis, IN: BradyGames.

Sumner, C., Schmidt, K., Shotton, B., & Owen, M. (eds). (2006). *World of warcraft dungeon companion*. Indianapolis, IN: BradyGames.

Washington, R. E. & Karen, D. (2001). Sport and society. *Annual Review of Sociology, 27*, 187–212.

Chapter 20
Cooperation, Coordination, and Trust in Virtual Teams: Insights from Virtual Games

M. Audrey Korsgaard, Arnold Picot, Rolf T. Wigand, Isabelle M. Welpe, and Jakob J. Assmann

Since their introduction in the late 1970s, MMOGs (massively multiplayer online games) have developed from relatively simple text-based games with hundreds of players into complex 3D environments with millions of players. In this process, teams and organizations within these virtual worlds have become increasingly important for the gameplay as players must cooperate, coordinate, and strategize their actions to be successful. The social dynamics of MMOGs have increasingly attracted the attention of scholars from many disciplines (Bainbridge 2007; Castronova and Falk 2009). As microcosms of social and organizational phenomena, virtual settings hold great potential for innovative research in the social sciences, although such research is still in its early stages (e.g. Picot et al. 2009; Williams et al. 2006). Accordingly, MMOGs can serve as living laboratories for the study of social systems in ways that purport implications for other important contexts.

Here, we apply the study of MMOGs to actual work organizations. Specifically, we make a case for how the study of MMOGs can inform on the dynamics and effectiveness of conventional and virtual teams in work organizations. We first briefly review the literature on workgroups and teams as well as research on virtual teams and organizations with particular emphasis on the role of information and communication technology (ICT). We then discuss how these essential elements and dynamics of group functioning are present in MMOG play, and how studying MMOGs can lead to important insights. Finally, we draw conclusions and give an outlook on other applications of MMOGs for research.

Effective Teams

A team is a collective of individuals working interdependently toward a common goal (Marks et al. 2001). Contemporary team effectiveness models employ an input-process-output conceptualization of group effectiveness (Ilgen et al. 2005). Inputs are general characteristics of the team and its members impacting the group's willingness and capability to work together toward team goals. These inputs are transformed through social processes involving cooperative and coordinated efforts.

W.S. Bainbridge (ed.), *Online Worlds: Convergence of the Real and the Virtual*,
Human-Computer Interaction Series, DOI 10.1007/978-1-84882-825-4_20,
© Springer-Verlag London Limited 2010

In turn, these processes render certain team outputs of effective teams, such as productivity and innovation. Below, we briefly summarize research on inputs and processes related to team effectiveness.

Team inputs contributing to effectiveness are the resources that enable a team to work more effectively. These resources include the individual and collective capabilities of the team, diversity, size, and leadership along with the skills and abilities relevant to the required tasks. Teams composed of members with requisite skills will be, all else being equal, more capable to perform the task. The degree to which the team is diverse on personal attributes is also a key input to group effectiveness, even if the attributes are not directly relevant to task performance. Diversity is a two-edged sword, for while diversity can lead to innovation and high-quality decision-making, social harmony, trust, and cohesion of a group can be adversely affected by diversity, particularly when team members differ in demographic and personality characteristics (Harrison et al. 2002).

Another essential group input is its shared knowledge structures, or the degree of shared understanding among team members. One important type of knowledge structure is the concept of shared mental models, referring to the extent to which the team shares an understanding of tasks and strategies for achieving tasks (Marks et al. 2000). Teams with strong shared mental models tend to communicate and coordinate more effectively and, consequently, perform better. Another important knowledge structure for teams is transactive memory systems (Lewis 2003), referring to the extent team members share an understanding of which members possess specialized knowledge and can be trusted to perform certain tasks. Like shared mental models, transactive memory systems facilitate coordination and performance (Zhang et al. 2007).

Leadership style is another important factor in guiding and motivating the team. For example, teams with charismatic leaders tend to cooperate and coordinate more effectively, in turn leading to more effective team performance (Lester et al. 2002). Further, teams performing better tend to trust each other more. Group size is a final input to team effectiveness. Larger teams have the potential for greater capabilities, but this advantage may be offset by greater coordinating challenges and greater potential for free-riding (Gist et al. 1987). Leadership is also a key input to team process and effectiveness.

Effective *team processes* are interdependent acts directed toward transforming team inputs to desired collective outcomes (Marks et al. 2001). These activities can be distinguished from those performed within an individual team member's job in that team processes describe how team members work together. While various team effectiveness models describe processes differently, two core processes of effective teams are coordination and cooperation (Ilgen et al. 2005). Coordination refers to the team's efforts to plan, sequence, and monitor interdependent actions of its members. Cooperation refers to team members' willingness to direct efforts toward mutually beneficial outcomes. These processes are significant predictors of team effectiveness (LePine et al. 2008).

Coordination requires gathering and evaluating information, structuring the task, and learning and adapting, which are all essential to effective performance.

Coordinating activities requires communication, and monitoring the actions of other team members' actions (Majchrzak et al. 2007). Thus, inputs that encourage effective communication and enable or encourage mutual monitoring can lead to effective coordination. However, various coordination mechanisms may be more or less effective under different task and reward systems (Welbourne and Ferrante 2008). Moreover, as shared knowledge structures form, explicit coordination activities give way to trust (Majchrzak et al. 2007). Mature, functioning teams can work from implicit shared knowledge structures; however, if membership changes, shared knowledge may be lost and, coordination and performance will thereby be undermined (Lewis et al. 2007).

Cooperation within a team requires team members to trust one another and the team (Deutsch 1958); thus, factors promoting trust will encourage cooperation. Team members must be confident in each others' ability and willingness to produce beneficial outcomes. Several factors can build or undermine trust and cooperation. As noted above, the inputs of teams, especially diversity within the team and the presence of strong leadership, influence the degree of trust and cohesiveness within the team, which in turn influences the level of cooperation within the group. In addition, communication can promote trust and cooperation (e.g., Buchan et al. 2006). Further, interactions within the group both reflect current levels of cooperation and shape future levels of cooperation. Research suggests that generosity directed at team members can promote cooperation, particularly in uncertain or "noisy" situations (Klapwijk and Van Lange 2009).

Inputs and processes leading to effectiveness unfold over time as the team matures (Marks et al. 2001). In early stages of the team's development, team members seek to establish clarity over tasks and about each other (Ilgen et al. 2005). Concerns over exploitation and incompetence tend to be salient as team members develop trust (or distrust) for one another. Lacking direct knowledge of each other, team members are particularly sensitive to "surface-level" diversity, relying on social or demographic categories to make inferences (Harrison et al. 2002). Later, groups transition into a functioning stage wherein norms, roles, and modes of interaction have been established. Shared knowledge structures become established and teams develop patterns of interaction and coordination that enable learning, adaptation, and performance (Marks et al. 2000). In addition, the deleterious effects of surface diversity on social harmony and cooperation diminish (Harrison et al. 2002) while the adverse effects of deeper, values-based dissimilarity become more apparent (Jehn and Mannix 2001).

Virtual Teams

The preceding review outlines the fundamentals of working in teams. The particular challenges to virtual work, however, have led scholars to view virtual teams as a unique phenomenon (Bell and Kozlowski 2002). In this section, we briefly review this literature by focusing on three core issues. The first issue is understanding the definition and nature of virtual teams. The Ssecond is the extent to which virtual teams are unique from conventional, collocated teams. The third is identifying the key conditions for effectiveness in virtual settings.

What is a virtual team? The prevailing view today is that virtualness is a characteristic of teams that varies along two primary dimensions (Martins et al. 2004). First, virtualness is determined by the reliance on information and communication technology (ICT). It is important to note that actual ICT use is often a choice made by team members (Kirkman and Mathieu 2005). Even teams that are physically present in the same location and are able to interact in a face-to-face manner may choose to rely on various forms of ICT to interact with one another. ICTs vary on a number of dimensions such as synchronicity and richness that have important implications for the functioning of groups and organizations, an issue we discuss later in the chapter further below.

Second, virtualness typically involves physical dispersion of team members. Teams may be physically separated for several reasons. A team may be headquartered in one location but some team members telecommute from other locations. Teams may also be dispersed because members or subgroups are located on more than one worksite. Teams may be dispersed because team members or subgroups are employed by different organizations. Dispersion takes on many forms and degrees. It can be represented by the average distance between team members, the number of distinct worksites, and the distribution of team members across those work sites (O'Leary and Cummings 2007).

Geographic dispersion has implications beyond physical distance. The greater the geographic dispersion, the greater the temporal differences in team members (O'Leary and Cummings 2007). Thus, geographic dispersion not only constrains the team's ability to opt for face-to-face interaction, but also affects the viability of synchronous forms of ICT as it becomes more difficult for temporally dispersed teams to find a common time to meet in a virtual context. Moreover, because ICT enables teams to span the globe, virtual teams are often culturally diverse. Finally, dispersion in virtual teams is often associated with more permeable boundaries in teams. Virtual teams are typically more fluid in that the composition of the team can change readily and the entire team may form and dissolve relatively quickly (Mowshowitz 1997).

What makes virtual teams unique? A major advantage of virtual teams and organizations is their ability to span boundaries within and between organizations. Members can be assembled into virtual teams so as to precisely meet the skill requirements of the task. Thus, virtual teams have the potential of being more capable than collocated teams (Blackburn et al. 2003). ICT frees teams from the constraint of traditional hierarchical decision-making and information structures, leading to greater empowerment and flexibility. As such, virtual teams also have the potential for better coordinated and collaborative work (e.g., Hossain and Wigand 2003).

With these benefits come certain downsides to virtual teams. Team members are vulnerable to social isolation (Kirkman et al. 2002) that can lead to stress and disengagement from work (Raghuram et al. 2001). Team members are also apt to feel they lack information about other team members, leading to uncertainty (Tangirala and Alge 2006). Because members of virtual teams are more loosely coupled and enjoy relatively greater autonomy, there is a significant risk of opportunism, free-riding, and antisocial behavior (Kurtzberg et al. 2005; Rockmann and Northcraft 2008).

Leadership of virtual teams poses its own unique challenges. Typically, team leadership serves two primary functions: task-based activities such as assigning roles, monitoring progress, and holding members accountable, and relational-based activities, such as motivating and supporting team members and managing conflicts. These activities are far more difficult when team leaders are not directly interacting and observing team members (Bell and Kozlowski 2002). ICT empowers and enables more complex forms of collaboration. Leaders of virtual teams must fulfill the task-based role through less directive means than in traditional command and control structures. Not surprisingly, scholars have identified leadership as a central challenge in virtual teams, as control is difficult when team leaders are not co-located with team members (Hertel et al. 2005).

What makes virtual teams effective? As with any team, virtual teams require certain structures and processes to perform effectively. Team members must possess the requisite task skills, and be sufficiently engaged and committed to the group and its goals. As well, the group as a whole must engage in core processes of coordination and cooperation. The characteristics and challenges of virtual teams pose a hindrance to core processes of teams. Largely, the success of virtual teams rests on their ability to overcome these hindrances. Consequently, factors contributing to cooperation and coordination, while not wholly unique to virtual teams, are especially critical to team success and worthy of particularly close scrutiny.

As noted above, effective teams develop shared knowledge structures that enable them to coordinate effectively. Development of these capacities requires experience and interaction among team members. To the extent that modes of communication are limited and team members cannot rely on direct observation of behavior, it may take teams longer to develop such capacities. A recent meta-analysis found that compared with conventional teams, virtual teams took more time to make decisions and made less effective decisions (Baltes et al. 2002). In the absence of direct experience, virtual teams must rely on ICT to explicitly share ideas about the group's goals and tasks and the capabilities of individual members. Virtual teams spending more time on task-based communication are more effective in coordinating their efforts (Kanawattanachai and Yoo 2007).

As noted above, numerous factors may enhance collective cooperation in teams, but in virtual settings, trust in the team and the leadership becomes especially vulnerable to the exploitation and incompetence of other team members. Structures and policies such as contracts, monitoring, and incentives may offset these risks. However, attempts to address this uncertainty and risk through behavioral controls and monitoring can undermine trust in virtual settings (Piccoli and Ives 2003). Alternatively, team members may trust each other and their leader because they believe that they are trustworthy – specifically, that they are competent, honest, and benevolent (e.g., Hossain and Wigand 2003). Forming such judgments requires observation, experience, and interactions, which are often hindered in virtual context. Thus, some face-to-face contact in the early stages of working relationships may be especially important to promoting trust and collaborative behavior in virtual teams (Bell and Kozlowski 2008). As well, richer forms of communication promote trust and a willingness to cooperate (Rockmann and Northcraft 2008).

In short, effective coordination and cooperation in virtual teams requires shared understandings and mutual trust, which, in turn, hinge on communication processes within the team and the effective use of ICT. In the following section, we discuss theories and research examining how this is achieved.

ICT: Social Presence, Media Richness, and Synchronicity

For many years, social science researchers investigated the effects of social presence as well as media richness on media choice and their respective actual effects on media use. Three main theories, social presence (Short et al. 1976), media richness (Daft and Lengel 1986), and media synchronicity (Deluca and Valacich 2008) theory, have developed to explain the choice and effects of communication media.

Short et al. (1976) developed *social presence theory* (SPT) well before the development of computer-mediated communication and online games as we know them today. According to SPT, communication media vary along the one-dimensional continuum of *social presence*, measured by the degree of *awareness* of the other person in a communication interaction. Face-to-face communication is considered to have the most social presence, whereas written, text-based communication, the least. SPT posits that communication is effective if the communication medium has the appropriate social presence required for the level of interpersonal involvement required for a task. Media with higher social presence are thus said to be preferable for important acts of communication or for important social tasks such as conflict resolution or building relationships.

Building on SPT, *media richness theory* (MRT) (Daft and Lengel 1986) posits that communication media differ in their ability to facilitate shared understanding. A medium's information richness is defined as the amount of information the medium could convey to alter a receiver's understanding, and is a function of (1) the medium's capacity for immediate feedback, (2) the number of cues and channels available, (3) language variety,; and (4) the degree to which intent is focused on the recipient (Daft and Lengel 1986). A phone conversation not providing visual social cues is less rich than video conferencing. MRT states that the information needs for performing a task should be matched with the medium's richness (Daft et al. 1987). The more uncertain or ambiguous a task, the richer a media format should be. An important implication of SPT and MRT is that, because they rely on less rich forms of communication with less social presence, virtual teams pursuing complex tasks should not fare as well as traditional teams relying on face-to-face interaction (Duarte and Synder 2001; Lipnack and Stamps 1997).

Media synchronicity theory (MST) focuses on how a medium's impact varies by how it is used and the context in which it is used (Deluca and Valacich 2008). The focal dimension of communication media is synchronicity, referring to the degree to which information exchanges between parties occur simultaneously. The most effective media choices must take into account the mix of two fundamental communication processes: conveyance (information transmission) and convergence (information processing). Synchronous forms of communication facilitate convergence by providing greater meaning. However, synchronous media are also more time-consuming and cumbersome and thus may limit conveyance. Media low in synchronicity (e.g., e-mail, listservs, bulletin boards, file sharing) are therefore more effective for conveyance, whereas media high in synchronicity (face-to-face, telephone) are more effective for convergence.

MST explains why virtual teams are sometimes more effective when using asynchronous collaboration media for complex tasks. Team characteristics and contextual factors influence conveyance and convergence demands and thereby determine which communication media is appropriate. For example, teams possessing shared knowledge structures may require less convergence in on-going communications. In such cases, asynchronous communication may be preferred because it enables more rapid decision-making and execution.

Theories of ICT provide insight into how to meet the challenges of virtual work. We maintain that integrating these literatures will contribute to knowledge and practice of working in virtual teams and organizations. However, conducting rigorous empirical research on virtual teams is difficult. Field studies of virtual teams are typically small in scale and often lack quantitative or objective data (e.g., Kankanhalli et al. 2007). Alternatively, laboratory studies allow rigorous quantitative data collection but are limited in replicating the range of ICT and social-psychological richness of virtual teams in work settings (e.g., Staples and Zhao 2006). MMOGs provide an alternative setting addressing the limitations of conventional research conducted in both field and laboratory settings. In the following section, we describe how MMOGs can be used to understand virtual team effectiveness. Moreover, we address how knowledge gained from MMOG research has direct implications for real-world organizations.

Using MMOGS to Understand Team Effectiveness

Like work teams, teams of players in MMOGs have a mission to reach, a common goal that demands coordinated distribution of scarce resources within a competitive environment. Players form groups, organizations, and networks requiring coordination and cooperation. Leadership and control mechanisms emerge to facilitate these processes. Thus, MMOG settings resemble real-world teams and small-to-medium enterprises (SMEs) striving for competitive advantage in the marketplace.

As a virtual setting, MMOGs provide platforms to investigate essential roles of ICT in virtual team effectiveness. Communication is a vital aspect of online game-playing, as it constitutes the vast part of all player interactions (Dickey 2007). Online games are essentially ICT applications that can be characterized in terms of social presence, media richness, real-time interaction, and lack of geographic boundaries (Lo et al. 2005). Various forms of ICT are utilized in online games: messages, IM, voice (using a microphone), LAN parties, and VoIP (software such as Ventrilo) are common. Many games offer a multiplayer universe with impressive visual and auditory effects. Thus, MMOGs provide a range of communication media differing in richness and synchronicity, enabling researchers to investigate how and why forms of communication influence team effectiveness.

One should note that MMOGs are far more than a laboratory for the study of virtual teams. MMOGs are highly engaging and psychologically meaningful to participants (Williams et al. 2008). Relationships between players can be compared to relationships between co-workers in real jobs (Yee 2006). Team members become colleagues and psychologically invested in their standing within the team and the game. Players learn social and organizational skills from MMOGS, such as decision-making and handling risk and failures (Reeves et al. 2008). Further, compared with traditional field or laboratory studies, MMOG research can be conducted on much larger numbers of groups using fewer resources. MMOGs also offer the potential to obtain unobtrusive archival data from games' electronic archives, avoiding biases resulting from self-reported measures or conventional laboratory experiments.

The preceding review highlights how research in MMOG settings can inform on structures, processes, and performance of virtual teams. We believe that such research could provide valuable insight into the emergence and persistence of trust and cooperation as well as the impact of different communication media for coordination and information management in virtual organizations. As an illustration, we discuss findings from a nascent program of research we are conducting using the MMOG called Travian (http://www.travian.com).

The game is a real-time strategy (RTS) game wherein players seek to build an empire. Players start out as chieftains of their own villages and seek to gain natural resources, build armies, and expand their realm. Expansion is achieved through conflict and cooperation. On the one hand, players battle over territories and possession of resources yet, they must also cooperate with selected other players to protect their territory and resources to successfully expand their reach. To do so, players form teams of up to 60 members. As teams grow, they form governance and leadership structures with differentiated roles within teams. The leadership of a team may invite new members or release existing members, as long as the team does not exceed 60 players. Games are timed to last approximately 1 year, at which time one team is deemed the winner based on the fastest completion of a certain building called "wonder of the world." Teams are equipped with a shared forum, a chat room, an in-game messaging system, and a regularly updated, shared news list showing most recent attacks on team members and members' attacks on other actors. Like virtual teams at work, teamwork and negotiation skills play a crucial role in this context.

We have used this setting to explore leadership and trust in virtual teams. For example, Picot, Assmann, Korsgaard, Welpe, Gallenkamp, and Wigand (2009) use a multi-level approach to study virtual leadership focussing on cultural and communication aspects and their impact on trust and performance. In a study of about 1,800 teams playing Travian in 23 different countries, the authors found that communication synchronicity and breadth uniquely contributed to building trust in leaders and that these relationships varied by culture. Further, teams that trusted their leaders performed better.

In another study also using the Travian setting, Assmann, Gallenkamp, Korsgaard, Picot, and Welpe (2009) viewed team leaders as founders of entrepreneurial ventures and examines the role of trust developing networks and growing newly formed organizations. The study indicated that founders who communicate openly were more trusted by the organization's members, and that trusted founders were better able to recruit talent and create larger organizations. The findings have implications for practice, as many entrepreneurial organizations utilize virtual networks. Therefore, entrepreneurs need to recognize the strategic importance of managing trust in ICT-enabled virtual context.

Other promising future research fields may include: studying internal structures of virtual teams and transferring such insights to the design of virtual organizations in general; investigating ethical issues of team work and business organizations such as deception, social loafing, or corruption also with the help of experimental designs for research in MMOGs; and deepening the insight into cultural differences between virtual teams operating in various regions and their impact on structures, processes, and performance of virtual teams.

Finally, the external validity of research results on virtual teams in MMOG environments deserves a closer attention. We recommend cross-validation of findings from MMOG research with virtual teams operating in work organizations. Such evidence would validate the role of virtual worlds and MMOGs for social science research.

References

Assmann, J., Gallenkamp, J., Korsgaard, M. A., Picot, A., & Welpe, I. (2009). *Trust in virtual entrepreneurs*. Paper presented at 28th Babson College Entrepreneurship Research Conference (BCERC), Babson College, Wellesley, MA.

Assmann, J., Korsgaard, M. A., & Welpe, I. (2008). Antecedents of trustworthiness in a virtual team environment. Presentation at the Academy of Management Annual Meeting, Anaheim, CA.

Bainbridge, W. S. (2007). The scientific research potential of virtual worlds. *Science, 317*, 472–476.

Baltes, B., Dickson, M., Sherman, M., Bauer, C., & Laganke, J. (2002). Computer-mediated communication and group decision making: A meta-analysis. *Organizational Behavior & Human Decision Processes, 87*, 156–179.

Bell, B. S., & Kozlowski, S. W. J. (2002). A typology of virtual teams. *Group & Organization Management, 27*, 14–49.

Bell, B. S., & Kozlowski, S. W. J. (2008). Active learning: Effects of core training design elements on self-regulatory processes, learning, and adaptability. *Journal of Applied Psychology, 93*, 296–316.

Blackburn, R., Furst, S. A., & Rosen, B. (2003). Building a winning virtual team: KSA's, selections, training, and evaluation. In C. B. Gibson & S. G. Cohen (Eds.), *Virtual teams that work: Creating conditions for virtual team effectiveness* (pp. 95–120). San Francisco, CA: Jossey-Bass.

Buchan, N., Johnson, E., & Croson, R. (2006). Let's get personal: An international examination of the influence of communication, culture and social distance on other regarding preferences. *Journal of Economic Behavior & Organization, 60*, 373–398.

Castronova, E., & Falk, M. (2009). Virtual worlds: Petri dishes, rat mazes, supercolliders. Games and Culture, *4*, 396–407.

Daft, R. L., & Lengel, R. H. (1986). Organizational information requirements, media richness and structural design. *Management Science, 32*, 554–571.

Daft, R. L., Lengel, R. H., & Trevino, L. K. (1987). Message equivocality, media selection, and manager performance: Implications for information support systems. *MIS Quarterly, 11*, 355–366.

Deluca, D. C., Gasson, S., & Kock, N. (2006). Adaptations that virtual teams make so that complex tasks can be performed using simple e-collaboration technologies. *International Journal of E-Collaboration. 23*, 64–85.

Deluca, D. C., & Valacich, J. S. (2008). Situational synchronicity or decision support. In F. Adam & P. Humphreys (Eds.), *Encyclopedia of decision making and decision support technologies* (Vol. 2, pp. 790–797). Hershey, PA: Information Science Reference.

Deutsch, M. (1958). Trust and suspicion. *Journal of Conflict Resolution, 2*, 265–279.

Dickey, M. D. (2007). Game design and learning: A conjectural analysis of how Massively Multiple Online Role-Playing Games (MMORPGs) foster intrinsic motivation. *Educational Technology Research and Development, 55*, 253–273.

Duarte, D. L., & Synder, N. T. (2001). *Mastering virtual teams* (2nd ed.). San Francisco, CA: Jossey-Bass.

Gist, M., Locke, E., & Taylor, S. (1987). Organizational behavior: Group structure, process, and effectiveness. *Journal of Management. 13*, 237–257.

Harrison, D., Price, K., Gavin, J., & Florey, A. (2002). Time, teams, and task performance: Changing effects of surface- and deep-level diversity on group functioning. *Academy of Management Journal, 45*, 1029–1045.

Hertel, G., Geister, S., & Konradt, U. (2005). Managing virtual teams: A review of current empirical research. *Human Resource Management Review, 15*, 69–95.

Hossain, L., & Wigand, R. T. (2003). Understanding virtual collaboration through structuration. In F. McGrath & D. Remenyi (Eds.), *Proceedings of the Fourth European Conference on knowledge management* (pp. 475–484). Oxford, UK: Oxford University.

Ilgen, D., Hollenbeck, J., Johnson, M., & Jundt, D. (2005). Teams in organizations: From input-process-output models to IMOI models. *Annual Review of Psychology, 56*, 517–543.

Jehn, K., & Mannix, E. (2001). The dynamic nature of conflict: A longitudinal study of intragroup conflict and group performance. *Academy of Management Journal, 44*, 238–251.

Kanawattanachai, P., & Yoo, Y. (2007). The impact of knowledge coordination on virtual team performance over time. *MIS Quarterly, 31*, 783–808.

Kankanhalli, A., Tan, B., & Wei, K.-K. (2007). Conflict and performance in global virtual teams. *Journal of Management Information Systems, 23*, 237–274.

Kirkman, B. L., Mathieu, J. E. (2005). The dimensions and antecedents of team virtuality. *Journal of Management. 31*, 700–718.

Kirkman, B. L., & Rosen, B., Tesluk, P. E., Gibson, C. B., & McPherson, S. O. (2002). Five challenges to virtual team success: Lessons from Sabre. Inc. *Academy of Management Executive, 16*, 67–79.

Klapwijk, A., & Van Lange, P. A. M. (2009). Promoting cooperation and trust in "Noisy" situations: The power of generosity. *Journal of Personality & Social Psychology, 96*, 83–103.

Kurtzberg, T. R., Naquin, C. E., & Belkin, L. Y. (2005). Electronic performance appraisals: The effects of e-mail communication on peer ratings in actual and simulated environments. *Organizational Behavior & Human Decision Processes, 98*, 216–226.

Lee, A. S. (1994). Electronic mail as a medium for rich communication: An empirical investigation using hermeneutic interpretation. *MIS Quarterly, 18*, 143–57.

LePine, J., Piccolo, R., Jackson, C., Mathieu, J., & Saul, J. (2008). A meta-analysis of teamwork processes: Tests of a multidimensional model and relationships with team effectiveness criteria. *Personnel Psychology, 61*, 273–307.

Lester, S., Meglino, B. M., & Korsgaard, M. A. (2002). The antecedents and consequences of group potency: A longitudinal investigation of newly formed groups. *Academy of Management Journal, 45*, 352–368.

Lewis, K. (2003). Measuring transactive memory systems in the field: Scale development and validation. *Journal of Applied Psychology, 88*, 587–604.

Lewis, K., Belliveau, M., Herndon, B., & Keller, J. (2007). Group cognition, membership change, and performance: Investigating the benefits and detriments of collective knowledge. *Organizational Behavior & Human Decision Processes, 103*, 159–178.

Lipnack, J., & Stamps, J. (1997). *Virtual teams: Reaching across space, time, and organizations with technology.* New York: Wiley, 261.

Lo, S.-K., Wang, C.-C., & Fang, W. (2005). Physical interpersonal relationships and social anxiety among online game players. *CyberPsychology and Behavior, 8*, 15–20.

Majchrzak, A., Jarvenpaa, S., & Hollingshead, A. (2007). Coordinating expertise among emergent groups responding to disasters. *Organization Science, 18*, 147–161.

Marks, M., Mathieu, J., & Zaccaro, S. (2001). A temporally based framework and taxonomy of team processes. *Academy of Management Review, 26*, 356–376.

Marks, M., Zaccaro, S., & Mathieu, J. (2000). Performance implications of leader briefings and team-interaction training for team adaptation to novel environments. *Journal of Applied Psychology, 85*, 971–986.

Martins, L., Gilson, L., & Maynard, T. (2004). Virtual teams: What do we know and where do we go from here? *Journal of Management, 30*, 805–835.

McGrath, J. E., Arrow, H., & Berdahl, J. L. (2000). The study of groups: Past, present, and future. *Personality and Social Psychology Review, 4*, 95–105.

Mowshowitz, A. (1997). Virtual organization. *Communications of the ACM, 409*, 30–37.

O'Leary, M., & Cummings, J. (2007). The spatial, temporal, and configurational characteristics of geographic dispersion in teams. *MIS Quarterly, 31*, 433–452.

Piccoli, G., & Ives, B. (2003). Trust and the unintended effects of behavior control in virtual teams. *MIS Quarterly, 27*, 365–395.

Picot, A., Assmann, J., Korsgaard, A., Welpe, I., Gallenkamp, J., & Wigand, R. (2009). *A multilevel view of the antecedents and consequences of trust in virtual leaders.* Proceedings of the Fifteenth Americas Conference on Information Systems, San Francisco, CA.

Picot, A., Reichwald, R., & Wigand, R. (2008). Information, organization and management. Berlin-Heidelberg, Germany: Springer.

Raghuram, S., Gamd, R., Wiesenfeld, B., & Gupta, V. (2001). Factors contributing to virtual work adjustment. *Journal of Management, 27*, 383–405.

Reeves, B., Malone, T., & O'Driscoll, T. (2008). Leadership's online labs. *Harvard Business Review, 5*, 58–66.

Rockmann, K., & Northcraft, G. (2008). To be or not to be trusted: The influence of media richness on defection and deception. *Organizational Behavior and Human Decision Processes, 107*, 106–122.

Short, J., Williams, E., & Christie, B. (1976). *The social psychology of telecommunications.* London: Wiley.

Staples, D. S., & Zhao, L. (2006). The effects of cultural diversity in virtual teams versus face-to-face teams. *Group Decision and Negotiation, 15*, 389–406.

Tangirala, S., & Alge, B. (2006). Reactions to unfair events in computer-mediated groups: A test of uncertainty management theory. *Organizational Behavior & Human Decision Processes, 100*, 1–20.

Te'eni, D., Sagie, A., Schwartz, D., Zaidman, N., & Amichai-Hamburger, Y. (2001). The process of organizational communication: A model and field study. *IEEE Transactions on Professional Communication, 44*, 5–20.

Welbourne, T., & Ferrante, C. (2008). To monitor or not to monitor. *Group & Organization Management, 33*, 139–162.

Williams, D., Ducheneaut, N., Xiong, L., Zhangm, Y., Yee, N., & Nickell, E. (2006). From tree house to barracks: The social life of guilds in World of Warcraft. *Games and Culture, 1*, 338–361.

Williams, D., Yee, N., & Caplan, S. (2008). Who plays, how much, and why? Debunking the stereotypical gamer profile. *Journal of Computer-Mediated Communication, 13*, 993–1018.

Yee, N. (2006). The labor of fun: How video games blur the boundaries of work and play. *Games and Culture, 1*, 68–71.

Zhang, Z.-X., Hempel, P., Han, Y.-L., & Tjosvold, D. (2007). Transactive memory system links work team characteristics and performance. *Journal of Applied Psychology, 92*, 1722–1730.

Chapter 21
Virtual Worlds for Virtual Organizing

Diana Rhoten and Wayne Lutters

There is tremendous promise in leveraging the dynamism of virtual worlds to rethink the practical experience of virtual organizations. Virtual worlds are rapidly maturing as complex socio-technical systems that support all manners of human activity. As such, they confront our traditional conceptions of virtual organizing, challenging us to consider bold new forms, structures, and processes. This chapter explores precisely this convergence between the practices of virtual organizations and the affordances of virtual worlds toward a greater potential for both.

This convergence largely began in the early 1990s, as fundamental research on computer-mediated communication and collaborative virtual environments attended to micro-level questions concerned with elements both technical (e.g., artifact representation, gaze management, and gesture recognition) and social (e.g., communication patterns, identity management). Applied research focused on the design, creation, and use of virtual information spaces to support a distance collaboration experience richer than videoconferencing. Initial forays into full-fledged, immersive, graphical virtual worlds were, however, quickly frustrated by expanding technical obstacles and shrinking industry investments.

In the last few years, enthusiasm for virtual worlds as an enabling technology for virtual organizing has been renewed. Thanks both to the scientific enterprise and the entertainment industry, technical barriers have been overcome, popular systems have reached critical mass, and the workforce has become more socialized to virtual interaction. This recent revival has also extended the idea of virtual worlds as platforms and places for virtual organizing that go well beyond work-related activities to domains as diverse as learning and research, politics and civic engagement, culture and religion. When compared with earlier days, this increasing trend toward convergence begs the need for not just social and technical attention but

D. Rhoten
Social Science Research Council
e-mail: rhoten@ssrc.org

W. Lutters
University of Maryland, Baltimore County
e-mail: lutters@umbc.edu

W.S. Bainbridge (ed.), *Online Worlds: Convergence of the Real and the Virtual*,
Human-Computer Interaction Series, DOI 10.1007/978-1-84882-825-4_21,
© Springer-Verlag London Limited 2010

rather a robust socio-technical engagement of macro-level questions ranging from immersive social presence to emergent social movements, from avatar representation to identity management, and from artifact creation to virtual entrepreneurship.

This chapter begins with a brief socio-technical history of this confluence of virtual worlds for virtual organizing. It then examines a collection of contemporary examples that demonstrate how virtual worlds have enabled new arenas for virtual organizing beyond just work or just play. It culminates by mapping the current research topography and a vision for future directions, suggesting the need for more in-depth analyses of such central tensions as user versus designer and realism versus fantasy.

The Socio-technical History of Virtual Worlds for Virtual Organizing

A *virtual organization* is a group of individuals whose members and resources are dispersed across time and space, yet who function as a coherent entity through the use of technologies, networks, and alliances (Giuliano 1982; Hedberg et al. 1997; Cummings et al. 2008). A *virtual world* is a shared, persistent, computer-simulated environment in which people act on and interact with others as well as artifacts through characters or avatars (Bartle 2003; Jakobsson 2003). Thus, whereas virtual organizations are inherently social structures, virtual worlds are essentially technical architectures. Here, we will step through key points in their history – the guiding vision, technical advances, and social transformations that enable the use of virtual worlds for virtual organizing. We begin with the confluence of at least three important trends in computing in the late-1980s and early 1990s: computer-mediated communication, telepresence, and virtual reality for gaming.

Early network service providers in the United States, such as CompuServ, Prodigy, and America Online, popularized *computer-mediated communication* (CMC) for the masses. They expanded their users' experience beyond the standards of asynchronous electronic communication, e-mail, UseNet news, and topical bulletin boards, to new forms of synchronous interaction. The "killer app" of this era was the chat room. While technically indistinguishable from the chat channels of earlier technologies such as ICQ, this shift in metaphor from a citizen's band radio toward the local pub was titanic. People began to view chat in terms of virtual spaces to inhabit not frequencies to tune in. This suggested both permanence and malleability, enabling persistent conversation and facilitating group identification. No longer was chat about point-to-point conversation, it could also serve as a locus for organizing. Star Trek fans now had their own rooms, lesbians had their own neighborhood café (Correll 1995), and political activists had their street corner soap boxes. Sure, in many cases it was just a textual label and a rich description of a room, but other social computing technologies would support a richer sense of place.

Some argue that a social movement grew out of these developments, CMC enabled community networks (Schuler 1996). These were often tied to a specific geographical region, such as the Cleveland Free-Net, Montana's big Sky Telegraph, or the heavily studied Blacksburg Electronic Village (Cohill and Kavanaugh 2000).

Concomitant with this evolution in the perception of synchronous CMC and engagement with physical geography came a rapid maturation in user-generated virtual spaces. Expanding the concept of the text-based exploration games of the early 1970s, such as *Colossal Cave Adventure*, with new object-oriented programming methods, users were able to create and navigate text-based worlds filled with interactive artifacts. These multi-user dungeons/domains (MUD) allowed users to create rich profiles for their characters and inhabit worlds of their own design, chatting with other users, taking public action, and expressing emotion. This embodied interaction brought a new dimension to the online chat experience as users were able to share in communal experiences.

Most agree that the first commercial marriage of chat and inhabited virtual spaces was LucasArt's *Habitat* in 1986. Habitat allowed users to control avatars in game to travel through over 20,000 regions, interacting with pre-defined objects and chatting freely (Morningstar and Farmer 1991). The Habitat-inspired family of supporting CMC architectures had a long and profitable life. Some of the later instantiations included the chat space *Club Caribe*, followed by the ground-breaking *WorldsAway* in 1994, which allowed user-modifiable avatars and movement within a 2D world. Users could "own" their own real estate and decorate it by modifying pre-defined objects. Different systems improved on this fundamental notion of visual chat in interesting ways. *The Palace* allowed users to upload their own avatars designed out-of-world and use personal images as the background for inter-action (e.g., a photo of their own city block or living room). Microsoft's Comic Chat had a number of key innovations, including automatic parsing of the world's interaction into an archive of story panes and an "emotion wheel" to more subtly control the facial expressions of the chat avatar.

This progression in computational support for CMC from largely asynchronous text message exchange, to real-time chat, to embodied user-created graphical worlds, laid the foundation for the virtual worlds under discussion in this book. During this time, researchers became deeply interested in investigating all of these incarnations of chat: the channel, the room, the MUD/MOO, and graphical chat spaces. Did they function as viable third places (Oldenburg 1989)? Did they exhibit the sociological properties of community (Wellman and Gulia 1999)? What were the properties of these communities (Rheingold 1993)? Could they be leveraged for community organizing (Schuler 1996)?

A second thread in this story is the evolution of the theory, practice, and compu-tational support for *telepresence*. The academic discipline of computer-supported cooperative work (CSCW), popularized in "groupware" applications, was fundamen-tally concerned with developing socio-technical systems to better support distance collaboration. Early research focused on collaborative editors, file sharing systems, and next-generation teleconferencing. A cross-fertilization of CSCW and CMC researchers fostered to an interest in developing immersive, 3D virtual worlds to support work at a distance. "Discussion of cooperative work in virtual environ-ments contains two themes: one that emphasizes the desire to collapse space and reproduce in full detail unmediated interpersonal communication and the other that seeks to enhance and extend through artificial means the range of interpersonal communication" (Biocca 1992: 13). These two visions for virtual worlds to accomplish real work – an extremely high-fidelity replication of physical interaction and a broad-suite of tools to enable collaboration in ways that go "beyond being there" (Hollan and Stornetta 1992), were at times competitive but ultimately complementary. Fundamental research in the former, for example authentic replication of eye gaze (Kobayashi and Ishii 1993), would enhance collaborative video spaces starting with Europarc's *RAVE* system (Gaver 1992), and myriad media spaces dispersed along the physical-virtual continuum such as Hydra, Montage, and Portholes (Mackay 1999). These would inform future designs of virtual worlds, including both technical (e.g., orientation and perspective camera alignment of avatars) and social (e.g., attention management, floor control) concerns.

Research in collaborative virtual environments (CVE) relied on rendered virtual worlds, mirroring the latter of Biocca's perspectives. Most of the foundational CVE research was completed in Europe in the early 1990s. Two of the earliest and most influential systems were *MASSIVE* of the University of Nottingham[1] and *DIVE* of the Swedish Institute for Computer Science.[2] These projects conducted basic research into the social and technical interplay in virtual worlds for collaborative work, engaging such issues as floor control, object identification, localized speech, attention, and awareness (Greenhalgh and Benford 1995).

None of this could have been fully realized without significant advances in *virtual reality* (VR) itself. Basic research on human perception in virtual spaces, optimization of individual user interfaces for VR, and interactive objects laid the foundation for CVEs. Simultaneous advances in dynamic translation for object-oriented programming, data structures for massively distributed data sets, and real-time graphical rendering vastly improved the stability, reliability, and user experience of virtual worlds. Unfortunately, due to global economic conditions, few of these systems matured into full-fledged commercial releases of virtual worlds for collaborative work (e.g., Microcosm [Isaacs 1998]).

While much CVE development went into stasis during the downturn, ground-breaking developments were happening in the entertainment industry. Capitalizing on all of these advances in embodied chat, virtual organizing, and coordinated behavior in virtual space, immersive 3D gaming environments exploded on to the scene. Breakthroughs in computer graphics, from real-time rendering to first person perspective based navigation popularized in *Doom*, allowed for compelling immersive experiences. The first wave of massively multi-player online games (MMOG) became the vanguard of virtual world innovation starting with *Meridian 59*, *Ultima Online*, and *Everquest* in the late-1990s (Achterbosch et al. 2008). This trajectory of virtual worlds for entertainment developed rapidly. Nearing the end of the first decade of the 21st century, the dominance of immensely popular MMOGs such as *World of Warcraft*, *The Lord of the Rings Online*, and *Star Wars Galaxies*, it could be said that the baton has been firmly passed from the research lab to the entertainment industry. But academic and industrial research is returning after its brief hiatus.

---

[1] http://www.crg.cs.nott.ac.uk/research/systems/MASSIVE/

[2] http://www.sics.se/dive

Contemporary research on virtual worlds as places neither exclusively for gaming nor for working is picking up at a rapid pace. Learning from such popular virtual worlds as *Second Life* and *Active Worlds*, a new wave of multi-faceted virtual worlds is emerging, from Sun's *Wonderland* and *Croquet/Cobalt* to *Little Big Planet* and *Metaplace*.

Current Trends in Virtual Worlds for Virtual Organizing

As stated earlier, we understand a virtual organization to be a group of individuals whose members and resources are dispersed across time and space, yet who function as a coherent entity through the use of technology, networks, and alliances. A virtual organization is typically characterized by functionally or culturally diverse external ties (Coyle and Schnarr 1995) and is often rapidly assembled, disassembled, and reassembled based on need (Grenier and Metes 1995; Lipnack and Stamps 1997). As such, virtual organizations are best understood in terms of the "collaborative networks" that span and the "combinatorial freedoms" that defy geographic location and institutional affiliation (Bleecker 1994; Mowshowitz 1994). Such networks can be informal, unplanned, and sporadic just as they can be formal, planned, and consistent, and they can apply to business processes, social movements, scientific collaborations, or political activities. For these reasons, it may be more useful to talk about the act of "virtual organizing" rather than the concept of the "virtual organization."

The act of virtual organizing across time and space is not a new social phenomenon. It could be argued that The Hudson's Bay Company (O'Leary et al. 2002), vertically integrated aspects of General Motors (Davidow and Malone 1992), Linux (Benkler 1992), and Innocentive (Lakhani and Panetta 2007) as well as the Invisible College (Crane 1972), the Mafia (Sifakis 1999), and even Burning Man (O' Mahony 2008) are all cases of virtual organizing. Advances in virtual reality research have yielded sophisticated graphical rendering capacities and network communication functionalities that have not only enabled the ideas "being there" and "being with" via virtual worlds but also lent credibility to the promise of one day going "beyond being there" (Hollan and Stornetta 1992; Schroeder 1996). At the same time, these and other advances in hardware and software have lowered the threshold of entry to virtual worlds such that these virtual realities are within the reach of most people. As such, today, virtual worlds are being adopted ever more frequently as platforms for virtual organizing, not only for working and for gaming as initially intended but also for scientific as well as religious, cultural, and political endeavors that borrow from both (Balkin and Noveck 2006).

Contemporary virtual worlds vary along the spectrum of developer-defined and user-generated content, with compelling examples at every step along the way.

- Developer-defined, closed worlds where users can only interact with what was previously engineered by the developers (e.g., *Habbo Hotel*, *Whyville*, *Club Penguin*, *Lineage*, *Halo*, *Everquest*, *Lord of the Rings Online*, *Age of Conan*)

- User-modifiable, quasi-open worlds, where the users can morph and personalize primitives, including scripting, macros, and some open API add-ons (e.g., *Spore, Sims Online, World of Warcraft, Little Big Planet, City of Heroes*)
- User-generated, open worlds where users interact with and through user-chosen objectives and activities, user-crafted content, and user-manipulated features (e.g., *Second Life, Forterra, Wonderland, Croquet/Cobalt, Active Worlds, There*)

These different genres offer a range of experiences in which to explore the contexts and artifacts of virtual worlds for virtual organizing, from actualized to imagined, stylized to customized, and inworld to interworld.

But, truth is, despite all these developments, we are still in the early days of virtual worlds, and the real test of the convergence between the social practices of virtual organizing and these different technological affordances of virtual worlds will be if, how, and why communities inhabit any of these environments over time and across space to sustain multiple complex social interactions, like "holding a conference," "organizing a tradeshow," or "organizing an architectural competition" (Bartle 2006; Damer et al. 2000). Below, we explore examples of early forays into virtual organizing within virtual worlds, gleaning patterns of what is and what may be yet to come.

In line with CSCW and CMC objectives for distributed work, many corporations have turned to virtual worlds to decrease transaction costs and improve the quality of interactions between distributed employees. The best-known case of corporate virtual organizing is IBM, which has had a presence in *Second Life* since 2006. IBM currently maintains more than 50 "islands" in that world, which it uses to host corporate meetings and employee events. In partnership with Linden Labs, IBM has also developed and tested "behind-the-firewall" environments for workplace training. Intel, Northrop Grumman, and the U.S. Naval Undersea Warfare Center have all also agreed to investigate this platform for corporate training and development (McCarthy 2009). Noting the growth potential of this market, start-ups such as Qwaq and Multiverse Network have begun to develop a line of boutique virtual worlds optimized specifically for corporate organizing, where employees can meet as avatars, view presentations, and conduct other business virtually. At the same time, some companies have opted to create their own in-house virtual world, including Sun Microsystems, which has developed its own software, *Wonderland*, so Sun teams from around the world can attend meetings without leaving their desks or offices, cities, or countries.

Beyond boosting internal productivity, we also see multiple examples of corporate virtual organizing for external commerce. Companies including brand names like Nike, Sears, Nissan, Phillips Design, Reuters, and ABN AMBRO have all adopted a customer-facing presence in *Second Life*. By hosting virtual showrooms and storefronts, giving away or selling virtual products, or holding focus groups and product seminars, these companies have organized hoping to leverage what is an inherently a distributed physical and virtual world customer base. Whereas companies have trended toward highly actualized contexts such as boardrooms and conference rooms with very literal artifacts from the physical world like Powerpoint slides and telephone systems when organizing for employees, they have begun to show some imaginative experimentation with the affordances of the medium when organizing for consumers. For example, the premier of Coca Cola's "Happiness Factory" movie (which is in and of itself about the virtual world deep inside a Coca Cola vending machine) at a red-carpet gala event in *Second Life* with glamorous movie star avatars and international press agents is but one demonstration of how virtual worlds can provide alternative realities. Another is "MTV's Virtual Laguna Beach" in *There* where users can live the MTV Laguna Beach television show alongside friends and fans.

But, the use of virtual worlds for virtual organizing is not limited to corporate acts alone. The longstanding tradition of religious organizing has also found a new venue in virtual worlds. In 2006, Bizarre Berry (the avatar of 37-year-old real estate broker George Byrd from Columbus, OH) built the First Unitarian Universalist Church of *Second Life* (FUUCSL). Why? Because he wanted "a place where people come and they hang out and congregate and they can make friends and find other people to talk to." Within its first 6 months, the FUUCSL attracted 180 members, holding biweekly worship services and sponsoring covenant groups. By 2008, the FUUCSL ratified its bylaws, establishing its purpose being "to organize as a religious community in *Second Life*" (Sutton 2007; FUUCSL Bylaws 2008). In 2007, the Jesuits also identified *Second Life* as the next missionary destination, a new land ripe for spreading their faith and organizing their parishioners. According to Father Antonio Spadaro of the Civiltà Cattolica: "This virtual *Second Life* is becoming populated with churches, mosques, temples, cathedrals, synagogues, places of prayer of all kinds. And behind an avatar, there is a man or a woman, perhaps searching for God and faith, perhaps with very strong spiritual needs" (Bompbard 2007).

Thus, similar to corporate organizing, much of the religious organizing is still very much about translating what's happening in the physical world to the virtual world, with the advantages interpreted primarily in terms of the functionalities of telepresence and immersion and the value understood almost exclusively as being about "being there" and "being with" rather than about "beyond being there." We did find, however, two examples that suggest greater leveraging of the modalities to transform religious movements; one is about customizable reality and the other alternative reality. First, experiencing Islamophobia in much of the physical world, Muslims have turned to virtual worlds to explain and expand the workings of Islam, whether it is at Islamicity in *Second Life* or in *Muxlim Pal* (the first virtual world dedicated to "enhancing Muslim lifestyle"). Second, taking greater advantage of the spatiality and playability of the virtual world environment to pursue more augmented religious reality experience, players in the game *Waco Resurrection* collect at the Waco standoff and interact with David Koresh as a "cult" community.

The present state of scientific organizing in virtual worlds is perhaps less developed (albeit more diverse) than one might expect. On the one hand, science, like business and religion, is using virtual worlds to take advantage of the medium to do in the virtual world that which they would do in the physical world. The National Science Foundation is using *Second Life* to host scientific review panels, and the Institute for Advanced Study at Princeton University has adopted *Qwaq* to organize regular meetings of internationally distributed astrophysics teams. There are small pockets of early adopters, however, that are also beginning to explore the possibilities of "unreal" world contexts for "real" world research activities. A prime example of this is the Convergence of the Real and the Virtual conference that led to this very book. Not only was Convergence the first scientific conference organized in *World of Warcraft*, it is also most likely the first scientific conference anywhere where attendees (shamans, rogues, elves, and warlocks) boarded pirate ships, commandeered zeppelins, and dodged hyenas between panels.

Surprisingly, however, there are still only the rare cases in which scientists have taken advantage of the simulation and visualization affordances of virtual worlds to advance the act of collective data analysis, an increasingly important interactivity in the organization of science (Rhoten 2004). The most promising example of not only distributed but also augmented data analysis we could find was *Second Earth*. By creating a KML importer, the National Oceanic and Atmospheric Administration has built a "3D mash up" of *Google Earth* and *Second Life* that allows data sets collected in the former to be represented and explored collaboratively in the latter. Beyond this one case, we found more examples of scientific data representation for educational purposes than of scientific data collaboration by research professionals.

Finally, as in the physical world, virtual worlds are experiencing their fair share of political organizing, manifest in social protests, political contests, and community quests alike. *Second Life* (again) has become the primary platform for virtual political organizing on behalf of workers' rights and citizens' rights. In 2007, an estimated 1,850 avatars converged on one of IBM's many islands to protest the threat of cuts in real-world worker pay bonuses at IBM Italy. Supported by global unions such as the International and European Metalworkers Federations (IMF and EMF) and UNI Global Union, the protest was not only successful in halting IBM's pay cuts in the physical world but also in demonstrating the potential of virtual worlds to organize for social change. On Union Island in *Second Life*, there is now a museum describing the IBM protest, which houses a replica of the trophy awarded to the IBM protest organizing team by the Netexploratuers, a recognition that honors the promise of the Internet for social impact.[3]

Second Life residents have also used the virtual world to protest against other "real world" current events in ways bounded by and not possible or imaginable in the physical world, including erecting memorials such as the Palestine Holocaust Memorial Museum, destroying the headquarters of the Le Pen party, and recreating protests in the image of the 1773 Boston Tea Party. Other political organizers have even gone not only interworld but cross-platform in their embrace of virtual worlds. People for the Ethical Treatment of Animals (PETA) began its virtual political organizing in 2007 in *Second Life* with a designer protest event, featuring Stella McCartney, anti-fur avatar accessories, and virtual-to-real dollar donations. In 2009, PETA took its movement to *World of Warcraft*, where it organized a "seal hunt" campaign. What we find most interesting about this latest PETA campaign, however, is the debate over its political purpose and the social and philosophical questions it raises about the future of virtual political organizing. On the one hand, the campaign

---

[3] SLUnionisland.org

was rumored to be a political demonstration to defeat hordes of in-game baby seal killers. On the other hand, it was purportedly designed to draw attention to the slaughtering of 338,000 baby harp seals on the ice floes of Canada. In discussing the link between conceptual innovation and political change, the political scientist William Connolly (Connolly, 1983: 39 in Cajvaneanu 2007) argued that "to understand the political life of a community one must understand the conceptual system within which that life moves." And, so how do we understand the political life of persons and personas participating in multiple conceptual systems that simultaneously take them to many theres and beyond simultaneously (Bartle 2003)?

The Future of Virtual Worlds for Virtual Organizing

The act of virtual organizing appears to be on the rise in a variety of different virtual worlds and across a host of domains. Understanding the confluence between these social practices and the technological platforms that support them demands deeper scientific research than is currently available today. And, while prognostication is always a perilous business, doubly so in the tumultuous space of social computing, we boldly but not blindly project a few key socio-technical trends worthy of interrogation.

First, we expect to see an increase in "born virtual" collaboration. Much of the current use of virtual worlds to support organizing – be it around work, religion, science, or politics – is still merely a creative extension of physical organizations, whether Nike, the Universalist Church, or NSF. In these instances, virtual worlds are primarily about telepresence, and are seen as means to expand a consumer base, connect employees, or engage an audience that would otherwise be imaginable, but simply unreachable. This is not surprising as one of the foundational CSCW findings is the need to establish common ground, rooted in common physical constructs and relationships, as a precedent for virtual collaboration. If virtual assets continue to increase in value, virtual professions become more financially feasible, and virtual lifestyles take over more of our daily lives, virtual organizing will naturally become more digitally native and wholly inworld – from assembling and managing teams, to producing and marketing virtual intellectual property, to protesting virtual corporate takeovers. This shift will raise significant social questions and raise interesting technical challenges. Work on this vein has begun with Ducheneaut et al.'s (2007) groundbreaking study of the organizational evolution of guilds in *World of Warcraft* and Ellis et al.'s (2008) exploration of game-based team building in *Second Life*. More research will be needed, however, especially on the acts of community "barn building" and the questions of "common grounding" in user-defined virtual worlds. Or what if there is a backlash against virtual worlds and in fact we see more organizing through alternate reality games (Kim et al. 2008) rather than immersive virtual worlds?

Second, and directly related to the first, even within our cursory review of virtual organizing examples (many of which still occur in *Second Life*), we sense a competing tension between high-fidelity recreations of the physical world and hyper-stylized imaginations of fantasy worlds as venues for different types organizing. On the one hand, we see a movement toward the fantasy landscape and game-based play of *World of Warcraft* for organizing new community-building activities like conferences and protests. On the other hand, we also note trends toward worlds that mimic or mirror reality when it comes to deepening existing professional collaborations. This raises for us the question of whether users are or will be seeking more *Matrix Online* or more *City of Heroes*, more *OLIVE* or more *Little Big Planet*, and the extent to which this preference is influenced more by the purpose, the participants, or the period of virtual organizing? Will the act of collaborative work turn more playful, or will collective play turn more workful in virtual worlds of the future? While Michael Heim (1998) argues that virtual worlds should each strike a balance between fidelity and fantasy, we wonder whether virtual worlds will in the future still externally differentiate themselves as actualized or fantasized, or whether they will begin to integrate both as aspects internally. In either case, there will be an increased need for research focusing on questions of social authenticity versus technical conformity of virtual worlds, and how people perceive, experience, and understand the "reality" of a virtual world. It will also beg future work on what aspects of "virtual reality" users seek more of – reproduced, alternative, augmented, simulated, or unbounded?

This bring us to our third trend. We cannot help but ask ourselves how much have we learned from the fate of textual worlds that is applicable to the future of graphical virtual worlds, at least in terms of personal customization versus mass commercialization. In the examples above, we see evidence suggestive of a trend toward specialized worlds optimized for particular sectors, constructed for single companies or dedicated to particular cultures. This social trend toward niche organizing combined with the technical emergence of affordable and accessible consumer-facing virtual world engines and development kits could take us in the direction of a future when greater numbers of smaller-scale, less-expensive, user-customized virtual worlds become as popular as personal websites, blogs, and profile pages. This view, however, stands in stark contrast to commercial sector development plans, which hint at massive infusions of dollars into large-scale, corporate-designer worlds. In 2008, MTV announced that it would invest $100 million into casual MMOs and virtual worlds, at the same time that Time Warner Investments identified virtual worlds one of its four major channels for new media investment and HiPiHi (China's response to *Second Life*) touted plans for an infrastructure to support up to 75 million simultaneous users (Wilson 2008). Whether headed toward a future of personalized customization or one of massive commercialization, more research is needed on the technological standards for the portability of virtual avatars and assets between platforms as well as on the social customs for the interoperability of personal identities and communities across worlds.

Building off this question, we come to our fourth observation. We sense a continued, if not growing, dominance of entertainment as the driver for innovation in both the social and the technical dimensions of virtual organizing around virtual worlds for the foreseeable future. Not only does interactive gaming have the most creative brainpower, financial resources and marketing to focus on the problem, they also have the luxury of failure. The surest sign of failure for a virtual world is the inability to achieve a critical mass of users. Many gaming worlds never catch on, such as *Tabula Rasa*. Yet, given their stability of capital, gaming companies can take the loss, learn their lessons, and move on to the next development effort. For many industrial experiments, the entire virtual world concept is swept out with the deserted servers as "just another fad." For academic worlds, such as *Arden: The World of Shakespeare*, the failure is even more catastrophic and costly, at least culturally and reputationally, if not also financially. Given the proclivity of game companies toward proprietary systems and rigid control of intellectual property and game player's increasing interest in user customizable worlds, we foresee a tension requiring further research. Will the future yield a hierarchy of virtual worlds that do not interoperate, with the proprietary systems being the most developed and sophisticated as well as most costly and least modifiable? Will this stratification of virtual worlds mirror the stratification we see in the real world, thus erasing many of the leveling benefits of being virtual? Or will there be a host of different worlds that do inter-connect to make up the larger Metaverse?

Research on virtual organizations and virtual worlds continues apace in their traditional academic and industrial venues, but more integrated efforts across these camps are needed in the future. For virtual organizations, there are communities of scholars concerned with the organizational issues of distance collaboration, ranging from the Academy of Management (most notably the Organizational Communication and Information Systems [OCIS] division) to ACM-CSCW and ACM-Group. For virtual worlds, ACM-SIGGRAPH remains the academic showplace for technological advances. Myriad other gatherings examine the behavioral side of virtual worlds, including sessions at the Association for Internet Research (AoIR) and mini-conferences (e.g., Persistent Conversation track) at the Hawaii International Conference on System Sciences (HICSS). The journals, professional publications, conferences, and workshops of these associations remain the best, albeit siloed, sources for cutting edge research on virtual worlds and virtual organizing. However, the recent debuts of the *Journal of Virtual Worlds Research* and the *Journal of Gaming and Virtual Worlds* in 2008 may offer new interdisciplinary and transdisciplinary venues for the integration of work at the confluence of virtual worlds for virtual organizing.

New work at the intersection of these social and technological trends could also be accelerated by recent increases in both public and private funding. Within the United States, the National Science Foundation, the leading public funder of information and computer technology research, has funded basic research on both virtual organizations and on virtual worlds for years within and across multiple disciplines, most notably the Human-Centered Computing program. Within the past few years, the notion of virtual organizations has garnered increased attention from other areas of the Foundation. The directorate for Engineering has sponsored a multi-year "Engineering Virtual Organizations" solicitation focused on designing topically targeted virtual organizations using cutting edge technology, and the Foundation-wide e-science initiative, "Cyber-enabled Discovery and Innovation (CDI)," included virtual organizations as one of its three focal areas. Finally, the most recent competition, called "Virtual Organizations as Sociotechnical Systems (VOSS)," clearly demonstrated the intersection of virtual organizations with virtual worlds to the point of receiving enough submissions to require a panel dedicated to the intellectual convergence. Alongside these public investments in research, several large-scale private foundations like the MacArthur Foundation and the Kauffmann Foundation are supporting research on and practice toward virtual worlds as a medium for organized social change. But today, the pace of these foundation efforts lags behind the pace of commercial development. Without better coordination across research and development as well as integration across disciplines, we could find ourselves at a new convergence defined by an old divergence between the social and the technical.

References

Achterbosch, L., Pierce, R., & Simmons, G. (2008). Massively multiplayer online role-playing games: The past, present, and future. *ACM Computers in Entertainment, 5*(4): article 9.

Balkin, J., & Noveck, B. (eds). (2006). *The state of play: Law and virtual worlds.* New York: New York University Press.

Bartle, R. (2006). *Designing virtual worlds.* New York: New Riders Publishing.

Benkler, Y. (1992). Coase's Pengion, or, Linux and the nature of the firm. *The Yale Law Journal, 112,* 369–446.

Biocca, F. (1992). Communication within virtual reality: Crating a space for research. *Journal of Communication, 42,* 5–22.

Bleecker, S. E. (1994, March–April). The virtual organization. *The Futurist, 28,* 9–12.

Bompbard, P. (2007). Gospel 2.0: Jesuits move into Second Life. *Financial Times,* July 26. Last retrieved May 1, 2009, (http://www.ft.com/cms/s/0/ceae9c60-3ba8-11dc-8002-0000779fd2ac. html?nclick_check=1)

Cajvaneanu, D. (2007). Virtual worlds: A political incubator. *ACM SIGMIS Database, 38,* 104–105.

Cohill, A. M., & Kavanaugh, A. L. (eds). (2000). *Community networks: Lessons from Blacksburg, Virginia.* Norwood, MA: Artech House.

Correll, S. (1995). The ethnography of an electronic bar: The lesbian cafe. *Journal of Contemporary Ethnography, 24,* 270–298.

Coyle, J., & Schnarr, N. (1995). The soft-side challenges of the virtual corporation. *Human Resource Planning, 18,* 41–42.

Crane, D. (1972). *Invisible colleges: Diffusion of knowledge in scientific communities.* Chicago, IL: University of Chicago Press.

Cummings, J., Finholt, T., Foster, I., Kesselman, C., Lawrence, K., & Rhoten, D. (2008). *Beyond being there: A blueprint for advancing the design, development, and evaluation of virtual organizations.* Arlington, VA: National Science Foundation.

Damer, B., Gold, S., de Bruin, J., & de Bruin, D.-J. (2000). Conferences and trade shows in inhabited virtual worlds: A case study of Avatars 98 & 99. In J.-C. Heudin (Ed.), *Virtual worlds: Proceedings from Second International Conference.* Paris: Springer.

Davidow, W., & Malone, M. (1992). *The virtual corporation: Structuring and revitalizing the corporation for the 21st century.* New York: Harper.

Ducheneaut, N., Yee, N., Nickell, E., & Moore, R. (2007). The life and death of online gaming communities: A look at guilds in World of Warcraft. In *Proceedings from 25th Annual ACM*

Conference on Human Factors in Computing Systems (pp. 839–848). San Jose, CA: ACM Press.

Ellis, J., Luther, K., Bessiere, K., & Kellogg, W. A. (2008). Games for virtual team building. In *Proceedings of ACM DIS 2008 Conference on Designing Interactive System* (pp. 295–304). Cape Town, South Africa: ACM Press.

Gaver, W., Moran, T., MacLean, A., Lövstrand, L., Dourish, P., Carter, K., & Buxton, W. (1992). Realizing a video environment: EuroPARC's RAVE system. In *Proceedings of the SIGCHI Conference on Human Factors in Computing Systems* (pp. 27–35). Monterey, CA: ACM Press.

Giuliano, V. (1982). The mechanization of office work. *Scientific American, 247,* 148–164.

Greenhalgh, C., & Benford, S. (1995). MASSIVE: A distributed virtual reality system incorporating spatial trading. In *Proceedings of the IEEE 15th International Conference on Distributed Computing Systems (DCS'95),* Vancouver, Canada, May 30–June 2.

Grenier, R., & Metes, G. (1995). *Going virtual: Moving your organization into the 21st century.* Upper Saddle River, NJ: Prentice Hall.

Hedberg, B. B., & Dahlgren, G. (1997). *Virtual organizations and beyond discover imaginary systems.* New York: Wiley.

Hollan, J., & Stornetta, S. (1992). Beyond being there. In *Proceedings of the SIGCHI Conference on Human Factors in Computing Systems* (pp. 119–125). Monterey, CA: ACM Press.

Isaacs, E. A. (1998). Microcosm: Support for virtual communities via an on-line graphical environment. In *Proceedings of the Conference on Computer-Human Interaction (CHI)'98* (pp. 5–6). Los Angeles, CA: ACM Press.

Jakobsson, M. (2003). A virtual realist primer to virtual world design. In P. Ehn & J. Löwgren (Eds.), *Searching voices - towards a canon for interaction design.* Studies in Arts and Communication #01. Malmö, Sweden: Malmö University Press.

Kim, J. Y., Allen, J. P., & Lee, E. (2008). Alternate reality gaming. In *Communications of the ACM* (pp. 36–42). New York: ACM Press.

Kobayashi, M., & Ishii, H. (1993). ClearBoard: A novel shared drawing medium that supports gaze awareness in remote collaboration. In *IEICE Transactions on Communications, Institute of Electronics* (Vol. E76-B, pp. 609–617). Tokyo: Information and Communication Engineers of Japan (IEICE).

Lakhani, K., & Panetta, J. (2007). The principles of distributed innovation. *Innovations, 2,* 97–112.

Lipnack, J., & Stamps, J. (1997). *Virtual teams: Working across space, time, and organizations.* New York: Wiley.

Mackay, W. (1999). Media spaces: Environments for informal multimedia interaction. In X. Beaudouin-Lafon (Ed.), *Computer-supported co-operative work, trends in software series* (pp. 55–82). New York: Wiley.

McCarthy, C. (2009). Second Life cracks whip on adult content. *CNet News,* April 21. Last retrieved May 1, 2009, (http://news.cnet.com/the-social/?keyword = virtual + worlds)

Morningstar, C., & Farmer, F. R. (1991). The lessons of Lucasfilm's habitat. In M. Benedikt (Ed.), *Cyberspace: First steps* (pp. 273–301). Cambridge, MA: MIT Press.

Mowshowitz, A. (1994). Virtual organization: A vision of management in the Information Age. *The Information Society, 10,* 267–294.

O' Mahony, S. (2008, November). *Using differentiation to establish organizational boundaries in the burning man and open source communities.* Philadelphia, PA: Association for Research on Nonprofit Organizations and Voluntary Action.

O'Day, V. L., Bobrow, D. G., & Shirley, M. (1996). The socio-technical design circle. In *Proceedings of the ACM conference on Computer Supported Cooperative Work (CSCW)* (pp. 160–169). New York, NY: ACM Press.

O'Leary, M., Orlikowski, W., & Yates, J. (2002). Distributed work over the centuries: Trust and control in the Hudson's Bay Company, 1670-1826. In P. J. Hinds & S. Kiesler (Eds.), *Distributed work* (pp. 27–54). Cambridge, MA: MIT Press.

Oldenburg, R. (1989). *The great good place: Cafes, coffee shops, community centers, beauty parlors, general stores, bars, hangouts, and how they get you through the day.* New York: Paragon House.

Rheingold, H. (1993). *The virtual community: Homesteading on the electronic frontier.* New York: Harper-Collins.

Rhoten, Diana. (2004). "Interdisciplinary Research: Trend or Transition?" Items and Issues 5(1):6–11.

Schroeder, R. (1996). *Possible worlds: The social dynamic of virtual reality technologies.* Boulder, CO: West View.

Schuler, D. (1996). *New community networks: Wired for change.* Menlo Park, CA: Addison-Wesley.

Sifakis, C. (1999). *The mafia encyclopedia.* New York: Checkmark Books.

Sutton, K. (2007). Going to church in Second Life. *UU World Magazine,* February 19. Last Retrieved May1, 2009, (http://www.uuworld. org/life/ articles /16206.shtml)

Wellman, B., & Gulia, M. (1999). Net-surfers don't ride alone: Virtual communities as communities. In B. Wellman (Ed.), *Networks in the global village* (pp. 331–366). Boulder, CO: Westview.

Wilson, C. (2008). Avatars, virtual reality technology and the U.S. military: Emerging policy issues. CRS Report for Congress (RS22857, April 9).

Chapter 22
Future Evolution of Virtual Worlds as Communication Environments

Giulio Prisco

Some users are mainly interested in virtual worlds as a means to escape everyday reality, while others see them as tools to do things faster and better in everyday reality. They are not very much interested in the metaverse as a replacement for the physical world, but see it as a communication tool for people in the physical world. Even *Second Life* (Rymaszewski et al. 2007), which is a very primitive Virtual Reality (VR) world by upcoming standards, can already be used as a telepresence and telecollaboration option much better, and much more immersive, than video-conferencing or other traditional forms of remote collaboration. If videoconferencing is one step below a critical threshold for suspension of disbelief, Second Life is already one step above. The evolution of VR will provide next generation telework platforms, which will really enable, and empower, global communities. Thus, its social and political importance will be huge. Further evolution of VR and other emerging technologies will result in science-fiction-like scenarios, from instant telepathic communication to full transcendence of biological constrains.

Metaverses

Virtual reality worlds are also known as Massively Multiuser Online – MMO – games or environments, or "metaverses." In his cult novel *Snow Crash* (1992), science fiction author Neal Stephenson detailed a vision of a future 3D Internet based on virtual reality – the Metaverse – where billions of users, represented by their avatars, routinely spend time for both business and entertainment. Wandering in a synthetic universe generated by bits changing value in computer circuitry and traveling on communication links, metaverse residents can see and talk to each other, attend dance parties and work meetings, build their own virtual dreams, and explore the dreams of other users. Stephenson's vision is beginning to take off, and

G. Prisco
Metafuturing
e-mail: giulio@gmail.com

W.S. Bainbridge (ed.), *Online Worlds: Convergence of the Real and the Virtual*,
Human-Computer Interaction Series, DOI 10.1007/978-1-84882-825-4_22,
© Springer-Verlag London Limited 2010

this is a good example of the often very important role of good science fiction literature in shaping our actual reality. In *Snow Crash,* the metaverse is centered around The Street, the first VR settlement mainly developed by hackers, with a number of popular attractions including the first and foremost virtual club, world famous across realities, the Black Sun. Of course, the fictional Black Sun has been rebuilt in many "real" virtual worlds. For example, it has been built in *Second Life* in the Stone Age of the platform back in 2006.

Virtual reality (VR) environments, or "worlds," are computer-generated environments that can give users the impression of "being there." A very general, rigorous definition of *virtual reality* has been given by David Deutsch:

> The term refers to any situation in which a person is artificially given the experience of being in a specified environment. For example, a flight simulator - a machine that gives pilots the experience of flying an aircraft without their having to leave the ground - is a type of virtual-reality generator. Such a machine (or, more precisely, the computer that controls it) can be programmed with the characteristics of a real of imaginary aircraft. The aircraft's environment, such as the weather or the layout of airports, can also be specified in the program. As the pilot practices flying from one airport to another, the simulator causes the appropriate images to appear at the windows, the appropriate jolts and accelerations to be felt, the corresponding readings to be shown on the instruments, and so on. It can incorporate the effects of, for example, turbulence, mechanical failure, and proposed modifications to the aircraft. Thus, a flight simulator can give the users a wide range of piloting experiences, including some that no real aircraft could: the simulated aircraft could have performance characteristics that violate the laws of physics: it could, for instance, fly through mountains, faster than light or without fuel. (Deutsch 1997: 98–99)

The best known examples of consumer VR are modern videogames for PCs and consoles powered by game engines. Players navigate near-photorealistic and even near-videorealistic computer-generated 3D spaces and hear computer-generated stereoscopic sounds that are "spatialized" – directional and fading with distance. Another common feature of modern consumer VR games is the possibility of sharing a VR world with remote players, for example in Valve Software's Counter-Strike, whose development began as a user-created modification, or "mod," of Valve's *Half Life 2,* or in the soon to be launched *Blue Mars* virtual world of Avatar Reality, powered by the current leader in game engine performance and visual quality Cry Engine 2 of Crytek. Game engines provide a simulated physics that allow players to have realistic interaction with physical objects, for example moving or breaking an obstacle, picking up an object, or driving a simulated vehicle.

Before its adoption by the gaming sector, VR technology had been developed by and used for the military and industrial simulation sectors. It can be said that most modern computer gaming technologies originated as spinoffs of military applications and simulation projects for the construction, oil, or air transport industries, not to mention space. Today, the trend seems reversed: New technology breakthroughs are generated by the gaming industry first, and then find their way to military and industrial applications. Current buzzwords are "low-cost simulation" and "serious games," which just means reusing gaming technologies and platforms for "serious" applications. This is due not only to the money available to the gaming industry, but also to its capability to attract and motivate young and brilliant engineers with a strong creative vein, who would never feel at home in a more culturally conservative sector. It is not surprising that smart young people are attracted by the computer gaming industry: in the words of Rudy Rucker (2005: 259), "Academia hasn't quite caught on to the fact that computer games represent the convergence and the flowering of the most ambitious frontier efforts of the old twentieth-century computer science: artificial intelligence, virtual reality, and artificial life."

A well-known example of modern consumer level VR is the popular virtual world Second Life (SL). Rather than a computer game, *Second Life* can be considered as a platform where "residents" collaborate at building a virtual world with the tools provided by the system. Residents build avatars, clothes, houses, vehicles, etc., buy and sell land and designer items, and organize events. *Second Life* is a "persistent" VR that does not disappear when a user logs off. Though the 3D graphics and simulated physics of *Second Life* cannot be compared with those of the best VR videogames, *Second Life* is a very interesting social phenomenon and it has probably been the first example of a successful, mass-market persistent VR world. Another example of massively multiuser consumer-oriented VR world is the immensely popular fantasy game *World of Warcraft* (Corneliussen and Rettberg 2008), of Blizzard. WoW, as it is often indicated, is the favorite pastime of more than 12 million paying users, who roam its dreamlike landscapes to defeat monsters and engage in solitary or collaborative quests, often learning strategy and collaboration skills in the process. Like *Second Life*, WoW is poor by modern gaming visual standards, but the visual quality of massively multiuser virtual worlds is clearly bound to improve.

More than a decade after *Snow Crash*, defined many of the Virtual Reality (VR) concepts used today, VR technology is beginning to catch up with science fiction literature. A few years after writing his novel, Stephenson said that his vision had not emerged in reality. This may have been a premature statement, and in 2009 we can see a growing number of operational implementations, with popular events taking place in a Metaverse, and an emergent economy consolidating. The best-known and most popular Metaverse implementation is Second Life.

Second Life was launched by Linden Lab in 2003, and enjoyed a few months of very positive, almost sensationalist press, in the first half of 2007. As it often happens, after hailing Second Life as the future of the Internet and something that would change the way business is done, the press has demonized it as a useless sink of time and money (Denton 2006; Bugeja 2007; Gardiner 2007; Naone 2007; Vallance 2007). Nothing new, and many readers will remember that about 15 years ago the press used to say the same things about the Internet. It is often said that many corporate headquarters and initiatives in *Second Life* are always empty of visitors and "desert," which is often true and due to a deep lack of understanding of new media by the business sector. On the contrary, many "home-made" virtual environments in *Second Life*, spontaneously created by users for fun, are vibrant communities always full of enthusiast regulars and visitors.

My company, Metafuturing SL, builds custom virtual environment for corporate and educational clients in many VR worlds, including *Second Life*, and I have seen many clients with a naive "let's build it, and they will come" attitude. The reality is that it takes a lot of work and dedication to build a virtual community, and most companies and academic departments just don't have the necessary resources and are not able to move fast enough. My experience is that, in order to build a successful VR environment with a positive impact on the core business, whatever that is, operational issues must be discussed with the client and taken into account at design stage.

One of the unique features of *Second Life* is the fact that all users, even those with only a minimum of 3D modeling and programming skills, are able to build new user created content for the virtual world. This has attracted many creative people to *Second Life*, and has been the main reason for its success. Even if new VR worlds, like the forthcoming *Blue Mars* and others still on the drawing board, will be much better than Second Life in terms of video-realistic graphics and accurate physics, and even stability and usability, I think the most creative users will stay in Second Life. Perhaps their main interest in alternative VR worlds will be as sources of inspiration for their Second Life creations.

Immersionists Versus Augmentationists

A very interesting feature of *Second Life*, not related to the technology of this specific VR platform but often discussed in the context of *Second Life* as a laboratory to study sociology and psychology in emerging VR worlds, is the divide between "immersionists" and "augmentationists." These terms were coined by Henrik Bennetsen in 2006 and used by many popular *Second Life* bloggers, including the declared immersionist Gwyneth Llewelyn:

> The first-generation SL residents were interested in *Second Life* as an "alternate reality," one that is disconnected from "real life" but bears some resemblance to it. In this alternate reality you would be able to be whomever you wanted to be – and requests for revealing your real life data are considered rude... A later generation, the "augmentationists," have a different point of view. They look at *Second Life* as an extension of real life – a tool, a platform, a communication medium, the second generation World-Wide Web in 3D. For them, anonymity is as silly as faking your voice on a phone call; just because you're a "phone number" you're not a different person.[1]

The debate between the two camps has generated some intense debates, for example after the introduction of voice chat in *Second Life* in 2007. Immersionists, who want to live a parallel *Second Life* (SL) completely separated by their Real Life (RL), prefer not to use voice because it would reveal information about their RL identity that they prefer to keep secret in SL. They also see voice as an unwanted intrusion of the real world in their "magic world." The immersionists loudly but unsuccessfully demanded a ban of voice in SL. I wrote an article about "Life 2.0: Augmentationists in Second Life and beyond," published online by the Institute of Ethics and Emerging Technologies,[2] where, while understanding the immersionists' point of view, I sided with the augmentationists on the basis of a point which is, in my opinion, very important: Having more options is always

---

[1] http://gwynethllewelyn.net/2006/09/17/the-big-controversies-in-second-life/
[2] http://ieet.org/index.php/IEET/more/prisco20070812/

good, even when the availability of an option causes some psychological distress to those who prefer not to use it. It is interesting to see how this important issue, which may become one of the most important sources of tension of our times as I will show in the last part of this article, was initially discussed in a VR world. In 2009, many immersionists define themselves as "Digital Persons" and value their alternate identity in a VR world more than their, often hidden, "real" identity. Sooner or later, they may begin to claim legal personhood, which will certainly cause some difficult but interesting problems.

I have many immersionist friends (too bad I will never meet them face to face in brickspace reality), and I find it very interesting to observe the development of their culture, but I am not much interested in immersionism myself. I am more interested in 3D Internet as an enabling technology for remote communication and collaboration. One thing that I do very much in virtual worlds is attending seminars and conferences. In May 2008, I participated in a scientific conference in *World of Warcraft*, of all places! It was a high-profile event organized by William Sims Bainbridge and John Bohannon who, in a *Science* magazine article titled "Scientists, We Need Your Swords," wrote:

> This will not be your typical conference. Sure, there will be sessions devoted to various research topics involving virtual worlds, panel discussions, social activities, and those conference goody bags that we've all come to love. But to attend this conference, you don't have to splurge on grant money or add to global warming by flying to another country. And in the goody bags, you won't find brochures, pens, or those quickly lost notebooks. Instead, each conference participant will receive (while supplies last) 10 gold pieces, a red "Sciencemag" shirt, a colorful conference tabard emblazoned with an infinity symbol, two extra bags for swag, a telescope, and a pet creature. Between sessions, there will be group field trips across landscapes inhabited by dangerous beasts –some earthly and extinct, others fanciful – an introduction to the world's auction-based economy, and finally a massive joint assault on an enemy city. (Beat that, Gordon conferences!) Anyone with an Internet connection can take part, from anywhere in the world. All you have to do is install the game, create a character, and join the guild called "Science" on the Earthen Ring US server. If that sounds scary, complex, weird, geeky, well... welcome to the future. At least, welcome to the future of scientific research envisioned by the conference organizers, William Bainbridge (a sociologist at the National Science Foundation) and about a dozen scientists whose research involves the 10 million people who spend time – scary amounts of time – in the Warcraft universe. (Bohannon 2008: 312)

The WoW conference was very interesting and gave me the feeling of being in a historic event (a very nice feeling), but WoW is not really a suitable platform for talks and conferences. *Second Life* is much more suitable and has a growing set of communication and groupware features, including in-world PowerPoint, voice chat, and streaming video, which, together with a mature in-world programming system and the ability to quickly import images and build 3D models, permit running professional and immersive VR events. If videoconferencing is one step below the "immersion threshold" necessary for suspension of disbelief, *Second Life* is already one step above: Those who participate in Second Life events often report having the impression of "being there" and "talking to people," as in conventional conferences, but they don't have to travel halfway round the world to attend.

A few weeks after the WoW events I had the honor of speaking at a *Second Life* conference on "The Future of Religions – Religions of the Future," a 2-day event examining how two of the twenty-first Century's driving forces, religion and technology, will continue to re-shape each other and, in the process, re-cast our understanding of "humanity" in the Third Millennium. This remarkable event was hosted by two SL social movements, Extropia, which is "a creative, collaborative community around a positive vision of the future brought about by human ingenuity" and the Al-Andalus Caliphate Project, which is "a multicultural community built around a reconstructed 13th Century Moor Alhambra." Centered on, but not limited to, virtual worlds and social networking technologies, speakers and panelists also examined changes precipitated by the biotechnology revolution, cognitive science, information technologies, and robotics.

At the conference, I announced the Order of Cosmic Engineers (OCE), a new cultural organization positioned at the interface of advanced science with philosophy, and very active in virtual worlds.[3] In some respects, the OCE is a Transhumanist association, because it shares with so-called Transhumanist or Extropian organizations a belief that technology can legitimately be used to improve human nature (FM-2030 1989). It is also a space advocacy group, a spiritual movement, a literary salon, a technology observatory, an idea factory, and a global community of persons willing to take an active role in achieving a sunny future. As engineers, we aim to build what cannot be readily found. Adopting an engineering approach and attitude, we aim to turn this universe into a "magical" realm. The Order of Cosmic Engineers held its opening event in *World of Warcraft* a few days later, has organized many seminars in *Second Life* in 2008 and 2009, and plans expanding to other VR worlds. Metaverse, here we come!

Despite the frequent announcements of the imminent demise and death of *Second Life* by the sensationalist technology press, *Second Life* is here to stay: history doesn't read the sensationalist press. And even if *Second Life* were to disappear tomorrow and be replaced by a much better VR platform, its Linden Lab creators have already won their place in the history of the Internet as the originators of the first commercially viable mass market metaverse for consumers.

Moving Beyond Second Life

The *Second Life* platform is being cloned in open source by the Open Simulator project, often called OpenSim, which in 2009 is advancing fast and beginning to receive press coverage similar to that of Second Life in 2007. OpenSim permits all virtual world operators with sufficient technical knowledge to install VR worlds similar to *Second Life* on their own servers. A few large companies are using OpenSim and providing some financial support to the project, which seems able to

---

[3] http://cosmeng.org/index.php/Main_Page

escape the doom of many underfunded open source projects and become a major player in the industry. Intel is using OpenSim for their initiative *ScienceSim*, linked to the Supercomputing conferences and probably the most mature implementation of OpenSim at the time of writing.

The promising new technology Open Croquet is emerging from research laboratories as a "Metaverse Operating System" and a candidate for future implementations. Its most recent implementation Open Cobalt is an open source, collaborative, distributed metaverse, which does not have to rely on central server maintained by large corporations, but is powered by the personal hardware of its users. The technology of Open Croquet is used by a very interesting VR environment for business collaboration and educational applications, developed by Qwaq Inc. Qwaq Forums are linked VR rooms with groupware technology such as shared whiteboards, collaborative document editing, videoconferencing, screen casting, etc. In the wake of Qwaq, other companies, most notably Sun Microsystems, are developing their own open source VR platforms for the business world, and it is to be expected that VR worlds will become a routine platform for business collaboration. In today's fast moving Internet, the most exciting new developments are usually produced by small companies for the consumer market, and the slow moving conventional business world needs time to catch up.

Driven by a huge market and multi-billion investments, the computer gaming industry is generating many important developments. At the recent game Developers Conference 2009, the gaming technology developer Crytek has announced that the forthcoming version of its game engine, Cry Engine 3, will be optimized for massively multiuser applications. Two near-videorealistic massively multiuser VR environments, both developed with Cry Engine technology, are scheduled to be available before the end of 2009: the already mentioned *Blue Mars*, and the next version of *Entropia Universe*, a science-fiction themed game from Mindark. Another very interesting announcement at the Game Developers Conference was that of the launch, before the end of the year, of the OnLive streaming gaming platform, which may start the era of cloud gaming or Gaming As A Service: visually rich, videorealistic games played "in the cloud" on high-performance servers, which accept remote user input and deliver streaming video to the player over the wideband Internet. Though the OnLive demonstrations at the GDC have been successful, many experts have expressed doubts about the performance and scalability of this technology over the current Internet infrastructure, and believe the operational deployment of streaming gaming technology will have to wait a few more years. Once available, however, video streaming gaming technology will enable users to play next-generation games with thin clients, thus eliminating the barrier of expensive personal high-performance hardware. I predict that video streaming gaming technology will have an important impact beyond the world of computer gaming, and facilitate the emergence of the future 3D Internet.

Most consumers still see virtual worlds on a computer screen, and navigate them via keyboard, mouse, and joystick. There are also more "immersive" user interfaces based on VR glasses, helmets, gloves, and force feedback devices that can give a much stronger impression of "being there." Once only available to professionals, hardcore gamers, and hackers, advanced VR interface gear has already entered the consumer market. In only a few months, low-cost VR interfaces will start appearing in retail stores, and I think they will soon become standard interfaces like keyboard and mouse today.

It is currently very difficult to create a high-fidelity virtual reality experience, due largely to technical limitations on processing power, image resolution, communication bandwidth, and interfacing technologies. However, those limitations are expected eventually to be overcome as processor, imaging, data communication, and interfacing technologies become more powerful and cost-effective over time. Of course, dedicated VR systems, for example combat and flight simulators developed for military applications, are still much more powerful than consumer VR and permit much more realistic VR experiences. However, as processing power, imaging technology, data communication, and software keep improving according to Moore's law, it seems inevitable that consumer-level VR will achieve the same performance soon.

VR worlds can be, and often are, imaginary worlds with little resemblance to the real world. At the same time, VR technology is frequently used to permit users experiencing remote locations in the real world, for example previewing holiday resorts and real estate. In VR-enabled telepresence applications, the computer generates an accurate, real-time rendering of a remote location by using data from cameras and sensor networks at the remote site. Telepresence is the best option to "go to" inaccessible or dangerous locations and, with forthcoming advances in VR technology, it will also become a more and more appropriate replacement for face-to-face meetings. The evolution of VR will provide next-generation telepresence platforms that will really empower global communities beyond today's provincial national boundaries. Thus, the social and political importance of VR worlds will be huge.

Moving Beyond First Life

Now I wish to offer some predictions on the evolution of virtual worlds. But I have written this essay for a printed book and the safest assumption is that, by the time the book is out, any short-term prediction that I make here will be obsolete. Last year, Google launched their own VR world called *Lively*, which made headline news. A few months later, Google unexpectedly retired *Lively*. I think Google intended *Lively* as a reconnaissance mission behind enemy lines in virtual territory, and retired after gathering some intelligence. This would imply that Google may launch their "real" VR platform anytime now. This, which would have a huge impact on the short-term evolution of virtual worlds, may happen or may not happen – I just don't know. One thing I know for sure is that the evolution of virtual worlds in the next few years will be turbulent and chaotic, with players coming and going, with highs and lows, but with a general trend toward better technology and realism. Making short-term predictions is difficult, but fortunately making longer term predictions is easier.

I have said that I don't take immersionism in current VR worlds too seriously, because really immersive technologies are not available yet. You cannot touch and smell things in Second Life. You can fly, but you don't feel the wind when you fly (I will skip similar considerations about virtual dating and sex). Sounds are noisy and broken, and virtual things happen on a small screen while real things happen all around. Your avatar on the PC screen does not feel pain, but if the PC falls on your foot you do feel pain, and you know that a real headache can spoil even the most wonderful virtual experience. Can VR be real, as real as brickspace reality or even more real? Let's see the trends.

There is a trend toward more and more realistic graphics, physics, and AI-driven behavior. There is also a trend toward more and more sophisticated and immersive user interfaces. With much better graphics and VR glasses able to simulate a deep spherical field of view around the user, virtual reality will begin to feel much more real. There is also an emerging trend toward the development of neural interfaces, that is, Brain to Computer Interfaces (BCI) able to read or write information directly from and to a user's brain. Science fiction? Transhumanist wishful thinking? No, science fact: prototype BCI devices are already available since a few years.

The first applications of neural interfacing have been in the medical field, where the best-known examples are the breakthroughs of Cyberkinetics, whose technology used in medical pilot projects has permitted severely disabled patients interacting with computers by thought. Now, this technology is finding its way to the consumer market, and companies like Emotiv Systems and Neurosky are preparing the launch of the first neural interface devices for computer gaming. I am hardly surprised to see that the first consumer applications of neural interfacing are developed for the computer gaming industry. In the computer gaming market, there is a lot of money; there will be even more money, and game companies are able to attract very bright and creative people everywhere. I am more and more persuaded that other "transhumanist holy grails," such as conscious artificial intelligence, will be first developed by the computer gaming industry.

So, we will soon be able to think our way in virtual worlds. If a computer can read information from our brains, it won't be long before it can also write information directly to our brains, and write it very fast: two-way neural interfaces that will make computer screens and headsets obsolete, a *Second Life* that goes directly to the brain bypassing the eyes, with today's Instant Messaging replaced by direct telepathic communication between minds. And when our virtual environments will contain artificial intelligences, perhaps smarter than us, we will be able to communicate with them at the speed of thought. For the medium- and long-term future, probably within the first half of the century, it is to be expected that advances in neurotechnology will permit developing direct interfaces to the brain that can bypass sensorial channels to make VR environments directly accessible to the brain. This will permit creating fully immersive VR environments with full sensorial stimulation, indistinguishable from physical reality. Let's call things by their name: These first baby steps to neural interfacing for consumers will lead to the ultimate transhumanist Holy Grail: mind uploading, the transfer of human consciousness out of the brain into much higher performance supports, where we will be able to interact and merge with each other and our AI mind children (Moravec 1988).

These mind boggling possibilities will probably cause debates similar in nature to the immersionists versus augmentationists debate in *Second Life*, but much deeper and more intense. There will be very radical changes of the "nature of the game," and of course there will be those who will prefer to stay in the old comfortable game instead of embracing change and moving on. They will conceive life only within the narrow area defined by the experiences of earlier generations, and resist change, even if nothing is going to change for them personally unless they want it to. But I repeat that having more options is always good, even when the availability of an option causes some psychological distress to those who prefer not to use it.

I am sure that nobody will force anyone to "upgrade," and there will be "immersionist" communities for persons who choose to remain immersed in human biology and its limitations. However, knowing that a large part of the human species has moved on beyond biology, and knowing that there is a new game going on in which they don't participate, is bound to have some mental impact on those who choose to stay behind, and create very significant social and political problems to solve. The coming debate on human enhancement is very important, as it will permit analyzing problems and devising solutions. I think these problems can and will be solved, and VR worlds can provide a useful laboratory for analysis.

References

Bohannon, J. (2008). Scientists, we need your swords!. *Science, 320*, 312.

Bugeja, M. J. (2007). Second thoughts about Second Life. *Chronicle of Higher Education* online, September 14, from (http://chronicle.com/jobs/news/2007/09/2007091401c.htm).

Corneliussen, H. G. & Rettberg, J. W. (2008). *Digital culture, play, and identity: A World of Warcraft reader*. Cambridge, MA: MIT Press.

Denton, N. (2006). A story too good to check. *Valleywag*. Retrieved December 12, from (http://valleywag.gawker.com/tech/second-life/a-story-too-good-to-check-221252.php).

Deutsch, D. (1997). *The fabric of reality: The science of parallel universes – and its implications*. New York: Allen Lane.

FM-2030. (1989). *Are you a Transhuman?* New York: Warner Books.

Gardiner, B. (2007). Bank failure in Second Life leads to calls for regulation. *Wired* online, August 15, from (http://www.wired.com/gaming/virtualworlds/news/2007/08/virtual_bank).

Moravec, H. P. (1988). *Mind children: The future of robot and human intelligence*. Cambridge, MA: Harvard University Press.

Naone, E. (2007). Money trouble in Second Life. *Technology Review* online, August 8, from (http://www.technologyreview.com/Biztech/19193/?a=f).

Rucker, R. (2005). *The lifebox, the seashell, and the soul*. New York: Thunder's Mouth Press.

Rymaszewski, M., Au, W. J., Ondrejka, C., Platel, R., Van Gorden, S., Cézanne, J., et al. (2007). *Second Life: The official guide*. San Francisco, CA: Sybex.

Stephenson, N. (1992). *Snow Crash*. New York: Bantam Books.

Vallance, C. (2007). Second Life online gambling crackdown. *BBC* online, July 27, from (http://www.bbc.co.uk/blogs/podsandblogs/2007/07/second_life_online_gambling_cr.shtml).

Chapter 23
The Future of Virtual Worlds

William Sims Bainbridge, Wayne Lutters, Diana Rhoten, and Henry Lowood

This book, like the May 2008 conference in *World of Warcraft*, ends with projections toward what the future might hold for virtual worlds. Every chapter thus far has included speculations about future directions, even while standing on data from the past. This last chapter, like the final session of the conference on which it is based, incorporates comments from dozens of participants into a stream of ideas. We have edited selected comments together with the panel's contributions. Our intention is to provide a portal from this book into a wider virtual community comprising researchers and residents in virtual worlds. The discussion surveys many recent lines of development, some of which have already been surveyed in scientific and historical literature, or by journalists (Au 2008; Castronova 2007; Guest 2007; Ludlow and Wallace 2007). Yet, many of the topics here have not received such attention. Considered as a set of socio-technical innovations, virtual worlds are not just about technical possibilities; they also inspired the participants to consider the economic bases for investing in those possibilities and the novel cultural, social, and artistic forms virtual worlds might offer.

Technical Innovations

The final session of the conference began in the technical realm with a provocative question: "Given that computer technology and Internet have stabilized, are current virtual worlds a technological dead end?" The premise of this question was that the

D. Rhoten
Social Science Research Council
e-mail: rhoten@ssrc.org

H. Lowood
Stanford University
e-mail: lowood@stanford.edu

W. Lutters
University of Maryland, Baltimore County
e-mail: lutters@umbc.edu

W.S. Bainbridge (ed.), *Online Worlds: Convergence of the Real and the Virtual*,
Human-Computer Interaction Series, DOI 10.1007/978-1-84882-825-4_2,
© Springer-Verlag London Limited 2010

technological curve of the technologies behind networked personal computing seems to be flattening out. Internet latencies are not lowering appreciably for people who already subscribe to broadband, broadband speeds in some countries are throttled by a variety of circumstances, and universal access to high-speed internet is far from being a reality in others. Still, participants disagreed, insisting that Internet speeds will increase, and the expansion of broadband to a much larger population base will make it possible for virtual worlds to make full use of that speed. The current populations of virtual worlds are constrained when only a minority of potential users has full access to this technology, which they cannot do when only a minority of their customers have it. As one participant put, the problem that virtual worlds face in this regard is not limits on technology, but "open access" to the technologies that are available.

Virtual worlds need people, in other words, both as users and as content creators. One participant suggested that user modifications ("mods") and the development of open-source platforms for virtual worlds would encourage new kinds of creativity, presumably by residents as much as by developers. Since the conclusion of the conference, the appearance of new open-source solutions such as Stanford University's Sirikata seems to confirm that this will be an important direction to follow. Virtual worlds of the future would also benefit from a better understanding of human communication and socialization that occurs in these environments. More collaboration among researchers such as social scientists and developers might be helpful in creating a sense of the opportunities along these lines. Other areas of technical development mentioned by a few participants included artificial intelligence and new interface and controller designs. For example, we are currently only at the beginning of the application of advanced artificial intelligence techniques to the problem of creating plausible and interesting non-player characters in game worlds, and it is very likely that in more open sorts of virtual worlds there will be currently unanticipated uses for AI-based agents or artificial life software. Thus, some participants were more intrigued by what they see as a current period of technological turbulence rather than flat-lined stability.

Several participants cited a particular aspect of *World of Warcraft* during the discussion of technical innovation in terms of open-source software development: the ability to run interface modifications (called *mods* or *add-ons*). These are software programs based on scripting languages that allow players to change their user interface and distribute these scripts to other players, who then have access to the same modified interface elements. WoW runs scripts written by players and other developers in the Lua language, although some features of Lua have been disabled to prevent users from gaining unfair advantages such as awarding themselves free money. As a scripting language, Lua supports open development of programs within an essentially proprietary framework. On the one hand, players not only change the game interface by using mods, but they also can change the mods they are using, if they are so inclined; on the other hand, several conference participants noted that WoW is not an open-source platform. Mods thus provide opportunities for rapid prototyping of innovative interfaces for human–computer interaction and information management. The thriving mod community has extended the interface aspects to the development of ambitious Web 2.0 solutions that incorporate data harvesting and open access to data gathered from gameplay. Given the immense popularity of the game, a large community of modders has assembled around WoW. Many of WoW's competitors also use Lua scripts or comparable software technologies. Some conference participants were skeptical that open source modding could compete with the professional work done by the developers of the most successful virtual worlds, at the very least because of the unavoidable costs involved. Issues also remain with respect to the relationship between developers and players around the co-creation of virtual world software implied by the use of mods (Postigo 2008; Taylor 2006a).

In terms of aesthetic and narrative technologies, virtual worlds are just scratching the surface of player enactment, participation, and co-creation. As new interface technologies are developed, such as haptic interfaces, profound changes in player expressiveness in virtual worlds are to be expected, such as incorporation of body movement, gestures, facial expressions, and other ways for player to act as puppeteers of on-screen avatars. Past efforts to escape the confines of the computer screen and experience full, immersive virtual reality have not been commercially successful. Still, our conference demonstrated that an already available game world such as WoW can handle 120 avatars gathered together in one virtual location. Virtual worlds with richer possibilities for content creation and avatar expression, such as *Second Life* seem to be limited to roughly a third that number, especially if voice communication is enabled. The developers of another game world, *EVE Online,* have claimed to support as many as a quarter million co-terminous users on its single supercomputing cluster, but that number is achieved only because players are distributed across a large number of interconnected servers, and therefore cannot interact directly. When it is possible for thousands of participants to gather together in virtual world, as is the case for many current academic conferences, we will have reached a significant milestone.

Virtual worlds are complex socio-technical systems. Historically, the creation of virtual worlds has been characterized by cycles of popularity and clusters of development and adoption. One participant argued that the last "major wave" occurred during the mid-1990 with the launching of new 3D worlds such as *Worlds Away* and *The Palace.* Other clusters of activity have included MUDs and 2D graphical spaces such as *Habitat* during the 1980s, the rise of both virtual reality and 3D games during the early 1990s, and the successful launching of several 3D games and virtual worlds around the turn of the new millennium. This pattern may follow the recognition of paradigm shifts inside the developer community, or it may be triggered by deeper economic cycles that influence both the rate of financial investment and the market for products or services such as on-line social spaces.

One innovation that might change business models in a more permanent fashion would be standardization of software-data platforms, permitting migration across worlds. An example of development in this direction that has intensified since the conference would be the OpenSim projects that have followed open-source access to the *Second Life* client and reverse-engineering efforts aimed at is server-side software. Interoperability would offer a distinct advantage for small virtual worlds, such as those organized by academic or artistic projects. These specialized and intensely focused groups would find that smaller-scale virtual worlds tailored to their needs would become viable, both technically and economically, as is the case today for websites. Moreover, content and experiences available in these worlds could be opened up to larger communities through portals between virtual worlds.

A disadvantage is that standardization might impede innovation. The most successful commercial virtual worlds might not recognize any particular benefits from interoperability with their less successful competitors. Standardization also might pay dividends across different worlds offered by a single company, such as the several massively multiplayer games offered by both Sony and NCSoft, though the same goal might be achieved through proprietary designs.

If we could move easily among virtual worlds in an open platform scenario, would players and creative residents migrate in a more permanent sense between these worlds? One participant in the conference discussion wondered "how models of labor would migrate between worlds in an open platform scenario." Or do worlds like WoW have such a strong sense of local culture that migration would be unlikely? Similar issues of migration between the real world and virtual worlds and the implications of such migration for real-world governmental policy have been explored by Castronova (2007). Some participants disputed the value of migration of avatars among virtual worlds, arguing that "translation" – switching among avatars created for their particular worlds – is more likely, and in fact is nothing new. This last observation reminds us that people may use different avatars to play different roles within a game, and to play in different games, as well. Since they used to switching in this manner, would they really find it natural, for example, to have their *World of Warcraft* Orc warrior represent them in a business meeting in *Second Life*?

Another important area of innovation for some years now has been the technology known as *augmented reality*, the combination of virtual and real world activity in fields such as virtual surgery and telepresence. Research, development, and theory-building has begun for pervasive live-action role-playing games (pervasive LARPs) that take place both in the real world and online (Gustafsson et al. 2006; Jonsson et al. 2006; cf. Stross 2007) and so-called alternate reality games (McGonigal 2008). Opinions were divided over whether augmented reality games would revolutionize gaming, but the foundation for such games in technologies such as pervasive and mobile computing, radio-frequency identification (RFID) tagging of objects, realtime reading of physiological data, and wireless geolocation of objects and people suggests at least the potential for a rich set of applications. However, augmented reality, LARPS and ARGs may not sufficiently offer the "escape" from daily life, which is so often a goal in entertainment, while real-world populations and authorities are likely to react with limited enthusiasm to the prospect of players chasing each other through streets and buildings with weapons that appear to have real effects. When distinguishing fantasy from reality becomes difficult both inside and outside virtual worlds, the implications for real and virtual communities must be carefully considered.

The Economic Basis for Virtual Worlds

The venue for this conference panel was a fort overlooking Booty Bay, a frequently visited harbor town dominated by pirates at the southern tip of the WoW region known as Stranglethorn Vale. A location depicting a pirate town owned by goblin capitalists seemed like the perfect location for the next discussion topic: Besides Blizzard's *World of Warcraft*, "are there really any long-term viable business models for virtual worlds?" Some doubts were raised immediately about the subscription model that governs access to *World of Warcraft*. Subscription-based on-line games have been in operation for a relatively short time; it seems likely that at some point new subscribers may be outnumbered by cancellations. One participant referred to the "planned extinction" of virtual and game worlds, with the necessity therefore of a fresh supply of new worlds to replace those that die out. The discussion around the question of sustainability drew on the analogies ranging from advertising and publication to the life and death of real-world communities and settlements.

Participants revealed that their physical locations during the conference were scattered around the globe, cutting a huge swath of the world from Australia through North America and Europe to Russia. While of course this represented a remarkable situation for an academic conference, it also suggested that there may be quite a bit of diversity in the ways that people gain access to the game. In the United States, a player generally begins by buying a boxed copy of the game, consisting of the software on CD-ROM or DVD-ROM discs and some documentation and additional printed materials, from a store or by downloading massive files from Blizzard directly via the Internet. Expansions to the game are acquired in the same fashion, with frequent updates and patches downloaded automatically when a player logs in to the game. In March 2009, the GameStop game store was selling the original *World of Warcraft* for $19.99, the *Burning Crusade* expansion for $29.99, and the *Wrath of the Lich King* expansion for $39.99. After a free subscription lasting for 1 month, players pay a monthly subscription fee to continue playing the game. For example, in March 2009 for US subscribers the monthly fee was $14.99 if paid month-to-month, $13.99 if paid every 3 months, and $12.99 if paid every 6 months. Blizzard justifies the monthly subscription model on its website:

> Unlike a traditional PC game, *World of Warcraft* is designed for ongoing growth, with exciting new content being added regularly. In addition to benefiting from regular expansive content updates from our ongoing live development team, *World of Warcraft* has its own dedicated server infrastructure and internal support staff. The entire game takes place online, in a persistent, ever-changing game world that can host hundreds of thousands of players at any given time of the day. As such, it requires much higher levels of support, maintenance, and network bandwidth than other games.[1]

All this is true, but it is also worth mentioning that WoW is vast as digitally rendered worlds go; the development and maintenance costs certainly exceeded what could be recovered by the ordinary sales price of a computer game, especially when considering the on-going service, server, and transaction costs. A person who tries WoW for a month or two has the choice of whether to continue or not; if they do stick with the game, they are going to spend far more than the cost of a standard boxed computer game. If they continue for a year or two, or more (currently more than 4 years, for many players), they are probably not going to complain much

---

[1] http://us.blizzard.com/support/article.xml?articleId=20510

about having paid far more than what they would have paid for a typical boxed title. However, it is apparent that to be based on long-term satisfaction, the success of WoW requires substantial commitment on the part of players over a long period. Considering that a number of other popular subscription-based MMORPGs exist, it is not clear whether there is much opportunity for new ones to enter the market, unless it is to replace older virtual or game worlds that have closed down. A given individual might be quite willing to subscribe to one or two, but not five or six, and the more players try out, the more their participation is temporary, resulting in a "churn" of customers that jeopardizes the businesses underlying these virtual worlds.

WoW's competitors are trying a number of methods for maintaining viable operations in response to the dual challenge of competition and the dominant position Blizzard holds in terms of subscribers. Sony offers a package deal of $29.99 per month to subscribe to all its PC-based MMORPGs: *EverQuest*, *EverQuest II*, *Pirates of the Burning Sea*, *PlanetSide*, *Star Wars Galaxies*, *Vanguard: Saga of Heroes*, and *EverQuest Online Adventures*.[2] *Anarchy Online*, launched in 2001, is one of the oldest continually growing MMORPGs and has tried a number of business models and profit strategies. Currently, players have the options of entering much of the world for free, purchasing access to the complete world for $19.95, and subscribing to the most advanced expansions for $5.00 per month. In addition, a few billboards in major cities of this vast virtual world advertise real products. Figure 23.1 shows 4 billboards, three of them "real:" an energy drink, a Microsoft "PC" advertisement designed to counter Apple's anti-PC campaign, and a remarkable but genuine recruitment poster for robots in the U.S. Navy. The fourth billboard, for Dreadloch armaments, is fictional. So, at least some part of Anarchy Online's income comes from advertising, a business model that has been very successful for

Fig. 23.1 Four advertising billboards in Anarchy Online

[2] http://station-access.station.sony.com/

Google and other online businesses but thus far has been a very minor factor for virtual world companies.

A very different model involves so-called "free to play" MMOs and virtual worlds that encourage purchasing virtual goods for use inside the world. Depending on the particular system, some companies rely on real-money transactions (RMT), which often take place outside the virtual space, while others use an in-world currency that is convertible to an external (real world) currency. A European example is *Entropia Universe*, where at the time of writing (late March 2009) ten "Peds" are worth one U.S. Dollar. Figure 23.2 shows one of the many *Entropia* banks. In *Second Life* at the end of March 2009, about 260 "Linden dollars" could be exchanged for U.S.$1. *Second Life* also charges taxes on "land" and small fees for services such as using server storage space to store screenshots or audio. It is possible that virtual shopping centers will attract real-world businesses; as in Neal Stephenson's novel *Snow Crash* (1992), which has inspired many designers of virtual worlds? Are in-world avatars likely to function as sales personnel serving other avatars representing customers? Will the resemblance of bookstores in 3D worlds to real-world bookstores make it easier to shop on-line, or will using an avatar to navigate virtual bookshelves be more difficult than simply visiting the Amazon.com website? The solutions devised to address practical questions such as this one will go a long way in determining the sustainability of virtual worlds as business platforms.

Fig. 23.2 An office of the Neverdie bank on the planet Calypso in *Entropia*

Cultural Transformation

As the conference panel turned to cultural issues, we began to consider complex cases of crossover between life – and death – in real and virtual worlds. The creation of memorials in a virtual world involves appropriation of game technology, and thus constitutes a performance of game-related skills and creativity, as well as grief and memory. An example of a new service virtual worlds might provide is the provision of living memorials for deceased persons, perhaps as avatars animated by artificial intelligences. In fact, Blizzard's creative teams have placed several memorials in the *World of Warcraft*, discretely and often without public notice. The best known is perhaps the Shrine of the Fallen Warrior, which can be found on a hilltop in the region known as The Barrens; it is a memorial to artist Michel Koiter. A similar shrine can be found southeast of Tarren Mill in the Hillsbrad Foothills, but we do not know whom it memorializes. Kyle the Frenzied, a lost dog at Bloodhoof Village, is said to be the fulfillment of a wish by a child with a life-threatening illness. Perhaps most striking is Caylee Dak, a level 70 Night Elf hunter in Shattrath City, a non-player character; it is an exact copy of the character played by Dak Krause, who died in 2007 of leukemia. Caylee is the goal of a quest that starts with a little girl named Alicia in Stormwind City, who gives the player a sentimental poem about life and death that must be delivered to Caylee, who then thanks and blesses the player.

Second Life also contains a large number of memorials in a way that is rather different from WoW, since these have been created by "residents" of the virtual world. These memorials include a duplicate of the Vietnam Veterans Memorial Wall in Washington, D.C.; a Starfleet Memorial for all the deceased Star Trek actors; and a rather commercialized version of the World Trade Center Memorial. There are also numerous shrines for prominent individuals, as diverse as Benazir Bhutto, Vannevar Bush, and Sir Matthew Busby. Several areas are comparable to virtual cemeteries, because they memorialize large numbers of ordinary people, but with the difference that they represent these people through diverse virtual displays rather than relatively uniform headstones. One can imagine a new industry consisting of companies that offer virtual world memorials that are rich and realistic expressions of the lives of deceased persons, charging an initial cost to create the memorial and perhaps a subscription or an endowment to maintain it (Fig. 23.3).

One of the first words used by several conference participants to describe the concept of a virtual world memorial service was "creepy," especially if the memorial was offered in the form of an avatar that looked and acted like the departed person. However, participants discussed the possibility that virtual world memorial services might be seen as part of a more general shift in attitude, such that people might learn, so to speak, to live with artificially intelligent surrogates for departed persons. Six months after the conference, the US Department of Defense held a small business research competition, "Virtual Dialogue Application for Families of Deployed Service Members," that explored the possibility of creating avatars that can interact with humans in lieu of unavailable persons. An example might be a soldier who is on overseas duty speaking with their child:

Fig. 23.3 The *Second Life* memorial for *Star Trek* actors

For instance, a child may get a response saying "I love you," or "I miss you," or "Good night mommy/daddy." This is a technologically challenging application because it relies on the ability to have convincing voice-recognition, artificial intelligence, and the ability to easily and inexpensively develop a customized application tailored to a specific parent. We are seeking development of a tool which can be used to help families (especially, children) cope with deployments by providing a means to have simple verbal interactions with loved ones for re-assurance, support, affection, and generic discussion when phone and internet conversations are not possible. The application should incorporate an AI that allows for flexibility in language comprehension to give the illusion of a natural (but simple) interaction.[3]

This announcement did not address the possibility that, if the parent were killed in action, the surrogate could continue to interact with the child. Well before such AI surrogates could be realized, existing virtual worlds like WoW could replace non-player characters with duplicates of characters belonging to people who had died, or who merely had stopped playing. For example, throughout its huge virtual territory, numerous guards patrol the perimeters of towns or walk up and down near gates, operated by very simple artificial intelligence routines and automatically attacking any member of the opposite faction who approaches. If they were replaced on a server-by-server basis, with roughly 500 WoW servers, some two million memorial characters could function across all of WoW. If the market would bear a subscription of $100 per year to support a memorial service linked to these characters (a bit more than half the cost of maintaining a playable character), Blizzard would earn two billion dollars a decade from it. Given that it could be accessed from anywhere in the world, a virtual graveyard or memorial site could

---

[3] http://www.dodtechmatch.com/DOD/Opportunities/SBIRView.aspx?id=OSD09-H03

become a monthly meeting place for far-flung families, especially if a suitable combination of good technology and sensitive aesthetic design was reinforced by a cultural shift capable of transforming the funeral and cemetery industry to make such "virtual" ways of mourning acceptable.

This is only one of many as-yet unrecognized social functions that virtual worlds could serve, and the example illustrates the important principle that traditional inhibitions and assumptions may prevent us from seeing opportunities that future generations would find quite appealing. For example, virtual worlds are beginning play a role in family dynamics, not merely serving as babysitters for young players, but providing an activity through which members of different generations interact in meaningful ways. In a significant but as yet uncounted number of cases, parents, and children actively quest together in gamelike virtual worlds, rather than sitting passively and watching television dramas. After children leave home as young adults, virtual world-based activities provide a powerful channel for sustaining the relationship with parents, akin to other kinds of social networks, such as the Facebook family. The interactions formed around these activities might transform familial relationships in potentially healthy ways, as parents accept reliance on skills exhibited by their children, and children learn to take on leadership roles within the family. Generations ago, most children played important economic roles, proverbially feeding the cows at a family dairy farm, gaining workplace skills, and developing self-respect in the process. While virtual worlds may not have the power to reverse the historical trend toward economic marginalization of children, they could reshape important aspects of the relationship between among children, parents and the wider world.

Social theorists have long speculated that modern society has progressively lost a sense of community and meaning (Tönnies 1957; Durkheim 1897; Bainbridge 2007); researchers have considered the possibility that virtual institutions such as long-lasting *World of Warcraft* guilds compensate to some degree for that loss (Ducheneaut et al. 2007). As several chapters in this volume have indicated, virtual worlds may yet become a major tool for education. Already, it may be the case that they are teaching leadership and management skills, without specifically being designed to do so; individual gamers take responsibility for organizing raids into enemy territory, or virtual world residents cooperate to build artworks and buildings. Starfleet Academy in *Second Life* has actually created some of its own short classes on leadership, admittedly based on a paramilitary model and lacking much connection to the conventional administrative science literature, but with serious intentions nonetheless. It is conceivable that some form of virtual psychotherapy might be developed to take advantage of specific characteristics of virtual environments. First steps in this new discipline have been taken, beginning with desensitization experiments currently carried out in game and virtual worlds to help returning military personnel who have suffered emotional trauma from their wartime experiences (Pair et al. 2006). All of these examples point to a willingness to use virtual worlds that touch significant aspects of human psychology, society, and culture.

Connected to education, but far transcending conventional notions of schooling, virtual worlds may become a significant factor in creating a global culture. We do not know where all the participants of the May 2008 WoW conference lived, but the list of nations from which they logged in includes: Australia, Canada, Denmark, Norway, Spain, Russia, the United Kingdom, and the United States. On a practical level, many virtual worlds serve people who speak different languages, although as T.L. Taylor (2006b) has pointed out, real-world assumptions about national characteristics sometimes are carried over to virtual world culture through disputes about language. Often, English is the lingua franca, for better or worse, and some *Second Life* participants whose English is poor compensate by using real-time automatic translation systems. For example, a Brazilian might type into the text chat system a sentence in Portuguese, which is then immediately transmitted in that language to all avatars in the area. Instantly, the translator renders it as well as it can into English, transmitting that text as well, at which point the original sender can try to augment the translation in his or her own flawed English. In the game *Tabula Rasa*, a player could laboriously switch between four languages of game content: English, German, French, and Korean. Sony's *Final Fantasy XI* has a complex built-in cross-language communication system based on phrase equivalence, but players have augmented this with a kind of pidgin that, among other things, allows players who can only speak in Chinese, Japanese, and English to play together (Nolen 2007).

National identity is another important aspect of personality that is possibly affected by diegetic cultures present in digital games. Many game worlds operate around vast conflicts that are explained through background narratives and rein-forced by the cultures and activities built into the world. The world of the *World of Warcraft* can only be understood in terms of relentless and total factional conflict. The factions – Horde and Alliance – that carry out this struggle are made up of people from different "real-world" nations. It is worth considering that the commitment of these players to one side or the other in the game world potentially erodes their personal sense of nationalism in two ways. First of all, they build allegiances that have nothing to do with the national boundaries in the so-called real world. Second, these virtual conflicts provide powerful expressions of the tragedy of war, something which is very real indeed; opponents can be seen as being just as noble as the mem-bers of one's own clan, and the coalitions existing in this world are clearly based on raw self-interest rather than lofty principles. The proliferation of fantasy ideologies in such games may end up undercutting the very notion of ideology, redefining all dogmas as aesthetic stances or rhetorical conveniences, rather than sacred truths. In considering such cultural and ideological changes, we are reminded of Castronova's (2007) argument that virtual world policies will deeply affect those in the real world, as more and more citizens "migrate" to places like *World of Warcraft*.

Can virtual worlds effectively promote a new global consciousness that converts every player or resident into a world citizen? Such a notion takes inspiration from efforts of virtual world residents to band together such as the United Federation of Planets of the *Star Trek* subculture in *Second Life*. This may, however, be a cultural possibility whose boundaries are set by available technology. At present, every virtual world is like a separate planet. In some cases, this is even the case among different servers that deliver the same game content, as in the numerous "shards" of *Ultima*

Fig. 23.4 The planetarium in *ScienceSim*

Online or *World of Warcraft*. Travel from one to another means leaving one world and entering another. Figure 23.4 illustrates this point through a snapshot of the spinning planets in the *ScienceSim* world. Thinking of virtual worlds (or even separate servers) as planets is an especially apt metaphor here, because *ScienceSim* is part of the OpenSim Project that uses essentially the same technology as *Second Life*. Yet, it is organizationally and economically separate from it. The goal of the project is to make it possible for people to host their own virtual worlds and travel from one to another.

One could certainly wonder whether virtual worlds will create social and cultural alternatives that then thrive in the "real world," for example building on the communal sharing of resources that takes place in so many of them. Again, Castronova (2007) has argued that gamelike virtual worlds could inspire people to demand that real world policy-makers provide real equality of opportunity and full employment, as most online games do. At the very least, the experimental universes in virtual worlds might be used to level clear critiques or initiate investigations of real world institutions – as film and theater often do – but we can be forgiven for doubting whether social forms born in online habitats can overcome the destructive forces that rage in real-world society.

If the real world fails to conform to human values developed online, some virtual worlds could declare political independence, like geographically defined nations. To some extent, this is the case already when mundane political authorities decide not to tax (or perhaps simply to ignore) the virtual commerce carried out entirely inside virtual and game worlds. One expression of the autonomy of virtual worlds is their treatment of property rights; for example, in *Anarchy Online* or *Star Wars Galaxies* people can "own" their own homes, so long as they pay virtual real estate tax, but not in WoW. Ownership means that these properties are assigned to in-world characters. In *Second Life*, "residents" not only own their virtual property in the virtual world, but their real-life counterparts – the typists behind the avatars – also acquire real-world intellectual property rights associated with these 3D objects.

To some extent, all current virtual worlds are organized as dictatorships, ruled by the sponsoring real-world corporations, but this need not be the case in the future when peer-to-peer systems democratize virtual world ownership. A possible exception is *EVE Online*, which has an advisory board of players whose electorate is all registered players. In any case, Ludlow and Wallace (2007) has argued that the corporations are practically incapable of effective governance in these virtual spaces. Tonn and Feldman (1995) have maintained that non-spatial government is possible, by organizing the world in terms of overlapping strata and diverse areas reflecting the different interests and orientations that people may have worldwide, rather than in terms of geographically defined nations, states, and provinces. Logically, many of these non-spatial governmental districts could be virtual worlds. Clearly, we have to consider the possibility that virtual worlds will exert an increasing impact on real-world politics and culture.

Conclusion

The future of virtual worlds holds many possibilities, and earlier chapters of this volume examined some of them in detail. An important question for cultural institutions is how much of the past of virtual worlds they will be capable of preserving for future study. The conference session began by probing this issue in terms such as whether any current online games will become permanent features of human culture, like chess or Monopoly. The range of views proved to be quite wide, from those who doubted whether even chess and Monopoly will survive, to those who thought that *World of Warcraft* and *EVE Online* might be preserved as living relics of our era, to those who imagined that many of the existing games and virtual worlds might live forever, constantly re-emulated and hence replayed as technology evolves. One thoughtful perspective held that no current virtual worlds will survive, because they are examples of technological innovation, so that inevitably they will continue to change. Monopoly emerged during the Great Depression, but it continued to be popular after prosperity returned because it reflects an underlying understanding of economic culture that still persists. However, the particular expression of Monopoly in terms of which cities or streets it represents is less important than the core game design. In this sense, participants in the session considered whether *World of Warcraft* might turn out to be an "immortal" total work of art, comparable to Richard Wagner's operas, for example, which continue to be performed despite sometimes enormous production expenses after a century and a half (Wagner, 1849). Similarly, a number of ancient Greek dramas are still performed more than 2000 years after their appearance.

Some culturally significant virtual worlds have already ceased to exist, including *Uru, The Sims Online, Matrix Online*, and *Tabula Rasa*. Perhaps, future computer technology will make it easy for digital libraries of virtual worlds to host hundreds of them, but not without active inhabitants, who may prefer to enlarge the meaning of the work rather than conserve it. As the conference was winding down, the Preserving Virtual Worlds project was launched, with funding by the U.S. Library of Congress; one of our panelists (Lowood) leads the project team at Stanford

University, one of four U.S. universities participating in the project. Projects such as this one will not only explore issues of software preservation of virtual worlds, but also develop techniques for documenting the events and activities that have taken place in these spaces.

In any case, virtual worlds are an important expression of contemporary human creativity, and could represent a cultural watershed of great lasting significance. Thus, preserving the history of the early years of this new medium will be valuable for scholars and students of history. The spirit of this book has been to examine the present diversity of virtual worlds with a mind to their future significance, but in so doing it also serves as a part of the historical record for future generations who will want to understand the origins of the worlds – real and virtual – that they inhabit.

References

Au, W. J. (2008). *The making of second life: Notes from the new world*. New York: Collins.

Bainbridge, W. S. (2007). *Across the secular abyss*. Lanham, MD: Lexington.

Castronova, E. (2007). *Exodus to the virtual world*. New York: Palgrave: Macmillan.

Ducheneaut, N., Moore, R. J., & Nickell, E. (2007). Virtual "Third Places": A case study of sociability in massively multiplayer games. *Computer Supported Cooperative Work, 16*, 129–166.

Durkheim, E. [1897] 1951. *Suicide*. New York: Free Press.

Guest, T. (2007). *Second lives: A journey through virtual worlds*. New York: Random House.

Gustafsson, A., Bichard, J., Brunnberg, L., Juhlin, O., & Combetto, M. (2006). Believable environments: Generating interactive storytelling in vast location-based pervasive games. *Proceedings of the 2006 ACM SIGCHI International Conference on Advances in Computer Entertainment Technology*, Hollywood, CA. June 14–16, 2006.

Jonsson, S., Montola, M., Waern, A., & Ericsson, M. (2006). Prosopopeia: Experiences from a pervasive larp. *Proceedings of the 2006 ACM SIGCHI International Conference on Advances in Computer Entertainment Technology*, Hollywood, CA, June 14–16, 2006.

Ludlow, P. & Wallace, M. (2007). *The second life herald: The virtual tabloid that witnessed the dawn of the metaverse*. Cambridge, MA: MIT Press.

McGonigal, J. (2008). Why I love bees: A case study in collective intelligence gaming. In K. Salen (Ed.), *The ecology of games: Connecting youth, games, and learning* (pp. 199–227). Cambridge, MA: MIT Press.

Nolen, C. W. (2007). Virtual pluralities: Cultural pluralism in a massively multiplayer online role-playing game. Senior thesis, St. Louis, MO. Washington University.

Pair, J., Allen, B., Dautricourt, M., Treskunov, A., Liewer, M., Graap, K., & Reger, G. (2006). A virtual reality exposure therapy application for Iraq war post traumatic stress disorder (pp. 67–72). In *IEEE Virtual Reality Conference (VR 2006)*.

Postigo, H. (2008). "Video game appropriation through modifications: Attitudes concerning intellectual property among modders and fans". *Convergence, 14*, 59–74.

Stross, C. (2007). *Halting state*. New York: Ace Books.

Taylor, T. L. (2006a). "Beyond management: Considering participatory design and governance in player culture". *First Monday* Special issue number 7. Retrieved May 2009 (http://firstmonday.org/htbin/cgiwrap/bin/ojs/index.php/fm/article/view/1611/1526).

Taylor, T. L. (2006b). Does WoW change everything? How a PvP server, multinational player base, and a surveillance Mod scene caused me pause. *Games and Culture, 1*, 1–20.

Tonn, B. E. & Feldman, D. (1995). Non-spatial government. *Futures, 27*, 11–36.

Tönnies, F. (1957).*Community and society*. East Lansing, MI: Michigan State University.

Wagner, R. (1849). *The art-work of the future*, (http://users.belgacom.net/wagnerlibrary/prose/wagartfut.htm).

The Authors

Jakob J. Assmann is a research assistant at the Institute for Information, Organization and Management, Ludwig-Maximilians-University Munich, Germany. He researches in entrepreneurship and organizational behavior. His research interests lie at the intersection of information systems, management, and psychology and mostly focuses on the impact of computer-mediated communication on cooperative behavior. His research and publications have addressed specific aspects of virtual cooperation, such as trust in and leadership of virtual teams. The majority of his studies were conducted using teams from MMOGs. Some of his works were presented at conferences such as the *Academy of Management Annual Meeting* and the *Hawaii International Conference on System Sciences (HICSS)*.

Jeremy Bailenson is the founding director of Stanford University's Virtual Human Interaction Lab and an assistant professor in the Department of Communication at Stanford. His main area of interest is the phenomenon of digital human representation, especially in the context of immersive virtual reality. His findings have been published in over 70 academic papers in the fields of communication, computer science, education, law, political science, and psychology. His work has been consistently funded by the National Science Foundation for over a decade, and he also receives grants from various Silicon Valley and international corporations. Bailenson consults regularly for government agencies including the Army, the Department of Defense, the National Research Council, and the National Institute of Health on policy issues surrounding virtual reality.

William Sims Bainbridge is the author of 18 books and about 200 articles in the areas of sociology of technology, social movements, and research methodologies. For his recent book, *God from the Machine*, he programmed a neural network multiagent system to simulate religious cognition and conversion in a large community. His book about a popular gamelike world, *The Warcraft Civilization* will shortly be published by the MIT Press. He spends well over a thousand hours each year doing observational research inside virtual worlds, and he is currently writing a book on how virtual worlds explore possible real futures for humanity. For the past 17 years, he has served as a program officer managing review of grant proposals in the social science and computer science directorates of the National Science Foundation. He has extensive experience in editing publications on the societal implications of nanotechnology, converging technologies, and human–computer interaction.

Jane Barnett recently submitted her Ph.D. at Middlesex University in London, England. Her work was supervised by Dr. Mark Coulson and Professor Nigel Foreman. Jane's research interests include examining how MMO game play affects players' psychological emotional states and these studies have recently received significant press coverage after a presentation at the British Psychological Society's Dublin conference in 2008.

Tom Boellstorff is Professor in the Department of Anthropology at the University of California, Irvine, and Editor-in-Chief of *American Anthropologist*, the flagship journal of the American Anthropological Association. He is the author of many articles and the books: *The Gay Archipelago: Sexuality and Nation in Indonesia* (Princeton University Press, 2005); *A Coincidence of Desires: Anthropology, Queer Studies, Indonesia* (Duke University Press, 2007); and *Coming of Age in Second Life: An Anthropologist Explores the Virtually Human* (Princeton University Press, 2008).

John Bohannon is an innovative science journalist and intellectual adventurer who contributes to the weekly journal, *Science*. His approximately monthly online series, The Gonzo Scientist, takes a look at the intersections among science, culture, and art. In true gonzo style, he does not shrink from making himself a part of the story. He played the key role in instigating the May 2008 scientific conference held inside *World of Warcraft*, and leading a team of scientists who examined the connections of Spore to real evolutionary science.

Richard Childers is a chief executive officer and one of the founders of Virtual Space Entertainment (VSE). For over 25 years, he has led digital production teams producing animation, interactive CD ROMs, software, games, web sites, and books. From 1993 to 1998, he was President and CEO of Computer Visualizations, Inc.; a multimedia publishing/production company he founded and grew to sales of over $2 million. He developed the three-dimensional visualizations for mass transit systems in Honolulu, Los Angeles, and Vancouver, as well as design studies for the National Science Foundation's new *Ahmenson South Pole Station*. He has recruited, trained, and motivated teams of up to 40 designers, producing over 25 finished commercial projects. His books have been published by Random House and Stewart, Tabori, and Chang. Over the years, he has won 11 major design awards including the Communication Arts Gold Medal and the I-Magic Platinum award. For the past 4 years, Richard has served as the Assistant to the President, Special Projects at the Academy of Art University.

Mark Coulson is a Chartered Psychologist and is Principal Lecturer in Psychology at Middlesex University, London. He gained his first degree in psychology from Nottingham University, and his Ph.D. in Biological Sciences from Cambridge University. His research focuses on positive psychology, the communication of emotion through body posture and movement, and online gaming.

Nicolas Duchenaut obtained his Ph.D. in 2003 from the University of California, Berkeley, and currently is a researcher in the Computer Science Laboratory at the Palo Alto Research Center. Using a combination of methods (including data mining and social network analysis) he studies and designs systems to better support collaboration in online spaces, with a recent focus on 3D virtual worlds and massively multiplayer games.

Niles Eldredge has been a paleontologist on the curatorial staff of the American Museum of Natural History since 1969. His specialty is the evolution of trilobites, and his main professional passion is evolution. Throughout his career, he has used repeated patterns in the history of life to refine ideas on how the evolutionary process actually works. The theory of "punctuated equilibria," developed with Stephen Jay Gould in 1972, was an early milestone. Eldredge went on to develop a hierarchical vision of evolutionary and ecological systems, and in his book *The Pattern of Evolution* (1999) he unfolds a comprehensive theory that specifies in detail how environmental change governs the evolutionary process. Concerned with the rapid destruction of many of the world's habitats and species, Eldredge was Curator-in-Chief of the American Museum's Hall of Biodiversity (May, 1998), and has written several books on the subject – most recently (1998) *Life in the Balance*. He has also combated the creationist movement through lectures, articles and books – including *The Triumph of Evolution ... And The Failure of Creationism* (2000). Eldredge is the Curator responsible for the content of the major exhibition *Darwin*, which opened at the American Museum of Natural History in New York on November 19, 2005. The exhibition travels to Boston, Toronto, and Chicago before going to the Natural History Museum in London in time to celebrate the 200th anniversary of Darwin's birth in 2009. His book *Darwin, Discovering the Tree of Life* (2005) accompanies the exhibition.

Nigel Foreman is a Professor of Psychology at Middlesex University in London. His research interests include spatial judgments in real and virtual world scenarios, learning history from virtual environments, and spatial cognitive skills and individual differences. He also founded Middlesex's virtual reality laboratory in 1999 to investigate applications of virtual environments (VEs) in environmental familiarity and spatial training and assessment in young people older people and in people with disabilities.

Michelle Roper Fox is a Senior Analyst for Education and Workforce Development projects for Energy Efficiency and Renewable Energy Programs at the US Department of Energy. Formerly, she was the Director of the Learning Technologies Program at the Federation of American Scientists (FAS). Her FAS work involved the research, development and evaluation of advanced technologies for learning and training including games and virtual worlds. While at FAS, Dr. Fox created and managed several technology projects and knowledge management initiatives that encouraged interdisciplinary collaborations and multi-institutional partnerships including the IMLS-funded *Discover Babylon* game and the NSF-sponsored *Immune Attack* game. She also contributed to the organization's efforts to develop a national research plan for learning science and technology and has worked on the initiative that created the new National Center for Research in Advanced Information and Digital Technologies that has been authorized as part of the Higher Education Act of 2008.

Martin R. Gibbs is a Senior Lecturer in the Department of Information Systems at The University of Melbourne. He teaches subjects in the social implications of information and communication technologies. His current research examines the role of information and communication technologies in people's everyday, nonworking lives, with a particular emphasis on understanding how people play, love, and congregate in the "space of flows." He has degrees in electrical engineering, the social studies of technology, and the history and philosophy of science. With colleagues he has published over 50 peer-reviewed papers on topics associated with technology and domestic life, community informatics, and the sociality of online games.

T. Ryan Gregory completed his B.Sc. at McMaster University in 1997 and earned his Ph.D. in evolutionary biology and zoology from the University of Guelph in 2002. He has been the recipient of several prestigious scholarships, fellowships, and awards, including the 2003 NSERC Howard Alper Postdoctoral Prize, which identified him as the top postdoctoral researcher in Canada in any field of science or engineering, and most recently a McMaster Alumni Association Arch Award (2005), an American Society of Naturalists Young Investigator Prize (2006), and the Canadian Society of Zoologists Bob Boutilier New Investigator Award (2007). Dr. Gregory carried out postdoctoral research at the American Museum of Natural History in New York and the Natural History Museum in London, England, before joining the faculty in the Department of Integrative Biology and the Biodiversity Institute of Ontario at the University of Guelph. Dr. Gregory's primary research interests include large-scale genome evolution, biodiversity, and genomic diversity, and macroevolution. His first book, *The Evolution of the Genome*, was published in early 2005. He is an Associate Editor of the journal *Evolution: Education and Outreach*.

Searle Huh is a Doctoral student in the Annenberg School for Communication at the University of Southern California. His primary interests are the activity and passivity of media users, enjoyment in video game play, and cognitive aspects of media use.

Henry Kelly is now the Principal Deputy Assistant Secretary for Energy Efficiency and Renewable Energy Programs at the US Department of Energy. From 2001 until 2009 he was the president of the Federation of American Scientists (FAS). Prior to joining the FAS, Kelly spent more than 7 years as Assistant Director for Technology in the Office of Science and Technology in the White House. There he helped negotiate and implement administration research partnerships in energy and the environment, information technology, and learning technology. These partnerships included new automobile and truck technology, housing technology, bioprocessing technology, and information technology. Kelly convened the President's Information Technology Advisory Committee and translated their advice into a large expansion and refocusing of federal information technology research. He also was instrumental in creating major federal programs in learning technology for children and adults, including an executive order accelerating the use of instructional technology for training federal civilian and military employees. Before his tenure at the White House, he was a senior associate at the Congressional Office of Technology Assessment; assistant director for the Solar Energy Research Institute; and worked on the staff of the Arms Control and Disarmament Agency.

M. Audrey Korsgaard is a Professor of Management and Organizational Behavior at the Moore School of Business at the University of South Carolina. She earned a B.A. degree in psychology from Rutgers University, and both M.A. and Ph.D. degrees in psychology from New York University. Dr. Korsgaard joined the faculty at the University of South Carolina in 1991, and previously served as a visiting professor at the A.B. Freeman School of Business at Tulane University. Her research centers trust, prosocial orientation and justice as explanatory frameworks for understanding interpersonal and intragroup cooperation. She has studied these issues in a variety of work settings, including supervisor–subordinate relationships, investor–entrepreneur relations, virtual teams, and joint ventures. Dr. Korsgaard was previously an associate editor of the *Journal of Management*. She also has served on editorial boards of the *Journal of Management, Journal of Organizational Behavior, Group and Organizational Management, and Entrepreneurship Theory and Practice*. She is an active member of the Academy of Management and the Society for Industrial-Organizational Psychology.

Yong Ming Kow is a doctoral student in the Donald Bren School of Information and Computer Sciences at the University of California, Irvine. He is studying modders, computer users who create functionality in a software product that is more suited to their own needs. He is interested in how modding culture can impact the future of software and product development. Prior to his doctoral studies, he owned a consultancy performing ethnographic and human computer interaction research in industrial and consumer products. Outside of his research work and studies, he is interested in meditation and has been learning to incorporate meditation into his work and life.

Julian Lombardi, Ph.D. is a virtual world architect who serves as assistant vice president with Duke University's Office of Information Technology, research scholar with the Duke program in Information Science + Information Studies, and adjunct faculty member with Duke's Department of Computer Science. His work has been focused on the design of computational systems that support deep collaboration and resource sharing across large numbers of users. A former biologist studying the evolution of complex dynamic systems, in the mid-1990s, he began designing and developing avatar-mediated virtual world technologies. He eventually founded VIOS, Inc., a venture-capital funded RTP-based 3D social software technology company. In 2002, he went on to manage a software research and development group at the University of Wisconsin-Madison. He joined Duke in 2005. Julian is also one of the six principal architects of the Croquet project (along with Alan Kay and others) and is now engaged in a National Science Foundation and Andrew W. Mellon-funded effort to develop Cobalt, an open source and multi-platform virtual world browser and construction toolkit designed primarily for educational/scholarly communities. Julian also teaches about virtual worlds at Duke.

Marilyn Lombardi, Ph.D. directs the Renaissance Computing Institute (RENCI) Center at Duke University, part of a major collaborative venture of Duke University, North Carolina State University, and University of North Carolina at Chapel Hill. She is also Senior IT Strategist for Duke University, a Senior Research Scholar with the Duke (ISIS) Program, a Scholar-in-Residence for the EDUCAUSE Learning Initiative (ELI), and author of the 2007–2008 ELI White Paper series on technologies in support of authentic learning. As a former humanities professor and author who co-founded a venture-capital funded Research Triangle Park-based 3D software technology company (ViOS, Inc.), Marilyn brings a multidisciplinary perspective to her work on scalable collaboration infrastructures in support education, research, and scholarship. Her work has been funded by the National Science Foundation (NSF) and the Ewing Marion Kauffman Foundation, and she has been an advisor in the areas of cyberinfrastructure, visualization, human–computer interaction, and the digital humanities for the NSF, the National Endowment for the Humanities (NEH), and the Council on Library and Information Resources (CLIR).

Henry Lowood has been a curator for history of science and technology collections in the Stanford University libraries since 1983; and for film and media studies since 2005. He has lectured in the Science and Technology Studies Program, the History and Philosophy of Science Program, and Film and Media Studies Program at Stanford. Since 2000, he has been leading How They Got Game: The History of Interactive Simulations and Videogames, a research project funded in the Stanford Humanities Laboratory. He is currently leading Stanford's team in the Preserving Virtual Worlds project funded by the US Library of Congress.

Wayne G. Lutters is an Associate Professor of Information Systems in the College of Engineering and Information Technology at the University of Maryland, Baltimore County (UMBC). He has recently served as a Program Director for Human-Centered Computing at the National Science Foundation. Dr. Lutters' research interests are at the nexus of computer-supported cooperative work (CSCW), social computing, and knowledge management. He specializes in field studies of IT-mediated work, from a socio-technical perspective, to better inform the design and evaluation of collaborative systems. Dr. Lutters earned his M.S. and Ph.D. in Information and Computer Science from the University of California, Irvine and his B.A. in both Cognitive Science and History from Connecticut College.

Mary Lou Maher is the Deputy Director of the Information and Intelligent Systems Division at the National Science Foundation. She joined the Human Centered Computing Cluster in July 2006 and initiated a funding emphasis at NSF on research in creativity and computing called CreativeIT. She is the Professor of Design Computing at the University of Sydney. She received her BS (1979) at Columbia University and her MS (1981) and Ph.D. (1984) at Carnegie Mellon University. She was an Associate Professor at Carnegie Mellon University before joining the University of Sydney in 1990. She has held joint appointments in the Faculty of

Architecture and the School of Information Technologies at the University of Sydney. Her research includes empirical studies and new technologies for design in virtual worlds and other collaborative environments, behavior models for intelligent rooms, motivated reinforcement learning for non-player characters in MMORPGs, and tangible user interfaces for 3D design.

Bonnie Nardi is a Professor in the Department of Informatics in the Donald Bren School of Information and Computer Sciences at the University of California, Irvine. Her interests are activity theory, interaction design, and social life on the Internet. Most of her research has concerned work, although she has also conducted a long term study of *World of Warcraft*. She has conducted participant-observation studies in offices, schools, homes, hospitals, laboratories, libraries, and virtual worlds. She is the author of many scientific articles and books, and is the co-author (with Victor Kaptelinin) of Acting with Technology: Activity Theory and Interaction Design (MIT Press, 2006).

Sachin Patil is a Research Associate in the Learning Technologies Program of the Federation of American Scientists (FAS), whose work focuses on human–computer interaction techniques in technology-enabled learning. He firmly believes that most of the hurdles in expanding the reach of learning technologies can be overcome, if there is an easily accessible dedicated platform that supports "plug and play" learning tools. Currently, he is developing a toolset for virtual worlds to enable them to become future authoring environments for e-Learning applications and training simulations. Patil earned his Bachelor's Degree in Electrical Engineering from Pune University in India, and holds a Masters Degree in Computer Science from George Washington University in Washington, DC.

Celia Pearce is a game designer, author, researcher, teacher, curator and artist, specializing in multiplayer gaming and virtual worlds, independent, art, and alternative game genres, as well as games and gender. She began designing interactive attractions and exhibitions in 1983, and has held academic appointments since 1998. Her game designs include the award-winning virtual reality attraction Virtual Adventures (for Iwerks and Evans & Sutherland) and the Purple Moon Friendship Adventure Cards for Girls. She received her Ph.D. in 2006 from SMARTLab Centre, then at Central Saint Martins College of Art and Design, University of the Arts London. She currently is an Assistant Professor of Digital Media in the School of Literature, Communication and Culture at Georgia Tech, where she also directs the Experimental Game Lab and the Emergent Game Group. She is the author or co-author of numerous papers and book chapters, as well as *The Interactive Book* (Macmillan 1997) and the forthcoming *Communities of Play: Emergent Cultures in Multiplayer Games and Virtual Worlds* (MIT 2009). Dr. Pearce has also curated new media, virtual reality, and game exhibitions and is currently Festival Chair for IndieCade, an international independent games festival and showcase series. She is a co-founder of the Ludica women's game collective.

Arnold Picot holds the chair of the Institute for Information, Organization and Management at the Munich School of Management at the Ludwig-Maximilians-

Universität, Munich, Germany. From August 2004 until May 2005 he was the Konrad Adenauer Visiting Professor at the Georgetown University Washington DC.

Arnold Picot's research and teaching activities focus on the management of information and communication. His research interests lie in the field of organization theory and management under the influence of new technologies, especially information and communication technologies and investigate new ways of market transactions, of organizing, managing, and working. He has backgrounds in new institutional economics and in experimental economic research and also addresses issues of telecommunications and media regulation. He is an editorial board and review member of various academic and professional journals, book series, and yearbooks, and the author of around 30 books and over 400 articles, book chapters, and monographs.

Giulio Prisco is an information technology and virtual reality consultant, as well as a futurist, writer, and transhumanist. His principal interests include: science, emerging technologies, IT, VR worlds, space, and futurestudies. Formerly a senior manager in the European Space Administration (ESA), he is a physicist and computer scientist. He recently resigned as Executive Director and Board member of the World Transhumanist Association but continues to serve on the Board of Directors of the Institute for Ethics and Emerging Technologies. He is also a member of the advisory board of the Lifeboat Foundation and a founding member of the Order of Cosmic Engineers.

Diana Rhoten is the director of the Knowledge Institutions program at the Social Science Research Council and former director of the Virtual Organizations and Cyberlearning programs at the National Science Foundation. Her research focuses on the social and technical conditions as well as the individual and organizational implications of different approaches to knowledge production and innovation. She is particularly interested in the implications that geographically distributed and intellectually diverse networks pose for traditional institutions of research and Education – particularly in light of the many emerging technological capacities before us. Rhoten's research has been supported by grants from the National Science Foundation, Macarthur Foundation, Ford Foundation, Teagle Foundation, and Fulbright Program. Examples of her work can be found in *Science, Nature, Research Policy, Comparative Education, Journal of Education Policy,* and *Annual Review of Law and Social Sciences.* She is currently co-editing a book titled *Knowledge Matters: The Transformation of the Public Research University* (Columbia University Press, forthcoming).

Walt Scacchi is research director of the Center for Computer Games and Virtual Worlds at the Institute for Software Research and research director of the Computer Game Culture and Technology Laboratory at the University of California, Irvine. His research interests include: organizational studies of software development in open source communities, networked computer games and meta-game environments, acquisition of open source software systems (including governance, procurement, systems engineering, deployment, operations and field support), computer supported collaborative work environments, organizational and software process modeling and simulation, and electronic commerce.

Kathryn Segovia is a Ph.D. student in the Communication Department at Stanford University. She worked under the direction of Dr. Jeremy Bailenson in the Virtual Human Interaction Lab at Stanford University while completing her bachelor's and master's degrees. Currently, she is continuing her work with Dr. Bailenson and is using virtual reality technology to study topics in legal psychology, such as false memories in children and moral identity. She hopes to pursue a career in academia or trial consulting.

Greg Wadley is an Associate Academic and Ph.D. candidate in the Department of Information Systems at The University of Melbourne. He teaches a range of subjects in system design, and has conducted research into online communities, particularly those coalescing around online games. His Ph.D. is an evaluation of text and voice communication in online virtual worlds. He holds degrees in Computer Science and Cognitive Science. In 2008, he visited PARC, California, where he conducted a study of collaborative building in *Second Life*.

Isabell M. Welpe is a senior research fellow at the Max Planck Institute of Economics in Jena, Germany, and is the Chair for Strategy and Organization at the Technical University of Munich in Germany. She researches and consults in strategy, entrepreneurship, organization theories, and organizational behavior. Her research interests lie at the intersection of economic and psychological concepts, the role of communication (technologies) for cooperative behavior, and their impact on organizational collaboration. Some of her research and publications have addressed aspects of virtual work, such as social software and leadership of virtual teams. Isabell Welpe teaches Strategy, Organization Theories, Human Resource Management, Empirical Research Methods, and Entrepreneurship. She has taught on the faculty of Claremont University, EM Lyon, Ludwig-Maximilians-University and the University of Berne, Switzerland. She is an editorial board and review member of several academic and professional journals and the author of several books and edited volumes as well as over 40 articles and book chapters.

Rolf T. Wigand is the Maulden-Entergy Chair and Distinguished Professor of Information Science and Management at the University of Arkansas at Little Rock. He is the immediate past director of the Center for Digital Commerce and the Graduate Program in Information Management at Syracuse University. Wigand researches and consults in information management, electronic commerce and markets, IS standards and the strategic deployment of information and communication technology. His research interests lie at the intersection of information and communication business issues, the role of newer information technologies and their impact on organizations and society, as well as their strategic alignment within business and industry. Some of his research and publications have addressed virtual organizations and teams, new ways of working, management, organizing, all leading to a virtual structure. He also has backgrounds in social network analysis and examining the gratification derived from video games. Wigand teaches Electronic

Commerce, Emerging Technology and Strategic Issues and Data and Privacy Protection. He has taught on the faculty of Syracuse University, Arizona State University, Michigan State University, Universidad Iberoamericana, Mexico City; Helsinki School of Economics and Administration; the University of Bayreuth, Germany; and the University of Munich. His research has been supported by the National Science Foundation, the German National Science Foundation (DFG), the Volkswagen Foundation, the International Social Science Council, Rome Laboratory, and other funding agencies. He is an editorial board and review member of almost 30 academic and professional journals, book series, and yearbooks. Wigand is the author of seven books and over 110 articles, book chapters, and monographs.

Dmitri Williams is an Assistant Professor at the University of Southern California Annenberg School for Communication, where he co-directs the Virtual Communities Program. His research focuses on the social impacts of online games. Professor Williams was the first researcher to use online games for experiments, and he has since focused on voice use and community. He has served as an expert witness to the US Senate and in federal court cases.

Nick Yee is a research scientist at the Palo Alto Research Center (PARC). His research interests focus on social interaction and self-representation in virtual environments. At Stanford's Virtual Human Interaction Lab where Nick completed his dissertation, he worked with Jeremy Bailenson in exploring how rules of social interaction could be broken productively in virtual environments via experimental studies. Nick is also well-known for his survey study of online gamers. Over the past decade, he has surveyed over 50,000 online gamers on a wide variety of issues, such as demographic differences, motivations for play, and relationship formation. He has also worked with a variety of companies, such as Sony Online Entertainment, analyzing server-side information from online games. Nick's work has appeared in *The New York Times*, *The Wall Street Journal*, and *Business Week* among other places.

Index

Printed by Publishers' Graphics LLC
BT20130312.19.19.60